D1322409

Simon Seb... history at
Gonville and ... ... Catherine
the Great & ... ...son, Duff
Cooper, and Marsh Biography Prizes. *Stalin: The Court of the Red Tsar*
... the History Book of the Year Prize at the British Book Awards.
... Stalin was the winner of the Costa Biography Prize, the Bruno
... y Prize for Political Literature, the *LA Times* Book Prize for Best
...raphy, Le Grand Prix de la Biographie Politique, and was short-
...d for the James Tait Black Memorial Prize. He is also the author
of a novel, *Sashenka*. Montefiore's books are worldwide bestsellers,
...blished in over 35 languages. *Monsters*, the companion volume to
...oes, is also published by Quercus. A Fellow of the Royal Society
... Literature, he lives in London with his wife, the novelist Santa
...ontefiore, and their two children. He is now writing *Jerusalem: the*
...*ography*, a fresh history of the Middle East.

...n Jones is a journalist and historian. Born in 1981, Dan grew
... in Oxfordshire, and conceived a love of history under the tute-
...ge of Robin Green, perhaps the only teacher to have set lectures
...n the Mid-Tudor Crisis to folk guitar melodies. In 2002 Dan took
... First in history from Pembroke College, Cambridge. His first
...ook, *The Peasants' Revolt*, is due for publication in 2009. His passions
include Welsh rugby, English cricket and American television. He
... a very amateur boxer. Dan lives in London.

Claudia Renton was educated at St Paul's Girls' School and Trinity
College, Oxford, from where she graduated with a First in Modern
History. As an actress she has appeared on stage with the RSC and
the Royal National Theatre, and on television for the BBC and
... She is also currently working on a biography of the Wyndham
...ers, to be published by Quercus.

Heroes

HISTORY'S GREATEST MEN AND WOMEN

SIMON SEBAG
MONTEFIORE

With Dan Jones and Claudia Renton

Quercus

First published in Great Britain in 2009 by
Quercus
21 Bloomsbury Square
London
WC1A 2NS

A CIP catalogue record for this book is available
from the British Library

ISBN 978 1 84724 379 9

10 9 8 7 6 5 4 3 2 1

Typeset by Ellipsis Books Limited, Glasgow
Printed and bound by Clays Ltd, St Ives plc

THIS BOOK IS DEDICATED TO MY CHILDREN,
LILY AND SASHA

Thank you to Anthony Cheetham, Chairman of Quercus, with whom I thought up this book; my peerless agent Georgina Capel; my co-writers Dan Jones and Claudia Renton, both gifted historians; Richard Milbank, Quercus's publishing director for non-fiction, the epitome of publishing grace under pressure and a font of knowledge; Mark Hawkins-Dady, a masterful editor, and his team; Nick Clark and Austin Taylor, for their admirable taste and design; Elaine Willis for her picture research; and for their wealth of ideas, help and suggestions: Jonathan Foreman; Adam Zamoyski, Robert Hardman; Dr Kate Williams; my parents Stephen and April Sebag-Montefiore; and loving thanks as always to my wife Santa.

List of Illustrations

Contents

Introduction

For heroes have the whole earth as their tomb.
Pericles

We live in an unheroic age, and an unheroic age has a desperate need to learn about heroism. The stories of the great heroes bring history to life. They inspire and teach us about values and the nature of responsibility, the bonds that keep societies together – but they are also wonderful and exciting stories that we should tell our children.

The election of Barack Obama as US President in 2008 ignited a wave of hero-worship in America and internationally: his youth and grace raised intense hope and enthusiasm not seen in the Western democracies since Jack Kennedy, or internationally since Nelson Mandela's presidency in South Africa. Obama faced crises as complex and grave as those faced by his heroes Franklin Roosevelt and Abraham Lincoln. Only time will tell if he will one day join historic heroes like JFK, FDR, Lincoln and Mandela – who all appear in this book.

The virtues of heroism are courage, tolerance and selflessness. Heroism involves the willingness to take risks, both to protect those who are weaker than oneself, and to defend freedom. Heroes feel an obligation towards something more than the pursuit of their own happiness. This book is a celebration of human courage, achievement, tolerance and creativity, but it is also a treasure-chest of stories and characters that we should all know. It can be read alongside its companion volume, *Monsters: History's Most Evil Men and Women*.

Some of our *Heroes* have names that resonate to us across the centuries, others have been unjustly forgotten. There are traditional, old-fashioned heroes – warriors and princes; there are remarkable women – empresses, actresses and adventuresses. There are artists and poets and ordinary people who demonstrated astonishing bravery. They include representatives of different faiths and nationalities: Christians, Muslims and Jews; Britons and Americans; Indians and Haitians; Albanians, Chinese, Russians, Arabs and Poles.

The rulers that I have included achieved more than the mere exercise of power. Alexander the Great and Napoleon deserve their place on this list, not just for their political and military genius, but for using their power for the greater good. The scientists here saved millions of lives, while the writers, composers and painters promoted tolerance and freedom. Many of these characters were flamboyant, even outrageous, livers of life. But they have the advantage, unlike presidents and generals, of never having ordered a single death.

Indeed, at times even the most heroic of politicians and soldiers are guilty of acts of ruthlessness. Some of my choices, I accept, are as heroic as they are monstrous: hero-monsters. Rameses, Constantine the Great and Peter the Great, Atatürk and Cromwell, Suleiman the Magnificent and Napoleon, could all just as easily appear in my book of *Monsters*. The important thing is to know their stories and judge for yourself.

The boxes that accompany each biography allow us to reveal intriguing aspects of the lives and times of our heroes. Thus Queen Elizabeth I teaches us about 16th-century cosmetics; Tchaikovsky about the birth of the ballerina; Thomas Jefferson about America's first Middle Eastern war; and Marshal Zhukov about the T-34 tank, the machine that won the Second World War...

The final hero of this book is the unknown Chinese youth who, alone, defied a column of tanks at Tiananmen Square in 1989, when China's Communists brutally crushed democratic students. I end the book with this anonymous hero because it is the unsung heroes – ordinary people who did extraordinary things – who should command our greatest respect.

Heroism is out of fashion. We ignore real heroes and hype worthless idols instead. The modern age of reality-TV and 24-hour-news often confuses public shows of emotion and suffering with real acts of heroism. We must make heroism fashionable again.

You won't agree with all of my choices. I confess I chose some characters because I simply couldn't resist their genius or spirit. If I had chosen only saints, then *Heroes: History's Greatest Men and Women* would be a dull read – and I hope, above all else, that this will be a book of entertainment as well as knowledge.

Simon Sebag Montefiore

Heroes

Rameses the Great

c.1302–1213 BC

I met a traveller from an antique land
Who said:– Two vast and trunkless legs of stone
Stand in the desert. Near them on the sand,
Half sunk, a shatter'd visage lies, whose frown
And wrinkled lip and sneer of cold command
Tell that its sculptor well those passions read
Which yet survive, stamp'd on these lifeless things,
The hand that mock'd them and the heart that fed.
And on the pedestal these words appear:
'My name is Ozymandias, king of kings:
Look on my works, ye mighty, and despair!'
Nothing beside remains: round the decay
Of that colossal wreck, boundless and bare,
The lone and level sands stretch far away.

Percy Bysshe Shelley, 'Ozymandias' (1819), inspired by the many ruined
statues of Rameses in the desert

Rameses II was the most magnificent of the Egyptian pharaohs,
whose long reign – over sixty years – saw both military successes
and some of the most impressive building projects of the ancient
world. He subdued the Hittites and the Libyans, and led Egypt into
a period of creative prosperity.

Some of the greatest wonders of the ancient world owe their
existence to Rameses: he typifies the old-fashioned hero-king,
admired for his conquests and great, monumental works. His reign
marks the high point of the Egypt of the pharaohs, in terms of
both imperial power and artistic output.

During the reign of Rameses' father, Seti I, Egypt had been involved
in struggles for control over Palestine and Syria with the Hittites

of Anatolia (modern Turkey). Despite some initial success, when Rameses inherited the throne in 1279 BC Hittite power extended as far south as Kadesh in Syria.

Having been a ranking military officer, in title at least, since the age of ten, Rameses was keen to begin his reign with a victory. However, his first engagement with the Hittites, at the Battle of Kadesh in 1274, was a strategic failure. Despite winning the battle, Rameses could not consolidate his position and capture the actual city of Kadesh. Undeterred, Rameses maintained his belief in himself as a soldier. In the eighth or ninth year of his reign he captured towns in Galilee and Amor, and shortly afterwards he broke through the Hittite defences, taking the Syrian towns of Katna and Tunip. No Egyptian ruler had been in Tunip for at least 120 years.

Despite these successes, Rameses found his advances against the Hittite Empire unsustainable, so in 1258 the two sides met at Kadesh and agreed the first recorded peace treaty in history. With typical ostentation, the treaty was inscribed not on lowly papyrus but on silver, in both Egyptian and Hittite. It went further than merely agreeing to end hostilities; it also established an alliance by which both sides agreed to help the other in the event of an attack from a third party. Refugees from the long years of conflict were given protection and the right to return to their homelands.

The treaty ushered in a period of prosperity that lasted until the later years of Rameses' reign. During that time the pharaoh indulged his greatest passion: building gargantuan monuments, many of which can still be seen in various parts of Egypt. The Ramesseum was a vast temple complex built near Kurna, which incorporated a school for scribes. It was decorated with pillars recording great victories, such as the Battle of Kadesh, and featured statues of Rameses that stood 56ft (17m) tall and weighed more than 1000 tons. On an even bigger scale were the monuments built at the great temple of Abu Simbel. Four colossal statues of Rameses, each more than 65ft (20m) high, dominate the vast façade of the temple, which also includes friezes and depictions of other Egyptian gods and pharaohs, and statues of Rameses' favourites and family. Among these was his favourite wife Nefertari, who had her own, smaller temple built to the northeast. Her tomb in the Valley of the Queens

Royal marriage in ancient Egypt

The great love match between Rameses the Great and his wife Nefertari was not quite typical of Egyptian royal marriage, but it was an intriguing episode in an institution that was of vital importance to the pharaohs – as to all royal dynasties. Although it was not normal practice for the ordinary people of ancient Egypt, from the time of the 13th Dynasty in the 18th century BC the pharaohs were expected to take a large number – sometimes even hundreds – of wives. The ranking of wives became a matter of political precedence, with the Great Royal Wife being a prestigious rank.

The legend of Osiris and Isis was a major influence. Osiris was a great god and the original pharaoh, who married his sister, Isis. They were said to have come to the world to educate, civilize and teach humans about the wisdom and greatness of the gods. By marrying his sister, Osiris ensured that the divinity inherent in the pharaohs was kept pure and passed through the generations to be enjoyed by his successors. As a result, there was little hesitation among the pharaohs in taking their female relatives as wives. Most commonly, it would be sisters or step-sisters who became royal wives. Seqenenre Tao II, Ahmose I, Amenophis I, Tuthmosis I, Tuthmosis IV, Rameses II, Merenptah and Siptah all took

features some of the most magnificent art of the entire ancient Egyptian period.

These monuments are only a few of the vast architectural projects of Rameses' reign. He completed the building work of his father, finishing the hall at Karnak and the temple at Abydos, and in the east built the frontier city of Per-Atum. He inscribed his name and records of all his great deeds on many of the monuments built by his predecessors. There is little of the surviving architecture of ancient Egypt that does not bear his mark.

One note of caution is worth sounding. It is possible that Rameses was the Pharaoh of Exodus, the ruler who cruelly enslaved the Israelites until their god sent the ten plagues that persuaded the pharaoh to release the Chosen People, led to freedom by Moses. If it were certain that his oppression was as vicious as described in

their sisters as wives. But any female relative was fair game. Amenophis II married one of his daughters, as did Akhenaten, while Rameses married three of his, and Sethos II married his aunt. Despite this practice, there seems to have been less genetic degeneration than might have been expected, perhaps because large broods of royal children in fact came from several wives, and not solely from those who were closely related by blood to the father.

Despite the divine implications for the royal succession, throughout Egyptian society marriage was a civil contract, rather than a religious one. These contracts gave wives some protection in the relationship. However, the balance of power was tipped in favour of the husband, and – in royal circles at least – affectionate matches such as that between Rameses and Nefertari were uncommon. Apart from Nefertari, only Queen Ty, the mother of the great though religiously unorthodox pharaoh Akhenaten in the 14th century BC, had the honour of being deified.

The practice of sibling marriage continued into the Graeco-Egyptian dynasty founded in 305 BC by Alexander the Great's general Ptolemy. Until the dynasty came to an end with the suicide of Cleopatra in the face of Roman conquest in 30 BC, it was common for Ptolemaic pharaohs to marry their sisters, and to rule with them in tandem.

the Bible, he would not belong in this list of heroes. But there is no evidence that Rameses was this pharaoh.

Rameses was idolized by later Egyptian kings, and his reign was a high-water mark in the military, cultural and imperial achievements of ancient Egypt. He died in 1213, when he was in his early nineties – an astonishingly old age for the time. After his death, Egypt entered a period of slow decline, culminating in conquests by the Persians, then by Alexander the Great, and finally by the Romans. But Rameses, above all the rulers of ancient Egypt, has given us – in the form of monuments of breathtaking magnificence – an enduring reminder of the glory and splendour of the land of the pharaohs.

Solomon c.1000–928 BC

*Blessed be the Lord thy God, which delighted in thee,
to set thee on the throne of Israel: because the Lord loved
Israel for ever, therefore made he thee king, to do
judgment and justice.*

The Queen of Sheba to Solomon, 1 Kings 10:8–9

Solomon was ruler of the Israelite kingdom in the 10th century BC at the apex of its splendour, power and wealth. He was the founder of Jerusalem's Temple, the king whose myth transcended the bare bones of biblical history to embrace astonishing abilities as a sage, poet, lover and tamer of nature.

The principal source for Solomon is the Old Testament (Jewish Bible or Tanakh), notably parts of 1 Kings and 1 and 2 Chronicles, written hundreds of years after his reign. According to the biblical account Solomon was the only son of David and Bathsheba, who was anointed king while his father was still alive in order to thwart the conspiratorial aspirations of a half-brother. King David had been a ruler of brilliance, a superb general, an empire-builder, conqueror of Jerusalem, and a poet – noble achievements marred only by his coveting of Bathsheba, another man's wife. But David's successes reached their apogee in the wise and decent reign of his son.

After inheriting the kingdom David had created, Solomon soon defeated his foes and built a booming commercial empire, exploiting the strategic location of Palestine – bridging the Mediterranean and Red Sea, Asia and Africa. With armies and merchants, he established a vast network of ports and overland trading routes. At home, he imposed his authority over the tribal loyalties (and frequent quarrels) of the Hebrew peoples through a quasi-federal organization, cutting across clan power bases.

It was a reign of unparalleled magnificence, in which Solomon reputedly fielded an army of 12,000 cavalrymen and 1400 chariots, and for his pleasure and prestige a harem of 700 wives and 300 concubines. Such biblical calculations are undoubtedly exaggerations, but possibly not by much. (In Megiddo alone, the remains have been discovered of stalls said to be for 450 horses.) Using marriage to strengthen alliances, Solomon wed the daughters and sisters of kings. His marriage to the daughter of the Egyptian pharaoh, for example, secured him the Canaanite city of Gezer. The biblical report that Solomon granted the visiting Queen of Sheba 'all that she desired, whatever she asked' has prompted three thousand years' worth of rumours that this included a child. Since Sheba was probably a prosperous kingdom that included modern Ethiopia and Yemen, this was another example of Solomon's shrewd *realpolitik*.

The biblical pinnacle of Solomon's achievement was the Temple he built to house the Ark of the Covenant. Described as a building of stone and cedar, with a magnificently carved interior and an exterior covered in gold, it was a wondrous testament to the greatness of Israel and of its god. After seven years' labour by an immeasurable quantity of men, Solomon was able to dedicate it, and it became the holiest place in the Jewish world, the memory of it cherished for thousands of years at the heart of the Jewish faith.

Solomon continued to build, and on a colossal scale, with cities and forts springing up throughout the empire. He constructed breathtaking palaces for his wives, a city wall for Jerusalem, and facilities to encourage foreign traders, including pagan shrines to make them feel at home.

But Solomon's heroic status encompasses much more than politics and grandiose building. Sayings and teachings bearing witness to his matchless wisdom and a rather modern 'emotional intelligence' appear in the Book of Proverbs, including his most famous judgment. Confronted in his court by two women each claiming to be the mother of the same child, Solomon proposed dividing the infant in half, correctly judging that the real mother would abandon her claim rather than see the death of her beloved.

As a poet, Solomon is credited with the writing of no fewer than 1005 songs, including the *Song of Songs* or *Song of Solomon*. Although Solomon does not appear to be the actual author of the *Song of Solomon*, it is apposite that some of the most beautiful love songs known to man are preserved under the name of this extravagant lover.

God was said to have granted Solomon power over all living creatures and mastery of the elements. The Tanakh and the Qur'an

The Ark of the Covenant

An oblong acacia box, four feet long and two feet broad and high, overlaid with gold within and without and surmounted by two gold cherubim was, in ancient times, the Jewish people's most sacred religious symbol. The biblical Ark of the Covenant, known in Hebrew as the *aron*, was the vessel built to hold the two stone tablets engraved with God's Ten Commandments to his people.

Built according to God's instructions after Moses came down from Mount Sinai, it had stood in the Sanctuary, the Jews' tented shrine in the desert. On acacia poles threaded through four golden rings the Jews carried the Ark with them through their years in Exodus, into the promised land of Canaan, and finally to Jerusalem, where Solomon built the First Temple to enshrine this most treasured possession.

The Ark had totemic significance for the Jewish people. The tablets it kept safe reminded them of the covenant they had made with God as his Chosen People. Guiding the Jews through their years in the wilderness, the Ark led them to triumph in their wars of conquest. When once the Israelites tried to fight without it, they were shatteringly defeated. When the Jews finally crossed the River Jordan into the Promised Land and saw Jericho's walls collapse, it was in the Ark's presence.

both cite his miraculous ability to speak the language of the birds and ants, and to control the winds. For good measure he was said to have a magic carpet and a magic ring, the Seal of Solomon, which gave him power over demons. In the Persian and Arabic stories that, in a later millennium, made up *The Arabian Nights*, Solomon is the wizard who imprisoned the *djinn* (genies) in jars and cast them into the sea.

There was, though, a price to pay for such magnificence, and Solomon's reign witnessed unprecedented demands on his people. Since subject peoples were too few in number to carry out the construction projects, forced labour and oppressive taxes became the norm among the Hebrews. And Solomon's tolerance of paganism, even among his wives, became intolerable to his people. When the king died, his empire fragmented into two rival kingdoms, Israel

The Ark was an incarnation of divine will. When the Philistines captured it and installed it in their pagan temple, a plague ravaged their city. When they sent it elsewhere, pestilence followed in its wake. In desperation the Philistines placed it in a cart pulled by two cows for return to the Israelites. Instinctively and unerringly, the cows headed straight for the Israelite camp. As King David bore the Ark in triumph to Jerusalem, the pagan who tried to lay his hands on it was struck down on the spot.

In the Temple built by David's son Solomon, the Ark was placed in the Holy of Holies, the sacrosanct chamber that only the High Priest could enter. At the Temple's consecration, the Jews, their god and their land forged an unbreakable compact. 'The glory of the Lord filled the House of God,' says the Bible, as God set up residence in Jerusalem. The Jews had kept their covenant, and God had fulfilled his promise to his people to give them a land of their own.

The Ark disappeared when the Babylonians razed the First Temple in the 6th century BC. In the Second Temple, a stone slab marked where it would have stood. It is said to be buried on the Temple Mount, to have been carried off by the Babylonians, to lie in a cave near the River Jordan, to have been raised to heaven. Its replicas, containing God's words inscribed on the Torah, are built into the wall of every synagogue, a perpetual reminder of the covenant between the Jews and their god.

and Judah – this was, the Bible has it, God's punishment for Solomon's breaking of his covenant, the construction of Jerusalem's Temple not being sufficient to outweigh his indulgence of paganism.

Nevertheless, the creation of a great political and commercial empire that tolerated religious diversity gave the ancient Hebrews a golden age, and projected Solomon himself into immortality.

Sappho c.630/610–c.570 BC

Dark Sappho! Could not verse immortal save
That breast imbued with such immortal fire?
Could she not live who life immortal gave?

Lord Byron, *Childe Harold's Pilgrimage* (1819–24), Canto 2, stanza 39

Sappho was the first and greatest female poet of antiquity. For two and a half millennia she has been an iconic figure, as a creator of ravishing lyrical poetry, the first female literary star and as the original lesbian – a word that derives from her native island of Lesbos.

Though little more than fragments of her work survive today, Sappho was greatly admired and imitated by both Greek and Roman poets in the centuries following her death. A sense of vanished beauty, combined with the mystery of her passionate relationships with young women, have combined to make her the source of numerous legends and the subject of many works of art, from paintings to poems and plays, right up to the present.

Many myths may have sprung up throughout the ages, but the hard facts of Sappho's life are tantalizingly elusive. She was born some time in the late 7th century BC, probably between 630 and 610. Her family seems to have belonged to the aristocratic class on Lesbos, a large Greek island in the Aegean Sea, close to the Turkish mainland. She had at least two brothers, named Larichus and Charaxus, and devoted a poem to the latter. The family probably lived in Mytilene, a significant city on the island. Sappho was said to be small and dark, and her friend the poet Alcaeus called her 'violet-haired, pure, honey-smiling'. Tradition holds that she married a wealthy man called Cercylas who came from the island of Andros. If this is true, then Sappho's famous poem mentioning a young girl called Cleïs probably referred to her daughter.

Whatever the case, Sappho lived a privileged life in the aristocratic circles of Lesbos. Her poems refer to ladies of the court, and to great social occasions such as festivals, parades and military ceremonies. She was probably exiled with the rest of her family to Syracuse in Sicily some time around 600, as a consequence of the turbulent politics of the time. Among the many legends surrounding her is one that tells how she ended her life by throwing herself off the Leucadian Rock out of love for a young sailor called Phaon.

Sappho had a great influence on the young women who surrounded her. She was the leader of a *thiasos*, a female community that met under her tutelage to develop religious knowledge and social skills. In Victorian times Sappho was portrayed as the head of a girls' finishing school, but the group was not as formal as that. It was more of a close community that prepared its young members for the demands of marriage and travel away from the island. Membership of Sappho's *thiasos* was an intensely personal and emotional experience. Aphrodite, the Greek goddess of love, sexual desire and beauty, was their guiding deity. Much of Sappho's poetry is dedicated to, or written about, the goddess. Clearly the choice of Aphrodite was related to the goal of marriage, but there were also passionate homoerotic bonds between the members, mirroring the close, sexually charged male bonds that existed in the societies of ancient Athens and Sparta. The atmosphere was certainly not one of sexual abandon, but homoeroticism was without doubt an accepted part of the initiation and bonding of the *thiasos*. This, together with the highly charged passion that runs through Sappho's poetry, have made her a symbol and heroine of female homosexuality – Sapphic love or lesbianism – throughout the ages.

Sappho created a huge body of work. She turned away from the epic, male tradition of telling tales of the gods and of great heroes, and instead developed a more intimate lyric style, in which the exploration of the poet's own feelings was of supreme importance. Sappho's poems, written in her native Aeolian dialect, were intended to be sung, usually by more than one voice, and accompanied by an instrument. She wrote erotic poems to and about her female friends but also explored every aspect of love, both male and female, including all of love's attendant emotions, from hate and jealousy to frenzied lust and trembling passion:

Lyrics from the ashes

Our knowledge of the works of Sappho and many other great writers of the ancient world has been immensely enriched by the discovery of an ancient rubbish dump at Oxyrhynchus, the site of an ancient town about 100 miles (160km) south-southwest of Cairo, on a canal fed by the Nile. The town grew to importance from the time of Alexander the Great's conquest of Egypt in the 4th century BC, and was ruled first by Greeks and then by Romans, finally being abandoned in the 3rd century AD.

Throughout this period the inhabitants would cart their rubbish out to a series of tips among the sand dunes beyond the town walls. Along with the usual household detritus, there were large amounts of written documents among the refuse, from administrative orders to papyri on military, religious and political matters. Household papyrus was valuable and used for a number of purposes. A well-used document might have household accounts on one side and a young scholar's transcriptions of the great poets on the other.

After the town was abandoned and the canal system had dried up, the drifting sands of the desert combined with more than a thousand virtually rainless Egyptian summers to bury and preserve the papyri. They were discovered in 1896 by the Oxford scholars Grenfell and Hunt, who found that just kicking through the sand threw up documents of immeasurable value. Buried in the tips were fragments and full copies of works by some of the greatest authors of the classical world. Some were already known. Some were fairer copies of the originals that had been passed down by the scribes of the Middle Ages. Others were lost treasures, unseen for more than a millennium.

Among the works found were poems and fragments by Sappho and her fellow lyric poets, such as Pindar and Alcaeus. Other finds included a whole host of previously lost works, including plays by the Athenian dramatists Menander and Sophocles, and books by the Roman historian Livy. Early copies of the Gospels of the New Testament also turned up, along with apocryphal books such as the 'Gospel of St Thomas'.

More than 70 per cent of the world's literary papyrus comes from Oxyrhynchus, and to date around 4700 texts have been edited, translated and published. More continue to be transcribed, with the aid of multi-spectral imaging to decipher otherwise illegible documents. The rubbish dump of the ancients has become a gold mine for the modern world.

My flesh runs with soft fire,
My eyes lose sight,
My ears hear nothing but the roar of the wind.
All is black.

Sweat streams off me,
Trembling seizes me,
The colour drains from me like grass in autumn.
I almost die.

In the 3rd century BC, long after her death, Sappho's verse was arranged into nine books, and she continued to enjoy great fame throughout the classical period. The philosopher Plato is said to have considered Sappho the tenth muse. Five centuries after her death the Roman erotic poet Catullus used Sappho's great poem 'To me he appears like a god' as a model for his own work.

Many of Sappho's poems were lost as the classical world began to dim into the Dark Ages, and for many centuries her reputation suffered at the hands of those who found her frankly expressed female eroticism both dangerous and offensive to their concept of femininity. The little of her work that does survive permits us a mere glimpse of her genius.

Cyrus the Great
590/580–530 BC

Cyrus the Great, king of Persia, was the founder of a powerful empire that dominated western Asia and the eastern Mediterranean for two centuries. He was a peerless ruler: a bold soldier and conqueror but a tolerant monarch who recognized the human rights of his subjects, permitted religious freedom and liberated the Jews from slavery. In the ancient world he was lauded as the model of a great king, even by the Greeks, and was something of a role model for Alexander the

Persian empires up to the ayatollahs

Persia, now known as Iran, is one of the oldest and greatest civilizations in the world and has existed in various guises for more than 2500 years. Although its boundaries are smaller today than in ancient, imperial times, Iran is still of immense strategic importance in world politics.

Cyrus the Great's direct successors, Darius the Great and Xerxes, presided over a realm that stretched from Greece and North Africa to the fringes of India. Their Achaemenid Empire survived for two centuries, until Alexander the Great – 'the accursed Alexander' to Persians – burned and raided his way through to Babylon, bringing about collapse and ruin.

Persia did not remain depressed for long. The Parthian Empire rose in the late 3rd century BC, controlling the Iranian plateau for five centuries and pursuing a fierce rivalry with the Romans, who eroded their territory but proved unable to defeat the powerful Parthian cavalry. Internal revolt, led by Ardashir I, founder of the Sassanian dynasty, brought down the Parthian Empire in AD 226.

The new Sassanian Empire fared better against Rome, and later the Byzantine Empire, but the centuries of warfare proved taxing, and a weakened Persia fell in the 7th century AD to energetic Muslim conquerors from Arabia. Persian-Islamic culture survived the Mongol invasions of the later Middle Ages, and the Safavid dynasty (1501–1722) established Shi'a rather than Sunni Islam as the state religion. There was a great flowering

Great. Today the Persian Empire lives on as Iran; in Cyrus' time it stretched from modern Israel, Armenia and Turkey in the west to Kazakhstan, Kyrgyzstan and the fringes of the Indian subcontinent in the east.

Cyrus was born in Persis, in modern-day Iran. His mother was the daughter of Astyages, king of the Medes in western Iran, whose empire was then the pre-eminent force in the Near and Middle East. As with other great heroes, such as Moses or Romulus and Remus, a legend was passed down about Cyrus' birth. Astyages had a dream that he interpreted as a sign that Cyrus would grow up to overthrow him, and so he ordered that the infant be put to death. But Astyages' adviser

of the arts under the Safavids, combining both religious and secular aspects of Persian culture, for example in the beautiful mosques, pavilions and gardens of Isfahan, and in the great tradition of miniature painting.

The Safavids were followed by the Qajar dynasty, which survived until replaced in 1925 by the Iranian Cossack general Reza Shah, a self-made charismatic martinet, who became the first shah of the Pahlavi dynasty. His drive to modernize in industry and infrastructure drew him to Germany, and in 1941 Britain and the Soviet Union – rivals for influence in the region in the 19th century – invaded Persia to secure Iranian petroleum and Russian supply lines through the Middle East. They forced the shah to abdicate in favour of his son.

For almost thirty years the pro-Western Shah Mohammed Reza Pahlavi ruled sumptuously, but with good intentions. Resentment against the corruption of his regime found a focus in the exiled Muslim cleric Ayatollah Khomeini, who, in 1979, returned to lead an Islamic revolution. The result was the Islamic Republic of Iran dominated by a Supreme Leader (Khomeini, until his death) and a repressive Shiite theocracy. There has been deep antagonism between Iran and the West ever since.

Since the 1990s Iran has strived to re-establish itself as a great regional power, this time by way of its nuclear ambitions and its cultivation of terrorist allies, such as Hamas and Hezbollah in Gaza and Lebanon, to threaten Israel. The US humiliation in Iraq since 2003 has emboldened Iran's provocative President Mahmoud Ahmadinejad, who, along with his master, Supreme Leader Ali Khamenei, seems determined on international confrontation.

Harpagus could not bring himself to murder a newborn child, so he gave the baby to a shepherd. By the time Cyrus was ten, his precocious gifts had brought him to the court of Astyages, where his identity was discovered. Astyages allowed the child to live, but had his brutal revenge on Harpagus by tricking him into eating his own son.

Whether true or not, the legend shows that from the start Cyrus was seen as the anointed redeemer of his people. In 559 BC he succeeded his father Cambyses I as head of the Achaemenid dynasty that ruled Persia, which was then restricted to an area of southwest Iran and subject to the Medes. In 554 Cyrus allied himself with Harpagus and led a rebellion against his cruel grandfather Astyages.

The revolt gathered momentum during the next four years, and when Cyrus marched against Astyages in 550, the Median soldiers defected. Cyrus captured the land of the Medes and made its capital, Ecbatana, his own.

Cyrus was not yet done with empire building. In 547 he conquered the kingdom of Lydia, deposing the famously wealthy king, Croesus (source of the phrase 'rich as Croesus'). This extended his domain throughout all Asia Minor, and drew in the Greek cities along the coast of the Aegean Sea. Having secured the western frontiers of his empire, Cyrus turned his attention to Babylonia.

Babylon was the greatest of the ancient cities, but it was governed by a tyrannical king, Nabonidus. As even the city's high priests had fallen out with their king, Cyrus was welcomed as a liberator when, in 539, he dug a canal to divert the River Euphrates and marched his army into the thousand-year-old capital. With Babylon came vast territories including Syria and Palestine, which gave Cyrus control over all of the kingdoms of the Middle and Near East.

Within twenty years Cyrus had assembled the greatest empire the world had ever seen. He realized that keeping his vast new domain together would require peaceful diplomacy, rather than oppression and violence. So instead of forcing Persian customs and laws on the newly conquered peoples, he set about creating a brand new Achaemenid culture, selecting the best elements from different areas to create a better whole. He employed Median advisers, mimicked the dress and cultural influence of the Elamites, and allowed religious freedom everywhere. He governed from three capitals: Ecbatana, the Persian capital Pasargadae, and Babylon.

In Babylon he freed the Jews who had been held there in slavery and allowed them to return to their homelands. As a result, he is the only Gentile to be named by the Jews as a messiah – a divinely appointed king. His reputation was further enhanced by the discovery in the 19th century of the 'Cyrus Cylinder', an artefact inscribed with details of Cyrus' conquests and his overthrow of tyranny, and declaring his belief in religious toleration and his opposition to slavery. It is recognized by the United Nations as the first charter of human rights.

Cyrus died on campaign in 530 BC, fighting nomadic tribes from the east. He was defeated by Tomyris, queen of the Massagetai, intent on exacting bloody revenge for the death of her son, who had been held captive by Cyrus. The inscription on Cyrus' great tomb in Pasargadae was: 'O man, whoever you are and wherever you come from, for I know you will come, I am Cyrus, who won the Persians their empire. Do not therefore grudge me this little earth that covers my body.' Cyrus was succeeded by his son, Cambyses II, whose short reign resulted in the capture of the only territory in the Near East that Cyrus had not added to his empire: the kingdom of Egypt. The Achaemenid Empire continued to expand and lasted for another two centuries, until the coming of Alexander the Great.

The Buddha c.563–483 BC

'Are you a god?' – 'No,' he replied.
'Are you a reincarnation of god?' – 'No,' he replied.
'Are you a wizard then?' – 'No.'
'Well, are you a man?' – 'No.'
'So what are you?' they asked in confusion.
'I am awake.'

Siddhartha Gautama, the Buddha, questioned on the road after his enlightenment

Encompassing the most fundamental aspects of human goodness, the Buddha's teachings of benevolence, toleration and compassion have a universal appeal that extends far beyond those who expressly follow him. His quest for enlightenment gave rise to a movement that is as much a code of ethics as a religion. It provides each of his followers with the ability and the desire to live a life of contentment and spiritual fulfilment.

According to legend, the Buddha was conceived when Mahamaya, the queen consort to the king of the Sakyas, dreamed that a white elephant had entered her womb. Born in a curtained enclosure in a great park in Nepal, the prince was originally called Siddhartha Gautama (the title Buddha – 'enlightened one' – was conferred on

Enlightenment and rebirth; or, Whatever next?

The Buddha's teachings gave rise to a movement that has spread across the world. But Buddhism itself is difficult to define. It is a religion without a creator god; it holds that there is rebirth but denies that we have an eternal soul; and its ultimate goal may be described as 'non-existence'. It is a system that does not preclude other religious beliefs and one that is presided over by monks and nuns who have no priestly role.

Even the term Buddhism is itself a Western one: in the East it is given a variety of names, including *dharma*, meaning 'natural' or 'universal law', and *sasana*, 'the teachings' (of the Buddha). The teachings that became dominant in Asia mutated subtly as they crossed borders and continents. Within a century of the Buddha's death, teachers estimated that there were over 80 varieties of Buddhism. The Buddha himself described his teaching as 'hard to see and understand, subtle, to be experienced by the wise'. It is primarily a matter of individual experience, a personal course of spiritual development. Yet there are certain fundamentals that remain consistent.

At the core of Buddhism lie the Four Noble Truths taught by the Buddha: all existence is suffering; the cause of suffering is desire; freedom

him later). His forename, meaning 'one whose aim is accomplished', was an allusion to priestly predictions that he would achieve greatness either as a ruler or as a religious teacher. Some scholars have suggested his birth was later than tradition holds, around 485 BC.

Seven days after his birth, Gautama's mother died. Eager that his son should follow the former, worldly path, his father had Gautama 'exceedingly delicately nurtured', shielding him from any sight of hardship. He seldom left his palaces (he had one for each season of the year), and on the rare occasions that he did, the king ensured that the streets were filled with young, healthy and cheerful people. Only when he was 29 did chance encounters, first with an old man, then with a sick man and finally with a corpse, alert Gautama to the existence of age, infirmity and death. This realization inspired a fun-

from suffering is *nirvana*; and *nirvana* can be attained by the eightfold path – a journey of ethical conduct, wisdom and mental discipline.

The Buddha described 31 levels of existence, rising from hell to the 26th realm of the greatest gods. The fifth and ideal level is that occupied by mankind, which gives its inhabitants enough awareness to be capable of seeking enlightenment and enough suffering to want to do so.

Without reaching enlightenment, every living thing, from insect to god, will be reborn time after time in the 'endless wandering' that Buddhists call *samsara*. When the Buddha achieved enlightenment, he saw back through 91 aeons of past lives, an aeon being approximately the lifespan of a galaxy. *Karma*, by which action and consequence are inextricably tied, does not bring an end to *samsara*, but it does determine where you end up in your next life.

The ultimate aim of Buddhism is enlightenment, the attainment of *nirvana*, which can put an end to the otherwise endless cycle of suffering and rebirth. The Buddha discouraged speculation about the nature of *nirvana*, a word that literally means 'quenching'. He taught his followers that posing such a question was like asking where a flame goes when it is blown out. More important, said the Buddha, is striving for its attainment. It is by fusing virtue and wisdom, leading an ethical life, and practising meditation and moderation that his followers can hope to achieve the enlightenment that brings a perpetual end to suffering.

damental aspect of his doctrine – that human existence is one of suffering.

Subsequently catching sight of a peaceful wanderer with shaven head and yellow robe, Gautama made the 'Great Renunciation', abandoning princely luxury in the hope that an austere religious life might bring greater spiritual fulfilment. Taking one final look at his sleeping wife and newborn son, he stole out of the palace in the dead of night to embrace the life of a wandering ascetic.

Gautama's search for spiritual enlightenment took him first to two renowned sages, but when his abilities outstripped his tutors', he refused their offer to become his disciples. Instead, accompanied by five ascetics, he retreated to the village of Uruvela, where he spent six years trying to attain his ultimate goal of *nirvana* – an end to suffering. Fasting and denial, however, proved unrewarding. With limbs 'like withered creepers' and 'buttocks like a buffalo's hoof', Gautama framed another of his fundamental tenets: the path to enlightenment lies in a life of moderation – the 'Middle Way'. It was a decision that so disgusted his ascetic companions that they deserted him. Left alone, the 35-year-old Gautama finally reached *nirvana* while meditating cross-legged under the Bodhi tree. As the watches of the night passed, he fought and triumphed over the devil, saw all his past lives and all the past and future lives of all the world, and with his soul purified emerged as the Buddha: 'my mind was emancipated … darkness was dispelled, light arose'.

The Buddha promptly converted the five ascetics and spent the rest of his life teaching the path to enlightenment. He trained his followers to convert others, and his community of monks (the title by which the Buddha addressed his disciples) flourished. Pressed by eager followers, he later instituted an order of nuns. A teacher beyond compare, the Buddha instinctively understood the capacity of each student. When, before his death, he asked his disciples if they had any doubts they wanted clarified, none of them did. Those who came determined to oppose him left converted. When even a famously murderous outlaw became a monk, the Buddha's opponents accused him of being some sort of magician who possessed an 'enticing trick'.

At the age of 80 the Buddha announced his intention to die and did so shortly afterwards, having eaten a pork dish prepared by a lay follower. Despite the pleas of his closest disciple, Ananda, he refused to appoint a successor. Undogmatic to the end, the Buddha held that his teachings should be treated as a set of rational principles that each person should apply for themselves. Resting on a couch – soon to be his deathbed – placed between two trees in a park, he instructed his disciples to let the truth that is *dharma* (natural order) 'be your Master when I am gone'.

The Buddha's greatness as a man shines through in every account of his life. His affection and respect for his disciples evoked in his community a loyalty at which kings marvelled. His every action bespoke a man of infinite wisdom, compassion and understanding. He also had a physical beauty to match his goodness of character. Contemporaries praised his 'beauty of complexion', 'sublime colour' and 'perfect stature'. 'Noble of presence', the Buddha had a quiet sense of humour that showed the humanity of a man whose respect for his fellow human beings was unlimited.

The Buddha called for people to seek enlightenment to raise themselves above suffering. Celebrating each person's potential to determine their own fortune, he deemed all individuals worthy of respect. His doctrine of non-violence, the inviolability of human life, tolerance, compassion and understanding has spread across the world. The Buddha is truly a hero whose greatness has enriched human lives.

Confucius 551–479 BC

A man who has regard to the old in order to discover the new is best qualified to teach others.

Confucius, *Analects* 2, 11

Confucius was the Chinese philosopher and teacher whose influence was felt – and continues to be felt – not only in his native China but throughout Japan, Korea and other countries of East Asia. He regarded learning as the true path towards individual self-improvement, but, in a manner that was to leave an indelible mark on all subsequent Eastern thinking, he also took an eminently practical view of his role. He saw culture and refinement, based firmly on tradition and correct ritual observance, as the keys to good governance and sought to put his ideas into practice by taking an active role in the administration of his country.

Confucius was born and grew up in the state of Lu (the modern-day Shandong province). 'Confucius' is a Latinized version of his name; in the East he is known as Kongzi or Kongfuzi (meaning 'Master Kong' – his family name). His exact birthday is not certain but is celebrated according to East Asian tradition on 28 September. His parents were impoverished aristocrats. His mother was 18 when he was born; his father was 70 and died when the boy was only three years old.

By the age of 15 Confucius had become an avid and dedicated

learner, with a prodigious appetite for the six disciplines of calligraphy, arithmetic, archery, charioteering, ritual and music. He was particularly noted for his incessant questioning of his teachers at the Grand Temple. As a young man he took various jobs, working as a cowherd, shepherd, stable manager and book-keeper. He married when he was 19 and dutifully followed tradition in mourning his mother for three years after she died when he was 23. He spent most of his twenties combining his working life with a devotion to education.

His knowledge of the six disciplines was bolstered by extensive study of history and poetry, and in his thirties he was ready to start

Sun Tzu and *The Art of War*

Confucius' teachings continue to resonate in China and throughout the East. But almost as influential is the philosophy attributed to his contemporary Sun Tzu (or Sunzi), whose treatise on war is still hugely important in military thought, business, politics and the psychology of human relationships.

Little is known about Sun Tzu's life (indeed, his authorship of the famous treatise is not certain). He is believed to have been a general for the state of Wu towards the end of the Spring and Autumn Period (770–476 BC). In *The Art of War* he distilled his military genius into an organized series of instructions and axioms that covered every aspect of waging a successful war.

One of the most striking things about this work is Sun Tzu's insistence that although 'the art of war is of vital importance to the state', it is often better to avoid battle, which he views as costly, disruptive and damaging to the population at large:

> *To fight and conquer in all your battles is not supreme excellence; supreme excellence consists in breaking the enemy's resistance without fighting.*

Where fighting cannot be avoided, preparation and knowledge of the enemy are all:

> *If you know the enemy and know yourself, you need not fear the result of a hundred battles. If you know yourself but not the enemy, for every*

on a brilliant teaching career. Before his day, teaching was usually carried out by private tutors to the children of the wealthy, or else it was essentially vocational training in administrative posts. Confucius took a radical new approach, advocating learning for all as a means of benefiting both pupil and society alike. He started a programme of study designed for potential leaders, reasoning that an educated ruler would be able to disseminate his learning to his subjects and so improve society as a whole.

Unlike many other wise men of the time, who shunned human interaction and were detached from society, Confucius engaged

victory gained you will also suffer a defeat. If you know neither the enemy nor yourself, you will succumb in every battle.

To forsake this advice because it necessitates going to the expense of gathering intelligence is simply wrong:

To remain in ignorance of the enemy's condition simply because one begrudges the outlay of a hundred ounces of silver ... is the height of inhumanity.

As Sun Tzu makes clear in many passages, attention to detail can win the battle before it begins: 'making no mistakes is what establishes the certainty of victory, for it means conquering an enemy that is already defeated'. And this, in theory, ought to minimize the damage done by battle:

The best thing of all is to take the enemy's country whole and intact; to shatter and destroy it is not so good. So, too, it is better to capture an army entire than to destroy it, to capture a regiment, a detachment or a company entire than to destroy them.

Though he could be dispassionate and ruthless about war, Sun Tzu stresses the need for violence and bloodshed only as far as is absolutely necessary. Enemy soldiers should be kindly treated and lengthy, destructive campaigns avoided in favour of swift victory. It is Sun Tzu's mixture of brilliant strategy and tactical analysis with a concern for human welfare that makes him relevant even to this day.

wholeheartedly with the government of his state. He served as a magistrate, rising to become assistant minister of public works, and then was promoted to the position of minister of justice. When he was 53, he became chief minister to the king of Lu, accompanying him on diplomatic missions.

But Confucius' influence on the king and his strict moral principles alienated him from the rest of the court, who conspired to obstruct him. Realizing that his message was going unheeded, Confucius left the court and went into self-imposed exile. During the 12 years of his absence, Confucius toured the states of Wei, Song, Chen and Cai, teaching and developing his philosophy. His reputation as the 'wooden tongue in the bell of the age' began to spread.

Confucius' thinking was partly a reaction to the extreme lawlessness of his age, a time of unrest in which neighbouring warlords were constantly in conflict with one another. His position was essentially conservative, emphasizing the importance of tradition, proper ritual observance and respect for elders and ancestors. He saw himself as a conduit of learning, who invented nothing but simply passed on received wisdom and encouraged self-inquiry and the personal quest for knowledge. He believed that rulers, chosen on merit rather than according to lineage, should not impose rules and govern by means of threats of punishment, but rather should develop their own virtues and so earn the devotion of their subjects.

Confucius' sayings were collected after his death in the *Analects*, which form the basis of what Westerners now call 'Confucianism' (the term does not translate meaningfully into Chinese). His most famous precept, the so-called 'golden rule', is mirrored in countless later moral systems (including Christianity). It is well captured in the following exchange:

> *Adept Kung asked:* Is there one word that can guide a person in life? *The master replied:* How about shu? Never impose on others what you would not choose for yourself.

The idea of shu (roughly, 'reciprocity') runs through Confucius' ethics, which are also underpinned by the notions of li, yi and ren. The concept of li equates approximately with ritual, yi with righteousness, and ren with kindness or empathy.

Confucius ended his exile aged 67, returning to the state of Lu to write and teach. Burdened by the loss of his son, he died at the age of 73; he is reputed to have taught more than 3000 students, 72 of whom became masters in their own right. Confucius' followers developed his sayings and ethics after his death, which soon came to dominate Chinese politics and culture. Confucius' influence has endured in the East for 2500 years, a dominance that even the advent of communism in China in the mid-20th century signally failed to eradicate.

Leonidas of Sparta

d. 480 BC

In the course of that fight Leonidas fell, having fought like a man indeed. Many distinguished Spartans were killed at his side — their names, like the names of all the three hundred ... deserve to be remembered.

Herodotus, *The Histories*, Book VII

The last stand of Leonidas and his 300 against the might of Persia spread the legend of Spartan bravery across the world. A peerless fighter of great courage, Leonidas sacrificed himself for Greek freedom. His intrepid defence at Thermopylae gave the Greeks the time and the resolve to defeat the massively superior Persian force that sought to overwhelm them.

For over a decade the Greeks had been fighting the Persians, who were determined to absorb them into their empire. Faced with Greek intransigence, the Persian emperor Xerxes assembled the greatest army yet seen. In 480 BC it crossed the Dardanelles on a bridge of boats, then swarmed along the coast towards the Greek heartlands. Xerxes' progress seemed inexorable, Greece's subjugation inevitable.

Ten years or so earlier, Leonidas had succeeded to the throne of Sparta, a city-state in the area of the southeastern Peloponnese known as Lacedemonia. The latter name gives us the word 'laconic', for the Spartans were renowned for their terseness of speech — as

The school for warriors

There was only one career for a male Spartan: as fighting machine. In an education system as ruthless as it was effective, Sparta raised men who belonged, as the Roman historian Plutarch said, 'entirely to their country and not to themselves'.

Sparta was frozen into an ancient constitution laid down in the 7th century BC by the semi-legendary King Lycurgus. Innovation was a mortal offence, individualism mercilessly eradicated. Foreigners were discouraged, money was replaced by iron bars, meals were taken in common. Nothing was allowed to divide the brotherhood of Sparta.

Sparta began selecting its warriors at birth. Inspecting all male infants, the council of elders weeded out the sickly and malformed, abandoning them on the mountainside to die. The sturdy, destined to protect rather than burden the state, were sent back to their fathers to be reared by nurses.

At the age of seven boys were taken into the care of the state, which set about transforming them into some of the toughest warriors the world has ever seen. The balletic grace of Sparta's soldiers was honed by years of gymnastics and athletics, all undertaken in the nude. So endlessly did Spartans indulge in such exercises that the Athenians gave them the nickname *phaenomerides*, the 'displayers of thighs'.

Boys were taught only the skills needed in war. Literacy was of no importance, and music only valued insofar as it encouraged heroic

exemplified by the dry, fearless wit that Leonidas and his fellows were to display.

It was said that the Delphic Oracle had prophesied to Leonidas that only the sacrifice of a king descended from Hercules could save his city from destruction. Leonidas, the seventeenth king of the Agiad dynasty, knew that his family claimed descent from Hercules and thus from Zeus. When representatives of the terrified Greek city-states met to confer at Corinth, Leonidas volunteered to lead his men to head off the Persians at the only choke-point left: the narrow pass of Thermopylae.

It seemed an unwinnable battle from the start. With the Athenians setting sail to fight the Persians at sea and the other city-states

thoughts. Cunning, endurance, stamina and boldness were all prized. The boys slept on pallets made of rushes they gathered themselves. They were kept hungry to encourage them to take the initiative and steal food; they were only punished if they were caught.

Flogging competitions tested their mental and physical stamina. Some boys died, but as long as they had betrayed no flicker of emotion they were commemorated with a statue. Pitched into battles against each other, the boys went at it with unremitting savagery. They spent long periods fending for themselves in the wild. As the 20-year-old soldier-citizens approached the end of their training, the elite were sent out to live a guerrilla existence, using *helots* (slaves) as target practice.

Service did not end with the Gymnopaedia, an interminable ceremony in which the boys stood naked for hours in the fierce heat of the midday sun. All young men had to live in barracks until they were 30. They were encouraged to marry, but they could only visit their wives by stealth. 'Some of them,' reports Plutarch, 'became fathers before they looked upon their own wives by daylight.' It mattered little: their education had produced an unbreakable bond. 'They neither would nor could live alone,' Plutarch continues, 'but were in manner as men incorporated one with another.'

'A city will be well fortified which is surrounded by brave men and not by bricks,' declared Lycurgus. Sparta's citizens did not work – that was for the helots, who outnumbered them 25 to 1. They were rather born and bred to fight, so in this respect the heroism of the 300 at Thermopylae should not surprise us.

apparently resigned to their fate and focusing instead on securing victory at the Olympics, Leonidas was given a force of just 7000 Greeks to combat the vast Persian army. Even Sparta – occupied by its own ceremonial games and wanting to reserve the mass of its troops to defend the Isthmus of Corinth, the gateway to the Peloponnese – only allowed its king 300 soldiers. Leonidas, who chose only men with sons old enough to assume their fathers' role, seemed in no doubt that he was going to his death, telling his wife: 'Marry a good man and have good children.'

The curt wit of the Lacedemonians spread the legend of Spartan intrepidity across the world. Asked by Xerxes' envoy to order his army to lay down its arms, Leonidas replied, 'Come and get them.' His men were no less defiant. When the Persians threatened to let loose so many arrows that the light of the sun would be blotted out, one Spartan commented, 'So much the better. We will fight in the shade.'

Xerxes was confident of victory after his scout reported that the Spartans appeared to be preparing for battle by performing stretching exercises and combing their long hair. But as wave upon wave of Persians tried to force their way through the pass the next day, they were cut down in their thousands. The oncoming Persians were forced to scale a wall of their fallen comrades, and then they found themselves in a death trap. After three days of hurling tens of thousands of men at the small band of Greeks, Xerxes withdrew to rethink.

Had it not been for the actions of one man, the Delphic Oracle might have been proved false. But when a Greek traitor called Ephialtes showed the Persians a hidden path that led behind Greek lines, the fate of Leonidas was sealed. Leonidas sent away the bulk of his army. With 700 Thespians who chose to stay, and 400 Thebans who deserted almost immediately, Leonidas and his 300 Spartans set themselves up as a rearguard to delay the Persian advance and protect the retreating Greeks. They knew they would die fighting.

They fought with spears. When their spears shattered they fought with swords. Once those were broken, they fought with teeth and hands until they fell. The historian Herodotus estimated that this tiny band inflicted losses of 20,000 on the Persians. When Leonidas' body was recovered, Xerxes, raging impotently at his ignominious victory, ordered that the dead king be decapitated and his body crucified. Forty years later Leonidas' remains were finally returned to the Spartans, to be buried with the honour they were due.

Leonidas' last stand inspired the Greeks to rally and fight for their freedom. Their subsequent victories over the Persians at sea (Salamis) and on land (Plataea) ensured that Xerxes was the first, and last, Persian sovereign to set foot on Greek soil. The suicidal bravery of the Spartans, so gloriously victorious in defeat, is commemorated in a famous epitaph inscribed on a stone marking the place where they fell at Thermopylae:

Go tell it in Sparta, stranger passing by,
That here, obedient to their laws, we lie.

Herodotus

?484–430/420 BC

[I write] in the hope of thereby preserving from decay the remembrance of what men have done.

Herodotus, The Histories, Book I

Herodotus was the West's 'Father of History'. An adventurous traveller, he used his gift for storytelling to recount the upheavals affecting the lands where Europe, Asia and Africa meet. He is best known as a hawk-eyed observer of the epic wars between Greece and Persia in the 5th century BC, but he also charted the growing rivalry between Athens and Sparta with an eye for both the minute detail and the broader view.

Herodotus was the first to employ many of the techniques of modern historical writing (or historiography), and although his credibility has sometimes been called into question, more often than not modern research has proved him right.

Little is known for certain about the exact chronology of Herodotus' life. He was probably born in Halicarnassus, which was then under Persian rule. He lived for much of his life in Athens, where he met the great Greek dramatist Sophocles. He left Athens for Thurii, a colony in southern Italy that was sponsored by Athens. The last event recorded by Herodotus took place in 430 BC, although it is not certain when he died.

If our knowledge of his life is sketchy, our understanding of Herodotus' times is exceptional, thanks to the work he undertook. He travelled extensively through Egypt, Libya, Syria, Babylonia, Lydia and Phrygia. He sailed up the Hellespont to Byzantium, visited Thrace and Macedonia, and journeyed north to the Danube, then travelled east along the northern coast of the Black Sea. In short, Herodotus took in most of the civilized world of the eastern Mediterranean and western Asia, and the boundaries of his intellect expanded as a result.

Herodotus' great work was his *Histories*. It is divided into nine books, each named after one of the Greek muses. The first five books concern the background to the Graeco-Persian Wars of 499–479 BC. The final four comprise a history of the wars themselves, culminating in the invasion of Greece by the Persian king Xerxes at the head of a vast army.

The books setting up the background to the wars are subtle works that give a wealth of geographical and political information about the Persian Empire and its rulers. They also chart the fundamental differences between Persian and Greek society, with a level of comparison that was unmatched by the city chroniclers who had been the writers of history before Herodotus. Herodotus notes how the Persian Empire, although made up of diverse peoples divided by religion, geography and language, nevertheless acts with a remarkable unity. The Greeks, by contrast, drawn from a relatively small pool of culturally homogeneous city-states, are prone to faction and infighting.

Such astute general observations help to provide an explanation for the events contemporary with Herodotus' own life, when the political rivalries and disputes within Athens affected the course of the bloody contests between the Athenians and the Spartans. This grand, thematic approach was something quite new in historical writing.

Woven in among the long-term, tidal movements of Persian and Greek societies in *The Histories* is a detailed account of four generations of Persian kings and their conquests. Herodotus first describes Cyrus the Great's expedition to Lydia, followed by Cambyses' conquest of Egypt and his stalled expedition to Ethiopia. After Cambyses' madness and death comes the reorganization and further expansion of the empire under Darius, and finally Herodotus recounts the great campaigns led by Xerxes against the Greeks.

Though Herodotus was not a military expert, he has some grasp of the basics. He understands the importance of the Persian navy to its army as it marched, and thus appreciates the significance of sea battles such as that in 480 at Salamis, where Greece's victory over the Persians marked a turning point in the war. Generally, however, Herodotus tends to attach great importance to the actions, personalities and squabbles of individual protagonists. Xerxes is portrayed as arrogant, petulant, savage and cruel, and Herodotus suggests that it was these defects of character that caused his invasion – which should have completely overwhelmed the outnumbered Greeks – to wither and fail.

The father of biography – Plutarch

The first example of the bad review in literature was Plutarch's critique *On the Malice of Herodotus*, in which he tried to expose the errors of the Father of History. Given the breadth of his historical sweep, Herodotus was bound to have made some mistakes, such as his claim in Book IV of his *Histories* that there were flying snakes in Egypt. But in many cases his conclusions have been proved correct by modern archaeologists. For example, historians now agree with his claim, long mocked, that the Etruscans of Italy were originally from Asia Minor.

But it was appropriate that the first historian's most vicious review was by Plutarch (AD 46–127), because the latter was the real creator of that other form of history, the biography. Many of his biographies are lost, but those that survive are remarkable for their profound understanding of character, historical accuracy and curiosity, which make them so readable and gripping even today.

Born in Boeotia, in Greece, to a wealthy family, Plutarch travelled widely and was a magistrate. He was well connected with the Roman emperors Hadrian, who appointed him Procurator of Achaea, and Trajan, who may have appointed him to govern Illyria. Plutarch's *Parallel Lives* of famous Greeks and Romans provides us with unforgettable portraits of figures such as Alcibiades and Mark Antony. In some ways he complements that other possible rival for the title of 'inventor of biography', Suetonius (AD 69–130), a contemporary Roman historian also connected with Hadrian and Trajan, whose compelling account of the crimes and debaucheries of the first *Twelve Caesars* is as sensationalist, mischievous and saucy as a modern tabloid newspaper.

Plutarch's work, however, is more considered than that of Suetonius. As he explained, 'It's not histories I'm writing but lives: indeed a small thing like a phrase or a jest often makes a greater revelation of a character than battles where thousands die.'

For Herodotus, pride always comes before a fall, but he empha-
sizes that such failures are not the punishment of the gods, but
rather result from human mistakes. This rational approach, in which
the gods did not intervene in the affairs of men, was a major innovation and formed the basis for the tradition of Western history. It
also made for some gripping stories.

Herodotus may be known as the 'Father of History', but he has
also been called the 'Father of Lies'. It is true that some of his tales,
such as that of the giant man-eating ants, are fables. But his methods
were those of a true historian: he compared his sources wherever
possible and showed no bias in favour of either the Greeks or their
opponents. He was also a consummate storyteller who brought his
protagonists to life, providing them with inspiring speeches and
dialogue, and often digressing with amusing anecdotes to illustrate
character. It was this gift of narration, allied to an ability to paint
on the broadest canvas, that made Herodotus the first historian,
and arguably one of the greatest ever.

Alcibiades

c.450–404 BC

It is wiser not to rear a lion's whelp, but if you do,
you must accept its ways.

The dramatist Aeschylus' verdict on Alcibiades (as represented by Aristophanes
in his play The Frogs)

Alcibiades was the gilded youth in the golden age of classical Greece,
who took centre stage in the life-and-death struggle that enveloped
Athens in the second half of the 5th century BC. A gifted politician
and brilliant military leader, he was uniquely blessed: well-born,
charming, good-looking, charismatic, quick-witted, eloquent. But his
great virtues were matched by deep flaws: vanity, unscrupulousness
and egotism. Hamstrung by his political enemies and by his own
shortcomings, he was in the end unable to harness his talents to save

his city from destruction. Yet his flashy brilliance and deadly charm somehow still fascinate us across the centuries.

At the time of Alcibiades' birth in or just before 450 BC, the city of Athens was at the height of its power and wealth. Less than 30 years earlier, the Athenians had led an alliance of Greek states to turn back the vast tide of Persian invaders rolling in from the East. But what had started as a voluntary league of equals had gradually been transformed into an Athenian maritime empire. Throughout Alcibiades' adolescence there had been growing tension and eventually, in 431, Sparta, a conservative state increasingly alarmed at the expansive imperial ambitions of Athens, could take no more and attacked, so precipitating the Peloponnesian War. This was to engulf the Greek world for the next 27 years and finally led to the total defeat of Athens.

Alcibiades' father had died in battle in 447, leaving the boy to be raised in the household of Pericles, the greatest Athenian statesman and heroic leader of the day. Alcibiades was a follower of the philosopher Socrates and his superb oratorical skills must in part have been due to the excellent grounding in rhetoric he received at the hands of Socrates and Pericles.

In 421, after ten years of indecisive fighting, Athens and Sparta negotiated the precarious Peace of Nicias. Piqued at being considered too young to take part in the peace talks, Alcibiades instead set about undermining them, first holding private discussions with the Spartan ambassadors and then attempting to ridicule them before the Athenian assembly. He was elected general in 420 and orchestrated a new alliance against Sparta, but his aggressive ambitions were thwarted two years later when the new allies were heavily defeated by the Spartans at Mantinea.

The defining moment of Alcibiades' career came in 415, when he once again took up the cause of the war party by championing an ambitious plan to send a major expeditionary force to attack the city of Syracuse in Sicily. His view prevailed and he was appointed one of the three generals to lead the expedition. However, as he was about to set sail, his enemies managed to embroil him (perhaps unjustly) in scandal when the *hermai* – sacred boundary posts positioned all around Athens – were mysteriously mutilated. The outrage was considered a bad omen for the mission, which nevertheless set sail with the charges unresolved.

Recalled to face trial, Alcibiades fled and was sentenced to death in his absence. Now revealing the full depths of his vengeance, he first persuaded the Spartans to send forces to reinforce Syracuse, which contributed to the catastrophic defeat of the Athenians two years later. Then he encouraged Sparta to build a fortified outpost at Decelea, in sight of the city of Athens. This cut off the Athenians from their homes, crops and silver mines, forcing them to live inside the city walls all year round.

Having caused trouble for Athens at home, Alcibiades moved east to Ionia (Asia Minor), fomenting revolts among Athens' subject allies. However, his scheming with Sparta came to an abrupt end when he was suspected of having an affair with the Spartan king's wife. In mortal danger, he defected once again, this time to Persia. Now in negotiation with the Persians, Alcibiades was involved in stirring up political unrest in Athens, where in 411 a new (albeit short-lived) oligarchic regime was set up.

Believing (unrealistic) promises of Persian assistance, the Athenian fleet reinstated Alcibiades as general. Between 411 and 408 he redeemed himself by leading the Athenians to a spectacular recovery with a series of military successes. Most notably, he inflicted a crushing defeat on the Spartan fleet at Cyzicus in 410 and helped Athens regain control over the supply route through the Black Sea.

The Greek trireme of the 5th century BC

In response to the Persian invasions of 490 and 480–79 BC the Athenians constructed several hundred triremes (galleys powered by three banks of oars), manned by crews drawn from the lower classes of society.

The Athenian navy played a crucial role in the Greek victory against the Persians at Salamis in 480 BC, which allowed Athens to create an Aegean empire based on naval superiority.

The Greek trireme was powered by some 170 oarsmen, and in addition to its captain and crew it carried a fighting force of archers and hoplite soldiers.

Invited back to Athens and cleared of any impropriety, Alcibiades was given complete command of the war on land and at sea. But following a naval setback at Notium in 406 (due to the disobedience of one of his subordinates – Alcibiades himself was absent), he lost his position. In 405, following a catastrophic naval defeat at Aegospotami – which occurred despite Alcibiades' warnings to the Athenian commanders – he returned to Persia, where he was murdered, probably at the instigation of Sparta, in 404.

Alcibiades was a mass of contradictions, capable of brilliance one moment and utter recklessness the next. He proved himself to be a superb military commander and a gifted politician; but he was also a flawed hero and capricious chameleon. At its times of greatest need, Athens could not trust him enough to make use of his colossal talents, leading finally to his own destruction and that of his city.

Aristotle 384–322 BC

Aristotle was, and still is, the sovereign lord of the understanding.

Samuel Taylor Coleridge

Aristotle was the philosophical giant whose astounding intellect laid the principal foundations of Western thought. He was the ultimate polymath: ethicist, physicist, biologist, psychologist, metaphysicist, logician, literary and political theorist. But Aristotle was no head-in-the-clouds speculator. Being tutor to Alexander the Great ensured that his feet stayed firmly on the ground.

The son of Macedonia's court physician, Aristotle spent 20 years studying under Plato at his Academy in Athens. His unquenchable thirst for knowledge prompted his tutor to comment that he needed 'a bridle', and Aristotle's enthusiasm shines through in his scientific works. His *History of Animals*, begun in the decade he spent travelling after Plato's death, is a complete record of every species of animal known to the Greek world; he charts innumerable organisms, using

Plato

Pupil of Socrates and teacher of Aristotle, Plato (c.428–347 BC) showed such vision and originality in his thinking that he stands as the second and central figure in the great triumvirate that laid the foundations of Western thought.

Born to a noble Athenian family, Plato could trace his ancestry back to the last kings of Athens. He was a disciple and fervent admirer of the plebeian Socrates, whose refusal to toe the line and temper his ideas brought about his enforced suicide for impiety and corruption of youth in 399 BC.

Disappointed by the demagogic democracy of Athens, Plato travelled abroad, to Italy and to Syracuse. On his return to Athens he founded in 387 BC the Academy, an institution that trained the greatest thinkers of the next generation, of which Aristotle was the brightest star. Teaching at the Academy until his death 40 years later, Plato wrote his greatest works, including the many Socratic dialogues featuring his inspirational tutor and the monumental *Republic*, in which he outlines the ideal state.

It has been said that Western philosophy exists as footnotes to Plato.

his minute observations to explain their structure. There are of course some errors (a bison, for instance, is unlikely to defend itself by projectile excretion), but this work of genius and tireless energy nevertheless paved the way for the science of zoology.

A willingness to refine or contradict previous doctrines and opinions; to pose questions to which he did not know the answers; to wrestle with his own ideas – in all these ways, Aristotle transformed the methodology of thought. His surviving works do not make easy reading. They are mostly fragments, used as notes when he lectured at the academies he established on his travels and at the Lyceum, the covered garden in which he taught on his return to Athens. The school of philosophy that Aristotle founded – the Peripatetic school – is believed to have been named after the Lyceum's walkway (*peripatos*), where he delivered his lectures with lucidity and wit. Greece's brightest youth flocked to learn from him.

The wealthy dandy who sported jewellery and a fashionable haircut championed the mind above all else. Aristotle's philosophy insisted on thought as man's greatest attribute. Philosophical speculation

An extreme rationalist, Plato was a proponent of the philosopher-ruler of the *Republic*, who would reign only according to reason. But as experience suggested that no man was capable of such restraint, he proposed that laws must rigidly circumscribe a ruler's actions. He adopted the ideas of Socrates in arguing that the Good is an immutable and fundamental concept or 'form'. While opinion may shift, Plato argued, knowledge is eternal and unchanging; goodness is objective, inextricably linked to justice and personal well-being.

Plato was the first major thinker to express the idea that the higher functions of the mind (*psyche*) are, or should be, in control of the base passions and appetites of the body. His belief that the soul is a prisoner inside the body was countered by Aristotle's view that it is an inherent part of the body. In the Middle Ages the brilliance of the disciple, known throughout the Western world simply as 'the Philosopher', overshadowed that of his visionary tutor. But in recent centuries thinkers have generally recognized the greatness of the man whom Aristotle so esteemed that he considered it 'blasphemy in the extreme even to praise'.

implied civilization: only when a person had secured everything else could he afford the luxury of pure, untrammelled thought. In his works on ethics Aristotle came to the conclusion that human goodness derives from rational thought – that 'the good of man is the active exercise of his soul's faculties in conformity with excellence'; it is an assertion of the uniqueness of mankind that has influenced our understanding of civilization ever since.

The reputedly lisping logician established a new vocabulary of thought. Aristotle made logic an independent branch of philosophy. Struggling to express his meaning more precisely, he coined new terms for his concepts: 'substance', 'essence', 'potential', 'energy'. He argued that as language is a distinctively human trait, it is therefore an expression of the soul. He developed the idea that analysis of our words is the key to understanding our thought. His system of syllogistic logic (e.g. 'All men are mortal; Greeks are men; therefore Greeks are mortal') was the cornerstone of logical analysis for over 2000 years.

At the age of 42 Aristotle returned to his homeland to prepare the

Macedonian king's 13-year-old son Alexander for his future as a political leader and general. Aristotle tried to instil in his charge two of Greece's greatest contributions to civilization: epic heroism and philosophy. How much of Aristotle's political theory he absorbed is open to debate. Aristotle's ideas were based on the belief that Greeks were superior to other races. While he recognized that governments must be chosen in accordance with their citizens' needs and capacities, he favoured the city-state ruled by an enlightened oligarchy as the best form of government. Such ideas may not have had much impact on Alexander as that autocratic ruler forged his empire. Nevertheless, Aristotle's beliefs were a vast advance on contemporary political concepts and they fundamentally influenced the development of Greek civilization.

In his *Poetics* Aristotle established the fundamentals of tragedy that would long be observed in drama: unity of action and a central character whose tragic flaw, such as *hubris* (excess of pride), brings about his downfall. Aristotle also identified a process of cleansing or purification (*catharsis*) in which the audience's feelings of pity and fear are purged by experiencing them vicariously through the actions played out on stage.

The death of Alexander in 323 BC released in Athens a wave of anti-Macedonian sentiment, forcing Aristotle to flee the city. Referring to the death of that other great thinker Socrates, Aristotle reportedly said he feared the Athenians would sin twice against philosophy. He withdrew to his mother's estates on the island of Euboea but died of a stomach complaint just one year later.

Aristotle was reputedly kind and affectionate. His will was generous to his children and servants. It makes reference (as his philosophy implies) to a happy family life. He described man as 'a monument of frailty', but the ultimate conclusion of his philosophy is optimistic. According to Plato, the soul is trapped in the body, desperate to escape the world of change and illusion. Aristotle argued instead that the soul is an inherent part of the body and that life is desirable for its own sake.

Aristotle's world view, like so much of his thought, delighted in man and celebrated his potential. He believed that 'All men by nature desire to know'. This colossus of thought was ceaseless in his desire to advance human knowledge. Even to say that Aristotle influenced Western thought is an understatement – he determined it.

Alexander the Great 356–323 BC

He would not have remained content with any of his conquests, not even if he had added the British Isles to Europe; he would always have reached beyond for something unknown, and if there had been no other competition, he would have competed against himself.

Arrian, *The Anabasis* (c.AD 150), translated as *Alexander's Expedition*, 7.1

Alexander of Macedon stretched the limits of the possible. In little more than a decade of brilliant military campaigning, he forged the greatest empire the world had seen, stretching from Greece and Egypt in the west to India in the east and taking in all or part of 17 modern states. It is said that he wept that there were no more worlds to conquer. With some justification, the statue erected to him after his death bore the legend 'I hold the Earth'.

Alexander was one of the greatest military commanders who has ever lived. Julius Caesar, a great general in his own right, was plunged into deep despair whenever he pondered Alexander's achievements. But Alexander is also heroic for his personal beauty, grace and courage and above all for his tolerance and chivalry.

Within two years of inheriting the Macedonian throne on the assassination of his remarkable warrior-king father, Philip of Macedon, the 4ft 6in (1.35m) 22-year-old had united Greece's disparate city-states under his leadership in order to wage war on the mighty Persian Empire. It was the Hellenic world's most prized dream, and a goal Philip had spent his life working towards.

Alexander set out on his mission in 334 BC. Within two years the Persians had been totally defeated in victories such as that at Issus, which showed Alexander's military genius and tactical virtuosity. He went on to establish himself at the head of his own empire, one that included not only Greece and Macedonia but also the entire Middle East, from Egypt and Asia Minor to Mesopotamia, Persia and beyond, into Afghanistan, parts of Central Asia and, on the far side of the Hindu Kush mountains, the rich valley of the Indus. Only the final, stubborn refusal of his Macedonian army to breach the limits of the known world prevented him from going further. When he died in Babylon, aged just 32, he was planning the conquest of Arabia and may have had designs on the western Mediterranean.

Alexander's rule united East and West for the first time. Perhaps influenced by his boyhood tutor, Aristotle, Alexander was determined to govern well. He ordered his ministers to 'break up the oligarchies everywhere and set up democracies instead'. He forbade his armies to plunder conquered lands, and he founded new cities galore – usually named Alexandria. The greatest of these, at

Cleopatra, last of the Ptolemies

Three Greek empires emerged from the violent power struggles of his generals after Alexander the Great's death: Antigonid Macedonia, Seleucid Syria and Ptolemaic Egypt, the latter founded by the most impressive of Alexander's successors, Ptolemy. By the 1st century BC these empires had been subjugated to Rome, although they were still notionally ruled by Greek dynasties.

The Ptolemies had adopted the Egyptian pantheon of gods and the ancient Pharaonic practice of sibling marriage. The teenage Cleopatra VII (69–30 BC) co-inherited the throne with her brother-husband Ptolemy XIII, but Cleopatra made clear her intention to rule alone. Forced into exile by her brother, she sought the support of Julius Caesar, the most powerful man in Rome.

Cleopatra smuggled herself to Caesar rolled up in a carpet. As soon as the highly intelligent and seductive queen tumbled out at his feet, Caesar was bewitched. Six months later, as he fled the lovers' combined forces, Ptolemy XIII drowned in the Nile. Cleopatra's youngest brother became Ptolemy XIV and her new husband.

Bearing a son called Caesarion, the Egyptian queen lived openly as Caesar's consort in Rome, causing a scandal. It was rumoured that Caesar intended to become king of Rome and make Cleopatra his queen. On the Ides of March in 44 BC Caesar was murdered by his political enemies, and Cleopatra fled.

the mouth of the Nile Delta, became for many centuries the intellectual and commercial centre of the Mediterranean world. Alexander wanted to create an empire fusing the best of both Greek and Eastern cultures. He recruited Persians into his armies and assigned Persian wives to his generals, sending back to Europe any Macedonians who resisted this enforced equality. He himself married the daughter of the dethroned Persian emperor.

Alexander was revered as a god in his own lifetime. He was reputedly a descendant of Achilles on his mother's side, and rumours of Alexander's supernatural abilities abounded, reinforced by his unnatural speed and apparent personal invincibility in battle. He was also a romantic idealist as well as a man of action. Described

Back in Egypt, with her co-regent Caesarion (Ptolemy XIV having died in mysterious circumstances), Cleopatra set about re-establishing her influence. The swashbuckling general Mark Antony, one of the Triumvirate who now ruled the Republic, summoned Cleopatra to his presence. Her breathtaking entrance – reclining, dressed as Venus on a gold-burnished barge – captivated Antony as effectively as the carpet trick had hooked Caesar. The great general abandoned his duties and Rome for a life of hedonism with Egypt's queen. But she was politically determined to use Roman backing to re-establish the Ptolemaic Empire.

The besotted Antony treated Cleopatra not as a protected sovereign but as an independent monarch. He gave her vast tracts of Syria, Lebanon and Cyprus, and appointed their children the monarchs of half a dozen countries. But Rome could not allow the re-emergence of an independent Ptolemaic empire. Pressed by Octavian, one third of the Triumvirate and half-brother to Antony's abandoned Roman wife, the Senate in Rome declared war on Egypt.

The lovers who had designated themselves gods were vanquished by Octavian at the Battle of Actium in 31 BC. Antony committed suicide, and Cleopatra, rather than facing the shame of being paraded in chains through Rome, had a venomous snake smuggled to her in a basket of figs. When Octavian's soldiers came for her, they found the great queen laid out on her golden bed, the pinpricks of an asp's deadly fangs on her arm. Cleopatra had wanted to be the greatest of her dynasty, but she turned out to be its memorable last.

by a friend as 'the only philosopher whom I have ever seen in arms', he loved poetry and music. As a boy he declared that if he could only save one possession it would be Homer's *Iliad*. He was always alert to symbolism. On first setting foot on the shores of the Persian Empire, in Asia Minor, his first act was to make a pilgrimage to Troy to honour his ancestor Achilles. He named Bucephala, a town on the Indus, after his beloved horse Bucephalus, which had died in battle.

Alexander also had a wild side, revealed in his proclivity for raucous behaviour. He drunkenly killed one of his officers in a row at a banquet, a crime he deeply regretted. His own death is said to have resulted from too much carousing. 'Sex and sleep alone make me conscious that I am mortal,' he reportedly declared. He had several wives and mistresses, but his great love was his boyhood friend Hephaistion.

Alexander could be ruthless. On succeeding to the throne after his father's assassination, he executed all rival claimants, including his infant half-brother. He executed one of his greatest friends for treason, and also the friend's blameless father. The latter was in fact one of his most faithful generals, but Alexander refused to run the risk of paternal vengeance. He enslaved the Tyrians after they resisted his siege of their city and razed Thebes to the ground, a warning to the restless Greek city-states of what they could expect from rebellion. Towards the end of his life he became increasingly despotic.

Alexander's treatment of his enemies, however, often demonstrated his nobility of spirit. When an Indian king demanded to face him in battle, Alexander fought and defeated him, but rewarded his honour with the restoration of his kingdom and that of a less fortunate neighbour as well. He treated the wives of Darius, the defeated Persian emperor, with 'the utmost delicacy and respect'. He allowed the Jews, Persians and others to worship as they wished.

Alexander changed the face of the world. When asked on his deathbed to whom he would leave his kingdom, Alexander replied: 'To the strongest.' After his death, the empire spanning half the world disintegrated. No one could match him.

Hannibal 247–c.183 BC

Let no love or treaty be between our nations. Arise, unknown avenger, from my ashes to pursue with fire and sword ... may they have war, they and their children's children!

The suicidal Dido, queen of Carthage, to her lover Aeneas, who has abandoned her to found Rome – in the words of Virgil's *Aeneid*

The Carthaginian general Hannibal was the man who came closest to bringing Rome to its knees. A commander of determination and resourcefulness, he devised novel strategies and tactics that are still studied today. He achieved the seemingly impossible in leading an army and more than thirty war elephants over the Alps into Italy, where he inflicted a series of crushing defeats on the Romans. To them he was their nemesis, a terrifying and ruthless figure, his very name evoking fear and dread and inspiring the phrase 'Hannibal is at the gates!'

Carthage, near modern-day Tunis, had been settled by Phoenicians in the 9th century BC, and the Carthaginians proceeded to build up their own trading empire in the region. It was in Sicily that Carthage first came up against its rival for power in the western Mediterranean: Rome. The consequence was the First Punic War, from which Rome emerged victorious in 241 BC.

Hannibal's father, the general and statesman Hamilcar Barca, had fought in this war, and it is said that he made his young son swear eternal hatred for the Romans. Hannibal fought alongside him as he conquered to build a new Carthaginian empire in Spain. In 221 BC, some years after his father's death in battle, Hannibal was appointed commander in Spain, and here, three years later, seeking revenge for his father's defeat by the Romans, he deliberately provoked the Second Punic War by capturing the city of Saguntum, an ally of Rome.

Determined on the complete destruction of his sworn enemy, Hannibal assembled 40,000 infantry, 12,000 cavalry and a contingent of war elephants. With this mighty force he crossed the Pyrenees and traversed southern Gaul and the waters of the Rhône to the foothills of the Alps. Historians argue about Hannibal's precise route, but whichever sequence of passes he used would have presented formidable obstacles. Not only did he have to contend with narrow icy paths, landslides and starvation, but he also had to fight off hostile local tribes. Eventually, after a five-month ordeal, Hannibal and the surviving half of his army arrived on the plains of northern Italy, ready to march on Rome.

The Alpine crossing had been made possible by the immense loyalty Hannibal commanded. Even Hannibal's staunchest enemies recognized his remarkable rapport with his men, who were drawn from many different peoples. As the historian Polybius remarked, his enterprises were 'desperate and extraordinary', but Hannibal never asked his men to do what he would not do himself. He had been only 26 when the army in Spain had elected him their commander, and in all his long career there is no record of mutiny or even a desertion among his forces.

Sometimes known as the 'Father of Strategy', Hannibal pioneered the idea that war could be won beyond the set-piece battle. A master of the ambush, he attacked the enemy's communications and seized cities and supplies behind its back. The Romans accused him of duplicity, but he was also masterly in open battle, as his overwhelming victories over the Romans at Lake Trasimene (217) and the bloodbath that was Cannae attest. His deployment of encirclement at Cannae (216), resulting in a reported 50,000 Roman deaths, was admired by Napoleon and Wellington and is still discussed by military tacticians. After this humiliation of Roman military prestige, some of Rome's allies in Italy deserted to the Carthaginian side.

Receiving negligible support from Carthage, Hannibal had to levy troops on the spot and provision his men himself. Eventually the Romans deployed guerrilla tactics too, wearing their enemy down. Hannibal continued to campaign, largely in southern Italy, with little help from his Italian allies. Despite winning some further victories, his army was never strong enough to attack Rome itself. In 207 his younger brother, Hasdrubal Barca, led another Carthaginian army into Italy to join with Hannibal in a march on Rome, but Hasdrubal was killed and his army defeated at the River Metaurus.

Elephants at war

Western history has indelibly associated the exotic fighting elephant with Hannibal's feat in leading more than thirty of them across the Alps. But the elephant had a long history as a war machine, effectively the tank of the ancient world. Clad in steel armour, with blades attached to their tusks and a 'howdah' full of warriors on their backs, they were a terrifying sight. No wonder the hostile Alpine tribes preferred to avoid the beasts during their attacks on Hannibal's column.

The war elephant originated in southern Asia, where a horde of pachyderms was an essential part of every Indian king's army. Alexander the Great was the first Hellene to encounter them in battle, when fighting the Persians at Gaugamela in 331 BC. In the centuries to come, his successors eagerly adopted the war elephant. When Pyrrhus of Epirus used elephants to invade Italy, he thereby introduced the 'Lucanian cow' to the Roman world.

When the Syrian Seleucids blocked the supply of Indian elephants, the Ptolemies and Carthaginians turned to the African elephant – not the giants of the savannah but the smaller forest variety. These animals were large enough to carry only their handlers, and, according to the Roman chronicler Polybius, they lacked the fighting spirit. In the nearest thing to a head-to-head contest between the two species, at Raphia in 217 BC, the African elephants turned tail and fled when faced with their larger, smellier Indian counterparts. Of Hannibal's 37 elephants, only his lone Indian one, Surus, survived the first Italian winter.

Impervious to arrows and fearsome in their bulk, elephants could wreak havoc in their enemy's forces. Horses bolted and fled in terror, and infantrymen were crushed underfoot. But their strength could be turned against their own side. At Hydaspes in 326 BC, Alexander forced back the enemy so that they were hemming in their own elephants. Panic-stricken, the exhausted beasts became ungovernable, and, trumpeting in distress, they trampled everything within sight in their efforts to back out of the human *mêlée*. The Romans learnt to sidestep elephants as they advanced – a method Scipio employed to great effect at Zama in 202 BC.

Despite their disadvantages, war elephants were still being used in India and Southeast Asia as late as the 16th century, when a Mughal chronicler marvelled at the 'dragon-mouthed rushing mountains' that 'ruined lofty buildings by shaking them and sportively uprooted strong trees'. However, with the advent of field artillery around this time, the elephant – once the terror of the battlefield – was outdated as a viable weapon of war. It was demoted to the humbler, if more peaceful, role of pack animal.

When, in 203, the Roman general Scipio Africanus mounted a counter-invasion of North Africa, Hannibal was recalled to Carthage, and the following year was defeated decisively by Scipio at the Battle of Zama. Charged by Carthage's senate with misconduct of the war, Hannibal entered politics, where his admirable administrative and constitutional reforms alienated Carthage's old elite; before long they denounced him to the Romans. Hannibal fled.

Hannibal spent his last years waging war against Rome for any prince who would have him. He served Antiochus III of Syria and then was heard of in Crete and Armenia. He ended up at the court of King Prusias of Bithynia, but the Romans had long memories and were set on revenge. Eventually they pressured Prusias to give Hannibal up, but the great general chose death over captivity. In the Bithynian village of Libyssa he drank the poison that he had long carried with him in his ring, and so evaded his old enemy one final time.

The Maccabees

2nd century BC

God forbid that we should forsake the law and our ordinances. We will not hearken to the king's words to go from our religion

1 Maccabees 2:19

The Maccabees, so named for their hammer-like military force, were five brothers – and their elderly father – who, against all odds, rebelled against and defeated an oppressive empire to win religious and political freedom – and establish their own Jewish dynasty. The Greek Seleucids, polytheistic descendants of one of Alexander the Great's generals, ruled a huge Middle Eastern empire that included Judea, where the Jews worshipped their one god. Foolishly breaking with Alexander's admirable tolerance, Antiochus IV, the Seleucid king of the Syrian Empire, took for himself the name 'Epiphanes' (meaning the manifestation of a divine being) and decided to crush the Jewish religion. He issued a series of decrees banning Judaism in all its manifestations. Observance of the Torah, the laws of keeping kosher, the practice of circumcision – all were forbidden on pain of death. In 168 BC the Jewish Temple, the holiest place in Jerusalem, was forcibly converted to a shrine to Zeus, while troops patrolled the streets and the countryside to make sure the Judeans were now worshipping Hellenic gods.

Many Judeans did comply with the new laws, while a minority fled. It was old Mattathias, a priest at the hill town of Modin, who initiated active resistance by lashing out at a Jew complying with the new orthodoxies and killing a soldier of the evil empire. With his five sons, Mattathias retreated to Jordan to marshal his Jewish forces into a formidable guerrilla army. People flocked to join them from across Judea, rightly sensing that in these men they had found the champions of their faith.

The events of 168–164 BC are testimony to their bravery and leadership. Having dispensed with the essentially suicidal refusal to fight on the Sabbath (a prick of conscience that had ensured early defeats for them), the rebels achieved dazzling victories against the Seleucids and the Jewish 'collaborators' ranged against them. Much of this success was thanks to the inspired leadership of the eldest son Judah, dubbed 'Maccabeus' ('The Hammer') before the name was applied to the family as a whole. A talented and sometimes ruthless general, he transformed an assorted band of the pious and the outlawed into a guerrilla crack force. Under his leadership they inflicted a series of crushing defeats on better-equipped troops who vastly outnumbered them.

Within three years the Maccabees had taken Jerusalem, and in 164 BC the now more accommodating Antiochus died and his successor sued for peace (albeit a temporary one). Vitally, Jewish freedom of worship was restored. The Temple was cleansed and rededicated in December 164 BC. Even though the oil for the Temple lamp had run out, the lamp remained alight for eight days, a miracle that inspired the joyful Hanukkah Festival of Lights, in which Jews still celebrate religious freedom from tyranny.

Having won the right to practise their religion, the Maccabees fought on for the political freedom that would protect it. The result was the creation of an independent Jewish state, with Mattathias'

The Jewish Temple

The Temple in Jerusalem has been the symbol of the Jewish faith, and the Jewish nation, for 3000 years. The First Temple, from the golden age of Solomon's reign in the 10th century BC, was, in its biblical descriptions, a dazzling edifice of gold and intricate carving created to house the Ark of the Covenant, which contained the Ten Commandments. It reputedly took seven years of labour and a workforce of 150,000 Canaanites and 30,000 Israelites to build. Benefiting from the materials and the expertise of Hiram of Tyre, the First Temple was a marvel that exalted God and his kingdom, and celebrated the commercial and cosmopolitan might of Solomon's empire.

In the centuries that followed, and amid the divisions and weaknesses of the Jewish kingdoms, the riches of the Temple proved too tempting for foreign kings. It was ruthlessly plundered by marauding armies, and in the 6th century BC Nebuchadnezzar II of Babylonia, who had already ransacked the Temple twice, destroyed it completely and deported the Jews to Babylonia. Fifty years later the Persian conqueror Cyrus II allowed the Jews to return to Jerusalem and rebuild their Temple.

The Second Temple was so plain that old men who had seen the First were supposed to have wept at the sight of it. But its sanctity and treasures were largely respected until the 2nd-century attempts of the Seleucid Antiochus IV to impose the Greek pantheon on the Jewish people and desecrate the Temple, an act the Jews could only refer to as 'the abomination of desolation'.

descendants at its head. Fighting to drive the Syrian Empire out of Judea, Judah was killed in battle. His successor, Jonathan 'the cunning', secured his brother's military achievements with diplomacy. As dynastic struggle and civil war consumed the Syrian Empire, Jonathan's astute appraisal of the political balance, and judicious offers of support, secured him substantial territorial gains. In 142 BC Simon, the youngest and by now the only surviving son of Mattathias, negotiated the political independence of Judea. It was the culmination of all his family had fought for. A year later, by popular decree, he was invested as hereditary leader and high priest of the state. This marked the establishment of the Hasmonean dynasty,

Resanctified by the Maccabees in 164 BC, the Temple was restored under their Hasmonean dynasty to some of its former splendour. But it was under King Herod the Great of Judea, from about 20 BC, that the Second Temple reached a height of magnificence that surpassed even the glory of the First.

Herod rebuilt it to impress his Roman overlords and ingratiate himself with his Jewish subjects. He publicly assembled all the building materials before he began the project. The body of the Temple, a replica of the ancient Temple but faced in dazzling white stone, was rebuilt in just over a year. Herod was extravagant with the surrounding structures. Great gates of silver, gold and bronze towered over magnificent courtyards, cloisters and porticoes. The Temple held Judea's highest court of law as well as the Holy Scriptures. 'He who has not seen the House of Herod,' reports the Talmud, the chronicle of Jewish Law, 'has never in his life seen a beautiful structure.'

This grandiosely renovated Second Temple was destroyed in AD 70/1, less than 50 years after its completion. Revolting against Rome's rule, the Jews took refuge behind the Temple's fortress-like walls. In the ensuing siege a Roman soldier, apparently accidentally, threw a burning torch into its grounds. All that remains today is the portion of stone known today as the Wailing Wall, still for Jews the holiest place in the world. The Temple Mount itself is sacred not only to Jews but also to Muslims, for it is the site of their Dome of the Rock mosque.

which took its title from Mattathias' family name. For the next century and a half, the Maccabees ruled over an independent Jewish state.

The Maccabees represent nobility, courage and freedom, as well as the audacity to resist an empire and the right of all to worship as they wish. In a David-and-Goliath struggle, a small band of warriors succeeded in defeating the mighty phalanxes of an arrogant despot.

Cicero 106–43 BC

There was a humanity in Cicero, a something almost of Christianity, a stepping forward out of the dead intellectualities of Roman life into moral perceptions, into natural affections, into domesticity, philanthropy, and conscious discharge of duty . . .

Anthony Trollope, in the introduction to his *Life of Cicero* (1880)

Cicero was a supreme master of the spoken word whose stirring calls in defence of the Roman Republic finally cost him his life. In his own day he was uncontested as Rome's finest orator, a statesman whose devotion and loyalty to the Republic was unquestioned. But he was also a man of exceptional intellect and refinement who has arguably exerted a greater influence on Western civilization than any other of the ancients.

In spite of being a *novus homo* ('new man') – none of his ancestors had attained the highest offices of state – Marcus Tullius Cicero went on to become one of Rome's leading statesmen. A brilliant youth who studied under the best minds of the day, he entered the law as a route to politics. He rose swiftly and was renowned for the brilliance of his mind and his dazzling oratorical skills.

Cicero was never troubled by false modesty, but the Roman people generally shared his high opinion of himself. An outsider to the patrician-dominated political system, he won election to the highest offices of state, in each case at the earliest permitted age. In 63 BC, after reaching the pinnacle of political preferment, the consulship, he quickly established himself as a national hero. Discovering the Catiline conspiracy, a patrician plot to overthrow the republic, Cicero successfully swayed the senate into decreeing the death penalty for the conspirators, trouncing Julius Caesar in debate in the process. When he announced their execution to the crowds with just one word, *vixerunt* ('their lives are done'), Cicero was hailed with tumultuous rapture as *pater patriae* – 'father of the country'.

Cicero was the greatest orator Rome ever produced. In the space of a few sentences he could move juries and crowds from laughter to tears, anger or pity. Using simple words he could expose the heart of a complex matter, but if required he could befuddle his audience with rhetoric, winning cases by, as he put it, 'throwing dust in the jurymen's eyes'. His renowned declaration 'Civis romanus sum' ('I am a Roman citizen') has come to encapsulate the defence of a citizen's rights against the overbearing power of the state. Cicero's highly distinctive speaking style transformed the written language. His ability to layer clause upon clause while maintaining his argument's clear line became the model for formal Latin.

A century after Cicero's death, Plutarch eulogized him as the republic's last true friend. In a time of civil unrest Cicero harked back to a golden age of political decorum. Idealistic yet consistent, he was convinced that virtue in public life would restore the republic to health. Refusing to be involved in political intrigue that might undermine the system, he rejected Caesar's offer to join him in the so-called 'First Triumvirate' of 60 BC. Cicero played no part in Caesar's assassination in 44 BC, but he seized on the end of his dictatorship to vigorously re-enter politics. Over the following months, taking his lead from the renowned Athenian orator Demosthenes, Cicero delivered the *Philippics*, a series of 14 coruscating orations against the tyranny of Caesar and against his faithful henchman Mark Antony. It was a magnificent, if ultimately forlorn, cry for political freedom.

After Caesar as dictator had encouraged the staunch republican to refrain from politics, Cicero turned to philosophy to keep himself amused. As a youth he had been tutored by the famous Greek philosophers of the day. His knowledge, as broad as it was deep, was unmatched in Rome. Cicero's treatise on the value of philosophy, *Hortensius*, was practically required reading in late antiquity. St Augustine credited it as instrumental in his conversion. The early Catholic Church deemed Cicero a 'righteous pagan'.

Cicero introduced to Rome the Greek ideas that formed the basis of Western thought for the next 2000 years. His works have sometimes been criticized as derivative, but he laid little claim to originality in his treatises. 'They are transcripts.' he wrote to a friend. 'I simply supply words and I've plenty of those.' It is a remarkably humble statement for a man who made such an

Julius Caesar, or, How to make it in ancient Rome

For every budding Roman politician the formal route to power was through the *cursus honorum*, or 'course of honours' – a sequence of year-long offices whose holders were elected in popular assemblies. After an obligatory decade of military service, a citizen could seek election to become a *quaestor*, administering public finance and (after 81 BC) enjoying automatic entry to Rome's supreme governing body, the Senate. Next was *praetor*, who engaged in judicial administration with many of the powers of a consul (including *imperium* – the supreme authority to command in time of war and to interpret the laws). After that came the consulship: two consuls, elected every year, enjoyed full *imperium*. From 180 BC a law decreed minimum ages for each office and the amount of time that should pass between holding them. The mark of a rising star was appointment *suo anno* ('in his own year') – at the earliest permitted age – a feat Cicero achieved for every office.

That was the system in theory. However, the heroic career of Gaius Julius Caesar demonstrates how military success and imperial conquest became the real route to executive power. Born *c.*100 BC, Caesar was well connected, good-looking, pleasure-loving, intelligent and bold. Elected consul in 61 BC, he managed to form the First Triumvirate with the powerful Pompey and Crassus to rule Rome peacefully. But he really made his name with his astounding nine-year conquest of Gaul and the West for Rome, a campaign he later recounted (in the third person) in his *Commentaries*, revealing his expertise as a historian.

extraordinary contribution to Western philosophy: he translated Greek works, invented Latin words to explain hitherto untranslatable concepts, and elucidated the main philosophical schools. His vast discourse amounted to an encyclopedia of Greek thought.

In the end, Cicero's inability to hold his tongue proved his undoing. When Octavian, Caesar's adopted son and the future 'Augustus', learned of Cicero's remark about him – 'the young man should be given praise, distinctions, and then disposed of' – it spelled doom for the orator. Octavian, Mark Antony and Lepidus formed the Second Triumvirate shortly afterwards, and Cicero was

In 54 and 55 BC he invaded, but did not occupy, Britain. In 53 the Triumvirate fell apart; Pompey dominated Rome and the Senate ordered Caesar to resign his command. Caesar's crossing of the Rubicon, the river that separated his own Gallic provinces from Italy itself, marked his bid for power. Pompey fled to Greece, and Caesar took Rome, where he was appointed dictator. Caesar defeated his enemies at Pharsalus in 48 BC. Pompey was afterwards murdered in Egypt, where Caesar, again dictator and consul, fell in love with Cleopatra and fought to establish her rule before moving on to defeat Rome's powerful foe King Mithridates of Pontus. Celebrating these four great victories, Caesar turned down the throne but received the title Father of the Country, *imperator*, dictator for life and consul for ten years, and he was declared to be sacred.

In 44 BC Caesar's monarchical ambitions led to his assassination by conspirators under his erstwhile supporters Brutus and Cassius. After they were defeated in a civil war, the empire was uneasily divided between Mark Antony and Caesar's great-nephew (and adopted son), Octavian. In 31 BC, however, Octavian defeated Antony at Actium, thereby uniting the Roman Empire. He created the superb civil service that ensured a *Pax Romana* for four centuries and founded a hereditary dynasty, the Julio-Claudians, who ruled until AD 68. Raised to *princeps* (emperor), and taking the name 'Augustus' (Sacred), this managerial genius 'found Rome in brick and left her in marble' – though his dynasty also produced the unhinged emperors Caligula and Nero. The very name 'Caesar' came to signify legitimate power, the German 'Kaiser' and Russian 'Tsar' being its derivatives.

declared an enemy of the state. Pursued by soldiers as he half-heartedly fled Italy, Cicero was brutally murdered, his head hacked off, and the hand with which he had written the offending speeches displayed in the Roman forum.

'There is nothing proper about what you are doing, soldier,' Cicero reportedly said to his assassin, 'but do try to kill me properly.' The rhetorical skill of the statesman was undimmed to the last. Ardent defender of the Roman Republic, transformative orator, sparkling intellect: principled and unbending in life, in death Cicero was dignified and fearless.

Jesus c. 4 BC—c. AD 30

Blessed are the poor in spirit, for theirs is the kingdom of heaven.

Blessed are those who mourn, for they shall be comforted.

Blessed are the meek, for they shall inherit the earth.

The first three of the nine beatitudes (blessings) delivered by Jesus in his Sermon on the Mount

Jesus of Nazareth was the founder of Christianity, whose followers believe that he was the son and earthly manifestation of God. He lived in Palestine during the Roman occupation, and after working as a carpenter he had a relatively short-lived public career in which he preached the coming of the kingdom of God and exhorted his followers to live lives of humility and compassion. He is also reported to have healed the sick and performed miracles. As a result of his activities, he was crucified, after which Christians believe he rose from the dead and ascended to heaven. His legacy, in the form of the Christian Church, not only underpins much of Western society and culture but also provides spiritual inspiration and guidance to millions of people worldwide.

The story of Jesus' birth is well known, but little is recorded of the rest of his early years. His parents were Joseph, a carpenter, and Mary, who is known as the Virgin, though the Gospels of the New Testament differ over whether Jesus was immaculately conceived. He was born in the town of Bethlehem during a census that took place at the end of the reign of the puppet king Herod the Great, who died in 4 BC. Various groups of pilgrims, including shepherds and 'wise men' from the East, visited him at the time of his birth.

Jesus was apparently a precociously intelligent child. As a young man he went to be baptized by his cousin, John the Baptist, a prophet who had predicted his arrival. Some time after this, Jesus became an itinerant preacher and healer, travelling the Jewish areas of Palestine and spreading his message.

The Gospels report that Jesus was able, usually by the laying-on of hands, to cure men and women of blindness, paralysis, leprosy, deafness, dumbness and bleeding. He was also famed for his powers of exorcism – he visited synagogues to cast out demons, thereby apparently curing both mental and physical ailments. It is said that he conferred this ability on his disciples.

Further attention and bigger crowds were attracted by Jesus' ability to perform miracles. Some of his most famous miracles included the ability to walk on water; to multiply small numbers of fishes and loaves to feed large groups of people; and to turn water into wine. When he cursed a fig tree, it withered, to the amazement of his disciples.

As well as performing miracles, Jesus preached. He spoke of the kingdom of God, in which eternal life awaited those who repented and believed in him. He approved of poverty as a state of grace and chose to surround himself with sinners and the deprived, asserting that he was sent to preach not to the righteous but to those who had strayed. Jesus also taught the forgiveness of enemies and the observance of a humble and pious moral code.

Jesus' actions during his adult ministry aroused fear and suspicion among the authorities, who were concerned at his increasing ability to draw large crowds. So when, around AD 30, Jesus went to Jerusalem for Passover, he was a source of considerable concern to the city's governors.

Roman troops were usually stationed in Jerusalem for Passover, as the crowds present spelled trouble. Soldiers would have watched Jesus' triumphant entry into the city, mounted on a donkey. But he created far greater concern when he entered the city's temple, turning over tables as people convened to pay the temple tax and buy sacrificial pigeons.

The Jewish authorities were understandably aggrieved at the disruption, so they conspired with one of Jesus' disciples, Judas Iscariot, to bring him down. After a final meal with his disciples – the Last Supper – at which they shared bread and wine, Jesus led his disciples to the Mount of Olives for prayer. Here, in the garden of Gethsemane, Jesus was arrested and taken before Caiaphas, the Jewish high priest in Jerusalem, who adjudged him guilty of blasphemy. Brought before the Roman prefect Pontius Pilate, Jesus was sentenced to death, probably in the interests of maintaining public order. He was flogged, forced to drag a cross through the

Prophets and messiahs in the age of Jesus

With the turbulent politics of Roman occupation, the Jewish lands in the 1st century AD were fertile ground for charismatic leaders armed with a spiritual message and ready to give a call to arms.

Jesus was born in the last years of Herod the Great, the Roman client king who tried to be a Jewish leader while simultaneously imposing Greek and Roman culture, a policy continued under his sons. This outraged the Jews, prompting some to violent rebellion, harshly put down. By AD 6 such rebellions had gathered spiritual momentum. Jewish sects becoming prominent included the Zealots, whose founding member Judas the Galilean led a messianic rising against the Roman government of Judea. In AD 66 his son (or more likely grandson) Menahem even captured the Roman governor's palace in Jerusalem.

The Jewish sect that seems to have most influenced Jesus was the Essenes, and Jesus may have been a member. Since the 1947 discovery of the Dead Sea Scrolls, we have learned much about the Essenes, a monastic group that criticized corrupt Judaism, harking back to the simplicity of Moses' law. Their mystical beliefs included a strong sense of eschatology – the idea that the world was approaching a time of judgment, with the attendant expectation that a messiah would be sent to lead the

streets of Jerusalem, and crucified outside the city in the company of two thieves.

Three days after Jesus' death, sightings of him began to be reported. He did not reappear as a ghost, nor as a reanimated corpse, but was transformed in some mysterious way. After visiting a number of his acquaintances and friends, Jesus ascended to heaven, leaving his followers the task of establishing the Christian Church.

After centuries of persecution, the Christian Church eventually became the dominant religious force in the Western world. While Catholics, Protestants and others have at times been responsible for appalling excesses in the name of their particular denomination or viewpoint, Jesus' philosophy of pacifism, humility, charity and kindness has endured through the ages. Judeo-Christian ideas provide

world towards the new age. It seems that John the Baptist was an Essene, emerging out of the desert around Qumran in the late AD 20s, although his beliefs and teachings went further.

John may have been Jesus' cousin, and the two met around AD 29: John baptized Jesus. John also baptized people in the River Jordan for the remittance of sins, and for some time before Jesus' rise to fame John had been predicting the coming of another prophet, greater than himself. John's criticism of the Jewish ruler Herod Antipas led to his beheading, but the Essenes continued to influence Jesus, and the early Christian Church borrowed some of its ideas and structure from the sect.

The historian Josephus tells us about another preacher in the AD 60s, named Jesus (the name is simply the Aramaic version of the Hebrew name Joshua), son of Ananias, who prophesied the doom of the Temple. He was arrested but escaped with his life. The prophet Jonathan the Weaver, a messianic figure who followed the example of Moses in leading the poor and desperate into the desert, was burned alive for his troubles. In AD 66 local tensions finally exploded in a brutal religious and nationalistic rebellion against Rome: the Jewish War. Its leaders, such as John of Gischala and his rival Simon Bar Giora, were harshly punished – and the revolt ended with the destruction of the Temple under Emperor Titus.

the inspiration for, and foundation of, much of Western political thought, government and law, morals, art, architecture, music and literature. Jesus' legacy is, quite simply, one of the most powerful forces in world history.

Marcus Aurelius

121–180

Every instant of time is a pinprick of eternity. All things are petty, easily changed, vanishing away.

Marcus Aurelius, *Meditations* 6.36

Marcus Aurelius was the philosopher-king of the Roman Empire, who exemplified the qualities he praised in his philosophical writings in a reign marked by principled and reforming rule over a vast and turbulent domain. He had an unselfish and pragmatic approach to governing his empire and did not shirk from sharing supreme power for the greater political good. His major written work, the *Meditations*, is an urbane and civilized commentary on life, expressing in a tender and personal voice a Stoic view of life, death and the vicissitudes of fortune.

Marcus Aurelius, born Marcus Annius Verus in AD 121, came from a family well acquainted with high office. His paternal grandfather was a consul and the prefect of Rome. An aunt was married to Titus Aurelius Antoninus, who would later become the emperor Antoninus Pius. And his maternal grandmother stood to inherit one of the largest fortunes in the Roman Empire. He also came from liberal stock: the emperors of the 1st and 2nd centuries were more sober, munificent and inclined towards good deeds than the flamboyant urban emperors of the previous, Julio-Claudian dynasty founded by Augustus.

Marcus was handpicked for great things. In AD 138 the emperor Hadrian had arranged for Marcus to be adopted by his appointed heir, Antoninus, which marked out the 17-year-old as a future joint emperor, along with another young man who would become the emperor Lucius Verus.

Marcus received his education in Greek and Latin from the best tutors, including Herodes Atticus and Fronto, one of the principal popular literary figures of the day. But practice in rhetoric and linguistic exercises did not fully satisfy such a bright young man, and he keenly embraced the *Discourses* of Epictetus. Epictetus was a former slave who had become an important moral philosopher of the Stoic school, which taught that it was through fortitude and self-control that one could attain spiritual well-being and a clear and unbiased outlook on life. Philosophy in general, and Stoicism in particular, would be the intellectual touchstones of Marcus' life.

When his adoptive father died in AD 161, Marcus was already well groomed to take over the imperial duties. But in accordance with his sense of honour and political intelligence, he insisted that Lucius Verus be made joint emperor with him. Although Marcus could easily have eliminated his rival, he realized that with such a diverse empire to govern it made sense to have a partner with the political authority to rule when required but without the seniority to be a threat to stable government. It was Marcus who carried out the serious work of government.

As emperor, Marcus continued the benign policies of his predecessors. He made various legal reforms and provided relief to the less favoured in society – slaves, widows and minors all felt the benefits of his rule. Although there was some concern over the gap between the legal rights and privileges enjoyed by *honestiores* and those enjoyed by *humiliores* (the better-off and worse-off in society), Marcus was generally committed to building a fairer, more prosperous empire for his subjects.

One thing that Marcus could not control was the caprice of fate in sending disease and war. While fighting the Parthians between 162 and 166, many soldiers contracted the plague, which spread throughout the empire. From 168 until around 172, Marcus (with Verus until his death in 169) was preoccupied with subduing the German tribes along the Danube, who were intent on marauding into the Roman Empire.

In spite of such engrossing problems, Marcus Aurelius remained a keen scholar of Stoicism, and in the last ten years of his life, in breaks between his campaigning and administrative duties, he wrote his *Meditations*. Written in Greek and randomly arranged just as they came to him, these are an eclectic selection of diary entries, fragments and epigrams in which he addresses the challenges of life at war, the fear of death, and the cares and injustices of everyday life.

The general sentiment of the *Meditations* is that overreaction and

The emperor's wisdom

'By a tranquil mind I mean nothing else than a mind well ordered.' This simple aphorism lies at the heart of Marcus Aurelius' philosophy. His devotion to the good ordering of his own mind produced the *Meditations*, his collected notes on self-improvement which have long been admired and studied as a model of personal discipline and control.

The wisdom of the *Meditations* is broad and varied. Collected below are some of the highlights, which illustrate the essence of Marcus Aurelius' thought.

In the morning, when you are sluggish about getting up, let this thought be present: 'I am rising to a man's work.'

If you are pained by any external thing, it is not this that disturbs you, but your own judgment of it; and it is in your power to wipe out this judgment now.

Look well into yourself; there is a source of strength which will always spring up whenever you look there.

Waste no more time talking about great souls and how they should be. Become one yourself!

How much time he gains who does not look to see what his neighbour says or does or thinks, but only at what he does himself, to make it just and holy.

If the weight is too heavy for you, do not complain; it will crush you and then destroy itself.

Nothing happens to anybody which he is not fitted by nature to bear.

The universe is change; our life is what our thoughts make it.

Think not disdainfully of death, but look on it with favour; for even death is one of the things that Nature wills.

Never let the future disturb you. You will meet it, if you have to, with the same weapons of reason which today arm you against the present.

You will find rest from vain fancies if you perform every act in life as though it were your last.

Alas! all this ceremony must end at last in stench and dust.

lingering bitterness are the most damaging responses to life's iniquities. 'If you are pained by any external thing, it is not this that disturbs you, but your own judgment of it,' he writes. 'And it is in your power to wipe out this judgment now.' Another typical injunction reads: 'A cucumber is bitter; throw it away. There are briars in the road; turn aside from them. This is enough. Do not add "And why were such things made in the world?"'

As the *Meditations* were written against the backdrop of war, mortality naturally features prominently in them. Marcus' position is clear: 'Do not act as if you were going to live ten thousand years. Death hangs over you. While you live, while it is in your power, be good.'

It is advice that Marcus followed throughout his life. Before he died on campaign in 180, he appointed as his successor his son Commodus, whose brutal tyranny only served to highlight the wisdom with which Marcus had ruled. Wherever possible, Marcus was a decent and just ruler, and blessed with a sense of political fair play that was lacking in many other Roman leaders. Of course, he was obliged to lead armies that visited violence on Rome's enemies. But in spite of all, Marcus Aurelius managed to articulate with greater compassion than any of his contemporaries a timeless vision of fortitude in the face of human injustice and mortality.

Constantine the Great c.285–337

In hoc signo vinces – 'In this sign shalt thou conquer'

The words accompanying the divinely inspired vision that appeared to Constantine before the Battle of Milvian Bridge, AD 312

The reign of the emperor Constantine the Great marked a watershed in the history of the Christian Church and the Roman Empire. The first emperor to convert to Christianity, he ushered in a period of religious tolerance and freedom. Spurred on by his faith, he was victorious in a series of wars and briefly reunited the Roman Empire. He was also responsible for a cultural renaissance, establishing a vibrant new capital in Constantinople and laying the foundations for a new age of Christian learning and prosperity.

When Constantine was born in the middle or late 280s, the Roman Empire had recently been divided by the emperor Diocletian into eastern and western halves. Constantine was the son of Constantius, a general who later, in 305, was to be proclaimed emperor of the Western Empire. As a child, Constantine was sent to Nicomedia (modern Izmit in Turkey) to be raised at the court of Diocletian, who had taken for himself the Eastern portion of the empire. Under Diocletian's rule, Constantine witnessed fierce persecution of Christians, which intensified after 303, and he began to appreciate how divisive a social and political issue religion could become.

In 305 a complex power struggle for control of both the Eastern and the Western parts of the empire began. Constantius died at York, in Britain, in 306, whereupon Constantine was proclaimed emperor by his troops. A capable soldier, Constantine set about consolidating his power, which was initially centred on Gaul. In 312 he crossed the Alps with an army, attacking and defeating the (self-proclaimed) supreme Western ruler Maxentius at the Battle of Milvian Bridge, and becoming the sole Western emperor himself. Milvian Bridge was a key moment in Constantine's religious development. Following a dream in which God appeared to him, he made his soldiers paint a Christian monogram on their shields. From this point on, his military campaigns became intricately bound up with his religious convictions.

In 313 Constantine met with the Eastern emperor Licinius, and the two men agreed the Edict of Milan, a historic proclamation that extended to all people the freedom to worship whatever deity they chose. For Christians, this meant that they were granted legal rights for the first time and were able to organize their forms of worship as they chose. The edict also restored all property that had been confiscated under the recent persecutions.

After the Edict of Milan, relationships between Constantine and Licinius deteriorated, and in 320 the latter once again began to persecute Christians in his portion of the empire. By 324 the clash of cultures had spilled over into civil war. Constantine led the devout, zealous people of fledgling Christendom into battle against Licinius' pagan forces of the ancient empire.

Emerging victorious from the war, Constantine reunited the whole of the Roman Empire under the banner of Christianity. At this high point in his fortunes he wrote that he had come as God's chosen instrument for the suppression of impiety, and he told the Persian king that through God's divine power he had come to bring peace and prosperity to all lands. Crucifixion was abolished, and the sanctity of saints' days and Sundays was observed.

Victory for Constantine was not simply a matter of bringing a new imperial religion into being – it was the spur for a cultural and spiritual renewal of the Roman Empire. He rededicated Byzantium, which from 330 was known in the West as Constantinople, and welcomed in a new age of building, learning and prosperity. The city was provided with a new senate and civic buildings similar to those in Rome.

Across Europe the new tolerance was matched by new construction. The Church of the Holy Apostles in Byzantium was built on the site of a temple to Aphrodite. In Jerusalem the Church of the Holy Sepulchre was built; in Rome the Church of St Peter was handsomely endowed with plate and property. The intellectual credentials of the church were reinforced when Constantine summoned the Council of Nicaea in 325 to deal with heresy.

Constantine's Byzantine Empire, known to the Turks as Rum (or Rome), increasingly became a Greek state, but it lasted a thousand years until 1453 and produced exceptional rulers such as Justinian (482/3–565). Constantine used Christianity to unify the state, but he was as ruthless as he was practical. In 326 he executed his son Crispus and his own wife Fausta for treason, thereby joining Herod the Great of Judea, Emperor Claudius, Ivan the Terrible and Peter the Great of Russia, and England's Henry VIII as royal killers of their own wives or sons – though only Herod and Constantine managed to kill both categories. (Royal murderers of brothers or nephews – from Charlemagne to Richard III – are numerous.)

Constantine himself was baptized on his deathbed – perhaps prompted by the realization that his position had often necessitated unchristian acts. He was, in every sense, the first Christian emperor. His new religion had sprung out of a commitment to tolerance and the founding of a state ideology. Though in its later history the Western church would sometimes stray from these founding principles, Constantine is justly remembered for introducing religious enlightenment and political empire-building on a heroic scale.

Constantinople, city of the world's desire

Constantinople, now known as Istanbul, was for thousands of years the focal point of the civilized world. It has been a great trading city, the centre of three empires, and the historic meeting point of East and West. It is a melting-pot of influences, taking the best from the Greeks and Romans, Christian kings and Islamic conquerors. It has also provided a natural focus for Turkish nationalists and those dreaming of closer European integration.

According to legend, Greek colonists from Megara founded the city in 667 BC, naming it Byzantion (Latinized as Byzantium) after King Byzas or Byzantas. It was chosen for its superb strategic location, standing on the only opening to the Black Sea and linking eastern and western trading routes.

After successive conquests by Persia, Athens, Sparta and Macedonia, Byzantium was attacked, badly damaged and then refounded by the Roman emperor Septimius Severus in AD 196. In 330 Constantine the Great rededicated the city as Nova Roma ('New Rome') and made it the hub of the united Roman Empire. Constantine added the star of the Virgin Mary to the city's existing symbol of a crescent moon, as now appears on the Turkish flag. He stands along with Peter the Great (St Petersburg) and Alexander the Great (Egypt's Alexandria) as the founder of a city that endures as one of the great metropolises of the world.

After Constantine's death Constantinople remained the capital of the

Muhammad 570–632

I have perfected your religion for you, and I have completed My blessing upon you and I have approved Islam for your religion.

Qur'an, sura 5

Muhammad was the founder of the Islamic faith. Muslims believe that he was the messenger of God and the last of his prophets and that he transmitted the word of God to his people in the form of

Eastern Roman Empire. Its greatest emperor, Justinian, beautified it (527–65), as Augustus had Rome. The Christian religion, Roman organization and its Greek language and outlook made Constantinople a wonderful fusion of social and cultural influences. For more than 1000 years it was known for its religious fervour, street violence and magnificent architecture, second only to Rome as a centre of Christian worship.

After its conquest and sack by crusaders in 1204, Constantinople began to decline. The city was virtually deserted in 1453 when it fell to the Ottoman sultan Mehmed II. Mehmed brought the city into the Islamic fold and set about regenerating it. People were transferred here from the Peloponnese, Salonika and the Greek islands. Justinian's great church, Hagia Sofia, was converted into a mosque. Suleiman the Magnificent embellished the city between 1520 and 1566.

A long period of stable prosperity in the new capital of the Ottoman Empire was shaken by the early 19th-century Westernizing programme of Mahmud II, who attempted to arrest the decline of his empire by introducing a range of externally inspired reforms.

When Atatürk established Turkey as a modern secular republic in 1923, Constantinople, now renamed Istanbul, lost its status as capital to Ankara. In the postwar years the city experienced massive population growth, placing huge pressure on its infrastructure. As Turkey and the European Union contemplate further integration, Western eyes are once again on Istanbul.

the Qur'an (Koran). For Muslims, the Qur'an and the collections of Muhammad's deeds and sayings together provide complete guidance on how to live a good and devout life.

While he founded Islam against a background of turbulent tribal feuding, Muhammad encouraged his followers to serve God with decency, humility and piety. His unification of Arabia under the banner of Islam, though at times violent, improved social conditions for many oppressed people. As in other religions, some of his followers have corrupted or misrepresented his teachings, but he is a hero for hundreds of millions of others. For these people his spiritual guidance remains the foundation of their lives.

Muhammad was born in Mecca in the year AD 570. H-his early years in the Arabian desert in the care of a Bedouin wet-nurse. Both his parents and his grandfather were dead by the time he was eight, and he grew up under the guardianship of his uncle Abu Talib. Muhammad grew into a handsome young man with a generous character and great skill at arbitrating in disputes.

As well as being a skilled negotiator, Muhammad was renowned as a devout and spiritual man. He would regularly retreat to the desert to meditate and pray. It was on one such retreat in 610 that he first claimed to have experienced the presence of the archangel Gabriel, who appeared to him with a command to begin his revelation of the word of God. Terrified, he told his first wife, Khadijah, of his experience. She and her blind Christian cousin, Waraqah, interpreted Muhammad's experience as a sign that he was God's prophet.

Arab conquests, east and west

When Muhammad died in 632, a loose, tribal Islamic community covered much of the Arabian peninsula. A century later, however, an organized empire stretched from the Indian subcontinent in the east to the Pyrenees in the west. Its conquering force dominated the civilized world.

The Islamic leaders after Muhammad were known as caliphs, from the Arabic *khalifa* meaning 'successor'. The first was Abu Bakr, Muhammad's father-in-law and one of his closest confidants. Between 632 and 634 Abu Bakr took swift action to unite the dissident Arab tribes and consolidate Muslim control over Arabia.

The Muslims split into two denominations: the minority Shiites believed their rulers should descend through Muhammad's daughter Fatima Zahra, married to his cousin Ali. The majority Sunni accepted the first four caliphs. On Abu Bakr's death, Muhammad's other minister Umar, his father-in-law and shrewd commander, became caliph and swiftly expanded the empire, defeating the Byzantines at the Battle of Yarmuk in 636, and taking Jerusalem, Syria, Lebanon, and then Egypt, Armenia, parts of North Africa, and swathes of Iraq and Persia (from the Sassanid dynasty). On Umar's assassination in 644, Uthman reigned, conquering Cyprus, more of northern Africa, the Caucasus, and finally crushing the Sassanids to conquer Persia. In the next 50 years, the Arab empire swallowed the last ... in the east, plus what are now Uzbekistan, Tajikistan,

Over the next few years, Muhammad continued to receive the revelations that would become the Qur'an and which Muslims believe are the direct word of God. Soon he began to preach to the people of Mecca, converting small groups of his friends and family and various prominent Meccans. He taught them that there was one God, deserving of their complete submission (the meaning of the word Islam), and that he, Muhammad, was God's true prophet. This was seen as disruptive by many of the polytheistic tribesmen of Mecca, and Muhammad's supporters were threatened and persecuted. Muhammad sent one group of his followers to Abyssinia (modern-day Ethiopia) to seek refuge.

In 619, the 'year of sorrows', Khadijah and Abu Talib died. It was around this time that Muhammad experienced the most intense

Kazakhstan and Pakistan. When Uthman was killed in a civil war, he was succeeded by Ali, who was himself assassinated in 661. He was succeeded as caliph by Uthman's kinsman Muawiyah I, governor of Syria and the founder of the Sunni Umayyad dynasty that would rule until 750.

The heir to the Shia tradition, Husain, son of Ali and Fatima, was killed at the Battle of Karbala (in modern Iraq, and where he was buried) in 680, a martyrdom mourned by Shiites to this day. (The Shia–Sunni schism still splits the Islamic world, as seen in the fearsome sectarian violence in today's Iraq.) Meanwhile, the Umayyads expanded westwards towards Christian Spain, which they called al-Andalus. The advance against the Visigoths in the Christian Iberian peninsula was led by the Moors (North African Muslims). From their starting point in Gibraltar, they waged a seven-year campaign that pushed Muslim influence as far north as the Pyrenees. Few regions held out, and it was not until 732, when the Franks under Charles Martel defeated the Muslim armies at the Battle of Tours, that the advance of Islam was finally checked.

Following the defeat at Tours, the wide empire of the caliphs began to creak. Though it had been very effectively controlled from various capitals, including Medina and Damascus, the sheer vastness of the territory began to tell, and from the middle of the 8th century the empire started to fragment. After 750, the Umayyads were overthrown by the Abbasids. But by this time Muslim influence was firmly rooted across the world, from India to Spain.

religious experience of his life. He felt the angel Gabriel transport him from Mecca to Jerusalem, and from there he ascended to heaven. Witnessing the divine throne of God and meeting prophets such as Moses and Jesus, he learned of his own supreme state among them. The form of daily prayer was also revealed to him. This two-part journey is known as *Isra* (Night Journey) and *Mi'raj* (Ascension).

Still persecuted in Mecca, in 622 Muhammad led his supporters out of the city in the Hijra, a great flight to the city of Yathrib, now known as Medina. There he was recognized as the supreme judge and arbiter, and his following grew. Nevertheless, tensions remained between Muhammad and the Meccans, and between 624 and 627 there was a series of battles between the two groups. In the first of these, the Battle of Badr, 313 Muslims defeated a force of 1000 Meccans. In 627 a truce was concluded following a great victory for the Muslims at the Battle of the Ditch.

In 629 Muhammad carried out the first *haj* (pilgrimage) to Mecca, a tradition still followed by hundreds of thousands of Muslims each year. In 630, when the Meccans broke the truce, Muhammad led a force of 10,000 of his followers to the city, capturing it and destroying the idols and images of the polytheistic tribes. By the following year he had extended his influence to most of Arabia, so bringing to an end what he called the 'age of ignorance'. After preaching his final sermon to 200,000 pilgrims in 632, Muhammad died, leaving Arabia stronger and united under the banner of Islam.

Muhammad's promulgation and interpretation of God's word were based on the virtues of humility, magnanimity, justice, meritocracy, nobility, dignity and sincerity. The concept of internal jihad – the inner struggle to live a better, more pious life – was far more important to him than taking up arms against enemies. He enhanced the rights of women – compulsion to wear the veil did not arise until well after his death – and slaves. He condemned Arab practices such as female infanticide; reformed tribal custom in favour of a unifying divine law; and denounced corrupt hierarchies and privilege. His name is the inspiration for countless beautiful calligraphic works and much exquisite Islamic poetry. His life and words are indispensable to the Muslim world. Despite the excesses carried out in his name by extremists, he continues to provide spiritual direction to millions of ordinary people. On the basis of Muhammad's achievements, it is little wonder that Muslims believe that he was the 'perfect man' – not divine but 'a ruby among stones'.

The Venerable Bede

673–735

The candle of the church, lit by the Holy Spirit, is extinguished.

St Boniface, on hearing the news of Bede's death

The 'Venerable' Bede was the outstanding English writer of the early Middle Ages, a master whose works were read by virtually every literate person for 1000 years after his death. He provided us with much of what we know about the early English Church and almost single-handedly invented the modern way of writing history. His dedication to knowledge and devout study made him famous in his own day, while his extraordinary skill in describing the world of the first millennium has ensured that he has kept his place in the literary pantheon ever since.

Plenty of medieval priests were called 'venerable', but fittingly it is with Bede that history has associated the description. It is an indication of the extraordinary piety and learning of the man who was England's proudest representative in a tradition of Christian thinkers. Bede wrote more than 30 works, ranging from collections of hymns and saints' lives to translations of the Gospels and Latin textbooks that educated generations of scholars well into the second millennium. We still rely on Bede's most famous work, his *Ecclesiastical History of the English People*, to tell us about the formative years of the English nation.

Bede was born to well-off parents in Northumbria and lived his whole adult life in the Monastery of St Paul at Jarrow, where he became a deacon at 19 and a priest by the age of 30. For the rest of his life he devoted himself to mastering all the learning of his day. 'I spent all my life in this monastery,' he wrote, 'applying myself entirely to the study of Scriptures.' The library at Jarrow was one of the finest in England, containing between 300 and 500 books – an impressive collection at a time when books were extremely valuable property. Bede studied all the Greek and Roman authors available, and from his late twenties he was applying himself to the important intellectual matters of the day.

Bede was a pioneer in medieval science, influencing thinking in the field with works such as *On the Nature of Things* and *The Reckoning of Time*. The latter, a treatise on chronology, made an important contribution to one of the burning questions of Bede's day: the age of the world. Traditionally the earth was supposed to be 5000 years old at

'Write quickly' – the death of Bede

Bede's legendary piety and heroic capacity for work were never better illustrated than on his deathbed. He continued working until the hour of his death, completing a number of valuable works, including a translation of St John's Gospel into Anglo-Saxon. A fellow monk at Jarrow, Cuthbert, gave a moving account of Bede's last days, which reveals the deep affection and veneration in which he was held:

Often he would thank God for sending him this illness, and would say, 'God chasteneth the son whom He loveth.' Often, too, he would repeat the words of St Ambrose: 'I have not lived so as to be ashamed to live amongst you; neither do I fear to die, for we have a good Lord.'

Besides the lessons which he gave us, and his psalm-singing during these days, he composed two important works – a translation of the Gospel of St John into our native tongue, and extracts from St Isidore of Seville; for he said, 'I would not that my pupils should read what is false and after my death should labour in vain.'

On the Tuesday before the Ascension his sickness increased, his breathing became difficult, and his feet began to swell. Yet he passed the whole night joyfully dictating. At times he would say, 'Make haste to learn,

the time of Christ's birth, but Bede calculated a new figure of 3952 years. He also applied his powerful intellect to the important and politically sensitive matter of working out the correct date of Easter.

Bede is rightly known as the 'father of English history'. He wrote numerous early saints' lives, including three full accounts of the lives of the early martyrs Felix, Anastasius and Cuthbert, and short accounts of 116 others. Rather than relating stories uncritically, Bede sought out original sources and records of his subjects. It was a technique which came to glorious fruition in the *Ecclesiastical History of the English People*, an 85,000-word account of the church in England which runs from Julius Caesar's arrival in Britain to the date of the book's completion (*c.*731). Bede went to great lengths to establish accurate dates, to include original documents and to cite his sources – methods that were centuries ahead of his time.

for I do not know how long I shall remain with you, and whether my Creator will not soon take me to Himself.'

When Wednesday dawned he desired us diligently to continue writing what we had begun. One of us said to him, 'Dearest master, we have yet one chapter to translate. Will it be grievous to thee if we ask thee any further?'

He answered, 'It is quite easy: take the pen and write quickly.' At the ninth hour he said to me, 'Run quickly and call the priests of this monastery to me, that I may impart to them the gifts which God has given me.' Then he begged every one of them to celebrate the liturgy and pray for him.

They all wept, mainly because he said that they would not see his face again in this world. But they rejoiced in that he said, 'It is time that I go to my Creator. I have lived enough. The time of my departure is at hand; for I long to depart and be with Christ.'

Thus did he live until evening. Then the scholar [Cuthbert] said to him, 'Dearest master, there is only one sentence left to write.' 'Write quickly,' he answered. 'It is finished. Raise my head in thy hand, for it will do me good to sit opposite the sanctuary where I used to kneel and pray, that sitting thus I may call upon my Father.' So he seated himself on the ground of his cell and sang, 'Glory to Thee, O God, Father, Son and Holy Spirit.' And when he had named the Holy Spirit he breathed his last.

Still working even in the final hours before his death, Bede managed to complete the first ever English translation of the Gospel of St John.

After his death in 735, Bede came rapidly to be regarded as a saint, and his writings were in huge and constant demand. Much of his work contained important truths on how Christian kings and bishops should act, and King Alfred used an English translation of the *Ecclesiastical History* (originally written in Latin) as part of his educational programme when he was attempting to unite the English people in one kingdom. Bede had always regarded the individual kingdoms of early England as having an Anglo-Saxon unity, and as the country became more politically united, his works grew ever more relevant. Indeed, a new type of script had to be developed at Jarrow as the monks worked frantically to meet the demand for copies of Bede's work. His fame even spread to the continent, and in the 14th century he was granted a place in paradise by the great Italian poet Dante in his *Divine Comedy*.

Some of Bede's forthright thinking about the traditions of the church led to his being accused of heresy in his lifetime, but this was soon forgotten in what was generally recognized as a blameless career. His celebrated contemporary Boniface said that Bede shone like a candle of the church by virtue of his knowledge of the Scriptures, and it was not long after his death before miracles began to be attributed to his relics.

The cult of Bede was adopted by his medieval fellows. His Latin style influenced his successors at the monastery at Jarrow. And his striving both for accuracy and intellectual truth in the writing of history has been passed down from generation to generation.

Charlemagne 768–814

Let peace, concord and unanimity reign among all
Christian people ... for without peace we cannot
please God.

Charlemagne, *The Admonitio* (789)

In a reign of over forty years, Charlemagne – literally 'Charles the
Great' – transformed his Frankish kingdom into a Christian empire
that extended from France's western coast eastward into Germany,
northward into the Low Countries, and southward into Italy.
Charlemagne was not only a conqueror; he also presided over a
court renowned for its artistic and scholarly achievements, especially in the preservation of classical learning.

Charlemagne succeeded to the throne jointly with his brother,
but the latter's death three years later left him in sole possession of the crown. His drive for power shored up by a sense of
divine purpose, Charlemagne set about building a Christian super-
state. He conquered Lombardy and, in a series of prolonged
campaigns, subdued and converted the pagan Saxons. A decade
later he conquered Bavaria, uniting the west Germanic tribes
into one political entity for the first time. His influence extended
still further. Campaigning from his Bavarian base, Charlemagne
turned the Avar principalities (in modern-day Hungary and
Austria) and the Slavic states along the Danube into dependants
of the greatest empire since that of the Romans. Only once,
when he made an unsuccessful incursion into Spain, was
Charlemagne's effort to dominate Europe thwarted.

Charlemagne's achievement raised him from king to emperor.
His coronation by the pope in Rome, at the Christmas mass of
AD 800, represented a revolution in papal policy. The papacy had
formerly aligned itself with the rulers of Byzantium, the eastern
successors of the emperors of Rome, but relations had soured.
In contrast Charlemagne, aware of the pope's power to bestow
legitimacy on a ruler, made strenuous efforts to keep on good
terms with the Holy See – particularly as he made ever bolder

incursions into northern Italy. It paid off. When Pope Leo III anointed him emperor, the papacy signified that it was turning its back on the East and would henceforth seek protection from the West. In the short term, Charlemagne's achievement of imperial status simply legitimized his control over Rome. But its ramifications echoed down the centuries. His imperial constitution, titles and practices became the model for France's future dynasty, the Capetians, and his empire evolved into the Holy Roman Empire, which was to play such an important role in European history until finally dissolved in 1806. Christendom's political and religious balance was transformed.

The so-called Carolingian Renaissance – named after Charlemagne himself – similarly transformed Western Europe's spiritual and

Imperial coronation

Pope Leo III's coronation of Charlemagne as emperor was one of history's most extraordinary Christmas presents. On Christmas Day AD 800, Charlemagne was attending mass in St Peter's Basilica in Rome for the consecration of his son, the future Louis the Pious, as king of Aquitaine. As Charlemagne rose from prayer, the pope slipped an imperial crown on his head. While the Romans present acclaimed him as 'Augustus and Emperor', the astonished Charlemagne, who a minute before had been kneeling at the tomb of the first pope, found himself with the current incumbent at his feet, 'adoring' him 'after the manner of emperors of old'.

According to the chronicler Einhard, Charlemagne's imperial coronation caught him completely off guard. Had he known what was going to happen, the emperor reportedly said, he would never have gone to the basilica that day. Charlemagne's outrage was perhaps slightly feigned, and the smoothness of the operation suggests that there was almost certainly an element of pre-planning.

The immediate beneficiary was Leo III. The previous year he had briefly abandoned Rome for Charlemagne's protection after his enemies, the Roman nobility, had attacked him in a procession and threatened to blind him and remove his tongue – an effective if somewhat extreme way of disqualifying him from office. The distant and fissile Byzantines, busy

cultural life, as Charlemagne strove to fulfil what he saw as his divinely sanctioned purpose: the creation of a truly Christian empire. From the early years of his reign, Charlemagne sent out appeals for copies of remarkable or rare texts, whether Christian or classical. Libraries and schools flourished in monasteries and cathedrals across his realms. At his court at Aix-la-Chapelle (Aachen) Charlemagne gathered together Europe's most eminent scholars to instruct a new generation of the clergy, seeking to set up a chain of learning that would ultimately disseminate this Christian culture to the people. Greek was revived, and the intensive learning of Latin became compulsory in all educational establishments.

Charlemagne's single-minded drive for empire did breed a certain ruthlessness. He had few qualms about dealing with

blinding each other as they tussled for the imperial throne, were no help. By making Charlemagne an emperor, Leo secured himself a powerful protector, placing Rome, as the chronicler Theophanes wrote, 'in the hands of the Franks'.

Leo also soothed his own wounded ego by setting the momentous precedent that the pope had authority to confer the imperial crown. It was an entirely illegal action. Christendom already had an emperor in Byzantium, and technically the pope had no right to create any more. Charlemagne, who had gone to Rome to 'restore the state of the church, which was greatly disturbed', found himself having to restore the political balance of Christendom, which Leo III's unilateral action had disturbed even more. Charlemagne even proposed marriage to the Byzantine Empress Irene – 'to reunite the east and west', although the plan came to nothing when Irene was deposed shortly afterwards.

Charlemagne adopted few imperial pretensions. When he made his will in 806, he decreed that his realm should be divided among his three sons. The Byzantines did eventually deign to acknowledge him as 'emperor' (although they refused to automatically recognize his successors). For his part, Charlemagne laid no claim to their throne. And when Charlemagne consecrated his own son emperor, he made it clear that he would do things differently. The ceremony was held in Aachen; and on receiving the crown from his father, Louis placed it firmly on his head himself.

rivals, even among his own family. His nephews mysteriously disappeared when they fell into his hands; he deposed his cousin in order to conquer Bavaria; and when his hunchback son Pepin rebelled in 792, he put down the revolt with brutal force. Having secured the pope's approval for his conquest of Italy by promising to increase papal territory, Charlemagne reneged on the deal, keeping Lombardy for himself. When the Saxons rebelled, after accepting his sovereignty and converting to Christianity, Charlemagne was merciless. He considered their rebellion apostasy as well as treason, and he put it down with a level of violence rare even in his own violent era: on one occasion he executed 4000 Saxons in a single day. Yet in general he respected the rights and traditions of the lands he conquered.

Charlemagne's empire did not long survive his death. Subsequent generations could not provide a ruler to match his ability, his charisma and his strength of purpose. Charlemagne had made vast strides in the establishment of sound legislative and judicial practices, but it was still the ruler rather than institutions that bound together the realm.

In the centuries after Charlemagne's death, Europe's monarchs often sought to enhance their own image by associating themselves in some way with his legend. France's Capetian kings had themselves anointed in the same manner as he had, while in Germany the Holy Roman Emperors claimed to be his true heirs. Almost a thousand years after Charlemagne's death, Napoleon was declaring himself his successor. Little wonder that one of Charlemagne's court poets described him as the 'King Father of Europe'.

Haroun al-Rashid

763/6–809

A goodly place, a goodly time,
For it was in the golden prime
Of good Haroun Alraschid

Alfred, Lord Tennyson, 'Recollections of the Arabian Nights' (1830)

Haroun al-Rashid was the remarkable caliph who reigned over the Arab Empire during its golden age. A lover of poetry, music and learning, Haroun's fabulous court has been immortalized, and fictionalized, in *The Arabian Nights*. Renowned for his generosity, his good humour, his liberality and his piety during his lifetime, Haroun is still revered as the greatest of the caliphs.

Haroun appears in many tales in *The Arabian Nights* as a man devoted to pleasure and sensuality, a ruler who only abandons his magnificent court when he sneaks out into the city at night for amorous encounters. The real Haroun was less sybaritic but equally compelling. His piety was of the rational sort. He encouraged singing, believing the Qur'an's ban on music did not extend to the human voice. A keen horseman, he built race courses and is said to have introduced polo to the Arabs. Feast days and hunting expeditions became occasions of unparalleled splendour.

The wealth that Haroun accrued from his empire fostered the pursuit of pleasure on a scale that no other kingdom could match. Occasionally he checked himself, murmuring: 'I ask pardon of God, I have spent too much money.' But his largesse was widely distributed: every morning Haroun donated at least 1000 dirhems to the poor, setting an example that his wealthy subjects emulated, and giving rise to rumours that Baghdad's streets were paved with gold.

Haroun made Baghdad the hub of civilization, earning it the name 'Bride of the World'. Believing that 'It is a disgrace for a ruler not to be learned', he was on a constant quest for knowledge, and also promoted learning and the arts among his own people. He endowed scholarships, invited wise men from every

The court of the caliphs

The court of the Abbasid caliphs in Baghdad was the marvel of the world. Ambassadors from other lands rubbed their eyes as they were shown elephants and lions decked out in brocade and satin, and gasped as they stood under the shade of a tree made of gold and silver, festooned with jewelled fruits. Proceeding through scores of courtyards, miles of marble arcades, innumerable chambers dripping with almost unimaginable wealth, they finally reached the caliph's presence. Here they were dazzled by the ebony throne and jewels so bright they seemed to eclipse the sun.

The caliphs embraced excess with abandon. When Haroun's son Mam'un married, the bride was showered with a thousand pearls. Haroun's 2000 singing and servant girls, 24 concubines and 5 wives seem moderate compared with the 4000 concubines of one of his descendants, who, in a reign lasting only a thousand nights, managed to sleep with every single one of them. Less successful was Mam'un's wedding night: the newly married couple found the scent of the precious ambergris candles irritating and ordered them to be removed from the bedroom. Mam'un himself subsequently withdrew when it became apparent that the bride's menstruation precluded consummation.

kingdom to visit Baghdad and encouraged his formerly introspective scholars to profit from their knowledge. Haroun initiated an age of translation, and mathematics, medicine, astronomy and engineering all flourished.

Haroun's great love was poetry. No mean poet himself, his knowledge of verse was unparalleled even by learned men – he frequently corrected them on a slipped word. Poets filled his courts and were handsomely rewarded. Poetry was such a consuming passion for Haroun that he gave it up when on pilgrimage as an act of self-denial.

Haroun's strength as a ruler lay in the personal loyalty he commanded. When he became the fifth Abbasid caliph in 786 at the age of 22, Baghdad's populace spontaneously crowded the streets to rejoice. He has been criticized for leaving a clan of

Legends of the harem abounded, and death awaited any man other than the caliph who gained entry to this shadowy, voluptuous kingdom. Fragranced with saffron and rosewater, each of the seven slave girls who attended Haroun at his daily siesta knew that sensuality could garner unimaginable rewards. Haroun's mother Khaizuran herself had risen from slave girl to powerful wife of the caliph.

Poets and musicians flocked to the court, which became the cultural centre of the Islamic world. Praising their ruler in language as lavish as his surroundings, the poets earned themselves considerable rewards. Musicians, hidden behind velvet curtains, provided the backdrop to long evenings of drinking and feasting.

Death could come suddenly amid the hedonism, for intrigues abounded in the shadows. The Barmakids discovered how quickly the fatal blow could be dealt. When Haroun eventually decided to move against the clan, he ordered his grand vizier Jafar to spend the night feasting; while thus occupied he received a stream of gifts from the caliph until the arrival of a messenger bearing Haroun's only request: the head of Jafar. At other times courtiers were lured into honey traps that propelled them, almost before they knew it, from the arms of a beautiful slave girl to the executioner's block. But the ambrosial delights of the caliphs' court made it a risk that courtiers were willing to take.

administrators, the Barmakids, to govern in the early years of his reign, and for being too influenced by his redoubtable mother, the former slave girl Khaizuran. Open and instinctively trusting, Haroun was content to accept the advice of his viziers and theologians. Leaving his administration in capable hands, Haroun preferred instead to undertake extensive tours of inspection across his vast territories, making himself personally known to his subjects. His forays through the streets of Baghdad were in fact more paternalistic than amorous; he was said to roam his capital in disguise to check on his people's welfare.

An autocrat, Haroun was hot-tempered but quick to feel remorse and rarely vengeful. His most ruthless act was his removal of the Barmakids from power. Yahya al-Barmaki had been Haroun's boyhood tutor, his first vizier, and the man he called 'father'. After 17 years of service in which Yahya and his family established a monopoly over the government of the caliphate, Haroun, in a lightning *coup d'état*, executed or imprisoned the entire clan and its clients. Romance has it that this was revenge for an affair between his vizier at that time, Jafar, and Haroun's sister. Perhaps more likely is that the Barmakids were contemplating an attempt on Haroun's throne. More characteristic of Haroun was his subsequent pilgrimage. The last of nine, this time he made the thousand-mile journey barefoot as penance for his acts against a family to whom he owed so much.

Haroun was one of the most respected rulers of his age, acknowledged by both of Europe's emperors. Charlemagne reportedly sent him gifts, receiving an elephant in return. The tribute of Byzantium's emperors, however, was secured by military force rather than goodwill: Haroun defeated the Byzantines several times. After Nicephorus I became Byzantine emperor, he tried to renege on the tribute owed to the caliphs and furthermore demanded reimbursement for the tributes made by his predecessor, Empress Irene. Haroun's response was simple: 'You will hear my reply before you read it.' The former civil servant Nicephorus was no match for the military skill of the caliph. After Haroun and his 135,000-strong army laid waste to Asia Minor and a parallel naval force overwhelmed Cyprus, the emperor capitulated and agreed to pay a yearly tribute of 30,000 gold pieces, each stamped with the head of the caliph and his three sons.

Haroun's death at the age of 47 cut short the reign of one of the most admired of the caliphs. He was perhaps not the most driven of rulers, but this excellent general and exquisite aesthete presided over one of the most cultured and learned periods in Arab history, and his fame has passed into literature and legend.

Eleanor
of Aquitaine 1122–1204

*No matter how bestial and obdurate a man might be, that
woman could bend him to her will.*

Richard of Devizes, *Chronicle of the Deeds of Richard the First* (late 12th century)

Eleanor of Aquitaine was the queen of two kings, and the mother
of two more. Her resilience, her courage and her obdurate will
made her legendary across Europe as a woman in a male-
dominated age who refused to submit to convention, and whose
every action expressed her determination to rule.

Eleanor was the matrimonial catch of Europe, beautiful and charismatic. On inheriting the duchy of Aquitaine at the age of 15, she
became the ruler of one fifth of what is now modern France. Her
grandfather, Duke William IX, had been a famous troubadour and
had made his court in southwest France a home of courtly love.
Coming from this permissive, secular environment, Eleanor was an
alien figure in the stiffer northern courts of England and France.

At the age of 16 Eleanor became the queen of Louis VII of France.
But she refused to be simply a consort. Louis's apparent transformation
from a mild-mannered, pious young man into an energetic ruler coincided with his marriage, and contemporaries suspected Eleanor's hand
lay behind the king's sudden willingness to crack down on his barons
and meddle in church appointments. When Louis went on crusade,
Eleanor – always willing to endure the hardships of travel – joined him.

But Eleanor had quickly become disillusioned with her husband:
'I thought I had married a king, and found I had married a monk,'
she lamented. When their marriage finally ended in divorce, with no
male heirs, Eleanor refused to retreat into a convent, as was expected.
Rather, she took her future into her own hands. She knew what a
prize her lands were. Having already thwarted two abduction attempts
by would-be suitors, she proposed marriage to Duke Henry of
Normandy by messenger. At the time of their marriage he was only
19, 11 years her junior. Just over a year later Henry succeeded to

The troubadours

The lovelorn Provençal poets of the 12th and 13th centuries created verse and music as brilliant as it was novel. Earthy, erotic, graceful and cultivated, the troubadours – literally 'verse writers' – found new ways of looking at love, and new ways of expressing it.

In the seductively permissive court of Aquitaine, a revolution in sexual attitudes took place. Courtly love – or, as the troubadours first called it, *amor de lonh*, 'love from afar' – transformed the way that men saw women. No longer were women regarded as possessions, transferred from a father's care to a husband's by marriage; rather, ladies became like lords to their pining vassals. Idolized and idealized they could bestow favour with a look or a smile, exercise power with merely a glance.

The intricate beauty of the troubadours' verse forms and unharmonized melodies, as they wallowed in the painful pleasure of unrequited love, transformed the European tradition of lyric poetry. The troubadour poets, such as Arnaut Daniel, Bernard de Ventadour and Jaufre Rudel, were famed for their lyrical elegance, their irreverent wit and their permissive ways. But none was so notorious as the ruler of the court in which they flourished: the man whose sybaritic wit and poetical genius earned him the title of the 'first troubadour'.

the English crown, as Henry II, and Eleanor became queen of England. Later, when Henry's bullying rule became intolerable, it was Eleanor who marshalled her sons into a rebellion against their father – a rebellion that she persuaded Louis to support.

Eleanor was a remarkable politician, whose tireless later work secured her sons' inheritance. She had always governed well in her beloved Aquitaine. As regent for Richard I, her favourite son, while he was on crusade, Eleanor demonstrated her capacity as a ruler. She thwarted repeated threats to his throne, including his brother John's rebellion. When the Holy Roman Emperor captured Richard, Eleanor secured his freedom via complex negotiations and by raising the vast ransom demanded. She also sent several fierce letters reprimanding the pope for his failure to protect a crusader. After Richard's death, Eleanor secured the succession of the unpopular John. Travelling

Duke William IX of Aquitaine (1071–1126), Eleanor's grandfather, was brazenly charming, an insatiable and irresistible lover. His poetry was the first to use the vernacular of the south, the *langue d'oc*. Mixing obscenity with charm, delicate seductiveness with boisterous humour, manipulating complex verse forms with insouciant ease, Duke William inspired and fostered the languishing brilliance of the troubadour poets.

'He made everything into a joke and made his listeners laugh uncontrollably,' reported the somewhat disapproving chronicler William of Malmesbury, who apparently felt that William's crusading misadventures should not be fodder for uproarious rhyming couplets. The excommunicated duke, who had tucked away two wives in convents, took for his mistress the aptly named Dangerosa, wife of one of his barons. His shield had her image on it: William wanted to bear her into battle as often as she had borne him into bed.

Unable to have children with his beloved Dangerosa, Duke William married his son to her daughter. The child of this marriage, Eleanor of Aquitaine, grew up in a court unique in Europe for its secularity, its abandon, its sheer *joie de vivre*, surrounded by poets and singers who idolized women as beautiful, brilliant, and able always to bend men to their will.

long distances across the Angevin lands, Eleanor successfully campaigned for the support of the barons of England and Normandy over rival claimants to the throne. At 80 Eleanor crossed the Pyrenees to choose personally from among her Castilian granddaughters a bride for Louis VIII to cement the Anglo-French alliance. Her judgment was unerring: Blanche of Castile, as queen of France, became a ruler as formidable as her grandmother had been.

Eleanor's life consistently tested her powers of endurance. Her independence provoked Europe's chroniclers to revile her as first an incestuous whore, then a shrew, censuring her 'pagan' southern wildness and her hold over Louis VII. When rebellion broke out against Henry II, Eleanor was the focus of the blame. 'The man is the head of the woman,' thundered the Archbishop of Rouen, publicly threatening her with excommunication.

Eleanor was kidnapped innumerable times: at the age of 20 by pirates when she was on crusade; 60 years later by local barons on her journey to Spain. Both her husbands imprisoned her. After Eleanor sided with her uncle Raymond over a matter of crusade tactics, Louis forcibly removed her from Antioch. When Henry II's men discovered that one of the rebel band they had ambushed was Eleanor, disguised as a man, the queen was incarcerated in England for over a decade.

A woman of indomitable spirit, Eleanor triumphed over every one of her enemies. She refuted allegations of barrenness by bearing Henry eight children, mostly boys. Henry's attempt to force Eleanor through imprisonment to renounce her Aquitaine lands in his favour failed. She out-waited and outlived him. On succeeding his father in 1189, Richard immediately ordered his mother's release. The vigorous reappearance on the political scene of this woman who had been shut away for so long turned her into a living legend: a ruler active into her eighties in an era when forty was considered a venerable age. Chroniclers lined up to revere her.

Eleanor's legacy was not unequivocally positive. The Aquitaine lands she bequeathed her sons helped to sow the seeds of centuries of Anglo-French hostility. But it was only her tenacity on behalf of her sons that held together the English crown's disparate lands. Formidable, outrageous and awe-inspiring, Eleanor's refusal to submit to contemporary notions of femininity altered Europe's political balance.

Saladin c.1138–1193

He was a man wise in counsel, valiant in war and generous beyond measure.

William of Tyre, *A History of Deeds Done Beyond the Sea* (1170)

The Kurdish-born sultan Saladin was the ideal of the warrior-king: a superb commander and a tolerant ruler devoid of fanaticism. Ruling an empire stretching from Libya to Iraq, Saladin drew together disparate elements of the Arab world in the struggle between Islam and Christendom for control of the Holy Land. Although he could be merciless in battle, he embraced the code of European chivalry, and in turn he was respected and admired by his enemies.

Saladin was born to a Kurdish family in Tikrit, now in northern Iraq (and much later the birthplace of the tyrant Saddam Hussein). Son of the local governor and nephew of the lieutenant of Nur ad-Din, ruler of Syria, young Saladin seized Egypt on his master's behalf in 1171. Three years later Nur ad-Din died, and Saladin took control of Syria as well.

Ruling from Damascus, Saladin extended his influence throughout the Arab world, building an empire based on a combination of political cunning, ruthless order, military prowess and wise justice and tolerance. He was occasionally troubled by the Principality of Antioch, the Kingdom of Jerusalem and the County of Tripoli – European-ruled states that had been established in the Near East by the crusaders. By 1177 Saladin had built up an army capable of opposing the Christian occupiers of the Holy Land – as holy to Muslims as to Christians. Yet at the Battle of Montgisard his army of 26,000 was surprised and routed by a far smaller crusader force.

This was the last major reverse in Saladin's struggle against the Christian interlopers. Though a truce was called in 1178, the following year Saladin resumed his *jihad* against the crusaders, besieging and capturing the castle the crusaders were building at Jacob's Ford, which presented a strategic threat to Damascus. Saladin proceeded to raze the castle to the ground.

During the 1180s Saladin was dragged into increasingly serious skirmishes with the crusaders, in particular Raynald of Chatillon. Raynald was little more than a pirate and a brigand, harassing Muslim pilgrims on *hajj* and showing a total disregard for the sanctity of the Muslim holy sites of Mecca and Medina. All this only served to fire Saladin's determination to win his holy war.

By 1187 he had raised sufficient forces to invade the Kingdom of Jerusalem. The Crusaders were annihilated at the Battle of Hattin, only a few thousand escaping the field. Saladin took Raynald prisoner and personally beheaded him. In October Jerusalem itself fell, ending 88 years of crusader occupation.

The fall of Jersusalem opened a new chapter in the history of the crusades: Saladin's rivalry with Richard I of England, known as Richard the Lionheart. Richard arrived in the Holy Land in June 1191, and the following month Acre fell to the crusaders. In September

Richard defeated Saladin at Arsuf but, with both sides' resources depleted, they agreed a truce in autumn 1192. Saladin demonstrated his tolerance by agreeing to allow unarmed Christian pilgrims into Jerusalem. Richard left the Holy Land shortly afterwards. Though the two never met again, and Saladin died the following year, the relationship between the two men passed into legend. Richard seems to have been genuinely struck by Saladin's skill, tolerance and magnanimity as a ruler and battlefield commander.

There is no denying that Saladin could be merciless towards prisoners of war. Like Richard, he thought little of massacring them if the conditions of war demanded it. Such were the standards of

Richard the Lionheart

More legends have accrued around Richard I (1157–99) than any other English king. His chivalrous rivalry with Saladin during the Third Crusade was the subject of famous ballads and tales across Europe, as was his long, Odysseus-like journey home. Richard was the archetypal Angevin king. Like the rest of his family, he had a furious temper and could be irresponsible and cruel. And, being an Angevin with huge European interests, he simply regarded England as another fiefdom to defend and a resource to fund his conquests. He is popularly remembered for being an incredibly energetic soldier, an extremely adept politician, and a romantic crusader hero; but in reality this uncouth, brutal warrior was no match for the heroic, chivalrous gifts and graces of his brilliant Islamic foe, Saladin.

Richard was invested with land and power from the age of 11, when he became Duke of Aquitaine. He became Duke of Poitiers four years later and immediately allied with his brothers and his mother, the redoubtable Eleanor of Aquitaine, in a failed rebellion against their father Henry II in 1173–4. A harsh lord, Richard himself provoked rebellion among his subjects in Gascony in 1183, and a few years later was rebelling again against his father, this time in alliance with Louis, the king of France and his mother's former husband.

By 1189, now aged 32, Richard was King of England, Duke of Normandy and Count of Anjou. But his focus was on Jerusalem, which Saladin had conquered in 1187. After mortgaging as much of his kingdom as he could and taxing England with the so-called 'Saladin tithe', Richard sailed for the Holy Land via Sicily in 1190.

medieval religious warfare. But chroniclers on both sides sang the praises of Saladin the lawgiver, just ruler and great prince. He could inspire men to take to the battlefield despite daunting odds, and he was courteous and chivalrous towards his Christian enemies.

After Saladin's death, the Muslim chronicler Baha al-Din called Saladin 'one of the most courageous of men; brave, gallant, firm, intrepid in any circumstance'. Saladin (real name, Yusuf Salah al-Din), Sultan of Egypt and Syria, left an Ayyubid Empire stretching from Lebanon to Yemen. The pre-eminent Kurd in history, he became a symbol of Arab pride in the 20th century, with revolutionary Egypt, Iraq and Palestinian groups adopting his Eagle of Saladin.

It was during the Third Crusade that the great tales of Richard's chivalry developed. He fought hard and bloody battles against Saladin's forces, conquering Acre and winning the battle of Jaffa, but he failed to take the main prize of Jerusalem. Despite their violent struggle, Richard and Saladin held for each other a great and chivalrous respect. Each thought and spoke with the highest regard of the other. When Richard was sick and thirsty, Saladin sent him fresh fruit and water, and when he was in need of a horse, Saladin sent him one of his finest.

During their peace negotiations, Saladin is said to have called Richard 'so pleasant, upright, magnanimous and excellent that, if the land [Jerusalem] were to be lost in my time, he would rather have it taken into Richard's mighty power than to have it go into the hands of any other prince whom he had ever seen'.

On his way back to England in 1192, Richard was shipwrecked, then kidnapped, and finally held hostage by the Holy Roman Emperor, Henry VI: Richard had been part of a continental alliance against Henry. England had to raise an enormous ransom of 150,000 marks for his release. He returned in 1194, welcomed as the scourge of wrongs perpetrated under his brother John, but he stayed only a month in the country before travelling to the Duchy of Normandy, this time to make war against Philip, king of France.

Richard was killed in 1199, shot by an archer while besieging one of his subject's castles in a quarrel over buried treasure. In keeping with his huge and enduring chivalric reputation, legend has it that he applauded the marksman before he died.

Frederick II of Hohenstaufen

1194–1250

He was an adroit man, cunning, greedy, wanton, malicious, bad-tempered, but at times when he wished to reveal his good and courtly qualities, consoling, witty, delightful, hard working.

Salimbene di Adam, Chronicle (1282–90)

Celebrated in his own times as the Wonder of the World, Frederick II, the last of the Hohenstaufen Holy Roman emperors, was a visionary leader who was really the first Renaissance ruler. Frederick was also king of Sicily, king of the Romans and king of Germany, and his leadership of the Sixth Crusade brought him the title of king of Jerusalem. A strong-willed, highly intelligent and charismatic ruler, his government and cultural practices were extraordinarily advanced for his era. But his attempts to extend his empire brought him into conflict with the papacy, turning Italy into a battleground.

Frederick's sharp mind and intellectual openness fostered ideas of governance that anticipated by half a millennium the enlightened absolutism of 18th-century monarchs. In his territories, particularly in Sicily, Frederick's codification of administrative and constitutional practice marked a move towards centralized government that would not be seen elsewhere in Europe for centuries. He was not always successful. In Germany, in particular, the obstreperous princes forced Frederick to agree to concessions that strengthened princely power at the expense of central control. But overall the ideas of this medieval emperor were startling in their modernity.

Frederick was equally singular in his cultural advancement. His upbringing in the open, cosmopolitan court of Sicily fostered in him a familiarity and a respect for different cultures, and as an adult he corresponded with Jewish and Muslim scholars. His rapport with Sultan al-Kamil of Egypt secured Frederick the throne of

Jerusalem. He also established at his court a 'republic of scholars', who pursued knowledge without obeisance to the traditional religious authorities. His reign saw the development of an Italian form for the poetry of courtly love: the sonnet. Frederick himself wrote a standard book on falconry, *The Art of Hunting with Birds*, which displays his keen intelligence and an impressive knowledge of both Islamic and ancient cultures. Poetry, philosophy, mathematics, the sciences, art and architecture all flourished. And fostering this intellectual growth was Frederick himself: captivating, impulsive, amiable, witty and tolerant − on his good days.

Frederick is most famous, though, for his clash with Rome. Papal policy had dictated his upbringing. His father, Emperor Henry VI, had challenged the popes for leadership of Christendom. After Henry's sudden death the curia ensured the division of his lands: two other candidates were installed in the German kingdom, while the infant Frederick was left with Sicily. His mother died shortly afterwards, and the four-year-old king of Sicily became a ward of the papacy. After his German replacements had proved too territorially ambitious themselves, Frederick was reinstalled as a teenager in his northern titles, but not before his erstwhile guardian, Pope Innocent III, had extracted from him promises of extensive papal privileges and numerous vows never to reunite Germany and Sicily under one ruler.

Frederick, however, refused to be a puppet. He saw the Holy Roman Empire as sacred and universal. His conception of imperial sovereignty drove him to extend his authority into the Italian states that lay between his northern and southern lands. When he crowned himself king of Jerusalem it only strengthened his sense of conviction as to the right of the emperor to lead Christendom.

Frederick's conflict with his former guardians overshadowed European politics for half a century. On one level the gigantic struggle was simply a personality clash between the piously intellectual Pope Gregory IX, elected in 1227, and the witty and worldly Frederick. When Gregory IX excommunicated Frederick in 1227 for apparently malingering rather than going on crusade, Frederick's decision to go anyway, and in the process crown himself king of Jerusalem, did little to improve relations.

At the heart of this bitter conflict lay the question of who would dominate Christendom: pope or emperor. With each side buoyed

Falconry

Frederick II's book *The Art of Hunting with Birds* married the knowledge of Europe, Arabia and the ancients with the emperor's own expertise. It was, he said, a text that had been germinating in his mind for thirty years. Frederick was not alone in his enthusiasm; the ancient art of hunting with falcons, hawks and eagles (although Frederick thought the latter a showy choice favoured only by novices) became a craze in medieval Europe, practised by men and women, rich and poor alike.

The sport demanded skill and patience. While the rich employed falconers to rear the birds, instruction manuals abounded for those keen to do it themselves. A bourgeois Parisian of the 14th century wrote a set of rules for his wife, advising her to take the bird on her gloved hand to market while she did her shopping. The notoriously nervy birds took some time to get used to people. Frederick II particularly recommended a bath as a means of soothing them; others preferred to spit a stream of water in the bird's face.

When he was not breaking new theological ground, the monk and philosopher Abelard recommended that falconers feed their charges on little birds, hens' flesh, finely chopped sheep's head and hard-boiled eggs mashed with sweet milk and served on a silver platter. But such coddling was only for the off-season. When the birds were being prepared for hunting, their rations were reduced to make them eager for the kill.

The spoils of the hunt were relatively unimportant. The sport's appeal was in the beauty of the art, the joy of the outdoors, the breathtaking elegance of the falcon in flight. But not everyone was a fan. The chronicler John of Salisbury, frustrated at the failure of attempts to stop the monastic orders from indulging in this healthy but unholy pursuit, described the sport variously as 'an activity characterized by self-indulgence and vice', 'a silly and very trying business' and 'a milder form of insanity'. But most were in accordance with the 15th-century Englishman who wrote to his brother that, 'If I have not a hawk I shall wax fat for default of labour and dead for default of company.'

up by a messianic belief in their cause, Italy became the battleground of papal troops and imperial forces. Missives, manifestos, papal bulls and insults flew across Europe. Frederick was again excommunicated. If he was the Wonder of the World to his admirers, he was henceforth Beast of the Apocalypse to his enemies. Two different popes, Gregory IX and Innocent IV, fled Rome, the former dying in exile. In 1245 Innocent IV fired the papacy's ultimate salvo: he announced the emperor was deposed. For the next five years it was all-out war. In the end it was death, not the papacy, that defeated Frederick. Fighting on against the almost insurmountable twin obstacles of excommunication and deposition, Frederick was regaining ground in both Italy and Germany when he died suddenly in 1250.

The death of this titan stunned Europe. Reported sightings of the excommunicated emperor abounded, each more fantastical than the last. For half of Christendom he was the Antichrist; for the other half, the Messiah. Taking into account his record of governance, his intellectual advancement and his struggle against the worldliness of a church determined to deprive him of his birthright, it is clear that he was the towering figure of his age.

Edward III 1312–1377 and the Black Prince 1330–1376

The greatest soldier of his age.

Jean Froissart, *Chronicles* (late 14th century) on the Black Prince

Edward III and the Black Prince were the father and son who personified the glory, energy, triumph and dynamism of English chivalry at its medieval apogee. Edward III was the most successful and heroic of English kings; the Black Prince – formally Edward, Prince of Wales – was the most chivalrous and celebrated knight in Europe. Together they ruled justly, conquered new lands, performed deeds of courage, won golden victories and left a legend. Along with King Henry V, they are the greatest princes in British history.

Edward III grew up under the shadow of his disastrously weak father Edward II, who was deposed and murdered in 1327 by his mother, Queen Isabella, and her lover Roger Mortimer. The two then ruled despotically until the sidelined king, aged just 17, arranged a successful *coup d'etat*. Mortimer was executed and Edward took power: dynamic, talented, athletic, just and energetic, he defeated the Scots; started the Hundred Years War by provoking conflict with France; won victory at Crécy in 1346; founded the Knights of the Garter, his celebrated order of chivalry; and extended the English *imperium* over vast swathes of France via the Treaty of Bretigny in 1360. Even if in old age he lost his grip, allowing his mistress Alice Perrers too much power, he remains one of England's greatest kings. At 13, the king allowed his son and heir, known as Edward of Woodstock, to start campaigning abroad. Command of his company was, in reality, shared with the more experienced earls of Warwick and Northampton, but there is no doubt that the young prince lent fire and aggression to the march across enemy territory.

When the English faced the French at Crécy, the king placed Edward's company in the thick of the fighting. The French fell upon the prince and his men, and it took every ounce of strength to batter them back. Although later stories tell of the king refusing to help until the prince had 'won his spurs', in fact Edward III realized that his son was in grave danger and sent reinforcements of 20 senior knights. But when they arrived, they found the prince and his companions catching their breath, having already repulsed the French. The following day's fighting secured victory – one of the greatest the English had ever scored.

A legend was born at Crécy in 1346, and it was a legend that the prince was keen to maintain. One of the allies of the French, King John of Bohemia, had demanded to be brought into battle despite being totally blind. Not surprisingly, he did not survive long. But the prince was impressed with his chivalry and adopted the Bohemian ostrich feathers as his own heraldic device in the dead king's honour. The ostrich feathers still form the crest of the Prince of Wales today.

Ten years later, in 1356, with a decade's experience of command behind him, the prince commanded another division of English troops to an even greater victory. Without his father to back him up, the prince was not particularly enthused by the idea of engaging the French king, John II; yet on 19 September he led his men into

The late-medieval knight

The idea that warfare in the Middle Ages was dominated by charges of mounted knights is false. Given the right conditions, well-trained cavalry *could* exert a decisive influence on the battlefield if they were skilfully used, but in many cases commanders in fact dismounted their knights.

The principal weapon used during cavalry charges was the lance. When riding into battle, the knight of the late Middle Ages would probably not have carried a shield. This was because the development of highly effective plate armour had by this time rendered shields largely superfluous.

battle about 5 miles (8km) from Poitiers. the prince used his tactical nous to outflank his enemies, charging downhill at them and engaging them in hand-to-hand combat. The French king was captured, and a victory even greater than Crécy was won.

Of course, further stories of the prince's chivalrous deeds sprang up almost immediately. It was said that he had deferred to the superior rank of his captive, King John, refusing to eat with him but rather serving him at table. The story is probably untrue but gives a further indication of the esteem in which the prince was held. John was ransomed for a vast sum, and for a while England was in the ascendant over its larger neighbour.

Poitiers marked the high point of the prince's career. As governor of Aquitaine he was hated for his harsh rule, and he also ill-advisedly became involved with Spanish politics in Castile. With his beautiful wife Joan, 'The Fair Maid of Kent', he gained a reputation for lavish indulgence and a lack of political finesse. Nevertheless, he did have a genuine sense of moral purpose, and he was adored by the people of London in particular, especially in comparison with his infinitely more ham-fisted brother John of Gaunt, who oversaw the government in the 1370s when both Edward and his father were too ill and old to contribute.

The woeful decline of England's fortunes under John of Gaunt and then under Edward's own son, Richard II, only serve to indicate just how much the Black Prince deserved Froissart's famous epigram. He really was the greatest soldier of his age.

Filippo Brunelleschi 1377–1446

It may be said that he was given by Heaven to invest architecture with new forms.

Giorgio Vasari, Lives of the Artists (1568)

The magnificent dome on the Cathedral of Santa Maria del Fiore, in Florence, is testament to the genius of one of the world's finest architects, Filippo Brunelleschi, who preceded other geniuses of the Renaissance such as Michelangelo and Leonardo da Vinci. As did many of his fellow and later artists, Brunelleschi sought to revive the forms of Greek and Roman antiquity, and in so doing he pioneered a dazzling new style of design.

In developing the tools to realize his vision, Brunelleschi achieved some remarkable feats of engineering. His inquisitive and unorthodox mind could solve puzzles that stumped the finest talents in Europe, and his legacy, the great dome that dominates the Florentine skyline, is still one of the most beautiful and iconic buildings in the world.

Born in Florence in 1377, Brunelleschi was a bright child, whose natural instinct for draughtsmanship led his father to place him as an apprentice to the master goldsmith Benincasa Lotti. He formed a close friendship with a fellow trainee, the sculptor Donatello, and learned the intricacies of the goldsmith's trade. As well as perfecting such skills as engraving and embossing, this also involved a study of mechanics, and by his early twenties Brunelleschi was a talented artist with a solid grasp of cogs, gears, wheels and weights.

In 1401 a competition was held to design the doors of the city's Baptistery. Although Brunelleschi entered a magnificent design, the competition was won by his rival Lorenzo Ghiberti. Piqued by the slight, Brunelleschi left Florence for Rome, where he and Donatello spent the next decade.

Rome's classical remains fascinated Brunelleschi. He spent his time observing, measuring and sketching the city's ancient buildings.

He was intrigued by Roman engineering, especially as embodied in the Pantheon, where the Romans had poured concrete over a timber frame to create a great dome. When word reached him that the authorities in Florence were looking for an architect to build a dome on the city's new cathedral, Brunelleschi began at once to plan his return.

Arriving back in Florence, Brunelleschi won a commission from the silk merchants' guild to build a state orphanage – the elegant Ospedale degli Innocenti, which was the first building in Florence to show classical influences. The powerful Medici family then employed him to remodel the Basilica of San Lorenzo.

Most doubted that doming the huge cathedral could be achieved – the recipe for concrete was long forgotten, and creating an elaborate interior scaffold seemed impossible. Yet Brunelleschi had been secretly working on plans, designs and technical ideas for the dome for years, and managed to convince the cathedral authorities that he had the technical expertise to match the task. To demonstrate his prowess he recommended a Europe-wide contest, which attracted master-architects from across the continent.

Brunelleschi's original and daring ideas for constructing a double-vaulted, self-supporting dome were far better than any other suggestions advanced, which included such bizarre schemes as filling the cathedral with a mixture of earth and coins to support the roof as it was built, then inviting the ordinary citizens to remove the semiprecious mud when work was completed.

Having been granted the commission, Brunelleschi set about the mammoth task. There was no way that an internal scaffold could be erected in the cathedral, so he invented a lifting machine that could be driven by an ox to hoist and lower brick and sandstone supports hundreds of feet up to the roof. To keep his workers safe and satisfied, he controlled the food and wine on site, building inns within the structure to cut down on the time spent travelling for refreshments in the baking heat of the Tuscan summer. A safety net allowed the builders to work at dizzying heights, and when there was a strike among the native craftsmen, he drafted in labourers from Lombardy to keep production going.

The dome took 16 years to build. In 1434 a visitor from Rome described it as 'a structure so great, rising above the skies, large

The Gates of Paradise

One of Filippo Brunelleschi's greatest rivals was the Florentine sculptor Lorenzo Ghiberti. The two were pitted against each other as young men, and a fiercely competitive relationship developed over the course of the next 50 years. Following their initial joust in a competition to build the doors of the Florentine Baptistery, both played an important part in building the stunning Renaissance city.

In 1401 a competition was announced to build a new set of doors for the Baptistery of St John, which was one of the oldest buildings in the city, dating back to the 3rd or 4th century AD. One existing set of doors had been designed by Andrea Pisano, who was commissioned in 1329 and whose work was completed in 1336. The panelling represented scenes from the life of St John the Baptist.

The new competition invited entrants to design a panel illustrating Abraham about to sacrifice Isaac, one of the most dramatic episodes in the Old Testament. Seven men entered – Brunelleschi, Ghiberti, Donatello, Jacopo della Quercia and three others. It was clear that the main contenders were Brunelleschi, then 23, and Ghiberti, who was only 21.

Both of the young men created stunning designs. Brunelleschi, who had just achieved the rank of master goldsmith, passionately believed that his was the finest. Indeed, his trial panel marked the high point of his career as a sculptor. But the city authorities awarded the victory to Ghiberti.

Ghiberti ignored the jibes of those who thought his work had only been commissioned because it was the cheapest. He toiled for the next 21 years to create the doors (known as the North Doors, though that was not where they were originally installed). They consist of 28 magnificently sculpted panels: 20 contain scenes from the New Testament, and the remainder are portraits of the 4 evangelists and 4 early Fathers of the Church.

As a reward, Ghiberti's next commission was to create another set of doors, this time destined for the east side of the Baptistery. For 27 years he laboured over what Michelangelo would call the Gates of Paradise. They contain ten stunningly realized scenes from the Old Testament, and utilize all the advances in perspective that had been developed during the early 15th century. The doors are surrounded by richly gilded decoration, with statuettes and busts of the prophets, and busts of Ghiberti and his father.

Ghiberti suffered disappointment when he was ejected from Brunelleschi's great dome project, but the Gates of Paradise are a technical masterpiece, one of the finest achievements of the Italian Renaissance.

enough to shelter all the people of Tuscany in its shadow, built without the help of any centring or of much woodwork, of a craftsmanship perhaps not even the ancients knew or understood'.

It was a unique achievement – two vaults weighing 37,000 tons, with more than four million interlocking bricks that kept the structure from collapsing under its own weight and holes to accommodate expansion and contraction with the change of seasons. The 66-ft (20-m) lantern on the very top shone a thin shaft of sunlight on to the cathedral floor, providing a means of checking that the roof was not moving.

When the pope consecrated the cathedral on Easter Sunday 1436, it was Brunelleschi's moment of triumph. The greatest architect of an age famous for producing brilliance in every field of the arts was eventually buried beneath his supreme achievement, where a statue of him still stands.

Joan of Arc
c.1412–1431

I have been sent here by God, the King of Heaven, to drive you, an eye for an eye, from the whole of France.

Joan of Arc, in a letter to the English forces besieging Orléans (22 March 1429)

France's national heroine, Joan of Arc, was a simple peasant girl who became a soldier, a martyr, and finally a saint. Convinced that God had told her to free France, she showed remarkable moral and military leadership and inspired the French to fight on against the English in the Hundred Years' War. Dressed in men's clothes, Joan defied convention, and the objections of both statesmen and churchmen, and in the end embraced death in her pursuit of the salvation of her country.

Joan was just 14 when she first heard the 'voices' of Saints Michael, Catherine and Margaret calling her to save France from the English. After half a century of war, the French seemed on the verge of losing the contest for their crown. Five years after the death of the Valois king Charles VI, his son, the Dauphin Charles, had still not been crowned, and the city of Orléans, the key to central France, seemed about to fall to the English.

Joan travelled across war-torn enemy territory to seek an audience with Charles, driven on by the persistent voices of the saints. Her quiet unbending determination gained her access to the Dauphin and persuaded him that he must reinvigorate the campaign against the English, and that it was God's will that he should be crowned at Rheims. She never disclosed what she had whispered to him that day, but it certainly convinced him that she had divine guidance.

Clad in white armour and wielding a battleaxe, Joan rode at the

Henry V and English archery

On 31 August 1422, at Bois de Vincennes outside Paris, Henry V of England succumbed to the grim fate of so many of his soldiers and died of 'camp fever' – most likely dysentery. Shakespeare's Young Prince Hal was just 34 years old and had succeeded his father to the English throne only nine years earlier. Yet Henry was young in years, not in experience. Indeed, such were the accomplishments of his brief life that he has been described by one modern historian as 'the greatest man that ever ruled England'.

When Henry came to the throne in 1413, the country had been riven for decades by dynastic wrangling, his father Henry IV having seized the throne from his cousin, the vicious and inept Richard II, whom he had had starved to death. Young Henry V, offering hope of a clean break with the past, rapidly set about doing his all to unite the country. A 'very English Englishman' himself, he aimed to nurture a sense of nationhood and national identity, abandoning the usual practices of his predecessors and reading and writing in English rather than in French. But even as a teenager he had commanded in battle, and his exceptional military prowess won him great popularity at home.

Henry set sail for France in August 1415 with a plan to capture a number of strategically placed towns in northern France that could be garrisoned and used as footholds for further conquests. By the end of September he had succeeded in taking the port of Harfleur, but as his

head of Charles's army to relieve the besieged city of Orléans. The English were routed, and other victories followed – as Joan was somehow sure they would. Hailed by the French as their saviour, and by the English as a witch, it seemed that the 'Maid of Orléans' must have some supernatural power, as the myth of English invincibility that had sprung up since Agincourt was conclusively shattered. In July 1429 the Dauphin was crowned as Charles VII at Rheims, with Joan in attendance.

Indefatigable, Joan urged on the vacillating Charles to push his advantage and press on to Paris. When Valois forces finally attacked the capital, Joan stood high on the earthworks, calling to the city's inhabitants to surrender to their rightful king. Undaunted by wounds

army had already been severely depleted by disease, he decided to return to England to regroup. On 25 October the English army of around 6000 found its path to Calais blocked near Agincourt by a far superior French force. Outnumbered by at least three to one, the thin English line was drawn up in a strong defensive position, forming a funnel with trees on either flank and several large groups of archers positioned along the line. When the French knights in heavy armour, on horseback, finally advanced, they found themselves increasingly constricted and caught in a deadly hail of arrows. Laying down their bows after the initial volleys, the English longbowmen then piled into the French, now hopelessly crushed together and in total confusion, and inflicted horrendous casualties. Henry's great victory was thus also the triumph of the powerful longbow of the English archers (many of them from Cheshire), whose sustained barrage of arrows was, in its terrifying and murderous way, the medieval equivalent of the machine gun.

Over the next few years, inspired by the leadership of their charismatic and dynamic young king, the English army rampaged through northern France, inflicting one devastating blow after another on the disorganized and divided French. Buoyed up by his successes, by 1420 Henry was in a position to impose a severe settlement on his adversaries, and according to the terms of the Treaty of Troyes the ailing French king Charles VI accepted Henry as his regent and future heir. Early death prevented Henry from fully exploiting his victories, but he was already guaranteed immortality as one of the greatest heroes that England has produced.

she received in the fight, she refused to leave the field – although the attempt to take Paris was not successful.

Captured by the Burgundians as she rushed to help the besieged town of Compiègne, Joan was sold to the English and tried as a heretic in Rouen, the seat of English power in France. Charles, eager for a truce with Burgundy and reluctant to be associated with a witch, was nowhere to be seen. At her trial the peasant girl faced up to France's greatest theologians, confident of her divine mission, while avoiding being tricked into criticizing the church. Joan was so impervious to the threat of torture that her interrogators decided that it would be useless to try.

But when the church threatened to hand her over to the secular courts, Joan – petrified and ill – confessed to heresy and agreed to put on women's clothes, choosing life imprisonment over a painful death. Within days of recanting, however, Joan changed back into men's clothes, saying the voices had censured her treacherous abjuration. Handed over to the secular authorities, the young woman barely out of her teens – who had always had a premonition of an early death – was burnt at the stake as a witch.

Joan's conviction was unwavering. Allowed to make her confession and receive communion, she died gazing at a cross held up by a priest, who, acceding to her request, shouted out assurances of salvation so that she could hear him over the fire's roar. So anxious were the English that no relic of her should remain to keep her legend alive, they burnt her body three times, then scattered her dust in the River Seine.

Twenty years later, safely installed on his throne, Charles VII ordered an inquiry into the trial. Joan's conviction was overturned. Five hundred years later, on 16 May 1920, she was made a saint by the Roman Catholic Church.

Ferdinand
Magellan 1480–1521

*... the whole earth hangs in the air ... a thing so strange
and seeming so far against nature and reason ... which is
yet now found true by experience of them that have in less
than two years sailed the world round about.*

Thomas More, *Dialogue Concerning Heresies* (1529), referring to Magellan's 1519 voyage

Ferdinand Magellan was a fearless and determined sailor who
achieved what Columbus had attempted: he sailed westwards from
Europe and reached the East Indies, thus making the first recorded
crossing of the Pacific Ocean. Although Magellan himself was killed
in the Philippines, one ship from his fleet of five, after experiencing appalling hardships, finally returned to Spain – becoming
the first to complete a circumnavigation of the entire globe.

Born to a noble Portuguese family, Magellan grew up around the
royal court. In 1495 he entered the service of King Manuel I, 'the
Fortunate', and enlisted as a volunteer on the first voyage to India
planned by the Portuguese viceroy Francisco D'Almeida.

Magellan took part in a series of expeditions to the East, as Portugal
sought to expand its trade routes and bring valuable spices back to
Europe, becoming involved in skirmishes en route and achieving promotion to captain. In 1512 he returned to Portugal. He helped to
take the Moroccan city of Azamor but was wounded during the fighting
and walked with a limp for the rest of his life. Even worse, he was
accused of trading with the Moors and subsequently fell from favour
with King Manuel.

It was clear that Magellan's career in the service of the Portuguese
crown was over. In 1513 he renounced his nationality and went to
Spain. In Seville he proposed to Charles V that he could reach the
Spice Islands of the East via the western passage that had eluded
Christopher Columbus some twenty years earlier. With the aid of
advances in navigation, diligent consultation with an astronomer and

the sheer guts to suggest travelling at a latitude of up to 75° S, Magellan was in a good position to trump Columbus. So in September 1519, with five ships and 270 men, he embarked on his historic voyage.

Magellan sailed across the Atlantic, sighting South America in November 1519. He then headed south, wintering in Patagonia, where he had to crush a dangerous mutiny led by two of his captains. He set sail again in August 1520.

In October Magellan found a channel leading westwards between the South American mainland and the archipelago to the south, which enabled his fleet to avoid the stormy open seas south of Cape Horn. He called this passage 'All Saints' Channel', but it is now known as the Strait of Magellan after the great navigator. As the ships passed through, the sailors were overawed by the great snowy mountains on either side. To the north was the southern tip of Patagonia, and to the south the islands they called the Land of Fire – Tierra del Fuego – because of the fires lit by the native people that burned on the shore. Once they had passed through the strait, they found themselves facing a vast expanse of open water. In honour of the steady, gentle wind that blew them across it, Magellan named the ocean the Pacific.

For 98 days Magellan's crew sailed northwestwards across the open ocean, spotting only an occasional rocky, barren island. They had little water, and what they did have was bad. They ran out of supplies and were reduced to eating mouldy biscuit, rats and sawdust. But still Magellan pushed onwards, saying that he would rather eat the ships' leather than give up. And that was exactly what the crew did, chewing leather from the yardarms.

In March 1521 they reached the Philippines, which Magellan originally named after St Lazarus. They took on supplies and reached the island of Cebu, where Magellan befriended the native king. By purporting to convert to Catholicism, the king managed to convince Magellan to become involved in his violent feuds with neighbouring islands, and it was in an attack on one of these on 27 April that Magellan was killed. The treacherous king then murdered two of Magellan's men before the crew could regroup and head home for Spain.

Only eighteen crewmen, four South American natives and one ship, the *Victoria*, made it around the Cape of Good Hope and back to Spain, plagued by contrary winds, harassment from the Portuguese, malnourishment and scurvy. Although Magellan was not among them,

Mapping the world

Magellan's great voyage really was a journey into the unknown, because there simply were no accurate maps or charts of where he intended to go. But it was explorers such as Magellan who provided the raw data for the great cartographers whose work is still so vital to us today.

The Babylonians were producing maps as early as the 3rd millennium BC but the first centre of map-making was the Greek city of Miletus, where in 500 BC Hecataeus produced the first book on geography. Mathematicians and philosophers like Pythagoras and Parmenides gradually came to the conclusion that the earth was a sphere, which Aristotle argued forcefully in 350 BC.

The most important cartographer of the ancient world was the Greek scholar Ptolemy, who produced his *Geography* in Alexandria during the 2nd century AD. Despite problems with scale, this work included the most accurate world maps of the time, with 8000 place names and their approximate geographical locations. It was still influential when Columbus set sail 13 centuries later.

Scholarship stalled in the European Dark Ages, and though Islamic and Chinese cartographers made some advances, it was not until the journeys of Marco Polo in the 13th century, and the voyages of Columbus, Vasco da Gama, Magellan and others in the 15th and 16th centuries, that map-making began to make leaps forward.

With the colonial and European wars of the 18th century, maps became even more important. Napoleon had begun a project to map all of Europe on a 1:100,000 scale before he fell from power. Britain's maritime pre-eminence led to the establishment of Greenwich as the international meridian line, from where all longitude was measured.

The Ordnance Survey in Britain and the Institut Géographique National in France led the way in national mapping, but even in 1940 American pilots were complaining that only 10 per cent of the world was mapped to any degree of useful accuracy. The Second World War led to advances in aerial photography, and the Cold War to the development of satellite technology, and today virtually all of the world's surface – apart perhaps from some remote parts of Antarctica – has been thoroughly charted.

by the time of his death he had travelled well past the longitude of his original voyages to the East, when he had visited the Moluccas. He had also discovered the holy grail of navigators and traders: a passage to the eastern Spice Islands via the western ocean. This in turn helped to pave the way for Spanish and Portuguese dominance across the globe during the 16th century.

Great explorers like Columbus and Marco Polo may have discovered the hitherto unknown parts of the world, but it was Magellan who joined them all together.

Babur 1483–1530

Wine makes a man act like an ass in a rich pasture.

Saying attributed to Babur

Babur was the nomad prince who emerged from a tiny Mongol kingdom to found India's Mughal dynasty and empire. Babur's reign was brief. But he was a talented conqueror and intellectual. His power over and respect for the myriad peoples whom he ruled created a vast empire of an incomparable cultural magnificence.

Claiming descent from Genghis Khan, the young Zahir-ud-din Mohammed was directly descended from the Turkic-Mongol conqueror Tamurlane (Timur). But the family had lost much of Tamurlane's empire, so he was for much of his youth a king without a kingdom. Called Babur by tribesmen unable to pronounce his real name, he inherited the tiny Central Asian state of Fergana at the age of 12. Having fended off his uncles' attempts to unseat him, Babur set out to conquer neighbouring Samarkand. The 15-year-old prince miscalculated. In his absence rebellion at home robbed him of Fergana, and when he marched back to reclaim it, his troops deserted Samarkand, depriving him of that too. 'It came very hard on me,' Babur later recalled of his nomad years. 'I could not help crying a good deal.'

Defeat strengthened Babur's resolve. By 1504 the hardened warrior had secured himself the kingdom of Kabul. From there he looked east into Hindustan's vast lands. After several attempts, Babur finally triumphed in 1526 at the Battle of Panipat, where his 12,000 men routed the sultan of Delhi's 100,000-strong army. Over the next three years he defeated the Rajputs, the Afghans and the sultan of Bengal, to become the unchallenged ruler of Hindustan. Thus did this descendant of Tamurlane carve out what was to become known as the Mughal Empire, after the Persian word for 'Mongol'.

Babur ascribed his astounding victories to 'the fountain of the favour and mercy of God'. Weaponry helped. Babur introduced to India the matchlock musket and the cannon, although initially they only earned him ridicule. As Babur's tally of victories attests, it soon became clear that with effective firepower his almost absurdly small armies could make huge inroads against opponents with a vast numerical superiority.

A supremely well-trained collection of Pashtuns, Persians, Arabs and Chaghatai Turks, Babur's men revered their consummate commander. He was a warrior of legendary strength – it was reported that he could run up slopes carrying a man on each shoulder, and that he had swum across every major river he had encountered, including the Ganges. The Mughal armies terrified their enemies and not without just cause, for vanquished combatants were beheaded and their heads strung up from parapets. Babur considered his son and heir Humayun's decision to have 100 prisoners of war shot at Panipat, rather than released or enslaved as was the custom, 'an excellent omen'.

In contrast, as a ruler Babur was merciful. The Muslim emperor ruled over an array of peoples with immense tolerance and respect. He never forced their conversion or sought to alter their practices. Preach Islam 'by the sword of love and affection', he told Humayun, 'rather than the sword of tyranny and persecution'. His clarity of vision and his humanity allowed him to see that his vast empire could flourish in all its diversity: 'Look at the various characteristics of your people just as characteristics of various seasons,' he told his son. An advocate of justice regardless of race or religion, he hated hypocrisy, describing it as 'the lies and flattery of rogues and sycophants'.

Babur's respect for his conquered lands helped to forge an exquisite and unique culture. Babur brought to India his Timurid inheritance: the skills and practices of the jewel-city of Tamurlane's old capital, Samarkand. The resulting fusion produced centuries of breathtaking art and architecture, such as the monumental Taj Mahal.

Akbar the Great

Babur's grandson Akbar the Great (1542–1605) was one of history's most original and gifted rulers, the greatest leader India ever knew. Ascending a shaky throne at the age of 13, he defeated his enemies with dazzling victories, extended his rule across Afghanistan, Pakistan and much of northern India, initiated works of art, including the Akbar-nama, created beautiful buildings and founded new cities, presiding over an era of astonishing achievement and prosperity.

But his greatest legacy was to establish a policy of tolerance and encouragement of other religions. Although himself a Muslim, he invited Hindus into his governments and family, preserved Hindu temples and debated religion with Hindus, Sikhs, atheists, and even Jesuits, founding his supra-religious 'Divine Faith' to unite all peoples. His tolerance laid the basis for Mughal greatness.

The great emperors Humayun, Akbar, Jahangir and Shah Jahan fostered a culture at which the world marvelled. Great monuments like the bejewelled Taj Mahal, Humayun's Tomb and the black marble pavilion of the Shalimar Gardens shimmered on the landscape. In the rose-rust sandstone of Akbar's city Fatehpur Sikri, literature experienced a golden age: beautifully illustrated books with handsome calligraphy recorded the feats of the age, or the works of the flourishing school of Hindi poetry. In Mughal India beauty assaulted the senses.

Himself a skilled author, calligrapher and composer, Babur initiated his dynasty's patronage of all these arts. He created magnificent formal gardens as a respite from India's ferocious heat. They were the first of their kind on the subcontinent, stocked with plants and fruits that he brought from his homelands to the northwest. Buried according to his wishes in the garden of Bagh-e-Babur in his beloved Kabul, the inscription on Babur's tomb reads: 'If there is a paradise on earth, it is this, it is this, it is this!'

Babur's flaw was his excess. He drank heavily and developed a notable fondness for marijuana. His extravagant generosity emptied his coffers. And when Humayun seemed mortally ill, Babur was said to have offered up his life in return for his son's. Babur's last words say much about the ruthlessness of the time and the

Each emperor had his own speciality. While Babur's formal gardens celebrated the earth and its fruits, his astronomer-astrologer son Humayun wondered at the sky. Jahangir echoed his grandfather's love of letters in his poetry and memoirs, while Shah Jahan created for his late, adored queen Mumtaz Mahal that majestic domed monument to enduring love, the Taj Mahal.

With the Taj Mahal, the cultural splendour of the dynasty reached its zenith. Shah Jahan was deposed by his son Aurangzeb, in whom the freeness and *joie de vivre* of his predecessors was transmuted into an iron will. What his forebears achieved in culture, Aurangzeb carved out in territory; under his rule the Mughal Empire reached its greatest extent. However, his intolerant Muslim orthodoxy alienated many of his Hindu subjects.

'After me, chaos,' Aurangzeb once declared. He was right, but he was not the last of the Mughal emperors. A series of puppet rulers followed him, driven here and there by the external forces of the Marathas, the Afghans, the Persians, the French and the British. Finally, in 1857, the last of the Mughal emperors fell. Bahadur Shah II, a pale imitation of his ancestors, was eventually deposed by the British and hustled out of Delhi in a bullock cart. The great dynasty of the Mughals had come to an end, but in the wonders of their art in ink and stone, the splendour of their legacy endures.

humanity of the man: 'Do nothing against your brothers,' he told Humayun, 'even though they may deserve it.'

Babur's extraordinary story is recounted in his personal journal, the *Babur-nama*, charting his progress from Fergana's boy-king to Mughal emperor. It encompasses battles, intrigues, flora, fauna, geography, peoples, poetry, art, music, polo matches and feasts. It also gives the first documented mention of the priceless diamond the Koh-i-Noor. Including in places even Babur's personal feelings, the *Babur-nama* is an astounding record of the era and a startling insight into the man.

Suleiman the Magnificent 1494–1566

I who am the sultan of sultans, the sovereign of sovereigns, the shadow of God on earth, sultan and emperor of the White Sea [Mediterranean] and the Black Sea ...

Suleiman the Magnificent writing to the Holy Roman Emperor, Charles V (1547)

Under the rule of Suleiman the Magnificent, the Ottoman Empire, which stretched from the Middle East to North Africa and Central Europe, reached its glorious peak. He expanded its borders, rooted out corruption, overhauled the laws, ruled with tolerance, patronized the arts and wrote fine poetry. His legacy was a vast, well-governed, culturally flourishing empire, which continued to thrive for a century after his death.

When Suleiman came to power as Ottoman sultan or *padishah* (emperor) in 1520, aged 26, he inherited an empire centred on Turkey, which had been strengthened by his father's acquisitions of Syria, Palestine and Egypt, as well as the two holiest Islamic cities, Medina and Mecca. Suleiman determined to expand this empire in every direction.

His first target was Belgrade. In the summer of 1521 Suleiman captured the Serbian city from the king of Hungary, striking a heavy blow against Christendom and opening the path for further expansion into Europe. By 1526 Hungary had more or less succumbed to the Ottomans, and though it took another 15 years for a formal partition of the kingdom to be realized, Suleiman now had a springboard from which to attack Vienna. None of the major European powers could afford to ignore such a vital and energetic empire-builder on their doorstep, and all began to court Ottoman support in their own power struggles.

Meanwhile, in the Islamic world, Suleiman set his sights on the western frontiers of the Persian Empire. The shah avoided a pitched battle, and in 1535 Suleiman entered Baghdad. The capture of the city, along with lower Mesopotamia and much territory around the Euphrates and Tigris rivers, meant that by the time a treaty was signed with the shah in 1554, Suleiman was indisputably the dominant force in the Middle East.

The final thrust of Ottoman expansion under Suleiman secured Tripolitania (part of modern Libya), Tunisia and Algeria, a vast territorial gain that secured forthe Ottomans a brief period of naval dominance in the western Mediterranean. Suleiman was now a key player in the battles between the kings Francis I of France and Charles V, the Habsburg emperor and king of Spain.

But territorial expansion was only one of Suleiman's ambitions. In the Muslim world his legal reforms earned him the title Suleiman the Lawgiver. In particular, he concentrated on the Sultanic *kanun* – a system of rules in cases that fall outside Islamic Shari'ah.

As well as being an energetic reformer, Suleiman was also known as a scrupulously fair and even-handed ruler. He promoted his servants on the basis on their abilities, rather than of their personal wealth, their family background or their general popularity. He promoted tolerance of both Jews and Christians – indeed, many of Suleiman's most important civil servants were drawn from the ranks of the empire's Christian slaves.

Suleiman was devoted to the arts. Not only was he himself a talented poet (many of his own aphorisms have become Turkish proverbs), but he also enthusiastically promoted artistic societies within the empire. Artists and craftsmen were given career paths, leading from apprenticeship to official rank, with quarterly pay, and Istanbul became a centre of artistic excellence. Among the many fine mosques and other buildings commissioned by Suleiman is the Süleymaniye Mosque in Istanbul, which is Suleiman's final resting place. During his reign, numerous bridges were built throughout the empire, such as the Danube Bridge, the Bridge of Buda, and the great aqueducts that solved Istanbul's water shortage.

Suleiman brought the Ottoman Empire into its golden age. By the time he died of a stroke at the Battle of Szigetvar in 1566, his conquests had united most of the Muslim world, with all the major Islamic cities west of Persia – Medina, Mecca, Jerusalem, Damascus and Baghdad – under the same ruler. Eastern Europe, the Balkans and the southern Mediterranean were also dominated by the Ottomans. There is no doubt that Suleiman fully deserved his Western nickname – the Magnificent.

Clash of the empires

The high-water mark of Suleiman's advance on Central Europe came in 1529, when he tried unsuccessfully to capture Vienna. This failure contributed to establishing the limits of Ottoman hegemony in the 16th century. The struggle for Vienna was one of the most notable of those battles that saved Christian Europe from invaders – going all the way back to the defeat of Attila's Huns at Châlons in 451, the Frankish victory over the Moors at Tours in 732, and the repulsion of the Magyars by the Germans at Lechfeld in 955.

In 1526 Suleiman had defeated Louis II of Hungary at the Battle of Mohács, giving rise to a dispute over the Hungarian crown between the Archduke of Austria, Ferdinand I, and Suleiman's own choice, the subservient Transylvanian noble John Zápolya.

Ferdinand was married to Louis II's sister and heiress, and he was also a member of the powerful Habsburg dynasty, headed by the Holy Roman Emperor, Charles V, ruler of Austria, Germany, the Low Countries and Spain. The battle for Hungary was thus a clash of two empires.

In spring 1529 Suleiman gathered an army of 120,000 men and marched them through Bulgaria. Bad weather caused the loss of numerous camels and bogged down the heavy cannon, but Suleiman managed to meet up with Zápolya and recapture several Hungarian

Elizabeth I 1533–1603

I thank God that I am endowed with such qualities that if I were turned out of my realm in my petticoat, I were able to live in any place in Christendom.

Elizabeth I, addressing Parliament (5 November 1566)

Elizabeth I, known as 'Gloriana', was England's greatest queen. During her reign England began to emerge as a modern nation and a seafaring power. She kept her country's religious divides in check,

fortresses, including the important city of Buda, before marching on Vienna.

Without support from Charles V, the archduke feared the worst. He left Vienna in the hands of the 70-year-old Niklas Graf Salm and fled to Bohemia. Salm, an experienced veteran, shored up the Viennese defences around St Stephen's Cathedral and waited.

When they arrived, Suleiman's troops tried to bombard the city's defences into submission. But the earthen reinforcements held firm. The Ottomans switched tactics and began digging trenches and mines to weaken the city walls. This, too, failed, and as a wet autumn approached, they attempted one final push.

Despite their superior numbers, the Ottoman besiegers were beaten back by the pikes of the Austrian defenders. Giving up hope, the Ottomans killed their prisoners and set off for home on 14 October, having to endure heavy snowfalls and skirmishing all the way.

Suleiman had missed his chance to advance into the heart of Europe. Charles V reinforced Vienna with 80,000 troops, and Suleiman had to be content with consolidating his territory in Hungary. The outer limits of the Ottoman Empire had been drawn, until the effort was repeated once more at Vienna in 1683, with similar results. Most of Europe was saved from Ottoman domination. Then in the 19th century, with the tables turned, the Ottoman Empire would be characterized as the 'sick man of Europe'.

presided over an unprecedented artistic flowering, and inspired her people to resist the aggression of England's mightiest enemy, Catholic Spain. And it was under Elizabeth that England's empire began to be formed, with the New World's Virginia being named after the redoubtable Virgin Queen.

Elizabeth had a difficult childhood. Her mother, Anne Boleyn, had been sent to the executioner's block by her father, Henry VIII, and she herself was declared a bastard. Henry had left the throne to his only son, Edward VI, a determined youth during whose short reign Protestantism was imposed on England. On Edward's premature death, Elizabeth's elder half-sister Mary took the throne, and with considerable bloodshed restored the Catholic faith and the pope's authority. Although Elizabeth clung to her Protestant beliefs, she was careful to make a pretence of Catholic practice. In the face of investigations by Mary's inquisitors, she learned the valuable political lesson of keeping her own counsel.

When Elizabeth succeeded Mary as queen of England in 1558, she further showed her political good sense by making the extremely capable Sir William Cecil (later Lord Burghley) her chief minister, and he continued to serve her until his death in 1598. One of the first challenges Elizabeth faced as an attractive, young and highly eligible queen was whom she should marry. Through her reign she had a succession of male favourites, most notably Robert Dudley, Earl of Leicester, but she never married. She herself claimed that she was wedded to her realm and could not give her love (or, indeed, obedience) to just one man. Whatever her inner feelings, it seems that she realized that marrying a foreign prince would threaten England with foreign domination, while marrying an English nobleman would sow dissension among the court factions and possibly plunge England back into the civil strife of the previous century, the time of the Wars of the Roses.

Elizabeth deployed a cautious approach to matters of religion. The Church of England that she created, although technically Protestant, blended both Protestant and Catholic elements. She expected people to conform outwardly, and to respect her position as head of the church, but was not concerned about their inner beliefs: 'I would not open windows into men's souls,' she said.

Such tolerance was not on the agenda at the Vatican, and in 1570 Pope Pius V excommunicated Elizabeth, denying her right to sit upon the throne of England. For some Catholics, the rightful queen of England was Mary, Queen of Scots, Elizabeth's Catholic cousin, who had been ousted from the throne of Scotland and taken refuge in England, where she was effectively put under house arrest. Mary became the focus of numerous Catholic plots against Elizabeth's life. After years of conspiracies, and numerous warnings by her councillors as to the threat Mary represented, Elizabeth had finally had enough, and in 1587 Mary was tried and executed.

By now, religious tensions across Western Europe were reaching boiling point. Outraged by the execution of Mary and by the raids of English privateers on Spanish ships and possessions in the New

Power and powder

One of the secrets of the success of Elizabeth's rule was the visual projection of status – the mask-like image that she created of herself, turning a young, then middle-aged, then elderly woman into an icon of cold beauty and dazzling power. It is an image that appears in numerous portraits of the queen. Before long, all the ladies of the court sought to adopt the red-gold hair, the grey, wide-set eyes, the ghostly pale skin, the thin eyebrows and the high forehead that their sovereign presented to the world. It was, of course, all artifice.

Female beauty, as the Elizabethans saw it, was difficult, if not impossible, to sustain naturally. Age, the elements and the relatively poor standards of personal hygiene, even at court, made the use of cosmetics indispensable. Many of the ingredients were unpleasant or even dangerous, but, in the pursuit of looking a picture, the ends justified the means.

Elizabeth had contracted smallpox in 1562 and, though she survived, she was ravaged by scars. This, combined with the wrinkles that came naturally with age, led her and the ladies of her court to cake their faces with heavy white make-up, the key ingredient of which was a mixture of white lead and vinegar. Lead is extremely toxic and can cause hearing loss, kidney damage and problems with the nervous system. As a result, other, less dangerous concoctions were sometimes used, such as pastes of alum, tin ash and sulphur, or foundations made from egg white.

To redden their cheeks and lips, ladies would use a number of pigments. Cochineal, which was extracted from a species of insect found in the New World, was much valued in Europe, while madder, a small shrub, was another common source of red dye. More dangerous was vermillion, which gave a red-orange tinge to the cheeks. Europeans had cracked the secret Chinese recipe in the 14th century and learned how to make it from the powdered mineral cinnabar. Cinnabar is a compound of mercury, and thus highly toxic, capable of causing madness and death. Mercury was also used as a facial peel, to slough off the top layers of skin and leave a softer complexion behind.

Another poison, belladonna, an extract of the deadly nightshade plant, was used to make eye drops. The toxic ingredient atropine would dilate the pupils, making the lady appear to be in a state of high arousal, with the side-effect of permanently blurred vision and the risk of blindness.

To complete the perfect appearance, ladies would dye their hair with a mixture of saffron, cumin seed, celandine and oil. Their eyebrows would be plucked thin, and the hairline plucked back an inch from its natural place, to give an artificially high forehead. It was painful, but such was the pursuit of beauty at the Elizabethan court.

World – not to mention the support Elizabeth was lending to the Protestant rebels in the Spanish Netherlands – Philip II of Spain, the champion of Catholic Europe, sent a massive Armada against England. The plan was for the fleet of 130 ships to sail from Spain to the Spanish Netherlands, where they would pick up a Spanish army under the Duke of Parma and head for England.

As the invasion fleet was spotted in the Channel in July 1588, beacon fires flared across England. The English navy, under the command of such men as Lord Howard of Effingham and Sir Francis Drake, made ready, while in Tilbury the queen herself addressed her troops with one of the most inspiring speeches in English history:

> I am come amongst you all, as you see at this time, not for my recreation and disport, but being resolved, in the midst and heat of the battle, to live or die amongst you all; to lay down for my God, and for my kingdom, and for my people, my honour and my blood even in the dust. I know I have the body of a weak and feeble woman, but I have the heart and stomach of a king, and a king of England too. And think foul scorn that Parma or Spain, or any Prince of Europe, should dare to invade the borders of my realm!

The English navy and the weather scattered the invasion fleet, to the eternal ignominy of Spain and the glory of Elizabeth.

A superb politician (and Latin scholar), Elizabeth ruled personally with astonishing intelligence, cunning, moderation and tolerance for 45 years until her death, keeping absolute control except in her dotage, when she overindulged a vain young favourite, Robert, Earl of Essex, who was executed for treason. No one except Winston Churchill so symbolizes the defiant, patriotic liberty of the English.

Tokugawa Ieyasu

1543–1616

*The study of literature and the practice of the military arts
must be pursued side by side.*

Tokugawa Ieyasu, *Rules for the Military Houses* (1615)

The tenacity and patience of Tokugawa Ieyasu, Japan's ultimate
shogun, laid the foundations for two and a half centuries of stable
rule by his dynasty. Tokugawa transformed his family from an
undistinguished warrior clan into the undisputed rulers of Japan,
ending decades of anarchy and civil war. As capable a governor
as he was a soldier, Ieyasu's flair for both administration and com-
merce ushered in a long period in which Japan could flourish in
peace.

A legend tells how once Ieyasu was asked what he would do to
a caged songbird that would not sing. 'I'd wait until it does,' the
general replied. The story encapsulates Ieyasu's extraordinary patience,
which was doubtless honed during his childhood years spent as
the hostage of powerful neighbouring clans. He was well cared for,
trained to be a soldier and a governor, and encouraged in his love
of falconry. But he was powerless. He could only listen helplessly
to the news of his father's murder and impotently look on as his
family's fortunes disintegrated.

When the leader of the clan that held him captive was killed in
battle, Ieyasu seized the chance to return home. Deftly exploiting
Japan's precarious political balance, he restored order to his family
and persuaded his former captors to release his wife and children.
In his family's small domain, Ieyasu consolidated his rule, demonstrating the administrative and legislative skill that would later
secure his grip over the whole of Japan.

Ieyasu's network of control spread outwards. His canny governance, disciplined armies and ability to spot the weaknesses of
others made him one of Japan's most influential *daimyos* (feudal
barons). He never overreached himself, however. Realizing after
a few minor skirmishes that he was not yet strong enough to

triumph on his own, he vowed fealty to Japan's dominant war-lord, Toyotomi Hideyoshi. He also avoided involvement in the disastrous military expeditions to Korea that incapacitated so many of his rival daimyos.

Ieyasu's domain became the most prosperous in Japan. He encouraged artisans, businessmen and traders to come to Edo, the fishing village he chose as his base. Edo flourished, growing into the bustling town and port that was later to be renamed Tokyo.

Ieyasu's willingness to bide his time secured him an unassailable power base. Finally, in 1600, at the Battle of Sekigahara, Ieyasu emerged triumphant over his rivals as the undisputed master of Japan. Three years later the imperial court appointed him shogun – the title borne since the 12th century by those warrior-governors who are the real power in Japan, the powerless emperors having only a ceremonial role as figureheads.

Ieyasu consolidated his clan's claim to the shogunate as diligently as he had consolidated his authority over his territory. After only two years as shogun he passed the title on to his son, thus establishing a hereditary claim that endured for 250 years. He made sure that no daimyo could become as powerful as he had by obliging all daimyos to spend long periods at court, thus undermining their ability to build up a local power base. When they were allowed to return to their own domains, Ieyasu kept their families as virtual hostages in Edo.

The small, stout Ieyasu trusted his maverick judgment to see him through. He appointed a falconer as a diplomat, and made an actor the director of mines. His enthusiasm for trading with the Europeans filled his vast warehouses with rice and gold. Will Adams, a Kentish shipbuilder who was shipwrecked by a typhoon on Japanese shores, became one of Ieyasu's most valued commercial advisers.

Ieyasu allowed nothing to threaten Japan's new-found unity and stability, and to this end in 1614 he suppressed Christianity and imprisoned all foreign missionaries. Long tolerant of Christianity, Ieyasu did not initiate the religious killings that his descendants practised – his motive was purely to prevent sectarian divisions among his countrymen. A stream of new laws established stringent control over every stratum of society, curtailing people's freedom of movement but ensuring a stability that Japan had not seen for a century. In 1615, in

The samurai tradition

In the samurai of Japan, exquisitely graceful swordsmanship and iron self-discipline were fused to create a ruthless and fearless warrior class, for whom fighting was an art and honour more important than life itself.

The samurai were initially vassals of their daimyo or feudal lord. But over time warriors and lords began to meld into a single elite warrior class. In the late 16th century the powerful leader Toyotomi Hideyoshi issued an edict that all peasants and townsmen give up their arms, and Tokugawa Ieyasu's stringent ordering of Japanese society confirmed the elite status of the samurai.

In 1615 Ieyasu ordained that all samurai should excel in learning as much as in arms. He demanded that they use their leisured existence to discipline the spirit via austerity, self-restraint and self-improvement. Samurai became scholars and calligraphers as well as warriors, and their mastery of the art of the sword was seen as an aspect of their mastery of the soul.

Their skill was breathtaking. Boys began training at five, fitted out in miniature versions of the ornate traditional dress, a sword thrust in the belt. Innumerable stories are told about the athletic grace and extraordinary skill of the samurai, able to judge within a ribbon's breadth the length of an opponent's sword, leaping and twisting through the air in attack and defence. For the samurai, the beauty of how they fought was of prime importance.

Honour to a samurai was paramount. If lost through carelessness or cowardice or defeat, the only redemption was death. Suicide was carried out ceremonially, in the ritual of *seppuku* or *hara-kiri*. Plunging the knife into his left side, the warrior would then draw it across to the right and finally sharply up. The hardy would then pull out their own guts as a final flourish. It was a far from rare occurrence. In the 19th century a vendetta resulted in 47 samurai being ordered by a court to disembowel themselves: they willingly obeyed.

Technology brought about the end of the samurai. Frustrated by the unwillingness of the highly conservative caste to adopt firearms, in the late 19th century Japan's new and Westernizing rulers, the Meiji, banned all samurai from wearing swords. This inspired one final, doomed revolt, the Satsuma Rebellion. But the spirit of the samurai lived on, from the kamikaze pilots of the Second World War to the masterful martial arts still practised to this day in Japan, where honour is still valued by many over material values.

his most ruthless act, Ieyasu secured Tokugawa pre-eminence by destroying his family's last rivals to the shogunate, the Toyotomi. Among those put to death was his own grandson by marriage.

The shogun died a year later, from wounds sustained in the battle that finally extinguished the threat of the Toyotomi. Ieyasu's tireless energy had secured him and his descendants unchallenged control of the country, bringing centuries of peace and prosperity.

Sir Walter Raleigh

c.1554–1618

Fain would I climb, yet fear I to fall.

Sir Walter Raleigh, line engraved on a window pane, according to Thomas Fuller's *History of the Worthies of England* (1662). Queen Elizabeth is said to have written beneath: 'If thy heart fails thee, climb not at all.'

Walter Raleigh was the 'perfect man' of the Elizabethan age – not only a consummate courtier and a dashing soldier, but also a poet, a scholar and an entrepreneur. His charisma and chivalrousness made him a favourite of Queen Elizabeth herself, while his boldness and drive took him across the Atlantic to establish the first English colonies in the New World.

Raleigh was brought up in Devon and studied at Oxford, later going up to the Middle Temple to study law. As a young man he fought in the French Wars of Religion, and in 1580 he put down an Irish rebellion in Munster (with considerable brutality, it must be said). His service in Ireland brought him to the attention of the royal court, where his relationship with Queen Elizabeth blossomed.

The most famous story of Raleigh's early relationship with the queen is that he lay down his cloak to allow Elizabeth to walk unblemished across a muddy puddle. A further story tells of the pair scribbling lines of a couplet to one another on opposite sides of a glass window. Though these stories may be apocryphal, they attest to his reputation as a romantic courtier.

Having earned the queen's favour, Raleigh was showered with rewards. He was given vast territories in Ireland, valuable trade monopolies, control over the Cornish tin mines, political positions in Devon and Cornwall, and membership of the House of Commons.

At the same time, Raleigh turned his attentions to the New World. In 1583–4 he organized expeditions to Newfoundland and Virginia (which he had flatteringly named after Elizabeth, the Virgin Queen). In Virginia in 1585 he established the first English colony in America, on Roanoke Island, in modern-day North Carolina. Though conditions were unpleasant and the settlers soon took the chance to escape the misery of food shortages and attacks by the natives, Raleigh's vision had started the process of English colonization, which eventually led to British domination of North America.

In 1587 Raleigh dispatched another expedition to Roanoke Island, but this second settlement was even less successful than the first – ships that were meant to resupply the colonists were held up by the war with Spain, and when a ship eventually arrived in 1590, the settlers had vanished. This was hardly Raleigh's fault – the queen had commanded all ships to remain in port to defend the realm against the Spanish Armada.

Raleigh played no memorable part in the defeat of the Armada. He stayed on dry land, organizing the coastal defences and raising men, but the victory at sea of Howard and Drake meant that these preparations were unnecessary. Thereafter Raleigh's star went into something of a decline. He incurred the fury of the queen after he secretly married a lady-in-waiting, Elizabeth Throckmorton, without royal permission. The queen turned to a new favourite, Robert Devereux, Earl of Essex. Elizabeth never trusted Raleigh enough to award him ministerial office.

In 1595 Raleigh sailed to South America in search of the legendary golden city of El Dorado. Unfortunately, there was little support for his plan to colonize the gold-mining areas that were discovered in Venezuela. Raleigh's main import to England was the fashion of smoking tobacco – a phenomenon that so shocked one of his servants that he doused Raleigh in a pail of water, believing his master had burst into flames.

When Elizabeth died in 1603, the throne passed to her cousin

Colonizing Virginia

When Elizabeth I granted Raleigh a ten-year mandate to colonize Virginia – an area that then extended from New York south to North Carolina – she initiated England's drive to establish permanent settlements on the eastern seaboard of what is now the United States of America. But it took many hard years of disease, violence, starvation and squalor before the colonies began to prosper.

Raleigh's first mission, led by Sir Richard Grenville, was primarily a voyage of exploration. The colonists landed on Roanoke Island in 1585 but, following a number of expeditions along the coast, relations with the Native Americans became strained. The colonists accused local tribesmen of having stolen a silver cup and punished them by attacking their village. Grenville left 75 people to establish the colony, promising to return with supplies in 1586. But when he returned he found that most of the colonists had deserted and made their way back to England on a ship captained by Sir Francis Drake.

Raleigh's second mission, in 1587, was led by John White, and on this voyage 121 colonists sailed to join the rump of 15 men left by Grenville's supply mission. But all they found was a single skeleton and information that a few survivors had fled north along the coast. Undeterred, White established his own colony, and within months he had a granddaughter – the first English child to be born in America. She was named Virginia Dare,

James of Scotland, who arrived with fixed ideas about Raleigh. He was accused of plotting the king's downfall and imprisoned in the Tower. In 1616 he was released, though not pardoned, and set off once again for Venezuela. He had promised the king that he could open a gold mine without offending the Spanish, with whom he was extremely unpopular (he had been involved in an attack on Cadiz in 1596). The expedition was a disaster, and when he returned to England, James I invoked the suspended sentence of death that had been hanging over Raleigh since his initial arrest in 1603.

Raleigh was also, in keeping with his image as the perfect courtier, a writer of both verse and prose. Much of his poetry is addressed indirectly to Elizabeth, while his prose narratives relate his adventures in the New World. In his *History of the World*, written while he was imprisoned in the Tower, he details the divine and providen-

and White took word of her birth back to England that year when he went to gather support and supplies.

After much delay, caused by the Spanish Armada, White finally returned to Roanoke in 1590, to find his colony eerily deserted. There was no sign of a struggle, yet 90 men, 17 women and 11 children, including his granddaughter, had vanished. Despite a wealth of theories, the fate of the 'Lost Colony' remains a mystery to this day.

Under James I, missions to the New World gained royal backing. In 1606 the Virginia Company was founded, with the right to settle anywhere in Virginia in the name of finding gold, silver and a river route to the Pacific.

In 1607 the company founded Jamestown on a marshy peninsula near modern-day Williamsburg. Though it was accessible by ship, it was wet, unpleasantly hot in summer, and home to disease-carrying mosquitoes. Dysentery and starvation ravaged the colony, and the Native Americans were relentless in their attacks. The colonists were reduced to feeding on cats, rats, shoe leather and even their dead companions.

Though sick and emaciated, the colonists somehow survived. In 1614 their situation improved with the marriage of John Rolfe – who pioneered the cultivation of tobacco – to the local chief's daughter, Pocahontas. Tobacco provided a sustainable trading commodity, and relations with the Native Americans eased. After three decades of failure, the seeds of prosperity had finally been sown.

tial history of kings from the Creation. However, he had reached only the 2nd century BC when the sentence of death was carried out against him. It was a sad and inglorious end to such a dashing and dynamic career.

Galileo Galilei

1564–1642

*I do not feel obliged to believe that that same God who has
endowed us with senses, reason and intellect has intended to
forgo their use and by some other means to give us
knowledge which we can attain by them.*

Galileo Galilei, 'Letter to the Grand Duchess Christina' (1615)

Galileo Galilei, one of the key figures in the scientific revolution
of the 16th and 17th centuries, helped to transform the way that
people looked at the world – and the universe beyond. A physicist, mathematician and astronomer, Galileo made fundamenl discoveries about the nature of motion and the movement of the
planets. He realized the importance of experimentation and held
that the physical world was best understood through mathematics.
His insistence that the universe should be analysed via reason and
evidence brought him into conflict with the Church, but his discoveries long outlasted the Inquisition that sought to suppress
them.

Galileo's father was a musician, and the young man may well
have helped with paternal experiments into the tension and pitch
of strings. His formal education took place at Pisa University, where
he matriculated in 1581, initially to study medicine. To his father's
disapproval, Galileo spent most of his time on mathematics and left
the university without a degree in 1585.

Galileo continued to study mathematics for the next four years,
earning money through private tuition until he was appointed to
a chair at the university in 1589. It was during this time that he
supposedly demonstrated his theory of the speed of falling objects
by dropping weights from Pisa's leaning tower.

His unorthodox views earned him the disapproval of the university authorities, and in 1592 Galileo was forced to move to
Padua, where he taught until 1610. Crippled by his family's financial demands after his father died, Galileo earned extra money by

The history of the telescope

Since its invention in the Netherlands in the late 16th century, the telescope has transformed our view of our place in the universe. In 400 years, telescopes have developed from funfair novelties – simple brass tubes with a pair of lenses – to multi-billion-dollar arrays of antennae, capable of detecting not only visible light but also all the other frequencies of the electromagnetic spectrum.

Using lenses to manipulate light was common in both Europe and parts of Asia from around the 13th century, in the form of eyeglasses. Around 250 years later the technology was applied in the Netherlands to building the first telescope, which could make distant objects seem close. The news of this novelty spread across Europe, and early telescopes were popular toys for the well-to-do. It was Galileo who exploited the potential of the new device for serious scientific work.

The lens-based, refracting telescope soon reached the limits of practicality: to get more magnification telescopes had to become longer and longer, up to 200 feet (60 m). The arrival of Newton's reflecting telescope in 1688 was crucial. This relied on mirrors rather than lenses to magnify light – and it was this invention, rather than his theoretical works, that earned Newton membership of the Royal Society.

Though the 20th century saw great advances in reflecting telescopes, it was the development of radio telescopes – and those that could detect other invisible frequencies, such as microwaves, infrared, ultraviolet, X-rays and gamma rays – that truly revolutionized astronomy. With such devices scientists have measured the temperature of the planets and mapped the surface of Venus, normally covered in dense cloud. They have found new cosmic objects like pulsars and black holes, measured the mass of faraway galaxies, and discovered quasars, brilliant cosmic objects that can be 'seen' from 10 billion light years away (so what we 'see' actually happened 10 billion years ago). They have also detected background radiation left over from the Big Bang – the moment that the universe began.

But telescopes using visible light still provide us with new information about the heavens. To escape interference from the earth's atmosphere, the 94-inch (2.4-metre) Hubble Space Telescope was put into orbit in 1990. Ever since some initial technical problems were rectified, it has transmitted back thousands of extraordinarily detailed and beautiful images of vast cosmic events across the universe, and has proved one of the most important instruments in the history of astronomy.

selling home-made mathematical compasses and continuing to tutor private pupils.

In 1609 Galileo heard of a strange device invented in the Netherlands that could make distant objects appear close. It was the telescope, and Galileo immediately set about building his own. Within a year he was investigating the heavens with a device that provided 20x magnification. It was a turning point in his career.

With his telescope Galileo discovered Jupiter's four moons and noted that their phases indicated that they orbited Jupiter. This evidence dented the Church-approved Ptolemaic model of the universe, in which all heavenly bodies orbit the earth. Galileo also saw stars that were invisible to the naked eye. He immediately published his findings in a short book dedicated to one of his illustrious pupils, Cosimo II de Medici, Grand Duke of Florence. As a reward, Cosimo brought him back to Tuscany in triumph.

With greater financial freedom, Galileo was able to move his investigations on apace. He studied the rings of Saturn and discovered that Venus, like the moon, went through phases – an indication that it moved around the sun. These discoveries committed him to the theory – proposed by Nicolaus Copernicus a century before – that it was the sun, and not the earth, that was at the centre of the universe.

Copernicanism was a dangerous concept for Galileo to flirt with, and around 1613 it earned him the attention of the Inquisition. He travelled to Rome to defend Copernicus's heliocentric model but was silenced, and in 1616 he was warned explicitly not to promulgate such ideas any further.

By 1632 Galileo felt unable to keep silent on Copernicanism any longer and published his *Dialogue*, which drew together all of the major strands of thought about the nature of the universe and discussed them through the mouths of several fictitious characters.

When he was dragged to Rome the next year and asked to explain himself to the Inquisition, Galileo argued that he had obtained ecclesiastical permission to discuss Copernicanism in a hypothetical way. Unfortunately, he had not obtained permission to ridicule the papal attachment to older arguments, which he had done quite unashamedly. The Inquisition sentenced him to life imprisonment.

Fortunately for Galileo, his imprisonment amounted to little more than enforced internal exile to the Tuscan hills, where he was free to continue his work in a more muted form. Though he was going blind, he continued to study, concentrating on the nature and strength of materials and smuggling another book out of Italy to be published in the Netherlands in 1638. He died four years later, aged 77.

Galileo was a brave upholder of the truth in a time of zealotry and persecution. His adherence to reason and observation, over-turning centuries of dogmatic assumption, helped to prepare the ground for the European Enlightenment of the 18th century. Beyond that, his methods permanently transformed the practice of science, and his work laid the foundations for the great paradigm-shifting theories of Newton and Einstein.

William Shakespeare 1564–1616

He was not of an age, but for all time!

Ben Jonson, 'To the Memory of My Beloved, the Author, Mr William Shakespeare' (1623)

It is almost universally acknowledged – and not just in the English-speaking world – that Shakespeare was the greatest writer ever to have lived. He was a peerless poet, playwright and storyteller, and his understanding of human emotions, and the complexities and ambivalences of the human condition, are unparalleled in litera-ture.

Famously, little is known about Shakespeare's life. He was born in Stratford-upon-Avon in 1564, the son of John Shakespeare, a burgess of fluctuating fortunes, and his wife, Mary Arden. William attended the local grammar school, and at the age of 18 he married Anne Hathaway, who was some years his senior and already pregnant. At some point in the ensuing decade, Shakespeare moved to London. He was probably a jobbing actor but began to make a mark as a poet and a playwright. By 1594 he was the established dramatist for the theatre company known as the Lord Chamberlain's Men (which renamed itself the King's Men after James I's accession).

For the next twenty years Shakespeare wrote play after dazzling play – comedies, tragedies, histories – which brought audiences flocking to the Globe Theatre on the south bank of the Thames. Shakespeare's fortunes flourished. He probably supported his father's application for a coat of arms and bought one of Stratford's largest houses, New Place. On his death in 1616, he was buried in the chancel of Stratford's parish church. There is little more that we know about Shakespeare's life.

But Shakespeare's works tell us all we need to know about the man. He has an extraordinary sympathy with men and women of all ages, from all strata of society, demonstrating a deep understanding of their faults and frailties, their kindnesses and cruelties, their loves and hates, their vanities and self-delusions. Joy and despair, anger and resignation, jealousy and lust, vigour and weakness are all depicted with searing honesty. There is the dangerous infatuation of first love in *Romeo and Juliet*, the destructiveness of middle-aged passion in *Antony and Cleopatra*, the heart-rending follies of old age in *King Lear*. Shakespeare also subjects the nature of power to his unflinching gaze: the burdens of kingship in *Henry IV*, the nature of tyranny in *Richard III*, the abuse of trust in *Measure for Measure*.

Shakespeare's characters are multifaceted, complex, ambiguous. Hamlet, faced with his father's apparent murder, is beset by moral qualms and indecision as to whether he should take revenge. Macbeth and Lady Macbeth seize the throne by violence and then become mired in bloodshed, guilt and madness. In *Twelfth Night*, the jolly, roistering characters play a trick upon the pompous, puritanical steward Malvolio, but the trick goes beyond a joke and plunges into cruelty. In *The Tempest*, possibly Shakespeare's last play, Prospero, having used his magic powers to bring those who have wronged him into his power, decides 'the rarer action is / In virtue than in vengeance'. And then, in what is often taken to be an autobiographical touch on Shakespeare's part, Prospero, the magus, abandons his magical arts: 'deeper than did ever plummet sound / I'll drown my book'.

All this wealth of human experience Shakespeare embodies in language of astounding power and precision, from soaring passages

Who was the real Shakespeare?

An undistinguished provincial who never went to university could not have written, so some have argued, some of the finest plays known to humankind. Despite considerable evidence to the contrary, claims have been made that either 'William Shakespeare' was a fabricated pseudonym or his identity was simply used by someone else.

The instigator of the trend was an American schoolteacher who claimed descent from Sir Francis Bacon, the lawyer, statesman and philosopher. The 'Baconian Theory' insists that Bacon co-authored the plays with a coterie of courtly writers such as Edmund Spenser and Sir Walter Raleigh. Unable to reveal their identities because of the controversial content of the plays, they left clues hidden among the texts.

Another candidate is the feisty dramatist Christopher Marlowe, a Cambridge-educated shoemaker's son who dabbled in espionage, and who was suspected of atheism and homosexuality. Conspiracy theorists insist that he did not die in a bar-room brawl in 1593, as is widely believed, but that he went underground to avoid the authorities and continued to write plays, using 'William Shakespeare' as a pseudonym.

A third candidate is the Earl of Derby, whose aristocratic status precluded him from dabbling in the theatrical world as a professional. He had a company of actors, and among his papers were found several poems authored by a 'W.S.' His wedding may have been the first occasion on which *A Midsummer Night's Dream* was performed.

A final favourite in some quarters is the Earl of Oxford, a poet, playwright (although no plays survive) and patron of an acting company. Oxford stopped producing poetry just before Shakespeare first went into print with the dramatic poem *Venus and Adonis* in 1593 (although his first plays had already been produced). The case for Oxford is, however, handicapped by the fact that the earl died in 1604, before at least a dozen of Shakespeare's works were written.

Despite all these ingenious arguments, Shakespeare's contemporaries seemed in no doubt that he was the author of his works, and in 1623 his former colleagues compiled the First Folio edition of his plays 'to keep the memory of so worthy a friend and fellow alive as was our Shakespeare'. Modern textual analysis backs up the theory that all the poems and plays are by a single author whose name was William Shakespeare.

of poetic intensity, through quick-fire witty dialogue, to the earthy prose of the common people who crowded into the pits of London's theatres. Shakespeare's richness of vocabulary is astonishing, drawing imagery from a range of fields and activities, from flora and fauna to warfare and heraldry, from astrology and astronomy to seafaring and horticulture. Puns and double entendres abound throughout his work, and virtually every line has layers of meanings. Not content with the vast vocabulary at his command, Shakespeare introduced many new words into English, from 'meditate' and 'tranquil' to 'alligator' and 'apostrophe'. He also gave us a myriad phrases that have entered everyday speech: 'Discretion is the better part of valour', 'At one fell swoop', 'In one's heart of hearts', 'Seen better days', and many, many more.

As a master of dramatic art, Shakespeare has no peer. Many of his stories were not original – they were drawn, for example, from Boccaccio's fables, or folk tales, or Plutarch's *Lives*, or the Tudor chroniclers – but it is what he did with them that counts. He not only gave the two-dimensional figures in these tales fully rounded characters, he also knew how to build up tension, to create a mood of impending doom, and then to heighten that mood by interleaving an apparently incongruous comic scene (as he does, for example, in *Macbeth*). He was also a master of the *coup de théâtre*, such as the moment in *Much Ado About Nothing* when the hitherto light-weight, bantering world of the play is overthrown by Beatrice's sudden injunction to Benedict: 'Kill Claudio'. Thus none of Shakespeare's tragedies are unremittingly tragic, nor are his comedies filled with non-stop laughter. At the end of *Twelfth Night*, for example, although all the lovers are paired off happily, the action closes with a melancholy song from the Clown, bringing us back to the quotidian world where 'the rain it raineth every day'. Such simple, poignant touches are typical of Shakespeare and mark him out, just as much as his complexities, as a writer of genius.

Oliver Cromwell

1599–1658

A man of a great, robust, massive mind, and an honest, stout English heart.

Thomas Carlyle, describing Cromwell in his edition *Oliver Cromwell's Letters and Speeches* (1845)

Oliver Cromwell took just twenty years to rise from obscure country gentleman to lord protector of England, Scotland and Ireland. His military genius was vital to Parliament's victory over Charles I in the Civil Wars. His political management – sometimes cajoling – of Parliament and the respect he engendered in the army helped to stabilize the fragile country after the king was beheaded. As head of state in the new Commonwealth, he pursued religious toleration and his foreign policy was successful and prestigious. He turned down the crown, but his burning commitment to God and the English people, rather than any personal ambition, marks him as the greatest king that England never had.

Cromwell was by birth a relatively lowly gentleman farmer from Huntingdon, now in Cambridgeshire. Both his own family and that of his wife were connected to various networks of puritans, and throughout his life he was deeply and sincerely devoted to carrying out the will of God as he saw it.

Cromwell first sat as an MP in the Parliament of 1628–9, making little impact. Charles I ruled without Parliament for the next 11 years, and Cromwell did not sit as an MP again until 1640. As tensions between Charles and the so-called Long Parliament began to build towards violent crisis, Cromwell's puritan and oppositionist credentials began to come to the fore. But he showed his real worth as hostilities broke out, first captaining a troop of cavalry at the Battle of Edgehill (23 October 1642) and the next year forming his regiment of 'Ironsides', who were victorious at the Battle of Gainsborough (28 July 1643). His handling of the cavalry at the Parliamentary victory of Marston Moor (2 July 1644) secured his reputation nationally – though Cromwell was not interested in fame, regarding military success as an expression of God's will in the

The execution of Charles I

On the cold morning of Tuesday 30 January 1649, after a last walk in St James's Park, King Charles I, wearing two shirts lest his shivering against the cold be misinterpreted as fear, mounted the scaffold erected outside the Banqueting Hall in Whitehall. He had been condemned to death as 'a tyrant, traitor, murderer and public enemy to the good of the nation'.

Charles, unrepentant and convinced that his death would make him a martyr for the Royalist cause, addressed the crowd. If his life was disastrous, his leaving it was heroic:

I think it is my duty to God first and to my country for to clear myself both as an honest man and a good King, and a good Christian. I shall begin first with my innocence.

In troth I think it not very needful for me to insist long upon this, for all the world knows that I never did begin a War with the two Houses of Parliament ... they began upon me ...

I have forgiven all the world, and even those in particular that have been the chief causes of my death. Who they are, God knows, I do not desire to know, God forgive them ...

For the people ... truly I desire their Liberty and Freedom as much as any Body whomsoever. But I must tell you, That their Liberty and Freedom ... is not for having share in government that is nothing pertaining to them. A subject and a sovereign are clean different things, and therefore until ... you do put the people in that liberty as I say, certainly they will never enjoy themselves.

Sirs, it was for this that now I am come here. If I would have given way to an arbitrary way, for to have all Laws changed according to the power of the Sword, I needed not to have come here; and therefore, I tell you ... that I am the martyr of the People ...

I have delivered my Conscience. I pray God, that you do take those courses that are best for the good of the Kingdom and your own Salvations.

After inspecting the axe, he said:

I go from a corruptible, to an incorruptible Crown; where no disturbance can be, no disturbance in the World.

Having given the executioner his final instructions, the king knelt down, and his head was severed from his body with a single blow.

struggle for English liberties. By now he was leader of Parliament's Independent faction, determined not to compromise with the Royalists.

Cromwell and Parliament's supreme military leader Thomas Fairfax created a disciplined new force, the New Model Army, which in the mid-1640s changed the course of the war in Parliament's favour. The victorious Battle of Naseby (14 June 1645) determined the outcome of the First Civil War.

Cromwell's political centrality emerged in the years 1646–9, when he became power-broker between army, Parliament and the now-captive Charles in an attempt to restore a constitutional basis for government. But dealing with the slippery and inflexible Stuart monarch, who at root would brook no compromise to (as he saw it) his divinely inspired kingship, exhausted Cromwell. When Charles temporarily escaped in 1647 and sought to restart the war with the Scottish Presbyterians in support, Cromwell's attitude hardened. Dispatching the Royalist Welsh and Scottish rebels in 1648, he backed the trial for treason of the king, a show trial that ended, predictably enough, in the execution of Charles on 30 January 1649. Cromwell reputedly gazed at the royal body and murmured 'cruel necessity'.

Cromwell was now the most powerful man in England – head of the army and chairman of the council of state that ruled the new 'commonwealth'. But pro-Stuart Scotland and Ireland remained to be tamed. Cromwell's name has been cursed in many quarters for his unflinching brutality in putting down the Catholic risings in Ireland during the autumn of 1649. His atrocities have probably been exaggerated, but he certainly treated the towns of Drogheda and Wexford ruthlessly, the incidents balanced by the many occasions on which Cromwell showed himself magnanimous and merciful.

In 1650–1 Cromwell led his armies to victory over the Scots at Dunbar and over Prince Charles's Anglo-Scottish adventure at Worcester (1651). The prince famously escaped to France, helped by disguise and a convenient oak tree, but his subsequent nine years of exile left Cromwell as king in all but name.

The 1650s were remarkable for their diversity of opinions, religious and political, and it fell to Cromwell to try to rein in the forces that might split the country apart. To his enemies, then and now, he was a military dictator, the former upholder of parliamentary rights who himself happily dismissed parliaments when they became inconvenient. But Cromwell had to bridge the radical, almost socialist, views among the army ranks and the deeply held traditions of 17th-century 'middle England', at core Royalist and conservative.

It could have all gone disastrously wrong, and it is to Cromwell's credit that he produced serious achievements. He ensured political representation from Scotland and Ireland. In wars with the Dutch and Spanish, the navy, under Admiral Blake, achieved notable success. As 'lord protector', so styled from 1653, Cromwell negotiated for the Jews to be allowed back into England, a historic decision. And he remained devoted to social justice for the poor.

In 1657 Parliament offered Cromwell the crown – his chance, had he so wished, to revert to a type of government everyone understood and to beget a dynasty. He declined the crown, and his death in 1658 and the resulting power vacuum under the leadership of his son, Richard, showed just how dependent Cromwellian England was on the talents, force and personality of the man himself.

The monarchy would return of course – but in the name of that old Stuart, Charles II. So ended the republican experiment, but not without marking Oliver Cromwell's place in history as a man of conscience, fearless leadership, military brilliance and sincere piety.

Samuel Pepys 1633–1703

The greatness of his life was open, yet he longed to communicate its smallness also.

Robert Louis Stevenson, *Familiar Studies of Men and Books* (1882)

Samuel Pepys was the author of one of the most vivid diaries ever written. For almost a decade Pepys – who held a senior position at the Admiralty – recorded his life and his world in engrossing detail, providing an extraordinary insight into what it was like to be alive in 17th-century London. Pepys himself comes over as a man of great curiosity, at once open-minded and sceptical, sensitive to both the comedy and the pathos of the human condition.

Above Two of the four colossal seated statues of Pharaoh Rameses II that decorate the façade of the Great Temple at Abu Simbel. Rameses' queen, Nefertari, stands at the foot of the left-hand statue. Originally carved out of sandstone cliffs above the River Nile between 1285 and 1265 BC, the temple site in its entirety was dismantled and relocated in a higher position in the 1960s to avoid submersion by the waters of the newly built Aswan Dam.

Right A brooding depiction of Sappho – lesbian icon and pioneer of lyric poetry – holding her poet's lyre, by the French artist Charles-Auguste Mengin (1853–1933). The word 'lyric' comes from the Greek *lurikos* ('for the lyre'), and was the name given in ancient Greece to verses performed to the accompaniment of that instrument.

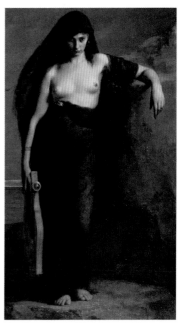

Above Detail of *The School of Athens* (1509–10) – a fresco by the Italian Renaissance artist Raphael showing the greatest philosophers, scientists and mathematicians of classical antiquity. Plato and Aristotle are standing in the centre: the former holding his Socratic dialogue *Timaeus*; the latter carrying a copy of his *Nicomachean Ethics*. Their gestures indicate their respective philosophical interests: Plato points upwards towards Heaven, while Aristotle gestures towards the earth.

Below A detail from a Roman mosaic depicting Alexander the Great at the Battle of Issus in Syria (333 BC), the second of his three great victories over the Achaemenid Persians. Despite his army being outnumbered by more than two to one, Alexander defeated a force led by the Persian ruler Darius III. Alexander's later victory at Gaugamela (331 BC) completed his overthrow of the Achaemenid Empire.

Right *The Baptism of Christ* (1448–50), a painting by the Italian Renaissance master Piero della Francesca (c.1415–92).

Below Milla Jovovich as Joan of Arc in a scene from *The Messenger: The Story of Joan of Arc* (1999), directed by Luc Besson.

Left Queen Elizabeth I in her coronation robes, *c.*1559, by an anonymous English artist. Elizabeth renounced her womanhood to become the epitome of a prince, a goddess-like figure presiding over a golden age in which England defied the power of Spain and embarked on the adventure of empire.

Right The so-called 'Chandos portrait', said to be of William Shakespeare, dated around 1610, and attributed to John Taylor (1580–1653).

Above A portrait of Catherine the Great, c.1770, by Fedor Stepanovich Rokotov.

Right Grigory Potemkin, by Giovanni Battista Lampi (1751–1830).

Left Wolfgang Amadeus Mozart by Barbara Krafft (1764–1825). The Swiss theologian Karl Barth once said of his music, 'When the angels sing for God, they sing Bach; but I am sure that when they sing for themselves, they sing Mozart, and God eavesdrops.'

Below Horatio Nelson, 1797, by Lemuel Francis Abbott (1760–1803). The portrait shows Nelson in rear-admiral's uniform, wearing the Star and Ribbon of the Bath and the Naval Gold Medal, awarded for his victory at the Battle of St Vincent (1797). 'I have always been a quarter of an hour before my time,' said Nelson, 'and this has made a man of me.'

Left *The Duke of Wellington* by Francisco José de Goya y Lucientes (1746–1828).

Right Jane Austen, in a copy of a watercolour by the novelist's sister Cassandra, *c.*1810.

George Gordon, 6th Baron Byron, portrayed in Albanian dress (1813) by Thomas Phillips (1770–1845). '"Whom the gods love die young" was said of yore.' So wrote Byron himself in Canto 4 of his *Don Juan* (1819–24).

He delights in the high life and the low and is unstintingly honest in depicting himself as a man with all-too-human needs and desires, yet beset by moral scruples and regrets.

Pepys's diaries are all the more remarkable because during his lifetime no one knew anything about them. To the world at large, Samuel Pepys, secretary to the Admiralty, Member of Parliament and president of the Royal Society, was a highly successful naval official who had risen from humble beginnings as a tailor's son. When he died in 1703 his contemporaries saw Pepys's legacy as the great library he bequeathed to his alma mater, Magdalene College, Cambridge. He was also admired for a lifetime of philanthropy towards educational establishments such as Christ's Hospital School, and for his achievements as a naval administrator who had tirelessly promoted meritocracy and efficiency. Pepys's most priceless legacy was only discovered over a century after his death, when the authorities at Magdalene employed an impoverished undergraduate to crack the diaries' seemingly impenetrable shorthand.

Pepys's descriptions of the disasters that befell England in the 1660s are some of the richest historical sources in existence. He charts day-to-day life during the Great Plague of 1665–6 and, from his perspective as an Admiralty insider, gives an invaluable insight into the Second Anglo-Dutch War of 1667. His almost hour-by-hour record of the Great Fire of London of 1666 is one of the finest pieces of reportage ever written.

Although Pepys largely owed his advancement at the Admiralty to royal favour, he never lets his diarist's eye be dazzled by the court. He can be as exasperated with the king as he is with his own servants, and more than once he vents his frustration that Charles II seems incapable of taking the duties of kingship seriously.

While most contemporary diarists were exclusively preoccupied with the spiritual or political sphere, Pepys's overwhelming interest is in more earthy matters. The diaries illuminate Pepys's fascination with the way humans behave, their greed, rivalries, ambitions, jealousies, and their fascination with scandal. The people he depicts might well be alive today, so vividly does he bring them to life.

What makes Pepys stand out above the average gossipmonger is that he also turns his unflinchingly honest gaze upon himself.

The Great Fire of London

In the early hours of a September Sunday in 1666, following a hot, dry summer, the unextinguished ashes of a fire under a baker's oven in Pudding Lane set fire to the house. The fire quickly spread, and a strong easterly wind and a city crammed with wooden houses made it almost impossible to extinguish the flames. Pepys was one of the first to realize that the only recourse was to demolish the buildings that stood in the fire's path. Five days later, when the blaze finally began to die down, the city smouldered in ruins and half of London's people were homeless.

Against the constant dull roar of the flames and the cracking of the buildings they consumed, for some people everyday life continued as normal. Pepys picnicked with his neighbours on a shoulder of mutton and then went to the bottom of the garden to check how far away the blaze was. And after talking to the authorities about how to quell the flames destroying the city, Pepys had to calm hot tempers at home: his wife had squabbled with the maid and sacked her.

As people piled into boats, borne down with as much as they could carry, others hoped that cellars and churches would provide a safe place for their possessions. Pepys and a friend buried their wine – and Pepys's prized Parmesan cheese – in the garden.

In the event, Pepys's house survived. But he was lucky. Although fewer than ten people died, London was gutted. St Paul's Cathedral was just one of the 89 churches destroyed; 400 streets covering 400 acres and containing 13,000 houses were all reduced to ashes. Robbers lurked among the ghostly ruins for months. Tourists came to gawp at the destruction.

The Royal Society's architects jumped at the chance to refashion the haphazard city along more orderly and elegant lines, with broad streets and grand vistas. But the ambitious plans of Christopher Wren, John Evelyn and Robert Hooke were thwarted by the obduracy of London's householders, all determined to rebuild their houses on their original patch of land. The architects were not entirely frustrated, however. From the ashes rose the glorious dome of Wren's greatest work, the new St Paul's, along with innumerable other fine churches, many of which still stand. And, as the authorities decreed, the new city was of brick not wood, with flat frontages replacing the overhanging eaves that had proved so conducive to spreading the crackling flames from house to house.

He never tries to show himself in the best light, nor does he conceal his flaws. This is no exercise in self-mortification or pious humility, however; rather, it reflects an all-consuming absorption in humanity, of which he is just the most familiar specimen. He records his own behaviour with almost scientific curiosity, including all the embarrassing, even mortifying, details that most diarists would leave out – for example, the occasion when his wife Elizabeth discovers him with his hand up her companion's skirt, or the combination of grief and guilty relief he feels at the death of a maverick brother. Pepys's record of his tempestuous relationship with his wife, whom he married for love, remains one of literature's most candid portraits of the Gordian knot of marriage. He writes of the blazing rows, the tearful confrontations, the nose pulling and the insults. Then there are the reconciliations, the long lie-ins spent chatting, and the sympathy for each other when sick. Pepys omits nothing: the presents he buys Elizabeth to try to assuage his guilt after yet another episode of philandering; even the details of their sexual relations, rendered problematic by a 'pain in the lip of her chose'.

After almost ten years, fearing his eyesight was failing, Pepys stopped writing his diary. It was, he wrote, 'almost as much to see myself go into my grave'. Although his eyes recovered, he never kept another diary like it, and none of his subsequent writings ever equalled his diaries for brilliance. Pepys lived out the rest of his life as a worthy man, who, despite his personal misgivings, remained unceasingly loyal to his royal masters through the Revolution of 1688. Much in Pepys's public life was admirable – but it was his private, intimate work of outstanding literature and reportage, writing diaries of such immediacy, originality and searing honesty, that demands the admiration of posterity.

Isaac Newton

1642–1727

Nature, and Nature's laws lay hid in night.
God said, 'Let Newton be!' and all was light.

Alexander Pope's famous 'Epitaph: Intended for Sir Isaac Newton' (1730)

Sir Isaac Newton is arguably the greatest scientist of all time. Along with such figures as Copernicus, Kepler and Galileo, he is one of the giants of the scientific revolution. His most influential work, *Principia Mathematica*, fundamentally altered the way in which scientists observed and explained the natural world.

Newton's main legacy was the fusion of mathematics and natural science, but he was a polymath who made significant contributions to philosophy, astronomy, theology, history, alchemy and economics. Without Newton, our understanding of the world would be unimaginably different.

Newton was born on Christmas Day, 1642. From an early age he seems to have taken firmly against the company of others. He formed a few close friendships in his life, but his general tendency to vacillate between shunning other people and picking fights with them appears to have been a peculiar part of his genius. It allowed him to focus his mind entirely on the scientific puzzles of the day.

As an undergraduate at Trinity College, Cambridge, Newton paid little attention to the syllabus set for him, largely ignoring the study of Aristotle in favour of the bright new scientists of his own day. The works of men such as René Descartes, Robert Boyle and Thomas Hobbes gripped him, and as he made notes on his reading, he began to question the world around him in ever greater detail.

It was at the age of 23 that Newton's intellectual star really began to burn bright. He called 1665–6 his *annus mirabilis* – his wonder year. He focused on various mathematical problems concerning the orbits of the moon and planets, developing in the process the theorem of calculus – a powerful mathematical tool vital to modern physics and engineering. The name 'calculus' was coined by the

German scientist Gottfried Leibniz, who developed the theory independently; Newton called it the 'science of fluxions'. In later life the two men argued bitterly over who could lay claim to the discovery. In any case, it is clear that even as a young man in the 1660s Newton was already a mathematical pioneer.

Leaving Cambridge to escape the plague in 1666, Newton started to study natural mechanics. In old age he claimed to have first understood that it was gravity that controlled the orbit of the moon when he sat in his orchard and watched an apple fall from a tree. Apocryphal or not, the story soon became part of Newtonian folklore; perhaps its most felicitous appearance is in Byron's *Don Juan*, where Newton is recorded as 'the sole mortal who could grapple, Since Adam, with a fall, or with an apple'.

Back in Cambridge, Newton was swiftly appointed Lucasian Professor of Mathematics. He was free to pursue his own course of studies, and as he worked he corresponded with other leading scientists and mathematicians, including Boyle, Robert Hooke and Edmond Halley. During the 1670s he spent much time on theology, exploiting his formidable knowledge of the Bible and developing original and radical views on the Holy Trinity. He also became interested in alchemy – the science of turning base metals into gold – and began to build up a huge library of books on the subject. But it was the appearance of the so-called Great Comet of 1680–1 that lay at the root of Newton's finest work.

In 1684 Newton began work on the project that would eventually become his ground-breaking *Principia Mathematica*. It was a work that would change both his life and the entire face of science. At its core lie Newton's three fundamental laws of motion:

◆ an object in a state of rest or moving in a straight line will continue in such a state unless it is acted upon by an external force;

◆ the acceleration of a moving object is proportionate to and in the same direction as the force acting on it;

◆ for every action there is an equal and opposite reaction.

From these relatively straightforward laws Newton produced an astonishingly comprehensive analysis of the operation of the natural

Theories of the universe

Newton's mathematical analysis played a vital role in developing a theory of the universe which explained the place of the earth among all the heavenly bodies in the vast expanse of space. He was one of a long line of scientists and philosophers who have attempted to tackle this question.

Early civilizations usually turned to religious, intuitive theories about the origins and nature of the universe. The ancient Chinese generally supposed that the earth was flat, but there was little agreement about the universe itself, which was variously dome-shaped, egg-shaped or infinite. Hindu tradition held that the earth was supported by a giant tortoise, Chukwa, or that the tortoise supported the elephant Mohah-pudma, who in turn supported the earth.

More rational analysis began with the ancient Greeks. Ptolemy, in the 2nd century AD, developed Aristotle's geocentric theory in which the sun, planets and moon moved around the earth. Ptolemy thought they were travelling in complex patterns, each within its own sphere, which explained their apparently erratic movements through the sky.

Nearly 1400 years passed before the Polish astronomer Nicolaus Copernicus suggested (in general opposition to Church teaching) a heliocentric model in which the sun was at the centre of the orbiting planets. In 1609 Galileo used telescopic evidence of moons orbiting Jupiter to confirm the Copernican system, while his German contemporary

world. He explained everything from the behaviour of small bodies and particles to the orbits of comets, planets and the moon. He put mathematics at the heart of the physical explanation of the world, where it remains to this day.

Newton's brilliance rapidly made him one of the most eminent scientists in Europe. But he felt unable to continue working in the strictly conventional religious environment at Cambridge and was relieved to be appointed to a key role at the Royal Mint, which gave him a secure financial position for life. In 1703 he became president of the Royal Society, London's most prestigious scientific community, and in 1704 he published *Opticks*, which dealt with the behaviour of light and the forces that attract and repel particles and bodies. The following year he was knighted by Queen Anne, the

Johannes Kepler derived his laws of planetary motion according to which the orbits of the planets were elliptical. Newton, in 1689, showed that it was gravity, working throughout the universe, that caused these elliptical orbits. He assumed that the universe was infinite, which seemed the only way of explaining why it did not collapse under its own cumulative gravitational pull.

In 1823 the German physicist Heinrich Olbers enunciated many people's doubts about an infinite universe by pointing out that with an infinite number of stars the night sky would be as bright as day. The theory of a finite universe was further strengthened in 1929, when the US astronomer Edwin Hubble noticed 'red shifts' in every direction of space, suggesting that the universe was expanding. Hubble's evidence was a major impetus behind the now widely accepted Big Bang theory, according to which the universe began in a gigantic explosion from a tiny mass of incredible heat and density and has been expanding ever since.

Whether there will be a Big Crunch, when everything collapses back together, continues to occupy physicists as they search for a unified theory of the universe. The feverish fluidity of the debate over the origins of the universe was neatly captured by the English humorist Douglas Adams in 1980: 'There is a theory which states that if ever anybody discovers exactly what the Universe is for and why it is here, it will instantly disappear and be replaced by something even more bizarre and inexplicable. There is another theory which states that this has already happened.'

first scientist ever to receive such an honour.

Amid all this achievement, Newton spent long periods of his later life engaged in furious debates and personal feuds with other European scientists. Yet for all his personal foibles, there was no one then or since who could disagree with the epitaph on his monument in Westminster Abbey: 'Let Mortals rejoice That there has existed such and so great an Ornament to the Human Race.'

The Duke of Marlborough 1650–1722

If I were young and handsome as I was, instead of old and faded as I am, and you could lay the empire of the world at my feet, you should never share the heart and hand that once belonged to John, Duke of Marlborough.

Sarah, Duchess of Marlborough, quoted in W.S. Churchill, *Marlborough: His Life and Times* (1938)

John Churchill, 1st Duke of Marlborough, was Britain's most brilliant soldier-statesman. He was one of the most successful generals in history, winning a string of glorious victories against the French and their allies in the War of the Spanish Succession that prevented Louis XIV and his Catholic absolutism dominating Europe in the opening years of the 18th century.

From early in his life, Churchill's career depended on James, the Catholic Duke of York, who later became the ill-starred James II. Churchill travelled with James when his brother, Charles II, sent the unpopular duke into exile in the 1670s. At this time James used Churchill as his skilled lobbyist at the royal court. Handsome, charming and clever, young Churchill was seduced by Charles II's voracious mistress Barbara, Duchess of Castlemaine, and once had to leap from her window when the king arrived. He was already showing himself to be a particularly talented soldier; he fought under the legendary musketeer d'Artagnan in 1673 and performed with the utmost bravery, earning himself personal praise from the French king, Louis XIV.

In 1677 Churchill married Sarah Jennings, a strong-willed woman who proved politically astute. As his military career progressed, the couple spent long periods apart, but the marriage was nevertheless an enormously successful one. From 1683 Sarah was the best friend of, and favourite adviser to, Princess Anne – later Queen Anne, a connection vital to Marlborough's future favour and fortune.

Although he had been a close confidant of James II, Marlborough was at heart a Protestant and had no difficulty in shifting his allegiance to William of Orange, who became joint monarch with his wife Mary II after the Glorious Revolution of 1688. He played an important role in the campaign against James's forces in Ireland in 1690, and though he was suspected for much of the 1690s of being a closet Jacobite (a supporter of James II), by 1701 William trusted him enough to appoint him commander in chief of British forces in the Low Countries.

It was under Queen Anne, who came to the throne in 1702, that Marlborough's career really took off. He was elevated to a dukedom and appointed captain general of the armed forces, taking command of the first campaign of the War of the Spanish Succession. From the very beginning, Marlborough was able to out-think, out-march and outmanoeuvre the French. During his first campaigning season he succeeded in pushing the French into a highly disadvantageous position. But it was the campaign of 1704 that saw Britain's greatest success.

Thanks to the complex European dynastic politics of the early 18th century, in 1704 Marlborough found himself commanding a combined army of British, Dutch, Hanoverian, Hessian, Danish and Prussian soldiers. Near the village of Blindheim (anglicized as Blenheim) on the River Danube in Bavaria, he came up against a force of French and Bavarian troops under the French commander Marshal Tallard. Tallard had more men and a stronger natural position on the battlefield, but he was no match for Marlborough. Throughout the Battle of Blenheim, fought on 13 August 1704, Marlborough completely outmanoeuvred the Franco-Bavarian army, personally intervening at crucial points of the battle and ensuring that his enemies were never allowed to exploit any small advantage. More than 20,000 of Tallard's men were killed or wounded, and Tallard himself was captured.

It was a resounding victory for Marlborough. After the battle was over, he scrawled a note to his wife on a tavern bill: 'I have not time to say more, but to beg you will give my duty to the Queen and let her know her army has had a glorious victory.' From that moment, Marlborough's fame spread throughout Europe. In England, as a reward for his success, Marlborough was granted funds to build the magnificent Blenheim Palace, near Woodstock in Oxfordshire.

At home, Marlborough was also the political partner of the chief

Prince Eugene of Savoy

Marlborough's most effective ally in his wars against France was Prince Eugene of Savoy, a brilliant soldier in the service of the Habsburg rulers of Austria and the Holy Roman Empire. Eugene's military contribution to the Grand Alliance was as significant as that of the English general: he was a superb strategist and had a remarkable ability to galvanize men to victory. Despite his small physical stature, he would regularly put himself in the thick of battle, and as a result he was injured many times during his career.

Eugene was born in 1663, the son of the Prince of Savoy, and brought up around the court of the French king, Louis XIV. His childhood was traumatic: his father died when Eugene was 10; several years later his mother was banished from the court.

Eugene's relationship with Louis XIV was extremely poor and dogged by rumours that the king was his real father. When Eugene abandoned a career in the Church for the military, Louis refused him a commission. Disgusted, Eugene left for Austria, where in 1683 the Ottoman Turks were besieging Vienna.

Having distinguished himself in relieving the siege, Eugene went on to win further victories at Buda and Belgrade. In 1697 he was given his first independent command and routed the Ottomans at the Battle of Zenta.

The next target was France. As the War of the Spanish Succession drew in nations across Europe, Eugene formed an alliance with Marlborough, and the two pre-eminent military minds were responsible for the resounding victory at Blenheim in 1704. Eugene also joined forces with Marlborough at the battles of Oudenarde in 1708 and Malplaquet in 1709.

From 1711, the alliance dissolved. Marlborough was recalled to England and Britain made peace with France in 1713. Eugene was left to fight on alone until Austria, too, made peace in 1714.

After turning his attention once again to the Ottomans, Eugene won his most spectacular victory at the siege of Belgrade in 1718. He annihilated a Turkish relieving force that outnumbered his own by four to one and captured the entire Turkish encampment.

Following the end of the Austro-Turkish War, Eugene retired to Vienna, where in 1714 he had begun building a majestic palace at Belvedere. He lived out his life as an elder statesman, reformer of the army, ruler of various Austrian provinces and one of the richest men in Europe. He died in his sleep in 1736.

minister Godolphin, making him a unique force in politics, in war and at court.

Other famous victories followed: Ramillies in 1706, Oudenarde in 1708 and Malplaquet in 1709. These were notably bloody affairs, but Marlborough's reputation soared. Throughout all of the campaigns between 1702 and 1710, Marlborough showed himself to be a shrewd tactician and a daring and confident commander, able to unify the forces of the disparate states of the Grand Alliance against the aggressively expansionist Louis XIV.

After 1710, domestic politics proved damaging to Marlborough. He and his wife lost favour at court, and the satirist Jonathan Swift aimed repeated barbs at the duke, accusing him of corruption. But, with the foresight of natural courtiers, the Marlboroughs simply aligned themselves with the elector of Hanover, who in 1714 became King George I and reappointed the duke as captain general.

But by now Marlborough's powers were fading. He suffered two strokes in 1716 and was thereafter largely confined to Blenheim. In 1722 a final stroke killed him, and he was buried in Westminster Abbey. A century later the Duke of Wellington declared, 'I can conceive of nothing greater than Marlborough at the head of an English army', and since then military historians have largely agreed that Marlborough was the finest general England has ever produced.

Voltaire 1694–1778

As long as people believe in absurdities, they will continue to commit atrocities.

Voltaire

The writer, philosopher, literary celebrity and friend of kings, François-Marie Arouet, better known by his pen name Voltaire, was the star of the Age of Enlightenment, one of the most influential men in Europe – and also one of the richest. His ridicule of the absurdities and atrocities of 18th-century Europe helped to give birth to the modern world – a world in which science and reason replaced superstition. Thanks to his indignation and energy, freedom of speech and of belief, and the even-handed administration of justice, came to be regarded as inalienable human rights.

Voltaire was famed even in his own time as a tireless multi-talented genius. He excelled as a playwright, a poet, a novelist, a satirist, a polemicist, a historian, a philosopher, a financial investor and a (sometimes sychophantic) courtier. Of his prodigious output of over 350 works, it is the slim satire *Candide* (1759) that most completely encapsulates his brilliance. Published, like most of Voltaire's work, to instant popular acclaim, it follows the hapless eponymous hero through a series of grim adventures as he clings to the conventional religio-philosophical piety that 'All is for the best in the best of all possible worlds' – despite increasingly conclusive evidence, as horror piles on horror, to the contrary. A devastatingly witty attack on everything from slavery to the professions, *Candide* exemplifies the power of Voltaire's razor-sharp pen to deflate pretension and hypocrisy.

Wiry, mischievous and wickedly brilliant, Voltaire was the changeling in an otherwise entirely conventional wealthy bourgeois

Torture and the Calas case

Leg braces, thumbscrews, the rack, sleep deprivation, pouring water on rags stuffed into the victim's throat to induce the sensation of drowning, hanging a victim by their arms with weights attached to their ankles – these were just some of the methods used in prisons across Europe in Voltaire's time to extract confessions from the 'guilty'.

Punishment could be still more gruesome. The execution in Paris, in 1757, of Robert Damiens, the man who tried to stab Louis XV, was incomparably grisly. First of all, as decreed by France's Parlement, the hand that had wielded the knife was burnt. The executioner then used pincers to tear away chunks of flesh, filling the wounds with molten lead. For over quarter of an hour, four horses, pulling in different directions, tried to dismember Damiens' broken body until finally his thighs and arms were severed with a knife. It was said that the would-be regicide was still just alive when his dismembered trunk was thrown on the fire.

Until the 18th century, torture was an accepted part of the judicial system. It was a means of wrenching the truth from the recalcitrant human will, a way of punishing the guilty in the most heinous way possible. The

family. He personally encouraged the rumours that his paternity lay elsewhere. By his late teens his acid wit – he once remarked of a rival poet's 'Ode to Posterity' that 'I fear it will not reach its mark' – had made him the pet of aristocratic society. Voltaire, the financial wizard, made a fortune from canny manipulation of the Paris lottery. Cirey, the Lorraine estate on which Voltaire spent ten years with his great love, the married and beautiful mathematics scholar the Marquise de Châtelet in the 1730s and 1740s, became a hothouse of intellectual debate and social mischief.

Voltaire's campaign against the monarchy's arbitrary practices was informed by first-hand experience: as a youth, his satirical pen had briefly landed him in the Bastille. A subsequent exile in London (1726–9) alerted Voltaire to the contrast between England's intellectual openness and the oppressive censorship of France. In his *Philosophical Letters*, published on his return to France in 1729, Voltaire embarked on a lifelong attack on the injustice and intolerance fostered by the Catholic Church and France's absolute monarchy.

thinkers of the Enlightenment saw it otherwise – as a barbaric practice that had nothing to do with justice, one that risked punishing the innocent as well as the guilty.

Inflicting such intense pain on a man, argued the Italian Cesare Beccaria in 1764, in one of the age's most influential tracts, would only compel the victim to 'accuse himself of crimes of which he is innocent'. Hearing of the case of Jean Calas, a Huguenot (French Protestant) from Toulouse who in 1762 was accused of murdering his son, then tortured to obtain a confession and finally broken on the wheel, Voltaire raged against the superstitious barbarism of the Catholic Church and its excessive judicial influence.

During the latter half of the 18th century, Prussia, Sweden, France, Austria and Tuscany all abolished judicial torture. In 1801, under Tsar Paul, Russia decreed that 'the very name of torture, bringing shame and reproach on mankind, should be forever erased from the public memory'.

It was far from a distant memory; but now torture was a shameful secret rather than a commendable practice. And while the bloodbath of France's Terror has totally sullied its name, Dr Joseph-Ignace Guillotin's invention for swiftly and painlessly beheading the condemned was meant to be a step away from the savage methods of the past.

Thereafter, Voltaire and the French authorities existed in an uneasy truce. He briefly held a court appointment as royal historiographer in the 1740s, although his rooms – 'the most stinking shit hole in Versailles' – disappointed him. But having come to the conclusion that 'I am very fond of the truth, but not at all of martyrdom', he spent most of his life away from the centre.

He based himself at Geneva from 1755, then, in 1759, settled at nearby Ferney in French territory, whose proximity to the Swiss border afforded him luxurious safety to exercise his pen. The pseudonyms he used were flimsy to say the least: he favoured 'the Archbishop of Paris' for his most virulent attacks on the church. But they allowed him to disavow authorship, with wide-eyed innocence, while the outraged authorities banned and burned his books.

Voltaire's outstanding achievement was his campaign for civil rights, waged under his motto '*écrasez l'infâme*' ('crush the infamy'). His calls for religious freedom and judicial fairness – for example in the notorious Calas case of 1762 – ushered in a new era. The deist Voltaire's *Treatise on Tolerance* (1763) expanded on his belief that reason should be government's abiding principle, and his assertion that religious freedom was not harmful to the state's well-being has become a fundamental principle of modern government. 'The right to persecute,' he declared, 'is absurd and barbaric.'

By now Voltaire's fame had spread across Europe: Frederick the Great and Catherine the Great, with whom he enjoyed a prolific correspondence, basked in his reflected glory, projecting themselves as adherents of 'enlightened absolutism'. Both repeatedly invited him to visit and he duly stayed with Frederick (1750–53), but the realities of the Prussian court soured Voltaire's rapport with the man he now described as a 'likeable whore', and who once described him as a 'monkey'. He resisted Catherine's invitations, but it was he who flattered her by dubbing her 'The Great'. Luminaries from across the continent flocked to see Voltaire, and at Ferney he became the self-described 'innkeeper of Europe'. The brilliant schoolboy, described by his father-confessor as being 'devoured by a thirst for celebrity', had become 'King Voltaire', revered and reviled in equal measure across Europe as the scourge of authority, injustice and hypocrisy. As he lay dying in Paris in 1778, his rooms were crammed with crowds of people, all determined to catch a last glimpse of a legendary man.

The shrine to Voltaire erected by the French revolutionaries in the Panthéon acknowledges their debt to him. It bears the inscription: 'He taught us how to be free.' Voltaire had begun the process of translating the ideals of the Enlightenment into reality, and his words became the first bomb thrown against the *ancien régime*. He once told a friend, 'I have never made but one prayer to God, a very short one: "O Lord, make my enemies ridiculous." And God granted it.'

Samuel Johnson
1709–1784

Here lies Sam Johnson: — Reader, have a care,
Tread lightly, lest you wake a sleeping bear:
Religious, moral, generous, and humane
He was: but self-sufficient, proud, and vain,
Fond of, and overbearing in dispute,
A Christian and a scholar — but a brute.

Soame Jenyns, suggested epitaph for Dr Johnson (1784)

Samuel Johnson was one of the most versatile, erudite and accomplished writers in the history of English literature. In addition to his remarkable and ground-breaking Dictionary, he also wrote copiously in a wide range of other genres: essays, literary criticism, travel writing, political sketches and satires, a tragedy, biography, poetry, translations, sermons, diaries, letters and pamphlets. He was a master conversationalist and a spiky, magnetic and brilliant figure in London society. Through the biography written by his disciple James Boswell, we can still appreciate one of the reigning personalities of literary history as though he were alive today.

Johnson's early years did not show much promise. As a child he suffered from both scrofula (tuberculosis of the lymph glands), which affected his sight, and smallpox, which disfigured his face, making him at best peculiar to look at. Throughout his life he was also prone to depression and had all manner of odd tics and twitches that now suggest Tourette's syndrome. Despite these disadvantages, the young Samuel was a bright boy and grew up in a family of booksellers in Lichfield. But poverty obliged him to leave Pembroke College, Oxford, after only a year, without taking a degree.

In 1735 he married Elizabeth Porter, a local widow twenty years his senior. Failing to obtain a teaching post, Johnson decamped to London in 1737 and began working for the *Gentleman's Magazine*, for which he wrote parliamentary sketches. He had already written a stage tragedy, *Irene*, and worked on satirical poems, biographies such as *The Life of Mr Richard Savage*, and a catalogue of the Harley collection of books and manuscripts.

It was in 1746 that Johnson began his *magnum opus*. He was commissioned to write a new English dictionary, and the project dominated the next nine years of his life. Nothing on such a scale had previously been undertaken, and the *Dictionary* proved to be a masterpiece of scholarship. It broke new ground in lexicography, encompassing a vast array of words from a gigantic pool of source material, and even made a good stab at discovering the etymology of many of the words that were included. The *Dictionary* was also a demonstration of Johnson's pithy and precise style. In a characteristic flash of witty self-deprecation, Johnson defines a lexicographer as 'a writer of dictionaries, a harmless drudge'.

The *Dictionary* was immediately recognized as a work of brilliance, and Johnson was awarded with an honorary MA from Oxford before the book was even finished. In the meantime he had continued to write copiously in other genres. His essays in *The Rambler* dealt with matters as varied as capital punishment, good parenting and the emergence of the novel, and are replete with eminently quotable epigrams – such as 'No man is much pleased with a companion, who does not increase, in some respect, his fondness for himself.' Johnson had the same gift as Oscar Wilde for pointing out, with razor-like wit, the contradictions inherent in human nature.

Johnson lost his wife in 1752. He never married again, but his house was a refuge to friends from a variety of odd backgrounds. Ex-prostitutes, indebted unlicensed surgeons, female writers – a particular favourite with Johnson – all stayed under his roof. But Johnson was just as popular in the higher strata of society, receiving

Johnson's Dictionary

After nine years' hard work, Johnson's *Dictionary* was finally published on 15 April 1755. It was an imposing work, weighty and expansive, and as a work of lexicography it far surpassed in scholarship and precision anything produced before. The first edition contained 42,733 headwords, and the definitions were illustrated with examples from a range of English writers.

The breadth of material was testament to Johnson's vast knowledge of the English language. The laconic, witty terms in which he couched his definitions – which were often mischievously opinionated – were a hallmark of the *Dictionary*'s unique genius. Here are a few examples:

Cough. A convulsion of the lungs . . . Pronounced *coff.*

Distiller. One who makes and sells pernicious and inflammatory spirits.

Dull. Not delightful; as, *to make dictionaries is* dull *work*.

Excise. A hateful tax levied upon commodities, and adjudged not by the common judges of property, but wretches hired by those to whom excise is paid.

Far-fetch. A deep stratagem. A ludicrous word.

Jobbernowl. Loggerhead; blockhead.

Network. Anything reticulated or decussated at equal distances, with interstices between the intersections.

Oats. A grain, which in England is generally given to horses, but in Scotland supports the people.

Patron. One who countenances, supports or protects. Commonly a wretch who supports with insolence, and is paid with flattery.

Pension. An allowance made to any one without an equivalent. In England it is generally understood to mean pay given to a state hireling for treason to his country.

Politician. 1. One versed in the arts of government; one skilled in politicks. 2. A man of artifice; one of deep contrivance.

Tory. One who adheres to the ancient constitution of the state, and the apostolical hierarchy of the church of England, opposed to a Whig.

Whig. The name of a faction.

patronage from the Treasury and conversing with men like the American founding father, philosopher and inventor Benjamin Franklin. In 1763 Johnson met the young Boswell in a bookshop and took him on as a protégé. Boswell was a devoted fan, and his biography tells us much about Johnson's life and scintillating conversation which otherwise might have been lost.

As his fame grew Johnson turned out another pair of fine works: an admired edition of Shakespeare's plays in 1765 and The Lives of the Poets, which came out between 1779 and 1781. Johnson was often tart, if not harsh, on his contemporaries – when asked to pick the better of the two minor poets Smart and Derrick, he replied that there was 'no settling the point of precedency between a louse and a flea'. But despite this gruffness, he had a warm heart and a fond regard for his friends. He died in 1784 and was buried in Westminster Abbey, a sign of the esteem in which he was held by his contemporaries – an esteem that has not diminished over the succeeding centuries. 'I hate a fellow whom pride or cowardice or laziness drives into a corner, and who does nothing when he is there but sit and growl,' he once said. 'Let him come out as I do, and bark.'

Frederick the Great
1712–1786

A man who gives battle as readily as he writes an opera ... he has written more books than any of his contemporary princes has sired bastards; he has won more victories than he has written books.

Voltaire, 1772

The outstanding soldier-statesman of his age, the paragon of gifted kingship, Frederick the Great prefigured Napoleon in terms of military brilliance, political genius and ruthless realpolitik. The most enlightened monarch of his day, Frederick was an aesthete and lover of the arts – an accomplished writer, composer, flautist and wit. Famed in his youth as a philosopher prince, on acceding to the throne in 1740, at the age of 28, this apparent milksop astonished Europe's crowned heads by becoming the most formidable ruler of the age.

With his typically wry wit, Frederick once declared that he had infected Europe with warfare just as a coquette infects her clients. Introspective and self-critical, Frederick's analysis and planning were always immaculate, his quick mind the first to seize the advantage on the battlefield. His martial qualities inspired in his formidably well-trained army the utmost respect and loyalty, despite the horrific privations his campaigns put them through. When Napoleon reached Berlin 20 years after Frederick's death, he paid homage at the great leader's tomb. As he entered, he declared to his men: 'Hats off, gentlemen! If he were alive, we would not be here!'

Frederick waged war to serve his state's interests, but he was never militaristic. He deplored war's effects and he abhorred hypocrisy. At other times he could be firmly pragmatic: 'If we can gain something by being honest, we will be it; and if we have to deceive, we will be cheats.'

In 1740 he boldly and ruthlessly invaded Austria's rich province of Silesia, unleashing almost twenty years of savage warfare across Central Europe, but he kept the territory. Europe's hypocritical old guard was quick to share in the spoils when Frederick initiated the partition of the increasingly anarchic Poland. 'She weeps, but she takes,' Frederick wryly commented of Empress Maria Theresa when she took her slice of Poland.

The man who refused to wear spurs because he thought them cruel to horses abolished torture within days of coming to the throne. He banned serfdom in all his new territories, and in an age when capital punishment was decreed for stealing bread, the famously liberal Frederick signed only eight or ten death warrants a year. He once reprieved a father and daughter from the death sentence for committing incest on the grounds that one could not be absolutely sure about the girl's paternity. The atheist Frederick's religious tolerance extended to welcoming the Jesuits to Prussia – a sect that crowned heads all over Europe were trying to expel.

The first of Europe's enlightened despots, Frederick was tireless in fulfilling his self-designated role as the first servant of the state. Every day he forced himself to rise at 4 am, ordering his servants to throw a cold wet cloth in his face if he seemed reluctant. Even such an early start as this barely gave him time to do all he wanted. At his court, which he filled with artists, writers, musicians and philosophers, he practised the flute four times a day, held concerts after supper, conducted a vast correspondence with philosophers and statesmen, wrote poetry, and administered the affairs of state.

His endurance was as striking as his luck. He was prone to fits of depression and despair, but he never gave up. 'Fortune alone can deliver me from my present position,' he declared at one point during the Seven Years' War (1756–63). The timely death of his inveterate enemy Empress Elizaveta of Russia in 1762 brought about a volte-face in foreign policy as his ardent admirer Peter III came

international friendship. Peter the Great established an annual gift of 48 a year. Once, when Peter decided to discontinue the gift, Frederick William refused to talk to the Russian ambassador until the practice was restored. The king tried breeding them, ordering giants to marry only giantesses, but had only limited success: all too often the children were of normal stature.

Prussia's king even turned to kidnapping giants. An operation to lift a prize Irish specimen off the streets of London cost £1000. On one occasion he nearly provoked war with England after he stole some Hanoverian giants and refused to return them. An exceptionally tall Austrian diplomat in Vienna only narrowly avoided an enforced career change.

The Giants were often of limited intelligence, but they were not entirely tractable. Despite their high pay and privileged treatment, some – especially those that had been abducted – tried to desert or commit suicide. When Frederick William suggested stretching them to make them taller, he was met with open rebellion.

Frederick the Great lacked his father's enthusiasm for the Potsdam Grenadiers – the first regiment he had commanded, as a 14-year-old. He considered them an expensive indulgence and disbanded them as soon as he came to the throne. A few were kept on as palace servants, but the rest of the lofty legion were sent on their way – 'huge weak-kneed loons', as one writer memorably described them, littering the roads of Europe as they traced their way home.

to the throne. Having teetered on the brink of total annihilation early in the war, Prussia emerged triumphant from it.

Frederick's insecurity may well have been instilled in him by his miserable youth. His father Frederick William I's contempt for his son was famous. 'What goes on in that little head?' the austere, violent, volatile Frederick William would demand suspiciously of his 'effeminate' son, whose lifelong love for all things French directly contravened his father's orders. Matters came to a head when the 18-year-old Frederick tried to flee his wretched existence. After he was caught and imprisoned, his best friend (and some say lover) Hermann von Katte was executed outside the window of his cell.

Prussia may have grown in grandeur but Frederick did not.

Towards the end of Frederick's life, a visiting dignitary encountered an elderly 'gardener' at the Sanssouci summer palace and had a friendly chat. Only later, when he was introduced to Prussia's king, did he realize who he had been talking to.

But he could turn nasty – in his wit, in his disciplining of his army, in his repudiation of his wife. He fell out spectacularly with his old correspondent Voltaire, who abused him in print as a miser and a tyrant. His pursuit of war to advance his country simultaneously exhausted its resources. His emphasis on the primacy of the state meant that his rule was never as enlightened as Voltaire had hoped.

Frederick's lifelong conservatism translated itself increasingly into rigidity with age. With typical self-deprecation, he frequently said that he had lived too long. But on his death Europe lost one of its greatest kings, a man in whom all the talents collided – an outstanding prince.

Casanova 1725–1798

Worthy or not, my life is my subject, and my subject is my life.
Giacomo Casanova

The name of Casanova or, to give his full name, Giovanni Giacomo Casanova de Seingalt, is synonymous with womanizing and wild living. Indeed, in his racy and scandalously frank memoirs, Histoire de ma vie jusqu'à l'an 1787 ('The Story of My Life up until 1787'), this tall, dark and handsome self-appointed hero presents himself as 'the world's greatest lover', describing his many conquests, as well as his early life, adventures and travels, in salacious detail. It may therefore come as a surprise to find that the notorious philanderer, who sired many children out of wedlock and was himself, it was rumoured, the illegitimate son of a Venetian nobleman, was also a highly cultured man – and that is his real claim to fame. Whether they are mainly fact or boastful fiction, his memoirs are the greatest ever written.

Precociously intelligent, Casanova attended the University of Padua from the age of 13, obtained a doctorate in law at the age of 16 (ironically, perhaps, his studies included moral philosophy), took holy orders, and also considered training as a doctor.

'The idea of settling down,' he wrote, 'was always repulsive to me.' The adventurous and talented Casanova was always on the move. He started out working in the church in Venice but was soon expelled under something of a cloud, due to his sexual appetites and dandified appearance. From there he had a short-lived career as a military officer, stationed in Corfu, then as a theatre violinist in Venice. He took a variety of jobs before leaving Venice in 1748, under suspicion of attempted rape (though he was later acquitted).

Born into a world of artists, con-artists and courtesans, Casanova represented a sparkling conflation of two 18th-century social types – the society fraud and the man of letters. He was one of the fascinating mountebanks and charlatans who entertained, mesmerized and swindled the royal courts of the age, claiming variously to be noblemen, necromancers, alchemists (who could turn base metals into gold), Kabbalists, magi and hierophants. The first of them was the so-called Comte de Saint-Germain (1710–84), who claimed to be 2000 years old and able to remember the Crucifixion (his valet claimed to remember it too); Louis XV gave him 10,000 livres. The ultimate was Count Alessandro Cagliostro (1743–95), born Giuseppe Balsamo in Sicily, who made a fortune in courts across Europe claiming, among other feats, that he could convert urine into gold and offer eternal life. His seductive wife, born Lorenza in Sicily, accompanied him as Serafina, Princess di Santa Croce. After a rockstar-style tour of Europe, Count Cagliostro was finally embroiled in the Diamond Necklace Affair that so damaged Queen Marie-Antoinette, and he died in 1795 in an Italian prison.

But it was also a very literary age, when the fame of witty letter-writers, such as Casanova, spread throughout Europe. The greatest letter-writer of the era (along with Voltaire) was the genuine high aristocrat Charles-Joseph, Prince de Ligne (1735–1814), Belgian grandee, Austrian field-marshal and international courtier, wit and socialite, who managed to be friends simultaneously with Emperor Joseph II, Catherine the Great of Russia, and King Frederick the Great. His hilarious letters were copied from court to court, and he finally died at the Congress of Vienna.

Passing himself off as the noble 'Chevalier de Seingalt', Casanova earned his living as the inventor of the Paris lottery, an agricultural adviser to the kings of Spain, an alchemist and a Kabbalist. He was repeatedly arrested for his debts and in 1755 for witchcraft and freemasonry – and then imprisoned for 15 months in Venice's Piombi Prison, known as the 'Leads', from which it was supposedly impossible to escape. Escape he did, however, across the rooftops, stopping for a recuperative coffee in St Mark's Square before disappearing in a gondola.

He travelled widely, through Italy, Austria, Spain, England, Turkey and Russia, meeting Catherine the Great, George III of England and Pope Benedict XII, not to mention Rousseau and Voltaire. Most of his income came from the grandees who admired his intelligence and wit, or – in the case of the women – sought and often received his attentions. Never married, he was engaged frequently. His lovers included courtesans, peasants, heiresses, sisters, countesses and many nuns, sometimes together. In 1776, overcome by debt, he became a secret agent for the Venetian Tribunal of Inquisitors, using the name 'Antonio Pratiloni' and snitching on heretics to the Catholic Church while living with a local seamstress.

Tales of derring-do and romantic trysts litter the memoirs, which are the main source of information about his chequered life. Heavily censored in earlier editions, they were not published in their full 'unexpurgated' 12-volume form until 1960; they paint a portrait of a lovable trans-European rogue and seducer. He wrote them as an old man looking back on an adventurous life, working as the librarian to the Bohemian Count Joseph Karl von Waldstein. Casanova was never one for letting the facts stand in the way of a good tale. Some of his dates simply do not fit: people are in the wrong places and die at the wrong times, and the pseudonyms he gives his various conquests make it impossible to be certain who was who. Unreliable, self-indulgent and shameless, the memoirs are nevertheless a literary classic, only half-true but a real picture of an entire epoch.

'I have lived as a philosopher,' declared Casanova on his deathbed, 'and died as a Christian.' It was rather less straightforward, and rather more interesting, than that.

Dangerous Liaisons

Casanova has become the historical prototype of the cultured libertine, living a life of brazen disregard for the ethical, religious and behavioural norms of conventional society. In France, a mini-genre of libertine fiction – anti-clerical, anti-establishment and often pornographic – flourished before the Revolution. Its typical products were a licentious mix of sexual titillation and contemporary satire. However, the cult of hedonism threw up one fictional masterpiece that is a sustained attack on the heartless amorality of the libertine and has outlasted all the other works of its type. *Les Liaisons dangereuses* (1782) was the only novel by the splendidly named Pierre Choderlos de Laclos (1741–1803), an artillery officer who moved in high society and rose to be a general under Napoleon. Perhaps Laclos' job as secretary to the notoriously sexually degenerate Louis Philippe II, duc d'Orléans, gave him special insights into the mind of the aristocratic seducer. In *Les Liaisons dangereuses* he certainly produced a technically brilliant and psychologically acute portrayal of 18th-century libertinage.

Written in the form of an exchange of sparklingly witty letters, the novel's exquisitely modulated plot anatomizes the seduction by two experienced libertines (and former lovers) – the vicomte de Valmont and the marquise de Merteuil – of the innocent Cécile de Volanges and her admirer the Chevalier Danceny, whose lives they thus destroy. Valmont pursues sexual adventure without moral scruple – until he falls in love with Madame de Tourvel, a devout young married woman he had intended merely to seduce. The sexual conspiracy, and its heartless manipulation of the feelings of others, has fatal consequences for the plotters. Valmont is killed by Danceny in a duel, while Merteuil – her machinations laid bare – is publicly ostracized and her hitherto ravishingly beautiful face disfigured by smallpox.

Fastidious critics have always claimed that to describe libertinism in such realistic detail was to celebrate it (and there is no doubt that Valmont and Merteuil's resourcefulness and way with words is as seductive to the reader as it is to their fictional conquests). But *Les Liaisons dangereuses* is, in the end, a novel of moral purpose and wise humanity. The smooth progress of the libertines' plot is derailed by the unforeseen irruption of true feeling, and Valmont and Merteuil are ultimately undone by a human emotion (jealousy) to which the ice-cold Merteuil had believed herself immune. One of Valmont's last letters to Danceny concludes with the poignant words: 'Believe me, it is only through love that we can be happy.' Whether regarded as a fictional harbinger of revolutionary change or as a ruthless dissection of the tired mores of a doomed aristocracy, *Les Liaisons dangereuses* remains a timeless and lacerating exposé of the hidden darkness of the human heart.

Captain James Cook

1728–1779

The ablest and most renowned Navigator this or any
country hath produced.

Sir Hugh Palliser's monument to Captain Cook, erected at Chalfont St Giles,
Buckinghamshire, after the news of Cook's death reached Europe

Captain James Cook was responsible for exploring and charting boundless areas of the Pacific hitherto unknown to Europeans. A creative captain as well as a fine navigator, he devised a diet for his crews rich in vitamin C, thereby preventing the outbreaks of scurvy that usually afflicted those on long voyages. It was curiosity and ambition as well as science that drove Cook to fulfil his desire to voyage not only 'farther than any man before me, but as far as I think it is possible for a man to go'.

Cook's achievements were remarkable given his beginnings. The son of a Yorkshire farm labourer, as a lad he was apprenticed to a grocer. This did not satisfy his restless spirit, and he set off for the port of Whitby. Here he signed on to serve on a merchantman and spent a number of years sailing on colliers up and down the east coast of England. Having acquired the rudiments of navigation, in 1755 he volunteered for the Royal Navy and rose swiftly through the ranks. During the Seven Years' War Cook achieved renown as a hydrographic surveyor, and his work charting the St Lawrence River and the coast of Canada was critical to subsequent British victories. His surveys and sailing directions concerning Newfoundland were used for well over a century.

Cook's observations of the solar eclipse of 1766 so impressed the Royal Society that, jointly with the Admiralty, it commissioned him to make a voyage to Tahiti to observe the transit of Venus – and also to explore and claim for Britain the undiscovered southern continent known as *Terra Australis*. The belief in the existence of such a continent – covering not only the South Pole but also extending far to the north into the Indian Ocean and the Pacific – had been held by geographers since the time of Aristotle. Cook's discoveries conclusively put the myth to rest: in circumnavigating New Zealand for the first time (1769), discovering Australia's east coast (1770) and sailing through the Torres Strait between Australia and New Guinea, Cook showed these lands to be separate entities. But the furtherance of science was only one of Cook's aims; he also claimed for King George III many of the lands he discovered – such as New South Wales and Hawaii (which he called the Sandwich Isles in honour of his patron, the Earl of Sandwich). During his second voyage (1772–5), he achieved the first circumnavigation of the Antarctic, and in so doing became the first person to cross the Antarctic Circle.

The scale of Cook's achievement owes much to his brilliant and fearless seamanship. Cook consistently continued his explorations when all others would have turned back. His navigation skills were considerable, and he also had the vision to draw on the knowledge of the region of the two Tahitians he employed on his voyages. Boundlessly tenacious, Cook was never content with what he had achieved. He invariably extended his voyages, and his willingness to exceed the orders given to him by the Admiralty was rewarded by the discoveries he made.

Cook's maps and charts were often the first accurate depictions of the coasts he explored: he completed the outlines of Newfoundland, the northwest coast of North America, New Zealand and Australia. His use of the K1 chronometer, which by keeping time more precisely enabled him to measure longitude more accurately, was groundbreaking, and his results are remarkable for their accuracy, given the frequently adverse conditions in which he worked and the limitations of the instrumentation available to him.

Cook's pioneering work on the prevention of scurvy earned him a medal from the Royal Society, who were also impressed by the scientific achievements of his expeditions, in particular the records of new flora and fauna made by the scientists he took with him. Cook – praised in the House of Lords as 'the first navigator in Europe' – was elected a fellow of the Royal Society and awarded a captainship and honorary retirement by the Royal Navy. This last, however, he accepted only on the condition that he could still make further voyages. For, despite having a wife and a succession of children, Cook's life lay at sea.

In 1776 he set sail for the South Seas once again. During this voyage, Cook determined to make an attempt to break though the apparently impassable Arctic ice and find a route back to Europe to the north of Canada. While waiting for spring to arrive, Cook wintered in Hawaii, and here he became caught up in a disagreement with the islanders. In the resulting skirmish, Cook, who had initially been deified by the Hawaiians as the incarnation of their god, Lono, was killed. His body, according to custom, was stripped of flesh, which was then burnt – or possibly eaten. His bones were distributed among various chiefs and only handed back to Cook's men after protracted negotiations. His remains were buried at sea, as was only fitting, the sea having been his whole life. The map of the Pacific was his legacy.

The *Endeavour*

The humble vessel in which James Cook made his first famed voyage of discovery began life as a merchant collier. Flat-bottomed, sturdy and far from speedy, the *Endeavour* was ideal for a voyage through uncharted, often shallow waters. Designed to be beached, she was perfect for a ship that hoped to land on unpeopled shores. The navy made some fairly significant tweaks, adding a third, observation deck and reinforcing the hull, but it did little to improve the elegance of the HM Bark *Endeavour*, so named to avoid confusion with HMS *Endeavour*, a more graceful naval ship that shared her name.

The *Endeavour* set sail from Plymouth on 8 August 1768. Three years later she limped back into harbour. The collier had taken quite a battering, having run aground on the Great Barrier Reef. Managing to draw the ship free of the reef, the crew then faced the prospect of sinking as, sieved by coral, the ship began to take on water. When finally they reached Batavia in the Dutch East Indies, it was, Cook reported, 'a surprise to everyone who saw her bottom how we had kept her above water' – some planks in the hull were just one-eighth of an inch (3mm) away from being shorn in two.

The *Endeavour*'s end is as obscure as her beginning was modest. She was refitted again, this time as a store ship, and was sold by the Royal Navy in 1775, buyer unknown. Some say she was sunk in American waters later that decade, suffering the fate in more familiar seas that she had so successfully avoided in uncharted ones.

But the unassuming vessel has not been forgotten. Two hundred years later the merchant collier that went to the ends of the world gave her name to the command module of Apollo 15, and subsequently to the fifth and final space shuttle, which was first launched in May 1992.

Catherine the Great 1729–1796

Be gentle, humane, accessible, compassionate and open-handed; don't let your grandeur prevent you from mixing kindly with the humble and putting yourself in their shoes … I swear by Providence to stamp these words in my heart.

Catherine's private note to herself on becoming empress (1762)

Catherine the Great was not only a successful politician, a triumphant empire-builder and a remarkable self-made woman of strong passions in a male-dominated age. She was also arguably the most humane ruler that Russia has ever produced. She ranks with Elizabeth I of England as one of history's outstanding female monarchs – though her achievements were even greater than Elizabeth's.

Catherine was certainly ruthless in her pursuit of power and admiration, self-indulgent in her famous love affairs and enormously extravagant in her enjoyment of arts and luxury – but she was also overwhelmingly benevolent, decent in her intentions, loyal to her friends, merciful to her enemies, tolerant of others, industrious, intellectual and enormously intelligent. Her success was against all the odds. She was not even Russian, had no claim to the throne and found herself, at the age of 14, thrown into a loveless marriage and the brutal bear pit of the Russian court.

She was not even named Catherine, being born Sophie of Anhalt-Zerbst, a minor German princess in the patchwork of little principalities that was the Holy Roman Empire, which served as a sort of matchmaking agency for the monarchies of Europe. In 1746 the Empress Elizaveta of Russia summoned Princess Sophie to St Petersburg to marry her heir, Grand Duke Peter. She converted to the Orthodox Church, took the name Catherine and learned Russian – but found her husband disappointing. Puny, poxy, prejudiced, foolish and cowardly, Grand Duke Peter was out of his depth as the Russian heir – and as Catherine's husband. He also was German, but while Catherine embraced all Russian culture, he despised and feared Russia. She immediately charmed the empress, won friends and admirers among the courtiers and the Guards regiments, and proved adept at politics. It is uncertain if Peter even consummated the marriage, but it is certain that he did not satisfy the passionate Catherine.

When no child was forthcoming, the empress herself arranged for Catherine to take her first lover, Serge Saltykov. A son, Grand Duke Paul, was born. Catherine was not beautiful, but she was handsome, small and curvaceous, with bright blue eyes and thick auburn hair. She went on to take other lovers, though she only had a dozen in her entire lifetime − almost 70 years − which hardly justifies her reputation as a nymphomaniac. She was never promiscuous, more a serial dater. She enjoyed sex but was more of a romantic who longed to settle with one man.

Amid the vicious rivalries at the Russian court during the Seven Years' War, Catherine's intrigues almost destroyed her. But she used her cunning and charm to survive, shrewdly taking Grigory Orlov, a popular Guards officer, as her lover. When Elizaveta died and her husband succeeded to the throne, Peter III took only six months to alienate everyone. On 28 June 1762, dressed in male uniform, Catherine seized power. By the rules of the day, Peter had to be murdered to protect her dubious claim to the throne; the Orlovs strangled him − and she knew she would forever bear the blame.

Once in power, however, she ruled cautiously and sensibly. She set about expanding Russia south towards the Black Sea, seizing territory from the Ottoman Turks. She called a legislative commission to study the abolition of serfdom and the making of proper laws. She corresponded with the *philosophes*, including Voltaire, who hailed her as 'The Great'. The huge peasant revolt of Pugachev and the realities of aristocratic rule meant that many of these ambitions ended in disappointment, but her rule was decent, sensible and orderly − she worked hard to make Russian law and society more merciful and humane.

When her long relationship with Orlov broke down, Catherine found the love of her life, who was also to be her partner in power. Prince Potemkin was a dashing one-eyed cavalry general who was as politically brilliant as she was; but where he was wild and imaginative, she was sensible and diligent. The combination worked. Their fiery sexual

Prince Potemkin

Grigory Potemkin was born of poor gentry near Smolensk in 1739, but he grew up to be so beautiful and intelligent that he was compared to Alcibiades. He was a scholar who, fascinated by religion, craved the priesthood, but instead he joined the Guards and helped bring Catherine to power. He fell in love with her but was ten years her junior, and she was still with her permanent lover, Orlov. She knew that Potemkin was so dominating, demanding, passionate and gifted that he would be a difficult partner. But when Catherine faced a political crisis in 1773, they embarked on a wildly sexual romance. Potemkin was much too energetic and talented to be a kept man. Instead, Catherine promoted him to the rank of prince, and he became her partner in power. As their passion, but not their friendship, dwindled they each took other lovers.

Like Catherine, Potemkin prided himself on decency, tolerance and humanity. As co-tsar and viceroy of the south, he annexed the Crimea in 1783 (becoming 'Prince of Taurida'), founded the naval base of Sebastapol and created the Russian Black Sea fleet. He also founded a series of cities, from Kherson to Odessa, then led Russian forces in the war against the Turks, in which he stormed Ismail, and conquered the southern Ukraine and Black Sea coast. But during his later years he became increasingly powerful, extravagant and bizarre.

'The most extraordinary man I ever met,' wrote the Prince de Ligne, 'constantly reclining yet never sleeping, trembling for others, brave for himself, bored in the midst of pleasure, unhappy for being too lucky, a profound philosopher, able minister, sublime politician or like a ten-year-old child, embracing the feet of the Virgin, or the alabaster neck of his mistress. What is the secret of his magic? Genius, genius and more genius.' This one-eyed giant enchanted and scandalized Europe like a sultan in *The Arabian Nights*, even seducing one princess by serving plates of diamonds instead of pudding. Pushkin hailed the 'glory of his name', while Stalin reflected: 'What was Catherine the Great's achievement? To appoint talented men like Potemkin to rule Russia.'

Potemkin died in 1791 on an open Bessarabian steppe, weeping over Catherine's letters. When she heard the news she collapsed: 'There'll never be another Potemkin.' Theirs was one of the great love stories of history, in a league with that of Napoleon and Josephine or Antony and Cleopatra, but more romantic and much more successful than either of those.

affair started in late 1773, recorded in the most outrageous and romantic letters ever written by a monarch. They probably married, secretly, but when their affair ended, Potemkin became her co-ruler and best friend. Together they fought the Turks, annexed the Crimea, built cities, out-witted the English, constructed a Black Sea fleet, bought art collections. Following Potemkin's advice, Catherine found love with a series of ever-younger favourites, whom she enjoyed teaching about the classics, but who played no political role. These young men usually humiliated the old empress by running off with a girl their own age, leaving Potemkin to comfort her. When he died in 1791, the ageing Catherine was heartbroken and allowed a talentless young lover, Platon Zubov, to replace him, leading to political mistakes, including the annexation of Poland and a bungled Swedish alliance.

Catherine's achievements – political, military and artistic – were colossal nevertheless. Her reign was a golden age, her vision of Russia essentially a liberal one, and her character exuded invincibility. Catherine the Great remains not only the paragon of Russian rulers, but history's most accomplished female potentate.

George Washington
1732–1799

The time is now near at hand which must probably determine whether Americans are to be freemen or slaves … The fate of unborn millions will now depend, under God, on the courage and conduct of this army.

George Washington, in his general orders to the Continental Army (2 July 1776)

George Washington, the first president of the United States and commander of the American army in the War of Independence against Britain, remains the paragon of the decent, honest – and hugely gifted – leader. Covered in glory, blessed with all the talents, equipped for the highest office and command, he was a gentleman who combined virtue and modesty with ambition to serve.

Legend has it that he turned down a crown, though in fact there was no sceptre to offer. He set the standards of probity and honesty for every president who followed him.

Born in Virginia in 1732 to a family of landowners who had emigrated from northern England in 1657, Washington started in public service as a brash young lieutenant-colonel in the Virginia militia. In May 1754 he commanded a small force in – and perhaps initiated – the opening engagement of the French and Indian War (at the Battle of Jumonville Glen), which would eventually become the worldwide Anglo-French conflict known as the Seven Years' War. A few days later he built Fort Necessity on the Ohio River, though when it was besieged by a larger French force, he was eventually forced to capitulate – the only surrender of his career. The next year he again fought the French, under British general Edward Braddock.

His natural talents, military and administrative, earned his promotion to colonel and commander-in-chief of the Virginian troops in 1755, aged only 23, and in 1758 he served under General John Forbes in the successful campaign to capture the French Fort Duquesne. Afterwards, Washington returned to his Mount Vernon estate, married a wealthy widow, Martha Curtis, and entered politics. In June 1774 he led the Virginia legislature's call for a continental congress to coordinate opposition to unpopular British colonial policies. In June 1775, after fighting had broken out, Congress unanimously elected him commander-in-chief of the Continental Army.

During the War of Independence, Washington managed to train the American army and to hold together all the different personalities and the differing characters of the states that made up the alliance, even in the face of defeat and adversity. Having forced the British to evacuate Boston in 1776, after a year-long siege, he committed mistakes in his defence of New York, losing the Battle of Long Island (the largest battle of the war) to General Howe and retreating, short of men and supplies, into Pennsylvania. Late in the year, however, he crossed back into New Jersey and took the British by surprise, defeating them at Trenton and Princeton.

But in 1777 his forces were defeated at the Brandywine in September and at Germantown in October, and Howe occupied

The men who would be king – from White Rajahs to King Zog

George Washington, being a good republican, always refused to consider any talk of a crown, following in the tradition of Oliver Cromwell and Julius Caesar, who both refused thrones.

Lesser men, usually vainglorious opportunists, have been less shy about crowning themselves – yet to found one's own kingdom in an exotic land must rank high in the fantasies of schoolboys everywhere.

Rudyard Kipling (1865–1936), who chronicled British India in his superb poetry and fiction, wrote 'The Man Who Would Be King', the story of an English soldier who founded a kingdom in Afghanistan and was killed for it. The tale is based on the American soldier, doctor and naturalist Josiah Harlan who, dressed as a Islamic fakir, helped seize the throne for various claimants, became commander-in-chief of the Afghan army and, in 1838, declared himself Prince of Ghor, heir to Alexander the Great, before being overthrown in an English invasion and dying in poverty in San Francisco.

But the most colourful and unlikely of such adventurers was Sir James Brooke (1803–68), a sea-captain who used a legacy to buy a ship, *The Royalist*, and successfully cleared the local seas of pirates for the Sultan of Brunei, whom he then threatened until that potentate granted him his own personal kingdom – Sarawak, with its headhunting tribesmen – to rule as absolute Rajah until his death in 1868. His life inspired not only Kipling but also Joseph Conrad's *Lord Jim*. Rajah Brooke was succeeded by his nephew, and these White Rajahs of Sarawak ruled increasingly like operetta autocrats until 1946.

The new independent nation-states of 19th-century Europe required monarchs, supplied by German princelings. Leopold of Saxe-Coburg established Belgium's monarchy (in 1831, surviving today), and Prince Otto of Bavaria became king of Greece (in 1833, but his Wittelsbachs were replaced by the Danish Glücksburgs who reigned from 1863 to 1924 and then from 1935 until King Constantine II was exiled in 1967). Prince Carol of Hohenzollern-Sigmaringen became King Carol I of Romania, ruling from 1866 until 1914, his dynasty lasting until King Michael's 1947 abdication was enforced by the Soviets. The Bulgarians crowned Prince Ferdinand of Saxe-Coburg-Gotha as Prince in 1887, then tsar in 1908. The last tsar of Bulgaria, Simeon II, reigned from 1943 until his removal by Moscow in 1946. Yet the elderly ex-tsar made an astonishing return to power, elected as prime minister of democratic Bulgaria from 2001 to 2005.

South America produced a string of self-made emperors. In 1821 Agustín Iturbide declared himself Agustín I of Mexico, but abdicated in 1823, and was later shot. In the 1860s Archduke Maximilian of Austria was precariously crowned emperor of Mexico by France, but was executed by republicans in 1867. More successful was the hedonistic Portuguese prince who became the real liberator of Brazil as Emperor Pedro I in 1822. He abdicated in 1831, returning to become King Pedro IV of Portugal, but his Bragança emperors ruled Brazil until the republic in 1889.

The most memorable self-made monarch was Zog: Ahmed Bey Zogu (1895–1961), ruthless chieftain and shrewd politician, became Albania's president in 1925, creating himself King Zog I and Scanderbeg III in 1928. He ruled with operatic flamboyance, married an Austrian princess who became his Queen Geraldine, and survived 56 assassination attempts – including one in 1931 at the Viennese opera after a performance of *Pagliacci* in which he drew his pistol and returned fire, the only head of state ever to do so in modern times. Fascist Italy invaded Albania, overthrowing Zog in 1939. Enver Hoxha's Stalinist dictatorship kept him in exile for the rest of his life.

Napoleon Bonaparte appointed his brothers Joseph, Jérôme, Louis, and his son to the thrones of Spain, Westphalia, Holland and Rome respectively. But the only lasting royal legacy of the Napoleonic era was the election to the throne of Sweden in 1810 of Marshal Jean-Baptiste Bernadotte, Napoleon's brother-in-law. He accepted the throne and in 1818 succeeded as King Charles XIV, reigning until 1844. The dynasty endures to this day.

Ibn Saud (1876–1953), desert warrior, father of 60 and founder, in 1932, of oil-rich Saudi Arabia, is the most successful self-made king. His son King Abdullah reigns today.

Philadelphia. Washington led his army to Valley Forge in Pennsylvania, where the weakened forces encamped through the winter of 1777–8, perhaps the lowest ebb of the revolutionary cause. It was Washington's personality above all that held together his broken army during that long winter. He used his almost dictatorial wartime powers with caution, tempered with bold action and skilled improvisation, common sense and respect for civil power. Aided by French entry into the war, in 1781 Washington commanded the superb Yorktown campaign against the British commander Cornwallis, whose army was besieged in the Virginia town which, after much bombardment, surrendered on 19 October 1781. This was to be the final major battle of the war.

After his victories, Washington retired to Mount Vernon. In 1787 he attended the Philadelphia Convention that discussed the creation of a new American government. Washington was elected president of the convention but refrained from joining the debate. The office of president of the United States was created to head the new government, and in 1788 Washington was elected to the post, winning re-election in 1792. As president, he attempted to maintain neutrality between the pro-French faction led by Secretary of State Thomas Jefferson and the pro-British faction of Treasury Secretary Alexander Hamilton, but he generally favoured the latter, angering those who supported the French revolutionary cause and wanted another war with Britain. When Washington's second term ended, he refused to stand for a third, setting a precedent that held for 140 years.

His calm, dignified leadership was followed by a civilized return to private life at Mount Vernon, where this democratic hero of talent and decency, the founder of a future superpower, died of a throat infection in 1799. His principled steadfastness is best summed up by the plausible story of how, as a boy, he chopped down his father's favourite cherry tree. When confronted, he confessed his guilt with the words: 'I cannot tell a lie.'

Thomas Jefferson

1743–1826

I think this is the most extraordinary collection of talent and of human knowledge that has ever been gathered together at the White House — with the possible exception of when Thomas Jefferson dined alone.

J.F. Kennedy, welcoming 49 Nobel Prize winners to the White House in 1962

Thomas Jefferson was a radical polymath who put into words the principles of the American Revolution and then put those words into practice as a statesman. Private, intense and simultaneously possessed of matchless generosity of spirit, grace and sensitivity, Jefferson was a man almost without compare who advanced the cause of liberty across the world.

Jefferson's intellect was second to none. The son of a wealthy Virginian planter, he could, at college and while studying law, as a close friend recalled, 'tear himself away from his dearest friends, to fly to his studies'. Gracious and charming in manner, he nonetheless had an intense dislike of oral debate and rarely spoke in public. But the intricate brilliance of the young politician was quickly noted in Virginia's colonial legislature.

Jefferson's power was in his pen. It is enshrined in the Declaration of Independence. As a delegate at the Second Continental Congress in Philadelphia in 1776, Jefferson became the chief author of the document repudiating British sovereignty. In his exposition he championed universal liberty and equality. It was the first charter of civil rights, the founding document of freedom. The stamp of Jefferson's peerless mind, his determination to secure liberty and his immense generosity towards his fellow men are apparent in the Declaration's every word.

Elected to the new Virginia House of Delegates, Jefferson was determined to translate his ideals into practice in Virginia's new constitution. He secured the abolition of primogeniture and entail. He tried in vain to introduce a scheme of universal education but

America's first Middle East war

In one of the first acts of his presidency in 1801, Thomas Jefferson refused to pay the pirate state of Tripoli the extortionate tribute it demanded in return for safe passage of American ships on the high seas. In so doing, he sent America for the first time into combat against an Islamic power in the Middle East.

Nominally vassals of the Ottoman Empire, but in reality independent states run by corsair dynasties, the regencies of Algiers, Tunis and Tripoli were known, along with the sultanate of Morocco, as the Barbary States. Unashamedly piratical, they existed very profitably on the revenue garnered from slave trading, looting, tribute and ransom.

The ships of the newly independent United States, now lacking British naval protection, were prime targets. Only substantial tributes could secure them some relief. By 1801 America was paying out 20 per cent of her annual federal revenue to the pirate states. When Jefferson assumed the presidency, he was determined to prove that war was preferable to tribute and ransom.

The Karamanli dynasty of Tripoli ruled what is now Libya. Pasha Yusuf Karamanli – like Colonel Muammar Gaddafi, Libya's dictator since 1969 – defied American power: 'I do not fear war, it is my trade.' Prospects initially looked bleak. In October 1803 the USS *Philadelphia* was shipwrecked and its crew taken captive by Tripoli. Infiltrating Tripoli harbour in February

later succeeded in founding the University of Virginia, which he considered among his greatest achievements. A deist himself, Jefferson pushed through a statute for religious freedom that established the complete separation of church and state, a division that lies at the very core of American democracy.

Jefferson's passionate belief in freedom at times made his liberalism somewhat anarchic. 'Was ever such a prize won with so little blood?' he asked during the early years of the French Revolution. He earned a reputation as a demagogic radical, but as the third president of the United States from 1801 Jefferson showed restraint and sensitivity in preventing the ideological schism that threatened to fracture the infant nation. He was an extraordinarily intense man,

1804, a daring young officer named Stephen Decatur set fire to the *Philadelphia* and thwarted the corsairs' hopes of turning the pride of the US fleet into a pirate ship. But his attempts to blow up Tripoli's fleet backfired, killing 11 US servicemen.

The erstwhile US consul to Tunis, William Eaton, managed almost single-handedly to reverse the fortunes of war. A maverick, educated at the elite Dartmouth College, fluent in Greek and Latin, a veteran of the Indian wars who could throw a knife with deadly precision from 80 feet, Eaton fulminated at the prospect of 'bartering our national glory for the forbearance of a Barbary pirate'. He proposed conquering Tunis with a force of 1000 marines. Then he suggested ways of enforcing regime change in Libya. The US secretary of state rejected both proposals.

Eaton acted unilaterally instead. He recruited a Karamanli prince, Hamet, in Egypt, and with 9 marines and a mercenary force of 400 he led his motley troop of Arabs and Christians on a 500-mile desert march to launch a surprise attack on Tripoli's second-largest city, Derna (modern Darnah). In the fierce pitched battle that ensued, Eaton and Hamet emerged triumphant. But Eaton's plans to make good his coup and march on Tripoli were thwarted. The pasha hastily offered the USA a treaty, which US naval officials immediately negotiated. Hamet was sent back to Egypt. Deeply disappointed, Eaton returned to America – a renegade hero whose role in American history has never been fully acknowledged.

but was almost incapable of animosity. 'We are all Republicans – we are all Federalists,' he declared at his inauguration.

The Republican Jefferson believed government's paramount duty was to protect the individual's right to 'life, and liberty, and the pursuit of happiness'. He deplored the Federalists' readiness to curtail civil rights in the supposed interests of the nation. But he concealed his extraordinary passions. His even-tempered approach quelled fears. Americans embraced Republican principles, realizing that Jefferson's protection of liberty would protect them too.

Jefferson's Louisiana Purchase of 1803 nearly doubled the size of the United States. This bold move, seizing on Napoleon's unexpected offer to sell French territory, was a decision taken (as Jefferson freely admitted) without constitutional authority. It was an act that secured America's stability and created what Jefferson called an 'empire for liberty'. It also earned him a landslide election to a second term as president.

The man who declared that 'all men are created equal' has been censured for his racial attitudes. Jefferson was a staunch opponent of slavery, yet he owned large numbers of slaves on his Virginian plantation. His only book, Notes on Virginia, revealed in its discussion of slavery a deep opposition to racial mixing and at times a surprising degree of racism.

Jefferson recognized his fundamental hypocrisy, based on an irreconcilable opposition between justice and self-preservation. 'We have the wolf by the ears,' he remarked of slavery to a friend, 'and we can neither hold him nor safely let him go.' Jefferson was no less anxious to shield his private life from posterity than from his contemporaries, but what we know of it shows the confusion of his attitudes. It has only recently been revealed that while ambassador to France (1785–9) Jefferson began a long relationship with his slave Sally Hemings (who was the half-sister of his beloved deceased wife Martha).

Jefferson's energy and creativity were phenomenal. He knew French, Italian, Spanish, Latin, Greek and Anglo-Saxon. At 71 he read Plato in the original (he thought it overrated). He collated Native American dialects. He was a keen archaeologist who pioneered new methods of excavation on the Indian burial mounds on his estate, and an oenophile who promoted the establishment of American vineyards. He smuggled back plants and seeds from his travels to enrich his new country. He invented a swivel chair and an early form of automatic door. He was a magnificent architect: his own constructions – the University of Virginia and his Virginian estate of Monticello – are now World Heritage Sites. His library, which he left to the American nation, became the Library of Congress.

At the White House President Jefferson greeted guests in his slippers. The 'sage of Monticello' welcomed visitors, only occasionally escaping to his retreat at Poplar Forest for the solitude he craved. All America wanted to sit at the feet of the Republican radical who had proved himself America's greatest architect. He died, like his old friend John Adams, on 4 July 1826, the 50th anniversary of the day their Declaration of Independence promulgated freedom across the world.

Toussaint Louverture c.1743–1803

The Spartacus ... whose destiny it was to avenge the wrongs committed on his race.

Comte de Lavaux, the French governor-general of Saint-Domingue, describing Toussaint

Toussaint Louverture was the founding father of Haiti. A plantation slave himself, he won his own freedom and went on to help emancipate hundreds of thousands of others and to found the world's first black state. He was a skilful politician and general who led the Haitian revolution from the early 1790s and drove the mighty European powers of France, Spain and Britain out of Haiti. Though at times his enemies found him harsh and uncompromising, he left behind a nation free from slavery and transformed by his enlightened leadership.

Toussaint once said, 'I was born a slave, but nature gave me a soul of a free man.' His early years demonstrated this perfectly. He was born François Dominique Toussaint to a father who had been shipped by French slave traders to Saint-Domingue (the French colony, later called Haiti, occupying the western third of the island of Hispaniola). Toussaint rose swiftly through the ranks of service under his owner, the Comte de Bréda. Naturally intelligent and fortunate enough to acquire a basic education in French and Latin, he rejected the voodoo beliefs of many of his fellow slaves and remained an ardent Catholic all his life. By 1777 he had served as a livestock handler, healer and coachman, finally becoming Bréda's plantation steward, a post normally reserved for a white man.

Toussaint won his freedom at the age of 34 and thereafter farmed a plot of 15 acres with 13 slaves of his own. The first uprising of the Haitian revolution broke out under the mulatto reformer Vincent Ogé in 1790, but Toussaint took no part. In August 1791 another revolt erupted as thousands of black slaves across Saint-Domingue rose in rebellion. Toussaint realized that this larger rising could not be ignored. After helping Bréda's family to escape and sending his

Bolívar and the liberators

Toussaint was just one figure in a line of inspiring liberators of the European possessions in Latin America who could also claim a place in our list of heroes.

Francisco de Miranda (1750–1816) is still an icon in Venezuela, where he led the struggle for independence. As a young man Miranda associated with the high aristocracy of Europe and while visiting Russia was rumoured to have had an affair with the Empress Catherine the Great. His lifelong dream was to unify South America in an empire called Gran Colombia. In 1806 he led a British-backed invasion of Venezuela; by 1811 the country had declared independence and Miranda assumed dictatorial powers. Facing a massive colonial counterattack, Miranda signed an armistice with Spain, which led to accusations of treachery. He was handed over to the Spanish and died in a Cadiz prison in 1816. Miranda is still known as 'The Precursor'.

Simón Bolívar (1783–1830) realized much of Miranda's dream of South American unification in a quest that encompassed most of the continent. The son of a wealthy mining family, in 1808 Bolívar joined the Venezuelan resistance movement. After Miranda's fall, Bolívar led the recapture of Venezuela in 1813 and was hailed as *El Libertador* ('The Liberator') on establishing the Second Republic. Bolívar next fought in Colombia and gained Haitian support for revolutionary conquests that, by 1821, had

own family to safety on the Spanish side of the island, he joined the rebel ranks.

There were more than half a million slaves on Saint-Domingue, compared to just 32,000 European colonists and 24,000 *affranchis* (freed mulattoes and blacks). Although the black army was a ragtag and ill-equipped bunch, their superior numbers and Toussaint's brilliant drilling in guerrilla tactics soon told. He gained the surname Louverture in recognition of his brilliant generalship (l'ouverture being 'the opening' or, in military terms, 'the breakthrough').

In 1793 war broke out between France and Spain. By this time Toussaint was a major figure in the black Haitian army. His leadership was widely admired and he had attracted talented allies such

resulted in the establishment of Gran Colombia. This federation, with Bolívar as president, covered much of modern Venezuela, Colombia, Panama and Ecuador. In 1824 he became dictator of Peru and in 1825 Bolivia was created. However, this vast empire proved unruly, and in 1830 he resigned; he died of tuberculosis before he could sail for exile in Europe. He is remembered as a hero throughout the Americas.

José de San Martín (1778–1850) fought for freedom in Argentina, Chile and Peru. Between 1812 and 1816 he played a major part in the establishment of an independent Argentina. In 1817 he crossed the Andes with an army – a feat comparable to Hannibal's crossing of the Alps. The following year he and the Chilean *libertador* Bernardo O'Higgins freed Chile from the Spanish. By 1822 San Martín had completed the liberation of Peru. After the death of his wife and perhaps to avoid a confrontation with Bolívar, in 1824 San Martín left South America for Europe, where he lived out his days in Belgium, England and France.

Bernardo O'Higgins (1778–1842) was the hero of Chilean freedom. He acquired his improbable name as the illegitimate son of a Spanish officer originally from County Sligo in Ireland. He studied in London and knew Miranda. From 1810 O'Higgins fought with the nationalist rebels, and in 1817 he joined forces with San Martín. After the Battle of Chacabuco in 1817, O'Higgins became the first ruler of independent Chile. He was deposed by a conservative coup in 1823 and lived the rest of his life in exile, dying in Lima, Peru.

as Jean-Jacques Dessalines and Henry Christophe, both future leaders of Haiti. Toussaint joined the Spanish and served with distinction in a series of engagements.

The following year the pressure told on the French and the revolutionary government in Paris declared an end to slavery. In what has been seen by some as an underhand about-turn against his former allies, Toussaint abandoned the Spanish and declared his new allegiance to France. The French governor of Saint-Domingue, the Comte de Lavaux, appointed him lieutenant-governor and the Spanish were expelled.

By 1795 Toussaint was widely seen as a hero. The freed blacks adored him, while the whites and mulattoes respected his hard but fair line on the economy, in which he allowed the return of émigré planters and used military discipline to force idlers to work. Favouring racial reconciliation between blacks and whites, he held the firm belief that – despite their history of oppression, enslavement and persecution – his country's blacks could learn valuable lessons from white people. His personal popularity and political shrewdness allowed him to outlast a succession of French governors.

His political cunning was in evidence in 1798–9, when after a series of secret negotiations Toussaint negotiated a British withdrawal from Haiti. The political settlement allowed Toussaint to sell sugar and buy arms and goods. He undertook not to invade British territories such as Jamaica but rejected their offer of conferring on him the title 'king of Haiti' – all his life he maintained that he was a true French citizen.

In 1801 Toussaint invaded the Spanish side of Hispaniola, overrunning the entire island, freeing the Spanish slaves and surprising the defeated non-blacks with his magnanimity in victory. He declared himself governor-general and strove to convince Napoleon of his loyalty.

Napoleon, however, was not to be convinced. He considered Toussaint an obstacle to the profitability of Haiti and an affront to the honour of France. In December 1801 Napoleon sent a powerful invading force under his brother-in-law General Charles Leclerc (accompanied by Napoleon's nymphomaniacal sister Pauline) to depose Toussaint.

Months of heavy fighting ended in May 1802, when Toussaint agreed to lay down his arms and retire to his farm. But he was not allowed to remain in his beloved country. He and his family were arrested and Toussaint was taken in a warship to France, where he was transferred in August to Fort-de-Joux in the Alps. Heartbroken and alone in a tiny dungeon, he wrote letters begging Napoleon for a fair trial. Napoleon never answered, and Toussaint died of pneumonia in 1803. It was a sad end to a great life, but his legacy – the Free Black Republic of Haiti – lived on.

John Paul Jones

1747–1792

I have drawn my sword in the ... struggle for the rights of men ... I am not in arms as an American, nor am I in pursuit of riches ... I profess myself a citizen of the world.

John Paul Jones, 4 August 1785, as he restored to the Earl of Selkirk a silver plate he had taken in a raid on the Kirkcudbrightshire coast seven years previously

The founder of the US Navy and a maverick fighting admiral, John Paul Jones had the rambunctious, ruthless energy to change the course of a sea battle and emerge victorious. His successes during the American War of Independence may not have been strategically decisive, but they gave the Americans confidence in the strength of their own sea power and earned Jones his reputation as the first hero of the American navy.

John Paul (as he was born) spent his boyhood in Scotland. At the age of 13 he was apprenticed to a merchant ship and sailed across he Atlantic to the Caribbean and the eastern seaboard of North America a number of times, at least twice on board slavers. He was an able and tough seaman, and his toughness sometimes got him into trouble: in 1770 he was accused of flogging a sailor so severely that he later died, and in 1773 he killed the ringleader of a mutiny in self-defence. To evade the consequences he became a Freemason, moved to America and assumed the surname Jones.

In 1766, following the outbreak of the American War of Independence, Jones fought against the British first on board the USS *Alfred*, then as commander of the 21-gun sloop *Providence*, conveying men and supplies from New England to New York and Philadelphia. His success in this, and in capturing and burning British prizes, led to his promotion to captain. He was sent to Europe in command of the *Ranger*, to take the war to the enemy's home waters.

Throughout the spring of 1778 Jones and his men harassed the English coast. Moving north, they raided the peninsula in Kirkcudbright Bay known as St Mary's Isle, part of the estate of the Earl of Selkirk in southwest Scotland, near to his own birthplace.

When his crew demanded plunder, Jones politely relieved the Countess of Selkirk of a silver plate with the family crest. Seven years later, when the opportunity arose, he returned it.

Following this episode, Jones sailed across the Irish Sea and captured the Royal Navy ship *Drake*, which he carried to France. Benjamin Franklin, the American diplomat stationed in Paris, rewarded him with command of the *Bonhomme Richard*, a much larger ship than the *Ranger*. Accompanied by four smaller ships, the *Bonhomme Richard* sailed for Britain, and on 23 September 1779 the American squadron intercepted two Royal Navy ships guarding a merchant convoy off Flamborough Head.

It was a confusing and hair-raising battle, lasting three and a half hours. At one point during the fight, the American ensign on the *Bonhomme Richard* was shot away. The captain of the Royal Navy frigate *Serapis* asked whether the *Bonhomme Richard* had struck its colours as

Famous corpses, lost and found

On 18 July 1792 John Paul Jones was discovered face down and dead on his bed in Paris. His body was buried at the St Louis cemetery, preserved in a leaden coffin in case either America or Russia wished to claim it. When neither did, its location was forgotten until 1905, when the US ambassador Horace Parker concluded a six-year hunt in the putrid crypts below the streets of Paris.

The body was shipped back to the United States with a naval escort of nine battleships. In 1913 Jones, to the thunder of 15 gun salutes, was finally and expensively laid to rest in a marble tomb beneath the chapel of the US Naval Academy in Annapolis, accompanied by a moving speech from former US president Theodore Roosevelt. Thus, Jones's body joined the many notable corpses to enjoy a life after death in the world of necro-politics.

After the Restoration of Charles II in 1660, Oliver Cromwell's body was exhumed and his head stuck on a pole – the traditional fate of traitors. Eventually, the head blew down in a gale and disappeared. After resurfacing in the 1770s, it was sold from one dealer to another, and in 1935 it was finally identified as the real thing. It was buried somewhere under the lawns (to avoid ghouls) in Sidney Sussex College, Cambridge, in 1960, three hundred years after leaving the ground.

During the French Revolution, in 1793, a shopkeeper broke into Cardinal Richelieu's tomb, broke off the head from the embalmed body and then, peeling off the skin, stole the Cardinal's face. It passed from

a sign of surrender, but was disabused when Jones, with legendary defiance, shouted 'I have not yet begun to fight!'

The *Bonhomme Richard* had its mainmast blown away and was holed below the waterline, but Jones managed to manoeuvre his battered ship alongside the *Serapis*, boarding and capturing it. Shortly afterwards his own ship sank. The other Royal Navy ship, the *Countess of Scarborough*, was also captured. Jones took his prizes back to the Netherlands and on to France, where he was hailed as a hero, awarded with the Ordre du mérite militaire and presented by Louis XVI with a gold-plated sword. Back in America, Congress passed a vote of thanks, and Jones took the only American ship of the line, the *America*, back to France.

The War of Independence over, Jones was engaged by the Russian empress, Catherine the Great, as a rear-admiral in the Russian navy to serve under her partner in love and power, Prince Potemkin, who in

---

owner to owner until 1866, when Emperor Napoleon III ordered it to be rejoined to its original owner.

After Napoleon's death in 1821, his body was kept on St Helena for twenty years, the headstone unmarked because the British would not consent to describe him as 'Emperor', preferring 'General'. When Louis-Philippe took the French throne in 1830, he backed attempts to honour Napoleon's will and have him buried by the River Seine. The body was returned to France in 1840 for an impressive military funeral and buried in a magnificent tomb on the Esplanade des Invalides.

Eva ('Evita') Perón was the wife and greatest political asset of Juan Perón, president of Argentina from 1946 to 1955, and after her tragic early death in 1952 support for her husband's regime waned. Those who ousted him from power were terrified that Evita's body would become the focus for Perónist opposition, such was the love and awe she had commanded, even in death. So her embalmed body was spirited into anonymous graves in Italy and Spain until the 1970s, when Perón returned to power. After his death in 1974, his widow and successor as president, Isabel Perón, brought Evita's body back to Argentina. It now lies in a tomb apparently secure enough to withstand a nuclear attack.

Organ thieves have often targeted famous heads, hearts and penises for profit. Napoleon's inch-long 'shrivelled object' was offered for sale at Christie's in 1969. There were no takers. In 2004 an object said to be Rasputin's penis (an impressive 12 inches/ 30cm) was put on display in St Petersburg.

1788 placed Jones in command of the ships-of-the-line squadron in his new Black Sea Russian fleet. Jones helped achieve a crushing victory in which 15 Turkish vessels were destroyed and 4700 Turks killed or captured. Russian losses were minimal. Jones helped blockade the Turkish fortress at Ochakov, enabling Prince Potemkin to capture it. Despite the intrigues of jealous rivals and Potemkin's irritation, Jones was hailed as a hero and awarded the Order of St Anne by Catherine.

In 1789 Jones took advantage of a two-year leave of absence from the Russian navy to tour the major European cities, ending up in Paris in 1790. There he remained, in retirement, until his death two years later.

Prince Talleyrand
1754–1838

It seems to me that one will do him no injustice in accepting him for what he claimed to be: the type, the representative, of the times in which he lived. But, good God! What times!

Baron de Vitrolles

Talleyrand was the undisputed grandmaster of diplomacy, an actor on the national and international stage whose political longevity is testimony to his genius as a statesman. Undeniably venal, supposedly amoral in character and capable of ruthlessness in pursuit of his goals, but also charming and witty, Talleyrand was surprisingly consistent in his admirable views. A champion of tolerance and liberalism, in government he advocated an English-style constitutional monarchy, in international affairs a balance of power and the rule of law. He remained all his life a dedicated enemy of power that was founded on conquest and force.

Born into an ancient noble family, Charles-Maurice de Talleyrand-Périgord was destined for the Church as a result of a 'dislocated foot', a disability that also prompted his parents to, effectively, disinherit him in favour of his younger brother. Talleyrand learned early on that charm and wiliness could more than compensate for his club foot.

Talleyrand seemed able to flourish in every circumstance. As the successful, if supremely decadent, Bishop of Autun, during the last years of Louis XVI (1754–93), he argued vigorously for the Church's privileges yet became the revolutionary clergyman who equally enthusiastically dismantled them. He was always a moderate. Through a timely departure abroad on diplomatic affairs (1792), he escaped the guillotine's worst excesses, living in England and America. On returning to a less bloodthirsty France in 1796, he managed to refute charges of counter-revolutionary behaviour, became foreign minister (1797) and struck up an alliance with the rising General Napoleon Bonaparte, organizing his seizure of power. As foreign minister, Talleyrand went on to help design Napoleon's rise to the position of Emperor of the French, serving as his grand chamberlain and becoming Prince of Benevento. He played his part in some of Napoleon's excesses – notably the kidnapping and execution of the Duke of Enghien and the disastrous Spanish adventure – but he grasped quickly that Napoleon's ambitions had become despotic and self-serving. Talleyrand, humiliated by the emperor who described him as 'excrement in a silk stocking', now worked to undermine him.

Above all, in an age dominated by war, Talleyrand wanted to secure peace and stability in Europe, even if the means involved mendacity and secret intrigues. At the 1808 Congress of Erfurt he secretly persuaded Russia to oppose Napoleon's European designs and henceforth helped Tsar Alexander I to overthrow Napoleon. (Talleyrand was also acting as matchmaker for Napoleon, brokering his marriage to Marie-Louise of Austria and securing a religious settlement with the pope.) On Napoleon's fall in 1814, Talleyrand supervised the capitulation of Paris, welcoming the conquering Alexander into his house, fostering the restoration of the Bourbon King Louis XVIII and forming a liberal ministry as premier.

Talleyrand's most audacious diplomacy, though, resulted in the 1815 Treaty of Vienna. Roundly defeated, and viewed in Europe as hopelessly aggressive and regicidal, republican France faced partition by the victorious allies. Talleyrand managed to gain France a place at the table and then fracture the anti-French alliance. The resulting treaty restored France to her 1792 borders, with no reparations to pay, effectively still a great power.

After Napoleon's brief resurgence and defeat at Waterloo in 1815,

Talleyrand again became prime minister, advocating a liberal monarchy on the English model. Forced out by ultra-royalists, he remained a respected grandee until another revolution overturned the stubborn Bourbons in 1830. He then returned in triumph under the July Monarchy of King Louis-Philippe to become ambassador to London in 1830, the glorious culmination of a diplomatic career of over 40 years.

In pure moral terms, Talleyrand suffers. He lived lavishly, courted bribes (offending the rather more correct American diplomats) and was exuberantly promiscuous, fathering at least four illegitimate children. But his principles were consistent. A co-author of the Declaration of the Rights of Man, he was a son of the Enlightenment who had praised its ideals since his seminary youth. His faith in a constitutional monarchy drove him to support the candidate who seemed most likely to secure it. This necessitated chameleon-like changes of alliance in the turbulence of revolutionary France and brought accusations of oppor-

Morning rituals of the old aristocracy

'No one who has not lived under the Ancien Régime,' once murmured Charles-Maurice de Talleyrand, 'will know how sweet life can be.' But those living in the France of Napoleon and the Bourbons who attended Talleyrand's daily semi-public *lever* – the last of its kind – were given a startling glimpse of the extraordinary pomp and precision of this vanished world.

Talleyrand devoted the first two hours of every morning to his *lever* – the serious business of rising. Like the monarchs of pre-revolutionary France, permanently surrounded by a horde of courtiers and onlookers watching and assisting his every move, Talleyrand made getting dressed a public event. His rooms were open to all who wished to attend – provided they were amusing, or at least furnished with up-to-date news and gossip.

Talleyrand's *lever* was an incomparable opportunity for networking and the exchange of information and repartee. Statesmen and society ladies, doctors, academics, financiers, on occasion the tsar of Russia, all were regular visitors to the prince's apartments. As 11 o'clock approached and men and women of all ages intrigued and debated the events of the day, Talleyrand limped into the room swathed in white flannel and nightcap, a mummified figure who slept in a bed with a deep hollow because he was terrified of falling out of it.

tunistic treachery. When Talleyrand called brie the 'king of cheeses', a contemporary remarked that it was the only king that he had never betrayed! But he was hardly unique in his dissimulation.

Although Talleyrand was modern in his beliefs, he belonged to an older French tradition in his methods. In this, he ranks alongside the two outstanding French statesmen of an earlier age: Armand Jean, Duc du Plessis, better known as Cardinal Richelieu (1585–1642), the brilliant minister of Louis XIII, and his Italian-born protégé Giulio Mazarini (1602–61), who became Cardinal Mazarin, lover of Louis XIII's widow Anne of Austria and prime minister of France, and who managed to restore stability at a time of civil war and train Louis XIV in statesmanship. These three politicians personify the ruthless subtlety and superlative style of French leadership at its best.

Diplomatic to the last, on his deathbed Talleyrand was reconciled with the Church and received the last sacraments.

The elderly Courtiade, the most famous valet of the age, directed proceedings. Two junior valets dressed Talleyrand's long grey hair as he sat in a chair by the fire. A sponge in a silver bowl was brought to him. After he had wiped his face, Talleyrand's hat was immediately set upon his pomade-drenched locks.

The man who kept the best table in France confined himself to a breakfast of a single cup of camomile tea, followed by two cups of warm water which he inhaled through his nostrils and expelled through his mouth.

Dressed from the neck up, the seated figure then had his legs unwrapped. The 'dislocated foot' about which Talleyrand was so sensitive was unashamedly revealed; his long, flat left foot and the stunted, gnarled right one were washed and dried. Pursued by his valets as he then meandered around the room, signing letters, listening to newspaper articles and issuing a stream of his famously understated *bon mots*, Talleyrand was unswaddled and helped into an array of clothes that were almost equally bulky.

Two hours after he had first limped into the room, Talleyrand, clad in a mass of cravats and waistcoats and several pairs of stockings, allowed his valets to add the finishing touch: his breeches. Fully dressed, his paperwork done, gossip exchanged, filled in on the news of the day, Talleyrand was ready to face the world.

Wolfgang Amadeus Mozart 1756–1791

I cannot write about Mozart. I can only worship him.

Richard Strauss

Born in Salzburg, Austria, Wolfgang Amadeus Mozart was the epitome of genius, a child prodigy who went on to become one of the most brilliant composers in the history of Western classical music. Leaping from one musical genre to the next, in his short life Mozart composed some of the greatest and most melodic compositions of all time.

As a child virtuoso on the keyboard Mozart was the musical wonder of his age, touring Europe's capitals and courts with his sister, Nannerl, under the direction of their father, Leopold, himself a musician who was quick to recognize his children's precocious talents. As both a fond parent and an assiduous publicist, Leopold dressed his children in the latest fashions and airily reported that: 'We keep company only with aristocrats and other distinguished persons.' Wolfgang began composing at the age of five, was a seasoned performer at seven, and had written his first symphony by eight. Of Mozart's early compositions, Leopold wrote with satisfaction, 'Imagine the noise these sonatas will make in the world when it says on the title page that they are the work of a child of seven.'

Even the sceptics realized that no trickery lay behind the child's precocity. By the still tender age of 13, Wolfgang was an artist of unrivalled musical understanding, of whom Johann Hasse (1699–1783), one of the era's eminent composers, was said to have remarked that 'he has done things which for such an age are really incomprehensible; they would be astonishing in an adult'.

Mozart's versatility was astounding. He wrote chamber music, operas, symphonies, masses; he virtually invented the solo piano concerto, and his use of counterpoint was as revelatory as his limpid melodies and subtle harmonic shifts. He composed with legendary speed – his magnificent 'Jupiter' symphony, No. 41 in C Major, was written in a mere 16 days, and he reportedly composed the overture to his opera *Don Giovanni* on the night before the work premiered. The range of his genius only increased over the years – from the exuberant violin concerti of his teens, dazzling operas such as *The Marriage of Figaro* and *The Magic Flute*, and masterpieces in late Classical style such as the Clarinet Quintet from 1789. His death at 35 left the musical world with the perpetual enigma of what might have been, had this sublimely talented composer lived to old age.

Fellow composers never wavered in their recognition of his genius. To Josef Haydn (1732–1809), the musical elder statesman of the time, he was 'the greatest composer . . . either in person or by name', while the 'magic sounds of Mozart's music' left Franz Schubert (1797–1828) awestruck. The public response was more capricious. Some judged his last three symphonies 'difficult', and other works were criticized for being 'audacious' or too complex. But he was held in high regard at the time of his death, and today layman and professional alike recognize what one conductor has described as 'the seriousness in his charm, the loftiness in his beauty'.

Mozart's princely patrons were less deferential. Perennially short of money, Mozart's frustration at his lack of independence and his pitiful wages often led to stormy relations. From 1773 he was engaged to compose at the Salzburg court, but in 1781, summoned to produce music for Emperor Joseph II's court in Vienna, he was angry to find himself in the role of a servant, with a correspondingly meagre salary. He angrily demanded his release, which was – as he wrote in a letter of June that year – granted 'with a kick on my arse . . . by order of our worthy Prince Archbishop'.

Throughout his life, Mozart displayed the same mix of playfulness and seriousness that shines through his music. He was an affectionate child, and his difficult relationship with his domineering father led him to constantly seek approval: visiting Vienna, the six-year-old Mozart apparently jumped into Empress Maria Theresa's lap for a hug. The adult Mozart, always physically small, retained this childlike manner in his wilful extravagance, his open and sometimes crude sexuality and the distinctive, scatological humour that had led the teenage Mozart to write to his first love: 'Now I wish

Who was the greatest composer?

From the formal structures of the Baroque style, to the wild musical Romanticism that came from the German *Sturm und Drang* ('storm and stress'), to the cool elegance of the Modernist movement – each era produces its particular champions, the composers whose chords and variations best embody the passions and preoccupations of their time.

While a difficult life is not essential to great artistry, certainly many composers had more than their fair share of strife. But despite, and perhaps because of, their difficulties, their music often triumphed. The underpaid Mozart and the fragile Tchaikovsky composed works of transcendent joy, and Beethoven's late works, composed as he was engulfed by deafness, are among the most sublime ever created. Even Shostakovich, in 1936 criticized by Stalin through the communist *Pravda* newspaper for composing Modernist music, managed a touch of sarcasm in the deliberately banal melodies of his Symphony No. 5 in D Minor – today wryly subtitled 'A Soviet artist's response to just criticism'.

Not all great composers had to struggle. Handel was a celebrity in Georgian England and Haydn was, during his lifetime, a revered figure, nicknamed 'Papa Haydn' by the musical establishment and fêted by the European aristocracy. Many composers whom we now consider great were not so famous in their own time but influenced later generations. The

a good night, shit into your bed until it creaks.'

The composer for whom, as he put it, composing was the only 'joy and passion' was no solitary genius. While in later years his relationship with his father deteriorated, his love for his wife, Constanze, was abiding – despite Leopold's disapproval. Nevertheless, after Leopold's death in 1787 Mozart, now permanently in Vienna, went through a period when he composed less. Fearing poverty, he produced a stream of begging letters to patrons, acquaintances and his fellow Freemasons. While never destitute, Mozart had to rely on income from teaching and performances of his works. He lived beyond his means, having a weakness for fashionable clothes while also paying off debts to friends and publishers.

contrapuntal style of the Baroque master J.S. Bach, considered somewhat outdated and provincial during his lifetime, fascinated Mozart and Haydn, and it was revived by the early Romantic composer Mendelssohn at a time when Bach was rarely performed.

The development of classical music from the early Baroque to the mid-20th century can, in fact, be seen as a 'chain' of composers, each handing on new discoveries and developments and taking music further. This chain travelled from Mozart, through Beethoven and on to Wagner, master of operatic High Romanticism, before the music of Stravinsky ushered in the era of Modernism with a kind of music that was previously unheard. After that, the avant garde of the 1960s and beyond composed music that broke all previous boundaries, from the atonal adventures of Pierre Boulez to the minimalism of Philip Glass and Steve Reich.

Legend has it that Lenin was so moved by Beethoven's *Appassionata* piano sonata that he could not listen to it again, for fear it would make him too weak for revolution. When Stravinsky's revolutionary ballet *The Rite of Spring* was premiered in Paris in 1913, fights broke out in the theatre in response to the dancers' interpretation of its paganistic subject. Music matters – it can undoubtedly strike to the soul's core. It can shock, delight, amaze, soothe, agitate – and even cause a riot.

But naming the 'greatest' of all composers is a fruitless task – we each have composers who strike a particular chord in our soul and whose music, for us, is the greatest ever written.

Mozart's last composition, the Requiem that became his own, is surrounded by mystery. Legend has it that Salieri, a jealous fellow composer, poisoned Mozart as he worked frantically on this composition, which had been anonymously commissioned by letter. But an acute attack of rheumatic fever (and a noble patron intent on passing off Mozart's compositions as his own) is probably nearer the truth. Even so, Mozart's modest burial – although not quite the pauper's of repute – sealed the myth of the neglected genius.

Admiral Nelson

1758–1805

Before this time tomorrow, I shall have gained a peerage, or Westminster Abbey.

Horatio Nelson, on the eve of the Battle of the Nile (1798)

Horatio Nelson was one of the most daring naval commanders in history, who, through a series of stunning victories, assured British supremacy at sea during the Revolutionary and Napoleonic Wars. He was adored in his own day, despite a complicated and very public love life, and has been celebrated ever since as the man who, by defeating the French and Spanish fleets off Cape Trafalgar in 1805, saved Britain from invasion. His death at the moment of victory wins him a special place in the pantheon of British military heroes.

When Nelson was 13, his uncle, a naval captain, took him to sea aboard the *Raisonnable*. For the next eight years Nelson learned the trade of a naval officer in the West Indies and on an expedition to the Arctic. He first saw action in the American War of Independence, and by the age of 21 he was captain of the frigate *Hinchinbrooke*. He was brave and often impatient; this endeared him to some but could make him unpopular.

When war broke out with Revolutionary France in 1793 Nelson was sent to the Mediterranean. He lost his right eye during the siege of Calvi in 1794, having been hit in the face by stones thrown up by enemy shot. In March 1795, as captain of the 64-gun *Agamemnon*, he took a leading role in taking two French ships.

The arrival of Sir John Jervis as commander-in-chief of the Mediterranean fleet was very useful to Nelson, for Jervis gave him free rein to exploit his natural abilities as a leader. During the Battle of Cape St Vincent, Nelson was at the head of the boarding party that took the Spanish ship *San Nicolas* and then the larger *San Josef*. It was unprecedented for an officer of Nelson's rank to throw himself into the heat of battle in such a manner, and he lapped up the public admiration that followed his success, along with the knighthood and promotion to rear-admiral.

Despite Nelson's personal fame, morale amongst the ordinary seamen of the Royal Navy was low, and 1797 saw mutinies in British waters. Nelson was given command of the *Theseus* and once again led raiding parties from the front, dragging his crew's spirits up by sheer force of character – something that became known as 'the Nelson Touch'. While attempting to storm the town of Santa Cruz, Tenerife, Nelson was seriously wounded, and his right arm had to be amputated. In 1798 he won a stunning victory over the French fleet at the Battle of the Nile. Although massively outgunned, the British fleet blew up the massive 120-gun *L'Orient* and took or sunk ten more ships of the line and two frigates. 'Victory is not enough to describe such a scene,' wrote Nelson, soon to be Baron Nelson of the Nile. All of Europe was watching, and the anti-French coalition was boosted immensely by the performance of the Royal Navy.

Between 1798 and 1800 Nelson spent much of his time in Sicily in the arms of Emma, Lady Hamilton, a liaison that caused great scandal, as the young Emma Hamilton was married to the elderly British envoy to Naples. Lady Hamilton bore Nelson a child in 1801, on the same day that Nelson learned he was to be posted as second-in-command of the British fleet off the coast of Denmark. In April the British demolished the Danish fleet at Copenhagen. During the battle, when his commander, Vice-Admiral Parker, raised a flagged signal for a withdrawal, Nelson famously ignored the order by placing his telescope to his blind eye.

Nelson was made a viscount, and in 1803 he was sent back to the Mediterranean as commander-in-chief of the fleet there. Much of 1804 was spent chasing the French fleet back and forth across the Atlantic – a pursuit that captivated the British public. On his return to London, he was mobbed in the street wherever he went.

In 1805 Nelson achieved his apotheosis. On 21 October he engaged the combined French and Spanish fleets, under his arch-enemy Admiral Villeneuve, off Cape Trafalgar. He took 27 ships to engage 33 enemy vessels, signalling by flag to his own men 'England expects that every man will do his duty.' Five hours of fighting began at noon, and, thanks to Nelson's bold and ingenious tactics, by 5pm the British were comprehensively victorious. But early in the battle Nelson had been hit by a musket shot, which punctured his lung and lodged in his spine. He died at 4.30pm, allegedly whispering to a comrade officer, 'Kiss me, Hardy.'

Only one British naval hero comes close to Nelson. Admiral Thomas

Powder monkeys and naval guns

A gun battle at sea was loud, confusing and violent. The huge shot that came from enemy cannon could rip holes in the sides of a ship, tearing human bodies to shreds in a single burst. But the heat, smoke and violent recoil from the cannon on deck could be just as dangerous. Firing the vast, heavy guns required enormous skill and bravery.

In battle, the ship's guns were under the command of the midshipmen and lieutenants who carried out the captain's orders. But in practice, success amid the smoke, noise and bloody drama of a sea battle was down to the skill of the gun crew.

The gunner – the man with the practical oversight of the ship's guns – was not a ranking officer but rather a 'standing' officer. Technically, like the boatswain and the carpenter, he was tied to a single ship for life. If he was married, his wife might well be aboard the ship and would look after the ship's boys.

Each gun had its own six-man team. The gun captain would aim and fire the gun. He was assisted by two men who would use long spikes to turn and raise the barrel. Another man loaded the gun and rammed the shot and powder into it, while a fifth sponged out the hot gun after every shot to make sure that no burning gunpowder or smoking waste material was left inside the barrel. If this man missed something, the gun could explode into action prematurely, killing or injuring the men who were firing it.

The sixth member of the team was known as the 'powder monkey'. He was the smallest and the youngest of them, often a boy aged just 10. His job was to run back and forth between the gun and the ship's magazine, where the gunpowder and charges were kept, keeping the team supplied with ammunition.

To fire a gun, a bag of powder and the shot would be loaded into the gun and rammed down tightly, one man keeping his hand on the vent hole to avoid any draft that might fan a flame and cause an explosion. The bag would be pricked through the vent hole, which was then filled with powder. On command – 'Fire!' – the powder was lit, and the cannon would explode with a thunderous roar, rocketing backwards and only being restrained by the thick ropes attaching it to the ship's sides. These ropes were of vital importance – a loose cannon careering around the deck could cause extensive damage and horrific injuries.

Cochrane, Earl of Dundonald, known as Lord Cochrane (1775–1860) enjoyed an even more extraordinary rollercoaster career. He frequently defeated the French during the Napoleonic Wars, who dubbed him the Sea Wolf. Cochrane later rose to prominence as a radical politician but became mired in a financial scandal and was dismissed from the Royal Navy. He took command of the Chilean navy, fought Spain and freed Peru, then commanded the Brazilian navy against Portugal, being raised to Marquis of Maranhao by Emperor Pedro I, and fought for Greece before being reinstated as a British admiral. The novelists C.S. Forester and Patrick O'Brian based their heroes, Horatio Hornblower and Jack Aubrey, on him.

Of those gallant Englishmen who perished in battle, including Harold II at Hastings (c.1022–66), Sir Philip Sidney (1554–86) at Zutphen, James Wolfe (1727–59) at Quebec and Sir John Moore (1761–1809) at La Coruña, Nelson remains the hero of the national pantheon.

The Duke of Wellington 1769–1852

Nothing except a battle lost can be half so melancholy as a battle won.

Duke of Wellington, in a dispatch from Waterloo (June 1815)

Arthur Wellesley, Duke of Wellington, was one of the ablest generals of his age, and – with Oliver Cromwell, Admiral Nelson and the Duke of Marlborough – stands among the greatest British military leaders of all time. His victory over Napoleon at the Battle of Waterloo, which he described as 'a damned nice thing – the closest run thing you ever saw', was a clash of the two most brilliant European generals of their day.

Wellesley, who was born in Dublin to an Anglo-Irish aristocrat, was not an exceptional young man, intellectually or physically. He gave up his one striking talent, for playing the violin, in 1793, burning his instrument in a fit of melodrama. He entered the army and relied on the patronage of his more successful eldest brother to rise through the officer

Redcoats, Tommys and Victoria Crosses

There is no greater heroism than courage under fire. Few deserve their place in this book so much as the 1354 individuals who have won the Victoria Cross, founded in 1856 to recognize 'some signal act of *valour*' performed 'in the presence of the enemy', its motto: 'For *Valour*'. The George Cross, founded by George VI in 1940, is its civilian equivalent, its motto: 'For *Gallantry*'.

Wellington's famous description of his Redcoat troops as the 'scum of the earth' belied his respect for their extreme courage – but no VC was available to recognize it. The medal's history began on 21 June 1854, during the Crimean War, when a Russian shell landed on the deck of the paddle sloop HMS *Hecla*, its fuse fizzing. It would have slaughtered many, but one Lieutenant Charles Lucas, aged 20, showing 'a remarkable instance of coolness and presence of mind', grabbed it and tossed it overboard. When Queen Victoria instituted the VC two years later, Lucas was the first to be honoured.

By the First World War, the VC was open to soldiers across the British Empire – and it has honoured individuals from over 20 nations. In 1914 a wounded Khudadad Khan, 26, became the first of 29 Indians to win the medal after steadfastly manning his howitzer at Ypres when all his crew lay dead. Often the medal is awarded posthumously: during the Second

ranks to the position of lieutenant colonel and head of his regiment.

Wellesley went to India in 1797, studying books on war and military tactics during the long voyage. The effort paid off. In 1802 he confronted a force of 50,000 French-led Maratha soldiers at Assaye. Through an unconventional choice of field positions and brave leadership in a bloody battle, Wellesley won against imposing odds. He later called it the finest thing he had ever done in the fighting line.

Returning home in 1805, Wellesley was knighted, married the short-sighted, timid Kitty Pakenham, and was sent for brief stints of duty in Denmark and Ireland, where he distinguished himself further. But it was his departure to fight the French on the Iberian Peninsula in 1808 that marked the start of Wellesley's ascent to greatness.

Here, the British Army had enough men to conduct defensive campaigns, and even to besiege large towns and castles, but insufficient strength to take advantage of these successes. Despite great

World War, Lloyd Trigg, 29, of the Royal New Zealand Airforce, refused to bail out of his burning plane. Flying within 50ft of a U-boat to drop his depth charges, he sank the Nazi submarine before crashing into the shark-infested sea, never to be seen again. Two VCs were won posthumously in the Falklands War of 1982, those of Colonel 'H' Jones and Sgt Ian McKay, both killed in action.

In 2005 Private Johnson Beharry, 26, born in Grenada and serving in the Princess of Wales' Royal Regiment, won the VC for a series of heroic acts in Iraq. In May 2004 his platoon was ordered to the rescue of a foot patrol in Al-Amarah, where a wave of rocket-propelled grenades shattered his Warrior armoured vehicle, injuring those inside. Private Beharry had no radio contact but knew that to halt would block everyone's escape, so he shut his hatch and advanced towards a barricade where he took more hits, which filled his vehicle with smoke. He opened his hatch, but it was destroyed by a rocket. Forced to drive another mile, he was exposed to enemy fire the whole time and sustained a 7.62mm bullet in the head. Beyond the ambush, he dragged the wounded from the vehicle before driving it back to base where, bleeding and exhausted, he finally collapsed. History repeated itself the following month, when another ambush left Private Beharry driving a damaged Warrior full of injured servicemen out of a conflict zone. This time his head wound induced a coma. As his VC citation states, 'Beharry displayed repeated extreme gallantry and unquestioned valour.'

British victories, at Vimeiro, Talavera, Busaco, Almeida and elsewhere, Viscount Wellington (Wellesley earned his first peerage after Talavera in 1809) was often frustrated in his ambitions to press on from Portugal into Spain.

By 1812 things had improved. Wellington fought his way to Madrid and persuaded the Spanish government to appoint him as *generalissimo* of its own armies. By 1814 the French had been pushed back to their own border. Wellington made sure his armies were better organized and better supplied than the French. He imposed superior discipline on his troops, and he did his best to respect the religion and property of the Spanish people, valuable lessons learned in India.

By now Wellington was the most famous man in England. He had won a dukedom, the ambassadorship to France, and the role as British representative at the Congress of Vienna. He was the recipient of honours from governments of Europe. But in 1815 he was to face the ultimate test of his military mettle.

Napoleon, who had been deposed and exiled to Elba in 1814, had escaped and begun to rally troops around him. Wellington was the only man in Europe considered worthy enough to command the allied forces against the emperor as he plotted to attack the Low Countries. Wellington was unimpressed by his own combined forces, calling them 'an infamous army, very weak and ill equipped'. He also had little knowledge of Napoleon's plans for the battlefield and was taken aback when French troops began to move on 15 June 1815. 'Napoleon has humbugged me, by God!' he exclaimed; but when the two vast armies met on 18 June, Wellington had arranged his forces into a defensive formation that was to prove extremely resilient against the waves of bludgeoning French attacks that Napoleon launched.

Throughout the long, hard battle, Wellington remained calm, though his Prussian reinforcements, under Marshal Blücher, arrived late and virtually every man of his personal staff was killed or wounded. 'I never took so much trouble about any battle, and was never so near being beat,' he wrote afterwards. But this victory, his last, was resounding, and Wellington was lauded right across the continent.

As a commander, Wellington was distinguished by his acute intelligence, sangfroid, planning and flexibility but also by his loathing for the suffering of battle. As a man, he was sociable, enjoying close friendships with female friends and a long line of affairs with high-born ladies and low-born courtesans, including a notorious French actress whom he shared with Napoleon himself.

After Waterloo, Wellington's prestige gave him great influence on government. By the 1820s he had been drawn into partisan politics, not his natural territory, although he was at heart a Tory and a reactionary. He served, with difficulty, as prime minister (1828–30), but he secured an agreement on Catholic Emancipation – political representation for Catholics, especially important for Ireland. However, his opposition to the clamour for parliamentary reform led him to resign the premiership. He was briefly prime minister again in 1834, holding every secretaryship in the government. In 1842 he resumed his position as commander-in-chief of the British Army, a post he held until his death.

A million and a half people turned out to see his funeral cortège make its way to St Paul's Cathedral in 1852. 'The last great Englishman is low,' wrote the poet laureate Alfred Tennyson.

Napoleon Bonaparte 1769–1821

Napoleon was a man! His life was the stride of a demi-god.

Johann Wolfgang von Goethe, *Conversations with Eckermann* (1828)

Napoleon Bonaparte bestrode his era like a colossus. No one man had aspired to create an empire of such a magnitude since the days of Alexander the Great and Charlemagne. Napoleon's ambition stretched from Russia and Egypt in the east to Portugal and Britain in the west, and even though he did not succeed to quite this extent, his brilliant generalship brought Spain, the Low Countries, Switzerland, Italy and much of Germany under French domination – albeit at the cost of two decades of war and some six million dead. Although his enemies regarded him as a tyrant – and indeed much about his rule was oppressive – Napoleon introduced to mainland Europe many of the liberal and rational values of the Enlightenment, such as the metric system of weights and measures, religious toleration, the idea of national self-determination, and the Napoleonic Code of civil law.

After an unruly childhood, a youthful military education, and service in his native Corsica during the French Revolution, Napoleon rose to prominence as an artillery expert in the defence of the town of Toulon against the British in 1793. Two years later he was in Paris, taking command of the artillery against a counter-revolutionary uprising. He boasted that he cleared the streets with 'the whiff of grapeshot'.

In 1796 Napoleon led a French army into Italy, driving the Austrians out of Lombardy, annexing several of the Papal States, then pushing on into Austria, forcing her to sue for peace. The resulting treaty won France most of northern Italy, the Low Countries and the Rhineland. Napoleon followed this up by seizing Venice.

Napoleon was now regarded as the potential saviour of France, and he ensured that the republic was reliant on his personal power within the army. The government welcomed the respite when

The Empress Joséphine

Joséphine was the love of Napoleon's life, and her name was the last word he is said to have spoken on St Helena. She was glamorous and extravagant, and though her tempestuous marriage to the emperor produced no heir, she was, by her first marriage, the grandmother of that enigmatic showman Napoleon III, the second and last Bonaparte emperor to rule France (1851–70).

Marie-Joséphine-Rose Tascher de La Pagerie – known as Rose – was born on Martinique in 1763, the child of an aristocratic sugar planter who fell on hard times. When she was 15 she moved to Paris to marry a rich young marquis and officer, Alexandre de Beauharnais.

The couple had two children, Hortense and Eugène, but Alexandre was embarrassed by his new wife's provincial accent and lack of urban sophistication, and he refused to introduce her at court. In 1785 the couple separated. Alexandre was guillotined during the Terror that followed the Revolution, and Rose was imprisoned. Shortly after her release she caught the eye of a young army officer, Napoleon Bonaparte, and in 1796 the couple were married by civil ceremony. Napoleon hated the name Rose, and thereafter his wife was known as Joséphine.

Joséphine was, initially, an indifferent wife. Napoleon's passionate love letters ('I awake full of you. Your image and the memory of last night's intoxicating pleasures has left no rest to my senses') often went

Napoleon sailed to Egypt to bolster French interests there at the expense of the British. In the campaign of 1798–9 he seized Malta, then defeated an Egyptian force four times as large as his own at the Battle of the Pyramids. Though the French navy lost control of the Mediterranean after Nelson's victory at the Battle of the Nile, Napoleon pushed through Egypt into Syria, until his army succumbed to disease and he was obliged to return to Paris.

In 1799 Napoleon seized control of France in the 'Coup of 18 Brumaire'. As First Consul, he improved the road and sewerage systems and reformed education, taxes, banking and, most importantly, the law code. The Napoleonic Code unified and transformed the legal system of France, replacing old feudal customs with a systematized

unanswered. When he was on campaign in Egypt, she began a flirtation with another officer. Napoleon threatened to divorce her and began taking mistresses himself. That the couple stayed together was thanks only to the sensible mediation of her son Eugène, who became viceroy of Italy under Napoleon.

During Napoleon's Consulate (1799–1804), Joséphine used her social standing to advance his position. She insisted they were remarried with religious rites on the eve of Napoleon's coronation as emperor, and at the ceremony in the cathedral of Notre Dame she became empress of France.

Joséphine's extravagance and inability to bear Napoleon an heir wore away at their marriage, and in 1809 Napoleon arranged – with her agreement – an annulment, on the grounds that a parish priest had not attended their second wedding. Napoleon married Marie Louise, the daughter of Francis I of Austria, and she bore him a son who became Napoleon's heir, the king of Rome, later technically Napoleon II and, after the fall of the Bonapartes, the Duke of Reichstadt.

After the annulment, Joséphine retreated to her private residence at Malmaison, outside Paris. She entertained lavishly, while Napoleon paid the bills. After the abdication she was visited by all the foreign leaders who occupied Paris and was supported by the admiring Tsar Alexander I of Russia, Napoleon's old rival. Unusually, she was beloved and respected by many – and deeply mourned when she died in 1814.

national structure and establishing the rule of law as fundamental to the state.

In 1804 Napoleon had himself crowned 'Emperor of the French', ostensibly to prevent the Bourbon monarchy from ever being re-established. His plan to invade Britain – which was funding his European enemies – was thwarted by Nelson's destruction of Napoleon's navy at Trafalgar. However, on land Napoleon seemed invulnerable, defeating the Austrians, Russians and Prussians in a series of stunning victories at Ulm (1805), Austerlitz (1805) and Jena (1806), ending the alliance of these powers with Britain and establishing the Confederation of the Rhine as a French satellite in much of Germany.

After this, Napoleon began to overreach himself. He made his brothers into kings, his marshals into princes. In 1808 he imposed his brother Joseph as king of Spain, provoking the Spanish to revolt. The British sent troops to support the Spanish, and for the next few years many French troops were tied up on the Iberian Peninsula. Undeterred, Napoleon looked east. Tensions were again rising with Tsar Alexander I, and in 1812 Napoleon amassed a *Grande Armée* of around 600,000 men to march on Russia. It was his moment of hubris. The Russians avoided engagement and retreated deep into the interior, implementing a scorched-earth policy as they went. When the Russians finally made a stand outside Moscow, at the Battle of Borodino, it was one of the bloodiest encounters in history. Though he took Moscow, Napoleon could not force the Russians to the negotiating table, and, with its lines of supply drastically over-extended, the *Grande Armée* was obliged to retreat through the bitter cold of the Russian winter. Only 40,000 men made it back to France.

Heartened by Napoleon's humiliation, the other European powers formed a new alliance against the French. The allies defeated Napoleon's forces in Spain and at Leipzig, taking Paris in 1814 and exiling Napoleon to the island of Elba.

But Napoleon was not done. Escaping from Elba in 1815, he made a triumphant progress north through France to Paris, telling the troops sent to stop him, 'If any man would shoot his emperor, he may do so now.' His old generals and their armies rallied round him, but the glorious 'Hundred Days' of his restoration came to an end on 18 June 1815 near the little settlement of Waterloo in what is now Belgium. As the Duke of Wellington, the British commander, conceded, it was 'the closest run thing'; but Napoleon's defeat was decisive.

The emperor was exiled to St Helena in the South Atlantic, dying of stomach cancer in 1821. Later, when Wellington was asked whom he reckoned to have been the best general ever, he answered: 'In this age, in past ages, in any age, Napoleon.'

Ludwig van Beethoven 1770–1827

Sweet sounds, oh, beautiful music, do not cease!
Reject me not into the world again.
With you alone is excellence and peace,
Mankind made plausible, his purpose plain.

Edna St Vincent Millay, 'On Hearing a Symphony of Beethoven' (1928)

Ludwig van Beethoven is one of the greatest composers of Western classical music. His music encompassed the transition between the Classical and Romantic styles, and his astounding contribution was all the more remarkable for being completed against the background of the encroaching deafness that plagued the last thirty years of his life. His nine symphonies raised the genre of orchestral music to a grand level, while his late-period string quartets and piano sonatas are some of the most transcendent achievements in classical music.

Born in Bonn, Germany, Beethoven was of Flemish descent. Both his father, Johann van Beethoven, and grandfather worked as court singers to the elector-archbishop of Bonn. Unfortunately, however, his father was also an alcoholic, who attempted to raise the family fortunes by touting his second son Ludwig as a child prodigy, somewhat unsuccessfully.

Unlike Mozart, Beethoven's genius took time to flower fully. Nevertheless, by the age of nine he was receiving composition lessons from Christian Gottlob Neefe, court organist at Bonn, becoming official assistant organist by the age of 14. Around this time Beethoven travelled to Vienna, and it is likely that he met Mozart and played to him. But his stay was interrupted by news of his mother's illness, and he was forced to return home to Bonn, where he found her dying of tuberculosis.

Beethoven now took charge of the family finances, largely because of his father's increasing incapacity. He began working as a musical tutor to the children of wealthy courtiers, as well as per-

Deafness and genius

The story goes that when Beethoven oversaw the first performance of his Ninth Symphony at the Kärntnertor Theatre in 1824, the soloists in the orchestra had to point out that the audience was applauding his work. Turning to see the silent adulation, he began to weep. He was by now totally deaf and never heard the work that had just been performed to such acclaim.

Beethoven had noticed the first symptoms from 1796, when he had begun to experience tinnitus, a constant ringing in his ears that made it difficult to hear and appreciate music or to engage in conversation. By 1802 there was little doubt that his condition was serious, and worsening. For a composer there could be nothing so destructive. Fully realizing the depth of his affliction darkened his mood. In the summer of 1802, in a letter discovered only after his death and known as the 'Heiligenstadt Testament', he wrote:

'O ye men who think or say that I am malevolent, stubborn or misanthropic, how greatly do you wrong me. You do not know the cause of my seeming so . . . for six years I have been in a hopeless case, made worse by ignorant doctors, yearly betrayed in the hope of getting better, finally forced to face the prospect of a permanent malady whose cure will take years or even prove impossible.'

All that kept him from suicide, he said, was his art, which made it

forming as a violist in the court orchestra and the local theatre. His positions allowed him to meet many influential nobles, including the Viennese aristocrat Count Ferdinand Waldstein, a skilled musician who became a friend and patron. Possibly at Waldstein's arrangement, Beethoven went to Vienna to study with the composer Haydn, lessons paid for by the elector, his employer. He left Bonn in 1792 and never returned.

Impressing the Viennese salons and nobility with his virtuoso performances on the piano, Beethoven performed widely and was considered a superb improviser – even greater than Mozart. His compositions at this time included piano sonatas, variations and concerti, as well as his first two symphonies, all of which show the influence of his own heroes, Mozart and Haydn.

The following years, up until around 1802, are considered

'unthinkable for me to leave the world forever before I had produced all that I felt called upon to produce'.

Although he could not hear the music he composed, Beethoven's gradual descent into deafness coincided with an increasing brilliance in his composition, with his middle-period works being characterized by themes of struggle and heroism, and those of his third period – the 'late period' – a time of total deafness, displaying a powerful intellectual depth.

By 1817 Beethoven was completely deaf, and for the latter part of his life he was able to communicate with friends only through written conversations. The resulting notebooks are unique historical documents, recording his thoughts and opinions on his music and the way it should be interpreted, and there are also written notes in the scores of his works.

At Beethoven's autopsy he was diagnosed as having a 'distended inner ear', which had developed lesions over time. Since then, other explanations have been suggested, including syphilis, typhus, the physical damage caused by beatings from his father and the effects of immersing his head in cold water to stay awake.

Posthumous analysis of Beethoven's hair revealed dangerously high levels of lead, certainly damaging to health, the effects of which may have contributed to his unpredictable moods. We may never know the cause of his deafness for certain; but what is beyond doubt is Beethoven's heroism in defying his condition to create a musical world of such timeless resonance today.

Beethoven's 'early period', during which he composed some significant piano works. Brilliant, fine compositions, they are not as innovative as the music of his later years. By now Beethoven's progressive deafness had become impossible for him to ignore. He was brought close to despair and, perhaps recognizing that his career as a virtuoso was over, began to focus on composition.

Settled in Vienna, he produced a series of masterpieces. His Symphony No. 3, completed in 1803, was originally dedicated to Napoleon Bonaparte, whose revolutionary zeal made him a hero to Beethoven. When Napoleon declared himself emperor in May 1804, the disillusioned composer angrily removed the dedication. Nevertheless, this dramatic, powerful symphony remained a landmark in Beethoven's musical development and when published in 1806 was suitably re-entitled 'Sinfonia eroica'.

Beethoven's middle period saw a rush of compositions that included the 'Waldstein' and 'Appassionata' piano sonatas, the Fourth Piano Concerto, the Razumovsky Quartets and the Violin Concerto, and also his first and only opera, *Fidelio*. His Symphonies Nos. 4 and 5 also date from this period, with the Fifth, its opening theme recognizable the world over, being a landmark in musical originality. Just as original is his Symphony No. 6, known as the 'Pastoral', in which woodwind instruments imitate the birds of the local countryside. The Symphonies Nos. 7 and 8 mark the close of a period filled with orchestral masterpieces.

Composing less in his later years, as complete deafness claimed him, Beethoven's late-period works, from around 1815 onwards, are marked by increased intimacy and emotional power. His final piano sonatas, opus 109, 110 and 111, are extraordinary virtuoso works, in which complexity is perfectly partnered with lyricism. On the other hand, his majestic Symphony No. 9, of 1824, explodes with the final movement's 'Ode to Joy', featuring a full choir and soloists – its soaring and exhilarating jubilance now used, somewhat absurdly, to drum up enthusiasm for the bureaucracy of the European Union. His last string quartets were completed in 1826, which coincided with the attempted suicide of Beethoven's nephew, to whom he was guardian. This, along with a bout of pneumonia and the onset of cirrhosis of the liver, probably contributed to his death in March 1827.

Prone to black moods and periods of emotional upheaval, Beethoven had difficulty maintaining relationships, and he never married – though a letter discovered after his death, addressed to his 'Immortal Beloved', has led many to speculate on the possibility of a secret, married lover. He was buried in great pomp, his funeral in Vienna befitting a composer who had become famous throughout Europe as one of the greatest of his, or any other, time.

Jane Austen 1775–1817

Like Shakespeare, she took, as it were, the common dross of humanity, and by her wonderful power of literary alchemy, turned it into pure gold. Yet she was apparently unconscious of her strength, and in the long roll of writers who have adorned our noble literature there is probably not one so devoid of pedantry or affectation, so delightfully self-repressive, or so free from egotism, as Jane Austen.

George Barnett Smith, in *The Gentleman's Magazine*, No. 258 (1895)

A parson's daughter who completed just six novels during her short life, Jane Austen emerged from deliberate anonymity to become English literature's best-loved female writer. Her gently ironic yet profound novels of love, manners and marriage transformed the art of writing fiction.

Acutely observed and subtly incisive, Austen's works are acknowledged as masterpieces. Her irony conceals a penetrating gaze, encapsulated in the famous opening line of *Pride and Prejudice* (1813): 'It is a truth universally acknowledged that a man in possession of a good fortune must be in want of a wife.' Austen's amused restraint was in marked contrast to the Romantic melodrama in fashion at the time, and the historian Macaulay thought that her well-constructed comedies of manners were the closest to perfection that writing could ever hope to reach.

The seventh child of eight, Austen spent her life among a large and affectionate family in Hampshire and Bath. 'Her life passed calmly and smoothly, resembling some translucent stream which meanders through our English meadows, and is never lashed into anger by treacherous rocks or violent currents,' wrote George Barnett Smith in 1895. She wrote about ordinary lives, about the petty dramas of lively provincial society, about the preoccupations, the squabbles, the complexities and the exhausting difficulties of unexceptional people. Sir Walter Scott (1771–1832), the best-selling author of *Ivanhoe*, was one of the few to recognize the extent of Austen's genius at the time, writing that she had 'the exquisite touch which renders ordinary commonplace things and characters interesting'. She pastiched the fashionable Gothic melodrama in *Northanger Abbey*, and broke away from the prevailing tradition that literature should be about great figures, great events or great dramas. Austen showed that the small and the conversational could be just as compelling, and her witty depictions of the elaborate matrimonial dances of the English gentry are thinly disguised social commentary, displaying a shrewd understanding of human motivation and social necessity.

Along the way, Austen produced some of literature's most memorable characters, drawn with her typical precision and intricacy. Aloof Mr Darcy, obsequious Mr Collins, flustered Mrs Bennet and her wry and long-suffering husband, Mr Bennet, populate *Pride and Prejudice*. Feisty, outspoken daughter Elizabeth Bennet is one of lit-

Debutantes and dowries; or, How to marry an English gentleman

'The Assemblies of Nottingham are, as in all other places, the resort of the young and the gay, who go to see and be seen; and also of those, who, having played their matrimonial cards well in early life, are now content to sit down to a game of sober whist or quadrille.' Thus, in 1814, was encapsulated the purpose of the endless round of entertainments that consumed the lives of England's gentry and aristocracy: to find matches for the new generation.

As the feminist writer Mary Wollstonecraft commented, a girl's 'coming out', at the age of 15 or 16, was purely 'to bring to market a marriageable miss, whose person is taken from one place to another, richly caparisoned'. The market they chose was of paramount importance. One prudent clergyman advised his step-sisters not to move to rural Oxfordshire, on the grounds that the location 'is but an indifferent one for young ladies to shine in'. Ambitious young women – or those with ambitious parents – would head for London.

No one was under any illusions about where they stood in the pecking order. It was unlikely that a provincial parson's daughter, such as Jane Austen, with her modest portion and limited connections, would even meet, let alone marry, a son of the high aristocracy. The daughters of the elite, carrying substantial dowries, were rigorously protected against the

erature's most engaging heroines, closely followed by the flawed but well-intentioned Emma Woodhouse of *Emma* (1816), who finds her equilibrium with the sensible and honourable George Knightley.

Austen's novels may end happily, but not without revealing the situation of women of her class and era. Marriage determined a woman's fate. As Charlotte Lucas's marriage to the ridiculous Mr Collins so eloquently demonstrates, almost any kind of marriage was deemed better than being an old maid. Elizabeth Bennet's decision to challenge this convention is presented as admirable, but daring. Whereas we know that Elizabeth's wit and charm will win her a husband (and a well-deserved place in the aristocracy), we also know that scores of women like Charlotte will not be so lucky and will have to compromise. Under a calm surface, Austen illuminates the prejudices, the scandals, the sheer misfortune and misunderstanding

adventurers who infiltrated London's society balls in the hopes of bagging themselves an heiress.

Parents and children alike were aware that choices were determined as much by financial considerations as by inclination. 'When poverty comes in at the door love flies out the window,' one gentlewoman reminded her daughter in 1801. The absolute minimum a gentleman could hope to scrape by on during this period was about £280 a year. But this would require a life, as one bride accepted, where 'we shall live in a quiet domestic manner and not see much company'.

Even an esquire on £450 a year would struggle to satisfy the social requirements of his class: a country household, lodgings in London, visits to the theatre and the opera, attendance at balls and pleasure gardens. One impecunious suitor complained to his beloved that: 'Every parent takes utmost care to marry his child [where there] is money, not considering inclination ... your papa no doubt may marry you to one [that] will make large settlements, keep an equipage and support you in all grandeur imaginable.'

Prudence ruled as much as passion. The lurking spectre of spinsterhood propelled many young women towards a match offering little but financial security. A century after Jane Austen wrote of the gentry's elaborate marriage dances, an Edwardian society hostess advised her son that his choice of wife 'ought to be submitted to your *judgement* before you give free rein to your affections'. 'Does this seem very cold-blooded advice?' she later asked. To the gentlemen and gentlewomen of the 18th and 19th centuries, it would have sounded eminently sensible.

that could leave women without a husband, and in the absence of a personal fortune, dependent entirely on the kindness of others for survival. Austen also suggested, through the successful social elevation of both male and female characters by means of marriage, that a stagnant but often snobbish aristocracy was in need of new blood.

The novelist who excelled in her treatment of love and marriage never herself married. She was, by all accounts, vivacious and attractive. The only surviving picture of her, a drawing done by her sister Cassandra, seems not to have done her justice. She had at least two semi-serious flirtations. At 26 she was briefly engaged to Harris Bigg-Withers, an heir five years her junior. Facing a lifetime with a man by all accounts as unfortunate as his name, Austen broke it off after less than a day. Rumours prevail of another, later attachment that was Austen's true love. Her beloved sister Cassandra, who also remained unmarried, destroyed much of her correspondence after her death.

Instead, Austen chose something her heroines never consider: a career. She had written since her childhood, producing stories, anecdotes and vignettes to amuse her family. In the upheaval after the family left her beloved childhood home, Austen stopped writing. Settling gratefully back in Hampshire with her mother and sister, Austen turned again to the works that she had begun a decade before. *Elinor and Marianne* became *Sense and Sensibility* (1811), and *First Impressions* became *Pride and Prejudice*. With the help of her brother Henry's negotiating skills, Austen's works were published under the authorship of simply 'a lady', with *Northanger Abbey* and *Persuasion* appearing posthumously in 1818. Famously private, Austen resisted attempts by the press and her proud family to make known the identity of this appealing writer, whose fans included the Prince Regent. Her authorship was made public only after her early death from, it is conjectured, Addison's disease.

In her short, uneventful life this extraordinary writer created works that resonate even more strongly today than they did in the early 19th century. The modern cult of Jane Austen continues apace, as fans try to discover more about the elusive novelist's life, and Hollywood films attempt to weave romantic tales out of the sketchy biographical details that exist. Many would agree, however, that her novels suffice. Discreet, ironic, witty and compassionate, Austen's masterful writing is the measure of the woman.

Lady Hester Stanhope 1776–1839

... the sort of woman that you sometimes see, I am told, in London drawing-rooms, — cool, decisive in manner, unsparing of enemies, full of audacious fun, and saying the downright things that the sheepish society around her is afraid to utter.

Alexander Kinglake, 19th-century travel writer and author of *Eothen*, who visited Stanhope in 1834

In an age when unmarried women of wealth were expected to live sheltered lives, Lady Hester Stanhope broke the mould. She was a daring, independent traveller, who journeyed in the Middle East and styled herself 'Queen of the East'. Refusing to be cowed by male convention either in Britain or abroad, she created a sensation wherever she went, blazing a trail for other women adventurers to follow.

Stanhope had the good fortune to be the niece of William Pitt the Younger. As a young lady she devoted herself to her uncle, and during his second premiership she acted as his official hostess and lady of the household. Her wit and beauty made a lasting impression on his guests, even if some of them found her to be more of a handful than they thought was quite proper.

When Pitt died in 1806, Stanhope was voted a pension by Parliament, which made her independently wealthy. After the loss of both her half-brother and a young man who might have been her fiancé at the Battle of La Coruña in 1809, she decided to use her modest means to take a long sea voyage, accompanied by her physician and faithful companion Charles Meryon. She travelled to Gibraltar, then on to Malta, where she met Michael Bruce, the son of a wealthy English businessman. Their romantic attachment meant a happy flow of cash from Bruce's father, and their travel plans grew grander as a result.

From Malta the couple travelled via Athens (where the poet Lord Byron jumped into the sea to greet Lady Hester) to Constantinople.

The life of the Bedouin

The Bedouin are a group of nomadic tribes that roam the deserts from the western Sahara to Syria, Jordan, Iraq and the Arabian peninsula. Although in the 20th century more and more Bedouin became integrated into nation-states, many are still attached to millennia-old traditions and ways of life.

The word 'Bedouin' comes from the Arabic *badawi*, meaning 'desert dweller'. Throughout history they have herded animals, spending the hot summer months close to fixed, cultivated settlements and the wetter winter months in the desert.

The 'royal' Bedouin tribes trace their ancestry back to the ancient Qaysis and Yamanis from the north and south of the Arabian peninsula. The fact that they herd camels marks them out as belonging to the top of the Bedouin hierarchy; lowlier tribes herd sheep and goats or cattle and make up their income by working as blacksmiths, artisans and entertainers. All the Bedouin have a reputation for great cultural sophistication in dance, music and, especially, poetry.

The traditional Bedouin household is based on the *bayt*, or tent, which is home to an extended family. The household often travels with other bayts in a group known as a *goum*, in search of grazing for the animals. Goums mark out their territorial boundaries with piles of stones and are loosely grouped together in the *ibn aam*, or descent group, a patriarchal group that forms a large block of the tribe as a whole, which is governed by a sheikh.

The Bedouin have a strong honour code, based on hospitality, generosity, courage and bravery. Gifts and charity must be given and cannot be refused. Women are expected to maintain their *ird* – an emotional concept roughly similar to virginity. Disputes are settled by tribal arbitration and offences punished with fines or by physical or capital punishment.

Trial by ordeal still exists, most commonly in the ceremony of *bisha'a*, in which an accused person must lick a red-hot metal ladle three times and then have their tongue inspected for scars or burns, which indicate a liar. Blood feuds, in which relatives of a murder victim must hunt down the murderer or kill one of his relatives, also still exist, although many Bedouin now prefer to seek justice in regard to serious crimes through the established national courts.

The Bedouin have always been a fiercely independent people, despising outside interference or structures and shunning fixed employment. Since the Second World War, however, their land and lives have been regularly encroached upon by the nations of the Middle East, and they have begun to integrate themselves more into employment, education and military service.

They stayed about a year before moving on to Cairo, which became their base for tours in the Holy Land and Lebanon. Having lost all of her clothes in a shipwreck off Rhodes, Stanhope had taken to wearing a Turkish male outfit, featuring a purple velvet robe, embroidered trousers, waistcoat, jacket and sabre. The strictly conventional citizens of Damascus were more than a little taken aback by this.

In 1813 Stanhope set off from Damascus with a Bedouin entourage, including 22 camels to carry her baggage, and travelled through the desert to the ancient ruined city of Palmyra, becoming the first European woman ever to set foot there. The Bedouin arranged a celebratory ceremony to crown her 'Queen of the Desert'.

After the journey to Palmyra, Michael Bruce returned to England, and Stanhope's steady flow of money began to dry up. She created a Turkish household in the disused monastery of Mar Elias, near Sidon in Lebanon. Though she was occasionally retributive towards villagers who angered her, she also gave refuge to hundreds of religious refugees during the civil wars in Lebanon.

In 1831 Charles Meryon also returned to England. Stanhope moved her household a few miles to the villa of Djoun. Desperately short of money, she was unable to sustain her previous lifestyle and died a virtual recluse in 1839.

Stanhope was the most famous of a succession of remarkable female travellers, but she was following a trail blazed in the early 18th century by Lady Mary Wortley Montagu (1689–1762) and by a lesser-known but equally heroic, and more beautiful, aristocratic adventuress in the later 18th century: the Countess of Craven, who was born Lady Elisabeth Berkeley (1750–1828), daughter of the Earl of Berkeley. With a curly auburn-blonde head of hair, a splendid figure and porcelain skin, she was strong, talented, brave and independent, and she became one of the first bestselling female authors. She married the Earl of Craven and swiftly became a famous London beauty, appearing in the metropolis's scandal-sheets. However, she started an affair with a French duke who was ambassador to London and was caught in *flagrante delicto* – though she was said to be 'democratic' in her taste for working-class lovers.

Faced with social destruction, she refused to follow the course of humble submission assigned to women of that time and embarked on a European trip of adventures accompanied by a young lover. She was simultaneously pursued by a royal suitor, the Margrave of Anspach, brother-in-law of Frederick the Great of Prussia. Her astonishing journey throughout the Russian and Ottoman empires was recorded in the bestselling book *Journey through the Crimea to Constantinople* (1789). She ended her literary, amorous and geographical journey by marrying the margrave, thereby joining the ranks of European royalty. She is a figure who deserves to be more widely known.

Lord Byron 1788–1824

A variety of powers almost boundless, and a pride no less vast in displaying them, – a susceptibility of new impressions and impulses, even beyond the usual allotment of genius, and an uncontrolled impetuosity in yielding to them…

Byron, as described by his friend and biographer Thomas Moore in his *Life of Lord Byron* (1835)

Lord Byron, the dashing, brilliant, brooding poet, was the quintessence of the Romantic hero. Women lost themselves trying to save him; society looked on in fascinated outrage as the aristocratic outsider defied their conventions. Shadowed by a permanent aura of depravity, irresistible in his vulnerability, mocking, witty, flamboyant and bold, Byron gave birth to a new image of the hero. Yet it is the incandescent, exuberant genius of the poetry that makes him immortal

George Gordon, Lord Byron, was, as he wrote in his unfinished masterpiece *Don Juan*, 'the Grand Napoleon of the realms of rhyme'. The poet who could dash off 60 to 80 stanzas after a hearty dinner hit the English literary landscape like a hurricane. When the first two cantos of his *Childe Harold* were published in 1812, they sold out immediately. 'I awoke one morning,' noted the 24-year-old poet, 'and found myself famous.'

Byron was the poster boy of the Romantic generation. The melancholic disillusionment of *Childe Harold* and the mordant, mocking irony of *Don Juan* satirized the hypocrisies and pretensions of society and mourned the failure of reality to live up to lofty ideals. Driven forward in searing, pounding rhythms, Byron's poetry embodied the spirit of the age:

> I live not in myself, but I become
> Portion of that around me; and to me,
> High mountains are a feeling, but the hum
> Of human cities torture

Everyone assumed that Byron was the lost and disenchanted eponymous hero of *Childe Harold*, restlessly wandering across the continent. The poet's history was indeed Romantic enough. Son of the profligate, charming Captain John 'Mad Jack' Byron, the boy was brought up in penury in Aberdeen by his widowed mother until the death of his great uncle transformed his fortunes. Brought back to England, the wild, club-footed ten-year-old inherited the magnificent ruins of Newstead Abbey and the title of Lord Byron.

Sitting in a corner, staring moodily into space, the slight, pale, beautiful Byron was a magnet for society's women. 'He is really the only topic almost of every conversation – the men jealous of him, the women of each other,' commented the political hostess Georgiana, Duchess of Devonshire. With his innumerable conquests, Byron cut a swathe through society – from Lady Caroline Lamb, who was so mad about the poet that when he was attending a party to which she was not invited, she would wait outside in the street for him, to Lady Oxford, the middle-aged hostess who encouraged her young lover's radicalism.

'Mad, bad and dangerous to know,' as Lady Caroline Lamb famously described him, the poet had no qualms about scandalizing society. 'It may be now and then voluptuous – I can't help that' was Byron's insouciant response to claims that *Don Juan* was a 'eulogy of vice'. Byron, living (by his own admission) in 'an abyss of sensuality', was infamous for his aura of tortured depravity and for the drinking orgies held with his friends, garbed in monks' habits, amid the Gothic ruins of Newstead Abbey. 'There never existed a more worthless set,' was the verdict of the war hero the Duke of Wellington.

A domineering mother and a childhood of sexual abuse by his nurse May Gray had thwarted his capacity for relationships; he

The Romantics – Keats and Shelley

In the late 18th and early 19th centuries Romanticism – that many-faceted movement, combining wonder at Nature with vivid self-expression, and exalting the artist-poet as visionary seer – captured the imaginations of writers and painters across Europe. John Keats (1795–1821) and Byron's friend Percy Bysshe Shelley (1792–1822) are two of English Romanticism's most enduring figures, both dying tragically young (Shelley from drowning, Keats from tuberculosis) and both having left behind a rich collection of verse that showed a striking inventiveness and creativity in the use of language.

Keats is largely remembered for the luxurious sensuality of his intensely descriptive poetry and for his fascination with death, which was not just a feature of his Romantic interest in further realms of being but a result of his having to confront illness at so young an age. The speaker in 'Ode to a Nightingale', one of the four great odes he wrote around 1818, sighs, 'Many a time / 'I have been half in love with easeful Death'. These are the ode's first and last stanzas:

My heart aches, and a drowsy numbness pains
  My sense, as though of hemlock I had drunk,
Or emptied some dull opiate to the drains
  One minute past, and Lethe-wards had sunk:
'Tis not through envy of thy happy lot,
  But being too happy in thine happiness,
That thou, light-wingèd Dryad of the trees,
  In some melodious plot
Of beechen green, and shadows numberless,
  Singest of summer in full-throated ease.

Forlorn! the very word is like a bell
  To toll me back from thee to my sole self!
Adieu! the fancy cannot cheat so well
  As she is famed to do, deceiving elf.
Adieu! adieu! thy plaintive anthem fades
  Past the near meadows, over the still stream,
Up the hill-side; and now 'tis buried deep
  In the next valley-glades:
Was it a vision, or a waking dream?
  Fled is that music: – do I wake or sleep?

Shelley, also intrigued by further states of consciousness and their relationship to the creative mind, found inspiration in a singing bird too, as expressed in his own famous ode, the 21-stanza 'To a Skylark'. In this elaborately constructed poem Shelley tries to present his ideal of art as a natural and 'unpremeditated' lyrical force.

Hail to thee, blithe spirit!
    Bird thou never wert –
That from heaven or near it
    Pourest thy full heart
In profuse strains of unpremeditated art.

Higher still and higher
    From the earth thou springest,
Like a cloud of fire;
    The blue deep thou wingest,
And singing still dost soar, and soaring ever singest.

In the golden light'ning
    Of the sunken sun,
O'er which clouds are bright'ning,
    Thou dost float and run,
Like an unbodied joy whose race is just begun.

The pale purple even
    Melts around thy flight;
Like a star of heaven,
    In the broad daylight
Thou art unseen, but yet I hear thy shrill delight –

Keen as are the arrows
    Of that silver sphere
Whose intense lamp narrows
    In the white dawn clear,
Until we hardly see, we feel that it is there.

constantly thirsted for new sensations and new lovers, whether male or female. He fell passionately in love and became equally swiftly disillusioned. Augusta Leigh, whose own daughter was probably Byron's, was the great love of his life, but she was also his half-sister. To all other women he could be monstrously cruel. He had an anguished relationship with his great friend Shelley's sister-in-law, Claire Clairmont, whom he made pregnant and then rejected. The much-loved daughter of this affair Byron placed in an Italian convent, where she died aged five. Byron's marriage to the humour-less Annabella Milbanke was a disaster. It broke down irretrievably after less than a year amid talk of Byron's marital violence, inces-tuous relationships and bisexuality – rumours so scandalous that they forced him in 1816 to leave England and the baby daughter of this marriage, Augusta Ada, never to return.

In Venice Byron swam home at night along the Grand Canal, pushing a board with a candle on it to light his way. The man who had kept a bear in his rooms at Cambridge lived in a palazzo that was a veritable menagerie. Shelley once listed the members of the household: 'ten horses, eight enormous dogs, three monkeys, five cats, an eagle, a crow, a falcon ... [and] I have just met on the grand staircase five peacocks, two guinea hens and an Egyptian crane'.

Visitors flocked to see the poet. Some found him grown fat and grey, but his vigour was restored by a passionate affair with a rad-ical young Italian countess. Restless once again, Byron launched him-self into yet another campaign: the fight for Greek independence from the Turks. He poured his money and his soul into the project. But at Missolonghi in Greece, weakened by a life of dissipation and excess, Byron caught a fever and died. Such was the end, at the age of just 36, of the poet whose magnificent defiance of petty con-vention had outraged and enraptured Europe for a generation.

Honoré de Balzac

1799–1850

I find people very impertinent when they say I am deep and then try to get to know me in five minutes. Between you and me, I am not deep but very wide, and it takes time to walk around me.

Balzac, in a letter to Countess Maffei (1837)

Honoré de Balzac was one of the most prolific of literary giants. His masterpiece, *La Comédie humaine*, is made up of nearly 100 works which contain more than 2000 characters and together create an alternative reality that extends from Paris to the provincial backwaters of France. Balzac's works transformed the novel into a great art form capable of representing life in all its detail and colour, so paving the way for the ambitious works of writers such as Proust and Zola. Balzac, the plump, amiable, workaholic genius, was in many respects the father of the modern novel.

As the unremarkable child of a beautiful but unpleasant mother and a self-indulgent father, Balzac did not seem marked for greatness. After school he worked as a legal clerk, but this did not excite a young man with grand ambition but little direction in which to channel it, and around the age of 19 he decided to become a writer. He went to Paris, determined to adopt a lifestyle appropriate to his new calling. He ran up great debts cultivating the image of a literary man about town, frequently dodging his creditors and flirting with bankruptcy.

One important thing was lacking: success. Balzac's first work, *Cromwell*, a verse tragedy about the leader of the English Common-wealth, was a failure that made his family despair. By 1822 he had written several more, equally unsuccessful, works. His output throughout the 1820s consisted of slushy or sensational potboilers and historical romances in the style of Sir Walter Scott. Some were published under pseudonyms, others under no name at all. None

Victor Hugo and Émile Zola

In the pantheon of French writers, Balzac's compatriots Victor Hugo and Émile Zola are his equals.

Best known outside France for his novels *The Hunchback of Notre Dame* (1831) and *Les Misérables* (1862), Hugo (1802–85) is remembered in his native land for his polymathic work as a poet, dramatist, novelist, essayist, painter, politician, human-rights campaigner and leader of the French Romantic movement.

An impassioned writer with a keen eye for political and social issues, between 1830 and 1841 Hugo produced a torrent of innovative poetry and drama that earned him election to the Académie française and a peerage. However, after the superficial chameleon Louis-Napoléon staged a coup d'état and established himself as Emperor Napoleon III, Hugo, a violent critic, was forced to flee the country. He settled in the Channel Islands and refused to return, even after an act of amnesty was passed in 1859, choosing exile until 1870.

Hugo's political pamphlets – *Napoléon le Petit* and *Histoire d'un crime* – were explosions of wrath against the right-wing regime of the emperor. Though banned in France, they were regularly smuggled in and played a role in undermining Napoleon III, whose regime was toppled in 1870 after defeat in the Franco-Prussian War. Hugo then returned, to political acclaim, and took office in the Third Republic, but he retired shortly afterwards and was mourned by the nation on his death in 1885.

Like Hugo, Émile Zola (1840–1902) was also a political activist, who may even have paid with his life for his courage. Between 1869 and 1893, taking Balzac's *Comédie humaine* as his model, he wrote a series of 20 novels called

gave any indication that Balzac was about to become a literary titan.

But around 1830 Balzac began to form a new and revolutionary concept of fiction. A few writers had toyed with the idea of placing characters across more than one book, but no one had applied the idea to their life's work. Balzac leapt at the concept, realizing that he could create a self-contained world that stretched across all his novels. When the idea came to him, he is said to have run all the way to his sister Laure's house on the right bank of the Seine, shouting 'Hats off! I am about to become a genius!'

With a focus for his efforts, Balzac swiftly began to produce work of real significance. He was a phenomenally energetic writer, routinely working for 18 hours at a stretch, fuelled by up to 50 cups of coffee

Les Rougon-Macquart, following the 'natural and social history of a family' and offering a panoramic view of French life in the middle years of the 19th century. Influenced by Darwinian thinking, Zola advanced, in prose and drama, the 'naturalistic' mode, which looked at people as products of their circumstances and environments. *L'Oeuvre* (1886), usually interpreted as a thinly disguised attack on Zola's childhood friend Paul Cézanne, tells the tale of a troubled artist who ruins his life trying to paint the perfect picture and finally hangs himself in front of his unfinished work. *La Terre* (1887) and *La Débâcle* (1892) are unsettling portrayals of the French peasantry and military respectively. *Germinal* (1885) portrays the world of the miners, *La Bête humaine* (1890) that of the railways, while *La Curée* (1871–2) and his notorious masterpiece *Nana* (1880) expose the sexual depravity and financial corruption of the Second Empire. Such novels earned him a reputation as a subversive, and on 19 occasions he was denied entry to the Académie française.

Zola's most important political stance came in 1898, with the publication of his open letter 'J'accuse'. It concerned the Dreyfus Affair, in which the Jewish-French army officer Alfred Dreyfus was sentenced to life imprisonment for espionage, his conviction based on specious evidence and supported by anti-Semitism in the French press and society. Zola's denunciation of high-ranking officers and politicians led to his prosecution for libel, and he was forced to flee to England. He returned in 1899 when the Dreyfus case was reopened, but he died in suspicious circumstances in 1902, supposedly poisoned by coal fumes from a blocked chimney but possibly a victim of foul play. Whatever the truth behind his death, Zola's activism was instrumental in undermining virulent anti-Semitism and rabid militarism in the French Third Republic.

a day. He described himself as a 'galley slave of pen and ink'; others called him a 'Napoleon of letters'. One story, *The Illustrious Gaudissart*, was produced in a single sitting – 14,000 words in a night. He was a furious amender of proofs from his publishers, revising and reworking his stories through six or seven drafts.

The tales that made up *La Comédie humaine* are characterized by Balzac's superb gift for storytelling, his rich sense of humour, and his delicate description of characters, scenes and places. In *Le Père Goriot* (1835), the tale of a penniless young provincial and the old man who gives up everything for his daughters, Balzac brings Paris to life almost as a character in its own right:

Left alone, Rastignac walked a few steps to the highest part of the cemetery, and saw Paris spread out below on both banks of the winding Seine. Lights were beginning to twinkle here and there. His gaze fixed almost avidly upon the space that lay between the column of the Place Vendôme and the dome of the Invalides; there lay the splendid world that he wished to conquer.

His imaginative gift and powers of description set the tone for the development of the 19th-century realist novel. As Oscar Wilde said, Balzac 'created life, he did not copy it'. The world of La Comédie humaine stretched from Paris to the French countryside, and its rich cast included sensitive portraits not only of young provincial men on the make in Paris, such as Rastignac, but also of young and old women, bureaucrats, politicians, courtesans, spinsters, nobles, peasants, actors and innkeepers – in his words, 'scenes of private life, Parisian life, political life, military life'. He also created the most unforgettable villain, the bisexual criminal mastermind turned police chief Vautrin, who was based on the real criminal-turned-police-chief Vidocq. It was Balzac who reflected that 'behind every great fortune lies a great crime'. The greatest works in this vast body of stories include Eugénie Grandet (1833), Le Père Goriot, Lost Illusions (1837), La Cousine Bette (1846) and A Harlot High and Low (1838–47).

From the age of 23, when he fell for the 45-year-old mother of some children he was tutoring, Balzac was in search of the ideal woman. He eventually found her in a Polish countess, Evelina Hańska, whom he married after a romantic correspondence that lasted 15 years. By the time he married her, in March 1850, Balzac had no more than five months to live. He died in August, killed by the strain of his punishingly indulgent working habits. At his funeral, the writer Victor Hugo remembered Balzac as 'among the brightest stars of his native land'. It was a fitting tribute.

Alexander Pushkin

1799–1837

The poet is dead: a slave to honour
Felled, by slanderous rumour
With a bullet in his breast, and thirsting for revenge
His proud head now bowed down.
The poet's spirit could not bear
The shame of petty calumnies ...

Mikhail Lermontov, from his homage to Pushkin, circulated secretly a few
days after the great poet's death

Alexander Pushkin is the heroic ideal of the Romantic poet. A genius
of exuberance, versatility, wit, poignancy and originality, a passionate and promiscuous lover of women, a victim of tyranny who
remained true to his art – he personifies the triumph of creativity
over the dead hand of bureaucracy. He helped create modern Russia
– its culture, its language, its very image of itself. He also wrote
history and short stories.

Pushkin is generally considered to be Russia's greatest poet.
Translation cannot do justice to the extraordinary way in which he
moulded the Russian language to his art, mixing archaic with
modern, vernacular with formal, and readily inventing new words
when old ones did not suffice. The profound simplicity of Pushkin's
poetry transformed the way that Russians – writers and ordinary
people – use language.

The brilliant and precocious son of an old noble family, Pushkin
became renowned when, as a 14-year-old schoolboy, his first poetry
was published. His romantic narrative poem *Ruslan and Ludmilla*, written
six years later, broke every literary convention of its day and was
a runaway success. The leader of Russian poetry's old guard, Vasily
Zhukovsky, gave Pushkin a portrait of himself inscribed: 'To the victorious pupil from the defeated master.' Barely out of his teens,
Pushkin was already recognized as Russia's pre-eminent poet.

Pushkin's astounding energy and drive transformed Russian literature. He cast off the stifling blanket of religion and censorship, creating works of extraordinary originality that laid the foundations of the modern Russian literary tradition. *Eugene Onegin* (1825–32) his great novel in verse, is considered by many to be the finest Russian novel ever written. Set in a Russian landscape with Russian characters, it was a decisive step away from the allegorical tradition and towards the realism later employed by Tolstoy, Dostoyevsky, Nabokov and Bulgakov.

The poet-revolutionary was the image of the Romantic hero. He was a sympathetic and social, rather than active, conspiratorial member of the aristocratic set later known as the Decembrists, who

Pistol duelling

Pushkin's fatal duel in the snow outside St Petersburg encapsulates the deadly glamour and poignancy of this ritual combat. It is said that d'Anthès had not intended to kill Russia's poet hero. But when Pushkin fervently rushed to his mark, d'Anthès shot to defend himself, resulting in the mortal wound.

In a sense it is no surprise that Pushkin met his end this way. The smallest of slights could provoke him to challenge another to a duel, for example when his uncle stole his dancing partner at a provincial gathering and even when a Greek expressed surprise that he had not read a particular book. 'Pushkin,' commented the wife of a friend, 'features in a duel almost every day.'

In Europe during the 18th and 19th centuries some questions of honour could only be settled by a duel. Three of England's prime ministers engaged in duels to settle matters of political controversy. The notoriously bookish Pitt the Younger was one of the two to do so while actually in office. The other, the Duke of Wellington, who duelled with the Earl of Winchilsea, was strongly criticized by the philosopher Jeremy Bentham: 'Ill advised Man! Think of the confusion into which the whole fabric of government would have been thrown had you been killed.' But for Wellington, Winchilsea's attack on the question of Catholic emancipation could be handled in no other way.

While his predecessors and successors made such combat illegal, Paul, the half-mad Russian tsar (1796–1801), was such an enthusiastic adherent

conspired to reform the oppressive autocracy of the tsars. The group's members were famed for their drinking, gambling and womanizing as much as for their liberal views.

Pushkin's work revolutionized the way Russians thought about their history and their drama, and especially the way they thought about their writers. Never one to play down his own achievements, Pushkin was one of the first Russian writers to make a collected edition of his various writings. Within a year of his death, a critic was able to declare: 'Every educated Russian must have a complete Pushkin, otherwise he has no right to be considered either educated or Russian.'

Russia's oppressive autocrats tried to break the will of the fiery

of pistol duelling that he proposed it be made the means of deciding the major questions of international politics. Europe's crowned heads should face each other in a pistol duel, he maintained, with their prime ministers acting as seconds. Napoleon did not respond to his challenge. France always disdained the pistol for the sword.

Participants in a pistol duel sometimes had almost no skill at all. In the famous duel of 1809 between Canning and Castlereagh, George Canning's second had to load and cock his pistol for him as the foreign secretary (and future prime minister) had never fired a pistol in his life. In many cases the duel was undertaken to restore honour on both sides, not to kill. The exception was Prussia, where 'deloping', or intentionally firing wide, was no less an act of cowardice than refusing a challenge; it suggested a man was asking for similar lenience from his opponent.

In the English-speaking world it was considered extremely bad form to deliberately aim at one's opponent. When the Duke of Wellington duelled, even the notoriously mad Winchilsea was of a mind with him and they both intentionally fired wide. In the 1804 Burr–Hamilton duel by the Hudson River, the US vice-president Aaron Burr did not. Shot by Burr, his Federalist opponent Alexander Hamilton (a brilliant treasury secretary) died the next day, and with him died Burr's reputation.

Returning to Russia, in a curious act of historical and literary symmetry the poet Mikhail Lermontov (1814–41), who so eloquently eulogized the dead Pushkin in 1837, also fell victim to a pistol duel.

radical. Pushkin was, in his own words, 'persecuted six years in a row, stained by expulsion from the service, exiled to an out-of-the-way village for two lines in an intercepted letter'. It was not all bad: he adored the exotic romance of Odessa, Moldavia and the Caucasus, which inspired him. He also managed several affairs, including one with Princess Lise Vorontsov, wife of the viceroy and a great-niece of Catherine the Great's minister Prince Potemkin. They had a child together and he wrote a poem to her called *The Talisman*.

But Pushkin was keenly aware of the oppressive hand of censorship and surveillance – and its potential to get worse. During the abortive Decembrist uprising of 1825, he could only look on helplessly as his generation's dreams of liberty were ruthlessly smashed by the dreary martinet Tsar Nicholas I. Finally, beaten down by almost a decade of censorship and exile, Pushkin was wooed into Nicholas's service with the illusory promise of reform. The tsar appointed himself as Pushkin's personal censor.

Imperial favour broke Pushkin even more effectively than imperial displeasure. Personally censored by the tsar, Pushkin was rendered almost speechless. The volatile radical poet fell increasingly out of favour at court, but, despite his increasingly desperate pleas to retire to a life of literary seclusion, he was not allowed to leave. His popularity still made him too much of a loose cannon. Besides, half the court, including the tsar, were infatuated with Pushkin's beautiful wife Natalya. His misery, drinking and gambling increased.

Pushkin's Romantic death, the result of a simmering romantic crisis, turned the hero into a legend. In February 1837 the creepy and sleazy French social climber Georges d'Anthès, having been frustrated by Natalya's decisive rejection of his approaches, publicly insulted her and challenged her husband to a duel. Pushkin, who had been itching to fight for months, accepted with alacrity. In the ensuing duel, Pushkin was fatally wounded, dying two days later at the age of 38.

The volatile, charismatic poet-radical who fought for liberty and died for love is revered in Russia almost as a god. His statue stands in Moscow's Pushkin Square, decked out with flowers even in deep winter. Pushkin had decreed in his great poem 'Monument' that 'My verses will be sung throughout all Russia's vastness / My ashes will outlive and know no pale decay . . . ' In this he proved a prophet too.

Alexandre Dumas père 1802–1870

*His successes ... resound like a fanfare. The name of
Alexandre Dumas is more than French, it is European; it is
more than European, it is universal ... Alexandre Dumas is
one of those men who can be called the sowers of
civilization.*

Victor Hugo

Alexandre Dumas's soaring imagination holds us spellbound. As
vividly drawn in life as one of his own characters, this master storyteller scorned literary pretension. Irrepressible to the end, he swag-
gered through a life that might have sprung straight from the pages
of his books.

Dumas's rip-roaring historical novels are crammed with romance,
adventure, courage and daring. At one moment comical and poignant,
the next mysterious and terrifying, they induce every emotion except
boredom. In The Count of Monte Cristo, The Three Musketeers and The Man
in the Iron Mask, Dumas created some of the most thrilling stories
ever written. He wove together history and fantasy, using scraps
gleaned from old books to embroider timeless characters and gripping plots. His fecund imagination has rendered the names
d'Artagnan and Dantès as familiar as Louis XIV and Richelieu.

He was the son of a swashbuckling Creole general (himself the
illegitimate son of a marquis) and an innkeeper's daughter. The general, a political outcast, died in his forties, leaving his indigent widow
to bring up two children on her own. When Dumas finally made
his way to Paris, the mixed-race, rambunctious provincial was mocked
for his frizzy blond curls and his antiquated dress. His father's erstwhile friends evaded his pleas for patronage. Only a stroke of luck
prevented an ignominious return to the countryside. Dumas's beautiful penmanship secured him a position as a clerk in the office of
the Duc d'Orléans (later King Louis-Philippe, 1830–48). It gave him

enough money and plenty of time to pursue the writing that he believed would make his fortune. His faith was vindicated. In 1829 his play *Henry III and his Court* made him famous overnight.

The self-styled 'king of the world of Romance' provided his audiences with a magical form of escapism. He was the champion of Romanticism, seeing the theatre as 'above all a thing of the imagination'and rejecting the cold orations and philosophical monologues of traditional French drama. His characters fought, wept, made love and died on stage with passion, the triumphant climaxes of his plays rendering his audiences delirious. When Dumas started writing novels, his imagination enraptured Paris. As *The Three Musketeers* and *The Count of Monte Cristo* appeared simultaneously, their daily instalments of

From the 'Black Marquis' to the *Dame aux camélias*

Given his ancestry, it is hardly surprising that Alexandre Dumas *père* specialized in tales of romance, derring-do, betrayal and intrigue. The fatherless boy who grew up in the small French town of Villers-Cotterêts was the son of the 'Black Marquis', a flamboyant and eccentric Napoleonic general whose integrity brought him only disgrace and provoked an early death.

Thomas-Alexandre Davy de la Pailleterie was the Creole son of a black slave girl and a minor Norman marquis. Born in French Saint Domingue in 1762 and raised by his mother's family after she died when he was 12, at 18 Thomas-Alexandre was taken by his father to France to be educated as befitted a nobleman. But when he joined the army as an ordinary soldier in 1786, he assumed his mother's surname Dumas in order to avoid embarrassing his father's family.

As the French Revolution overturned the strict hierarchy of France's *ancien régime*, he rose up the army ranks. Dumas's daring and skill in campaigns in the Vendée, in Italy and in Egypt had earned him the rank of general by the age of 31. But in 1802 he was ordered to put down the slave rebellion in Saint Domingue, and when he refused, Napoleon made his displeasure all too clear.

Politically disgraced, Dumas retired to the countryside, to the wife he

action and melodrama were instant talking points. Despite their tendency to melodrama, his characters were so exuberant that they still pulse with life today – the musketeers Aramis, Porthos, Athos and D'Artagnan (with their motto 'One for all, and all for one'), the sinisterly beautiful Milady de Winter, and Edmond Dantès, the count of Monte Cristo himself.

At the height of his success Dumas was Paris' uncrowned king. His image was on medallions and etchings. His workrooms were strewn with flowers and bursting with visitors. Extravagant, exuberantly dressed in capes and sporting flashy canes, with a menagerie of outlandish pets and an endless stream of still more glamorous mistresses, Dumas was the perfect subject for caricature. It was not

had first met when he was billeted at her father's inn in Villers-Cotterêts in 1789. Dogged by poverty and ill health, in 1806 the giant of a man died, leaving behind a widow and a small son and daughter.

The son did not share his father's enthusiasm for marriage. When he was 20, Alexandre Dumas moved to Paris to make his fortune and quickly took up with the first of many mistresses, Marie-Catherine Labay, a dressmaker who lived in the rooms opposite him. Young Alexandre, the child of this affair, was six years old before his father formally recognized him and won custody of him in a vicious legal battle. (Father and son, both Alexandre and both writers, are distinguished as *père* and *fils*.) His father cherished him and gave him the most expensive education possible (although he could not prevent his son's classmates from taunting him for his mixed-race heritage). But his mother's distress at losing her son was an experience that the adult Dumas *fils* (1824–95) would revisit in his work.

The son adored his father but was different from him in almost every way. Dumas *fils*, a member of the Académie française, wrote moralizing novels and plays that made him the darling of the French literary establishment. His love affair as a youth with the young courtesan Marie Duplessis, one of the celebrated beauties of her time, inspired his best-known work, *La Dame aux camélias* (1848), in which a young man falls in love with a beautiful girl of pleasure. His father ends it and she dies of tuberculosis. Verdi made it into the opera *La Traviata* (1853), and there have been eight film versions starring actresses from Sarah Bernhardt to Greta Garbo and Isabelle Huppert.

always kind and it was often racist. But his generosity, his child-like sensitivities and his bombastic naivety earned him as much love as ridicule.

The critics sneered at Dumas's popularity, at his readability, at his prodigious and varied output. He was never elected to the bastion of France's artistic establishment, the Académie française. He was attacked in print for being no more than the foreman of a 'novel factory' because he used collaborators. Assistants did indeed research and draft his work, but it was he who brought about the literary alchemy. Furiously scribbling away in his shirtsleeves, he injected the romance, suspense and humour that gave his work its magic. Dumas had no time for academic introspection. The self-styled 'popularizer' wrote to entertain, to enchant and consume, to dispel the mundaneness of life. He succeeded. 'It fertilizes the soul, the mind, the intelligence,' wrote Victor Hugo, one of France's other titanic men of letters. Dumas 'creates a thirst for reading'.

Dumas was always blithely unconcerned by the sniping of others less successful than himself. He abandoned his tenuous claim to the title of marquis; his name was title enough. He had his motto – 'I love those who love me' – carved in huge letters on Monte Cristo, the opulent château he built to celebrate his success.

His lifestyle was precarious. Debts forced him to sell Monte Cristo. On his deathbed he remarked wryly: 'I came to Paris with 24 francs. That is exactly the sum with which I die.' His action-packed cape-and-sword romances became less fashionable as literary styles changed. But he was undaunted by his oscillating fortunes. Irrepressible and indefatigable, he continued to write. He founded magazines and he lectured. He even participated in Garibaldi's campaign to unify Italy.

When Dumas died, at the home of his devoted son at Puys near Dieppe, it was, in the words of one young journalist, 'as though we had all lost a friend'. The 'affectionate and much-loved soul' was also the 'splendid magician' who created works that gave 'passage into unknown worlds'.

In 2002, President Jacques Chirac of France presided as Republican Guards dressed as the Musketeers moved Dumas's body to rest in the Panthéon. 'With you,' said the president, 'we *were* D'Artagnan and Monte Cristo!'

Benjamin Disraeli

1804–1881

*Mr Disraeli ... has always behaved extremely well to me,
and has all the right feelings for a minister towards the
sovereign ... He is full of poetry, romance and chivalry.
When he knelt down to kiss my hand, which he took in both
of his, he said 'in loving loyalty and faith'.*

Queen Victoria, letter to her daughter Crown Princess Victoria of Prussia (4 March 1868)

The greatest showman of British leaders, the most literary, and one of the wittiest, Disraeli – known appropriately by everyone, even his wife, as 'Dizzy' – matured from an adventurer into a heroic statesman, superb parliamentarian and virtuoso orator. Under him, the Conservative Party developed its guiding ideology that was to endure for over a century: fervent support for the monarchy, the empire and the Church of England, but also a commitment to achieving national unity by social reform. And although baptized a Christian in 1817, he remains the only British prime minister to have come from a Jewish background (let alone a Sephardic Moroccan one), a source of pride throughout his career.

Most of Disraeli's political achievements came late in life. The son of the writer Isaac d'Israeli, he was best known in his early years as a rakish literary figure, Byronic poseur and financial speculator. (Indeed, he and Winston Churchill remain the only outstanding literary figures among British leaders.) 'When I want to read a book, I write one,' he once said; his books included romantic and political novels – the most famous being *Coningsby* – which often earned him substantial sums of money. He was famed for his extravagant dress sense and bumptiousness, which made him as many enemies as friends. His financial life was rackety, his sex life was shocking and, at one point, he lived in a *ménage-à-trois* with the lord chancellor Lord Lyndhurst and their joint mistress, the married Lady Henrietta Sykes. It was all a far cry from the sobriety of his arch-opponent, the Liberal leader W.E. Gladstone, with whom he had a fiery, combative relationship. He married late – childlessly but happily.

Disraeli entered Parliament in 1837. Before long he was recognized as a brilliant speaker and a tricky character. In 1846 he was instrumental in splitting the Conservative Party, by opposing the repeal of the Corn Laws in defiance of his leader, Robert Peel. When the Conservative Party formed a minority government in 1852, the Earl of Derby appointed Disraeli as chancellor of the exchequer. But his first budget was rejected by Parliament, and Derby's government resigned after just ten months. Disraeli served twice more as chancellor under Derby, in 1858–9 and 1866–8.

It was in 1867 that Disraeli – now in his sixties – made his first

Democratic dynasties

If Disraeli was the self-made exception to the Victorian aristocratic age, his foreign secretary at the Congress of Berlin, Lord Salisbury, personified hereditary democratic power. Even in today's meritocratic democracies, many outstanding statesmen have been members of dynasties. As Indian and American politics particularly continue to demonstrate, the brand-name security of hereditary rulers continues to tempt the voting populace.

Britain's earliest, and longest, political dynasty is surely the Cecils. William Cecil (1520–98), later Lord Burghley, was a gifted statesman. He served as Elizabeth I's chief secretary (from 1558) and lord treasurer (from 1572 to his death), the wise architect of many of her triumphs. His son Robert succeeded him as secretary and eased the succession of James I of England, who raised him to the earldom of Salisbury and lord treasurer in 1608. Over 300 years later, another Robert Cecil, 3rd Marquis of Salisbury (1830–1903), progressed from foreign secretary to become a great imperial prime minister no fewer than three times (he was succeeded by his nephew, Arthur Balfour, hence the saying 'Bob's your uncle!'). Even today the Cecil family looms large in the Conservative Party, with Viscount Cranborne their leader in the House of Lords for part of the 1990s.

The Pelhams provided two competent British prime ministers in Henry (1743–54), and his brother Thomas, Duke of Newcastle, who succeeded him. Two other dynasties provided four of Britain's wartime titans: William Pitt, 1st Earl of Chatham, led the country adroitly (1757–61) in the Seven

great contribution to posterity, when he and Derby vigorously pushed through the 1867 Reform Act. This nearly doubled the number of people entitled to vote (although it did not enfranchise any women) and had the effect of underpinning the two-party system in England, lining up Conservatives against Liberals. When Derby became so ill that he had to resign the premiership in 1868, Disraeli was the natural choice to lead the Conservatives and the government. But his premiership was short. Gladstone's Liberals returned to power at the end of the year.

After another six years of opposition, Disraeli was prime minister once more (1874–80). 'I have climbed to the top of the greasy pole,' he said. This time the Conservatives had a majority. Queen

Years' War and again in 1768, while his son William Pitt the Younger became chancellor at 21 and prime minister at 24. He led the nation during the French Revolutionary and Napoleonic wars from 1783 to 1801 and from 1804 until his death in 1806, presiding over the victory of Trafalgar. With a two-century gap, the Churchills produced probably the two most inspiring contributors to national prestige: John Churchill, Duke of Marlborough (1650–1722), and Sir Winston Churchill (1874–1965).

In the United States, one family, the Roosevelts, delivered firstly the swashbuckling Theodore, president 1901–9, who was energetic, irrepressible and courageous. He led his Rough Riders in the Cuban War, was elected Republican vice-president, and succeeded the assassinated McKinley in 1901, being re-elected in 1904. He busted monopolistic trusts, dominated South America and won the Nobel Peace Prize for mediating between Russia and Japan. His name also inspired a new children's craze – the teddy bear. His cousin Franklin remains simply the greatest US president.

In fact, America has a taste for dynastic politicals. John Adams was the second president, 1797–1801, and his son, John Quincy, was the sixth, 1825–9. William Harrison was the ninth president, 1841, and his grandson Benjamin the twenty-third, 1889–93. But for assassination, a presidential Kennedy dynasty might have materialized in the 1960s. In our own era, there have been two Bush presidencies (George H.W. Bush, 1989–93 and George W. Bush, 2001–9) and after Bill Clinton's presidency (1993–2001), Barack Obama nominated Hillary Clinton as Secretary of State.

Victoria adored him – in contrast to Gladstone, whom she loathed. In 1876 Disraeli gave the queen the title of Empress of India, and he was created Earl of Beaconsfield. In foreign affairs he successfully impressed upon Europe and the world that Britain was indeed 'Great'. He protected British shipping interests and the route to India by arranging the purchase of a controlling stake in the Suez Canal. In European politics he played a canny hand to contain Russia's ambitions as the Ottoman Empire, the so-called 'sick man of Europe', declined.

One of Disraeli's most influential achievements was in creating an imperial ethos for the British Empire. He sang the virtues of *Imperium et libertas* (empire and liberty), and he saw Britain's mission as not just to trade and establish colonial settlements, but also to bring British civilization and values to the diverse peoples of its ever expanding dominions. He was convinced of Britain's unique and pre-eminent position in international politics, and to an extent his belief was vindicated at the Congress of Berlin in 1878, where his cunning and flamboyance dominated the attempts to solve the Russo-Turkish problem and the nationalist aspirations in the Balkans, securing peace and resisting Russian territorial ambitions. He also brought Cyprus under the British flag. 'The old Jew is the man,' said the German Chancellor, Bismarck. The 'old wizard' Disraeli received a hero's welcome following the congress.

Throughout his political career, Disraeli maintained an intense feud with Gladstone, whom he called 'that unprincipled maniac ... [an] extraordinary mixture of envy, vindictiveness, hypocrisy and superstition'. The feeling was mutual. Gladstone compared Disraeli's defeat in 1880 to 'the vanishing of some vast magnificent castle in an Italian romance'. Though Gladstone outlived Disraeli and served as prime minister a total of four times (the last time in 1892–4) he never had the same charm, vision or style. For Disraeli was not simply a tenacious politician and parliamentarian; he was a great statesman.

Giuseppe Garibaldi

1807–1882

Anyone who wants to carry on the war against the outsiders, come with me. I can offer you neither honours nor wages; I offer you hunger, thirst, forced marches, battles and death. Anyone who loves his country, follow me.

Garibaldi to his followers when fleeing Rome, as described by Giuseppe Guerzoni, in *Garibaldi* (vol. 1, 1882)

Maverick general of irregular troops and irrepressible liberator of peoples, Garibaldi led an almost incredible life of battle and adventure. But his cause was as heroic as his exploits: the liberation of the long-subdued disparate states of Italy from the shackles of corrupt tyrants and hidebound empires. In this process, known as the Risorgimento, Garibaldi led his Redshirt followers to decisive victories over the Spanish Bourbon and Austrian Habsburg dynasties that still ruled much of Italy.

Garibaldi was born in Nice, which from 1814 to 1860 was part of the Italian kingdom of Piedmont-Sardinia. He ran away from home in order to avoid a clerical education but was then reunited with his father in the coastal trade, becoming a sea captain in his early twenties. In his mid-twenties he joined the Young Italy movement, influenced by the nationalist republicanism of Giuseppe Mazzini, conspiring in an anti-monarchical uprising in Genoa in 1834. The plot was discovered; Garibaldi fled, but, drawn to other liberation causes, he travelled to South America.

There he fought for the rebellious state of Rio Grande Sol, which was trying to secede from Brazil. He lived a life of hardship and danger. During one campaign he met his beloved Creole partner Anna Maria Ribeiro da Silva ('Anita'), later mother of three of his children. She followed him when he received command of an Italian legion fighting for Uruguay against Argentina. Leading these first 'Redshirts', he won a reputation as a masterly guerrilla commander.

In 1848, as Europe caught fire with revolution, Garibaldi returned to Italy to offer his services in the struggle against Austrian hegemony.

Spurned by Piedmont (he was, after all, still a wanted man there), he took part in a republican experiment in Rome that saw Pope Pius IX flee the city, and he organized the brave, but hopelessly outnumbered, resistance to the French and Neapolitan forces that restored the pope in 1849.

Garibaldi and several thousand followers retreated across central

Peter the Great and other Fathers of their Peoples

Very few men can truly claim to be, as Garibaldi was, the 'father' of a nation. **King David**, the biblical king of the Israelites, was undeniably one such. He lived around 1000 BC, a superb soldier-statesman, a virtuoso harpist, a poet and a psalm-writer. He killed the Philistine champion Goliath, married the Israelite King Saul's daughter and became best friends with Prince Jonathan. Making himself king after the deaths of both Saul and Jonathan (David's lament to them still sings to us across the ages), he conquered much of present-day Israel, Syria and Jordan, took the Jebusite city of Ophel and founded Jerusalem, making it sacred by placing the Ark of the Lord there. Unfortunately, he also arranged the death of Uriah the Hittite so he could marry his wife Bathsheba (great men have great flaws too) and lost his son Absalom in a foolish rebellion; but he had the political wisdom to nominate Solomon as his heir.

The only English monarch known as 'the Great' is **Alfred** (849–99), in many ways the English David. A remarkable organizer and general, Alfred became king of Wessex in 871 at a time when Viking invasions had consumed the Anglo-Saxon kingdoms of Northumbria and Mercia and were threatening the borders of Wessex . When the Danes intensified their attacks in the late 870s, Alfred retreated into the Somerset Levels, from where he waged an effective guerrilla war against them. By the 890s, he had defeated the Danes on land and at sea, formed a restored kingdom, founded the English navy, built many of the towns that have now become great English cities and established a codified law and administration. He was the first to call himself king of all the Anglo-Saxons.

Tamara (1160–1213) inherited the kingdom of Georgia in the Caucasus from her father Giorgi III, but after coming to the throne in 1184 she founded the modern Georgian nation, conquering an empire that extended into today's Turkey and Persia, and oversaw its golden age, the flowering

Italy, evading French and Austrian forces but suffering many losses – including his beloved Anita. Garibaldi himself made it to the coast of Tuscany, going into five years of exile as a trading skipper in New York and Peru.

Finally, in 1854, Garibaldi was able to return to his Piedmontese homeland, where he planned a united Italian monarchy (instead

of building, poetry and chivalry. Tamara was as adept at internal politics as she was in foreign policy and military planning. She patronized the 'Georgian Shakespeare', the poet Shota Rustaveli (who was in love with her), and was rightly known as the 'King of Kings' and 'Queen of Queens'.

Skanderbeg (1405–68) was father of the Albanians. As the Ottomans conquered the Balkans, this young prince was sent to Istanbul, as a Muslim convert, and promoted by the sultan to general. Skanderbeg rebelled in 1443, renouncing Islam; he created an effective army of 10,000 warriors, united the Albanian tribes and defeated superior Ottoman armies to rule for over 25 years as an independent prince. Finally, Sultan Mehmed II himself led a force that devastated Albania, as Skanderbeg lay dying in 1468. The country did not re-emerge from Ottoman rule for over four centuries.

The astonishing **Peter the Great** (1672–1725) remains the father of the Russian state and empire. Energetic, visionary and exuberant, he was a colossus in brains and stature; but also ruthless, drunken, brutal and eccentric. Son of Tsar Alexei, Peter succeeded jointly with a weak-minded brother, Ivan, in 1682, but his sister, regent Sophia, ruled until she was overthrown by Peter in 1689. Peter dominated his co-tsar (who died in 1796), then ruled on his own with imagination, courage and innovation. He organized the army, founded the Russian navy and conquered Azov in the south. He set off on his 'great embassy' to learn Western ways, training as a boatbuilder and engineer in Holland, until he was recalled to suppress the rebellion of mutinous Muscovite musketeers, many of whom he personally executed and tortured. He launched the Great Northern War against Sweden (1700), founded St Petersburg (1703), decisively defeated the Swedish invaders at Poltava (1709), unhappily lost Azov to the Turks (1711), married his mistress – the camp-follower Catherine (1712) – and moved the government to St Petersburg. He tolerated no opposition, having his dissident son tortured to death and sending his wife the head of a young man suspected of flirting with her. Peter declared himself the first Russian 'emperor' in 1721.

of a republic) with King Victor Emmanuel II and his powerful prime minister Cavour. Napoleon III of France backed the plan. In 1859 Garibaldi, now a Piedmontese major-general, led Alpine troops into action against the Austrian Habsburgs in northern Italy, capturing Varese and Como. Austria ceded Lombardy to Piedmont.

In early 1860 Piedmont angered Garibaldi by returning Nice and the Savoy region to the French, in return gaining the sovereignty of the central Italian states. Garibaldi's thoughts turned to the south, the so-called Kingdom of the Two Sicilies, backward, impoverished and ruled by the Bourbons. With a mere 1146 of his Redshirts, and tacitly supported by Emmanuel and Cavour, he landed in Marsala, Sicily in May 1860 and soon captured Palermo. He forced 20,000 Neapolitan soldiers to surrender and declared himself a very popular 'dictator'. He then crossed the Straits of Messina, entered victoriously into Naples and forced King Francis II to flee. Garibaldi handed over his conquests to Victor Emmanuel, recognizing him as king of Italy. He had nearly achieved his vision of a united Italy; only the French-defended Papal States and Austrian-ruled Venetia remained outside the new kingdom.

Two ostensibly private campaigns by Garibaldi to take the Papal States, in 1862 and 1867, came to nothing, the first leaving him injured at the Battle of Aspromante, ironically by troops sent by Victor Emmanuel to intercept him. (In contrast, the 1867 campaign was secretly funded by the king.) But more success came in the north, when Garibaldi led Italian forces – allied to the Prussians in a wider war – against the Austrians at Bezzecca (21 July 1866). By complex treaty negotiations, Venetia was ceded to the nascent Italian kingdom.

The Papal States finally surrendered to Italian government troops in September 1871, the last piece of the Italian jigsaw, but Garibaldi played no part. His last adventure was in support of the French against the Prussians in 1870–1. Retiring to Caprera, the island he had acquired in the 1850s, he lived peacefully – as politician, memoirist, novel-writer, but always a living legend who, on his death in June 1882, plunged Italy into mourning.

Mazzini had the philosophies, Cavour the strategies and Victor Emmanuel the crown, but it was Garibaldi, the swashbuckling patriot, who created a nation.

Abraham Lincoln

1809–1865

We here highly resolve that the dead shall not have died in vain, that this nation, under God, shall have a new birth of freedom; and that government of the people, by the people, and for the people, shall not perish from the earth.

From Lincoln's address at the dedication of the National Cemetery at Gettysburg
(19 November 1863)

'Honest Abe', the president who saved the Union and freed the slaves, is a legend of American history. Truly good as well as truly great, this gaunt, austere figure, who rose from the Kentucky backwoods to lead his nation, evinced a humble charm that has made him loved as much as he is admired.

With almost no formal education – off-and-on schooling 'by littles', as he put it – Lincoln's journey from the one-room Kentucky log cabin of his birth to the White House is the blueprint for the American Dream. His father and much-loved stepmother were almost illiterate, so he essentially educated himself. The lowly one-time 'rail-splitter' taught himself law, established a flourishing Illinois practice, and – defending his well-known non-attendance at church – entered politics. First a Whig, then a founding member of the Republican Party, in 1860 Lincoln became the 16th president of the United States.

Lincoln's leadership may in the end have kept the states united, but his election was the catalyst for their split. In 1858 Lincoln famously declared: 'A house divided against itself cannot stand. I believe the government cannot endure permanently half-slave and half-free.' Lincoln's preference for freedom was well known, and even before he took office in 1861, seven Southern states declared themselves a new nation – the Confederate States of America. Respecting the Constitution, Lincoln would not open hostilities – it was the Confederates who initiated civil war when they fired on Fort Sumter – but refusing to countenance permanent secession, he was firm in his resolve: the Union would not be broken.

Lincoln wanted to save the Union both for its own sake and to preserve an ideal of democratic self-government that he saw as an exemplar for the world. In his 1863 Gettysburg Address, Lincoln bound the nation 'conceived in Liberty and dedicated to the proposition that all men are created equal' to the principles of democracy and equality on which it had been founded in 1776: 'this nation,' he proclaimed, 'shall have a new birth of freedom; and . . . government of the people, by the people, and for the people, shall not perish from the earth'. Lincoln reaffirmed a vision of the nation and its identity that endures to this day.

Lincoln's wartime leadership ensured the Union's victory. The struggle demanded extreme measures. Using emergency wartime powers, Lincoln suspended habeas corpus, blockaded Southern ports and imprisoned without trial thousands of suspected Confederate sympathizers. His opponents, including the 'Copperheads' lobbying

Assassinated presidents and prime ministers

In the 19th and 20th centuries, as republican and democratic forms of government have developed, so has the periodic habit of assassinating civilian political leaders. In the late 20th and early 21st centuries, a number of European prime ministers, both in likely trouble spots (Serbia's Zoran Djindjic, 2003) and in unlikely ones (Sweden's Olof Palme, 1986), paid the ultimate price for their public careers. Despite Britain's long tradition of prime ministers since Robert Walpole (1721–42), the first, only one premier has fallen prey to an assassin's bullet – the Tory Spencer Perceval, in the House of Commons lobby, 1812. In contrast, outrunning the would-be assassin has almost become part of the territory for any US presidential hopeful.

In 1865 Abraham Lincoln had the dubious honour of becoming the first US president to expire in this fashion. Sixteen years later, in 1881, in the waiting room of a Washington D.C., railway station, President James Garfield was shot twice in the back by Charles Guiteau, a civil servant whose petition to become ambassador to France had been refused. Garfield, who had been president for just four months, survived another 12 weeks of doctors poking unsterilized fingers into his wound. His assassin was hanged and the civil service's system of appointments was reformed.

for peace within the Union, violently criticized him, but, given the time and the circumstances, his methods were relatively humane. His innate magnanimity is clear in his treatment of the defeated Confederates: 'let 'em up easy,' he told his generals.

As the Union army's commander-in-chief, the former lawyer displayed an instinct for strategy that belied his lack of military training. After several false starts, in Ulysses S. Grant he found a commander who instinctively understood his vision of how the war should be pursued: 'I cannot spare this man,' was Lincoln's reported response to criticism of Grant. 'He fights.'

While Grant pursued the conflict with aggressive and highly successful campaigns, Lincoln travelled around the country inspiring fighters and followers alike. The eloquence and integrity of his addresses reached a climax at Gettysburg, where he dedicated the nation's future to those who had died in its name.

Popular president William McKinley was elected to a second term in 1900. The following year, at the Pan-American Exposition in Buffalo, New York, the anarchist Leon Czolgosz shot him in the chest and abdomen. The president who had brought the United States out of isolation and forged America's empire in the Spanish–American War was also admired for his devotion to his epileptic, mentally fragile wife, Ida. As he fell, McKinley, who died a week later, whispered to an aide: 'My wife, be careful ... how you tell her – Oh, be careful.'

The Tippecanoe Curse seemed to be coming true: the president elected every 20th year would be killed or die in office. (The founder of the curse was William Henry Harrison, the ninth president, who died in office – of natural causes – in 1841. He was known as 'Old Tippecanoe' for his victory over Native Americans at the Battle of Tippecanoe in 1811.)

In 1963 in Dallas, Texas, a sniper, said to be the ex-Marine Lee Harvey Oswald – but rumoured by others to be a Mafia or Soviet hitman – shot President John F. Kennedy. The first bullet hit the president in the neck, the next in the head. JFK – the golden president elected in 1960 – died in hospital 35 minutes later, and a host of conspiracy theories were born.

The 40th president, Ronald Reagan, was luckier: he survived a bullet in 1981, even though, in a typically self-deprecating observation, he 'forgot to duck'.

Lincoln had been 'naturally anti-slavery' since his youth, and it had been the issue that made him leave the law and re-enter politics in 1854. It was the Civil War that turned Lincoln into an outright abolitionist. His 1862 Emancipation Proclamation used his wartime powers to free all slaves in the rebel states. Bringing black support and enlisting soldiers for the Union cause, it was a decision as politically justifiable as it was morally sound. For Lincoln it was a triumph: 'I never, in my life,' he said, 'felt more certain that I was doing right, than I do in signing this paper.' Anxious to prevent a peacetime revocation of his emergency decree, Lincoln secured in 1865 the Thirteenth Amendment that enshrined in America's Constitution the freedom of all its people.

Shot in the back of the head by the Southern radical John Wilkes Booth as he attended the theatre with his wife Mary on 14 April 1865, Lincoln became America's first president to be assassinated in office. Some confusion surrounds the words spoken by John Stanton, the Secretary of War, as Lincoln breathed his last. But truly Lincoln belongs both 'to the angels' and 'to the ages'.

Charles Darwin

1809–1882

The more one knew of him, the more he seemed the incorporated ideal of a man of science.

T.H. Huxley, in *Nature* (1882)

Along with Copernicus, Newton and Einstein, Darwin stands as one of a small handful of scientists who have brought about a fundamental revolution in our ways of thinking. Before Darwin, the account of creation as described in the Bible was almost universally believed. After Darwin, a vast, chilling wedge of doubt was hammered into the claims of religion to explain the universe and our place in it. He altered radically the way we think about ourselves.

As a boy, Darwin was quiet and unassuming, with a keen interest in collecting minerals, coins and birds' eggs. After an unexceptional schooling he was sent to university in Edinburgh to study medicine. He found the dissection of dead bodies repellent and left without taking a degree, but his interest in natural history and geology had blossomed and it continued when he went on to study at Cambridge.

After Darwin graduated in 1831, his professor of botany recommended him to the Admiralty for the position of unpaid ship's naturalist on board HMS *Beagle* as it made a five-year surveying voyage around the world. The *Beagle* took Darwin around the coasts of South America, across the Pacific to the Antipodes, then on to South Africa, before returning to England. The experience opened his eyes to the wondrous variety of life forms around the planet – and the differences and similarities between them.

During the voyage Darwin read Charles Lyell's revolutionary *Principles of Geology*, which argued that geological features were the result of slow, gradual processes occurring over vast aeons of time. This 'uniformitarianism' was at odds with the orthodox 'catastrophism', which argued that such features were the result of sudden, violent upheavals over a relatively short timescale – and so conformed with the church's view that the earth was of very recent creation, as described in Genesis. On his travels Darwin collected more evidence in favour of Lyell's theory, such as fossil shells in bands of rock at a height of 12,000ft (3660m).

By the time Darwin reached the Galapagos Islands, a remote archipelago off the west coast of South America, his mind was open to new ways of thinking about the natural world. He had already noticed how the rheas – the large flightless birds of the South American pampas – looked like the ostriches of Africa, and yet were clearly different species. In the Galapagos he collected specimens of finches from the different islands, which were similar to each other yet also subtly different. Back home, closer study made it clear that the finches from the different islands were actually different species. Darwin realized they must all have had a common ancestor, but over time they had undergone a process of transmutation.

Ideas of evolution were not new, although they were not widely accepted. Darwin's own grandfather, Erasmus, had held

Soapy Sam versus Darwin's Bulldog

Less than a year after Darwin and Russell had presented their earth-shaking paper at the Linnaean Society, a much anticipated debate took place in Oxford during the annual meeting of the British Association for the Advancement of Science. On 30 June 1860 around a thousand people crowded into a room in the university's Museum of Natural History to hear Samuel Wilberforce, Bishop of Oxford, enunciate the Church of England's position on the theory of evolution.

Bishop Wilberforce (1805–73) – known as 'Soapy Sam' because of his unctuous manner and slippery debating skills – spoke for a full half hour. He ended his address by asking Thomas Huxley (1825–95) – the distinguished biologist who was to speak in defence of his friend Darwin – whether he was 'related by his grandfather's or grandmother's side to an ape'.

When Huxley rose to speak, he asserted that 'a man has no reason to be ashamed to have an ape for his grandfather'. He continued in a cool and quiet manner to demolish his opponent: 'If there was an ancestor whom I should feel shame in recalling, it would rather be a *man*, a man of restless and versatile intellect, who, not content with an equivocal success in his own sphere of activity, plunges into scientific questions with which he has no real acquaintance, only to obscure them by an aimless rhetoric, and distract the attention of his hearers from the real point at issue by eloquent digressions, and skilled appeals to religious prejudice.'

The debate was a key moment in the acceptance of Darwin's theory, and Huxley for ever after became known as 'Darwin's Bulldog'. It would become clear – if it was not always reassuring – to the majority of people that religion could no longer explain the physical world; that was now the province of science. The insecurities engendered by this sense of a God-inspired world replaced by a clinically amoral Nature is invoked, poetically, in Matthew Arnold's masterpiece of a few years later, 'Dover Beach' (1867):

The Sea of Faith
Was once, too, at the full, and round earth's shore
Lay like the folds of a bright girdle furl'd.
But now I only hear
Its melancholy, long, withdrawing roar,
Retreating, to the breath
Of the night-wind, down the vast edges drear
And naked shingles of the world.

the view – shared with the French scientist Jean-Baptiste Lamarck (1744–1829) – that species evolved over time by inheriting acquired characteristics. What Darwin himself came to realize was that animals (and plants), in order to survive, adapt over time to changes in their natural habitat, and if they are geographically isolated for long enough these adaptations will become so pronounced that the rhea of South America, for example, emerges as a different species from its cousin, the African ostrich.

Darwin's big breakthrough followed his reading in 1838 of Thomas Malthus's *Principles of Population*, which argued that human population growth is always checked by limits in the food supply, or by disease or war. Darwin realized that the variations or adaptations he saw in animals resulted from the 'struggle for existence', in which those individuals who possessed or inherited a characteristic that better fitted them to survive in their environment were more likely to breed and pass on this favourable characteristic. He called this process 'natural selection'.

It was an idea of great simplicity, and yet of enormous explanatory power. Through the 1830s, 1840s and 1850s Darwin continued to amass evidence, reluctant to put his theory before the public, aware as he was of the devastating impact it would have on religious belief and the comforting notion of a moral and purposeful world.

Darwin agonized and prevaricated, suffering more and more from the psychosomatic, but nevertheless painful, illnesses that were to plague him for the rest of his life. Then in 1858 he received a letter from a young naturalist, Alfred Russell Wallace, who had, it was clear, independently come up with the idea of natural selection. On 1 July 1859 the two presented a joint paper at the Linnaean Society in London. And in November of that year Darwin published *On the Origin of Species by Means of Natural Selection*.

It was a knock-out blow to the old, comfortable certainties. Any reasonable, thinking person found it almost impossible to dissent, such was the compelling nature of the argument and the overwhelming volume of the evidence. The big guns of the Church of England were wheeled out to mount a counteroffensive, but to no avail. In place of 'All things bright and beautiful, all creatures great and small' came, as Tennyson had foreseen, 'Nature, red in tooth and claw'.

The implication that man and the apes must share a common

ancestor was obvious. Darwin made this explicit when, in 1871, he eventually published the long-awaited sequel *The Descent of Man*. No longer did humanity possess some special status as God's appointed steward on earth, separate from and superior to the other animals. Man was now just one beast among many. It was a bleaker world view that Darwin bequeathed to us, but it was also more intellectually honest and showed us that there was still as much – or more – wonder and mystery in a Darwinian universe.

Charles Dickens
1812–1870

In literary matters my dividing line is: do you like Dickens or do you not? If you do not, I am sorry for you, and that is the end of the matter.
Stanley Baldwin

Charles Dickens was the English writer of his age. Rambunctious, touching, tragic and comic by turns, his novels captured the public's imagination like no others before or since. He transmuted the realities he saw into an enthralling and encyclopedic social panorama of hypnotic power. His works, effectively, constitute a world, such that even those who have read little of the author know what is meant by the term 'Dickensian'.

The master storyteller wrote a canon of classics. His books weave together darkness and light, romance and melodrama, the terrifying and the tender; one moment they are gruesome and fantastical, the next tear-inducingly funny. From the debtors' prison of *Little Dorrit* (1855–7) to the workhouse and thieves' dens of *Oliver Twist* (1837–8), to the machinations of the Chancery Court in *Bleak House* (1852–3), Dickens created a vision of London as a pulsating, living organism, which even today dominates our conceptions of the Victorian metropolis. From the moment his first major work, *The Pickwick Papers*, was serialized (1836), and a print run of 400 mushroomed to 40,000, he was established as the writer who understood the English better than anyone else.

Dickens's rudimentary schooling was cut short at 15 by the profligacy of his father, an erstwhile naval clerk. The boy who had wanted since childhood to be an actor and who was remembered by his schoolfellows for his 'animation and animal spirits' became instead a reluctant legal clerk. In spring of 1833 Dickens, by now a journalist (a more exciting but 'wearily uncertain' career), got an audition at Covent Garden Theatre but failed to keep the appointment on account of illness. An accident of fate, perhaps, because that summer he began to write. By the following year, under the pen-name 'Boz', Dickens was winning in print the fame that he had previously hoped for on the stage. His love of the theatre clearly influenced his work. Later he would adapt classics such as *A Christmas Carol* (1843) for the stage. But he never renewed his application to Covent Garden.

The colourful names of Dickens' characters were of paramount importance to him. He could not begin a new book until he had them right. He kept lists of those with special potential and scribbled down myriad variations. Martin Chuzzlewit was nearly Martin Sweezlewag. With age his work grew darker and more serious, but comedy was never far off. Frequently seized by hysterical mirth at the most inappropriate times, Dickens was always quick to see the ridiculous side of things.

Dickens-mania gripped rich and poor alike. Instalments of his works were read out to crowds of the urban poor, who had clubbed together to hire the latest episode from the circulating library. Dickens made the public laugh and he made them cry. His characters were as real to them as life. At New York Harbour, crowds pressed around disembarking passengers to ask about the fate of *The Old Curiosity Shop*'s Little Nell. Her death inspired hysteria; the Irish nationalist Daniel O'Connell was allegedly so enraged that he threw the book out of a train carriage window.

'I have great faith in the poor,' Dickens wrote to a friend in 1844. 'I shall never cease, I hope, until I die, to advocate their being made as happy and as wise as the circumstances ... may admit.' In his fantastical exaggerations the radical philanthropist showed the bleakness that faced so many. For some readers, it was an illustration of their lives; it made others realize how wretched such lives

The real Fagin and the Victorian underworld

In 1849 the journalist Henry Mayhew, founder of *Punch* magazine, began a series of articles for the *Morning Chronicle*. They would eventually become the mammoth four-volume *London Labour and the London Poor*, a work that shocked his middle-class readership with its unflinching picture of the realities of London's slums and which influenced radicals, reformers and writers, among them Charles Dickens.

Mayhew revealed the dark underside of the city, a world of crime, filth and depravity. Interviewing chimney sweeps and flower girls, beggars and street entertainers, pickpockets and prostitutes, Mayhew depicted a world, as the writer Thackeray described it, 'of terror and wonder'. He spoke of the 'pure-finders', who gathered dog faeces to sell to tanners. He introduced his readers to the 'mud-larks', children who made their living scavenging around the banks of the cholera-infested, sewage-filled Thames for coins and wood or for coal dropped from the barges.

Mayhew let his subjects speak in their own words and reported his findings with a humanist's eye. He told of Jack, a West End crossing-sweep, 'a good-looking lad with a pair of large, mild eyes'; of his friend 'Gander', who earned extra money with his acrobatic 'catenwheeling'. He described their room in the lodging house that was as clean as it could be and the

could be. One American reviewer considered Dickens' works a force for reform far more effective than anything the 'open assaults of Radicalism or Chartism' could achieve.

Dickens knew how quickly a man could slide into degradation. At the same age at which Oliver Twist is confronted with the terrifying darkness of the world, Dickens had become a child labourer. His time in a blacking factory, necessitated by his father's bankruptcy, was brief. When the family's fortunes recovered some months later, Dickens returned to school. His parents never spoke of it again. He himself kept it a close secret. But the memory never left him. He wanted always, he said, 'to present [the poor] in a favourable light to the rich'. His enduring fear of a return to poverty compelled him to work ever harder.

Left Alexander Pushkin, by the Russian portraitist Orest Adamowitsch Kiprenski (1782–1836).

Right Abraham Lincoln photographed in 1864 by Mathew Brady (1823–96). Lincoln sat on a number of occasions for Brady, who had risen to prominence as a photographer of the American Civil War. His photographs of the battlefields of Bull Run, Antietam and Gettysburg, as well as of senior Union and Confederate officers, provide a valuable documentary record of that conflict.

A caricature of Charles Darwin with the body of an ape that originally appeared in *The Hornet* magazine in 1871.

Above Sarah Bernhardt, born Henriette-Rosine Bernard, in a painting, *c*.1876, by Georges Clairin (1843–1919).

Right Oscar Wilde, photographed in cape and hat at the time of his arrival in America in 1882. When asked at Oxford what he proposed to do after taking his degree, Wilde replied: 'Somehow or other I'll be famous, and if not famous, I'll be notorious.'

Sir Winston Churchill flashes his famous 'V for Victory' sign to the crowd outside 10 Downing Street on his return from a visit to Washington, 1943.

Above Pablo Picasso and his then lover Françoise Gilot, photographed by Robert Capa in the South of France, 1951. Picasso's nephew Javier Vilato is in the background.

Right The writer and journalist George Orwell, Old Etonian and socialist. Born Eric Blair, he derived his pseudonym from George, patron saint of England, and the River Orwell in Suffolk, on whose banks he had once lived.

Above Anne Frank, May 1942, in a picture from her own photo album. Just two months after this picture was taken, her parents took the family into hiding.

Opposite top John Fitzgerald Kennedy and his wife Jackie arrive at the White House, 24 May 1961. In their presidential 'Camelot', JFK was implicitly cast in the role of King Arthur, and his glamorous wife as Queen Guinevere.

Opposite bottom A hero of our time: Nelson Mandela photographed the day after his release from prison, 12 February 1990.

Above US civil rights leader Martin Luther King Jr waves to supporters from the steps of the Lincoln Memorial, 28 August 1963. It was here that King delivered his famous 'I have a dream' speech.

Below A Chinese man stands alone to block a line of tanks heading east on Beijing's Chang'an Avenue in Tiananmen Square, 5 June 1989. The Chinese government crushed a student-led demonstration for democratic reform, killing an unknown number of demonstrators in the strongest anti-government protest since the 1949 Chinese revolution. The name 'Tiananmen', ironically, means 'Gate of Heavenly Peace'.

old woman who cared for them as well as she was able. He told the story of the drunken prostitute China Emma, the 'shrivelled and famine-stricken' woman lying in 'a hole … more like a beast in his lair than a human being in her home'.

In this world lived the model for *Oliver Twist*'s Fagin. One of London's most notorious pawnbrokers and 'fences' (receivers of stolen goods), Ikey Solomon became famous for his farcical escape from Newgate Prison. After he was arrested in 1827 for theft and receiving, the hackney coach that was intended to carry him to jail was in fact driven by his father-in-law. As the coach took a detour through Petticoat Lane, a gang of Solomon's friends overpowered the guards and set Ikey free.

Solomon fled to New York, but, in lieu of the notorious criminal, the authorities transported his wife and children to Tasmania. 'Determined to brave it all for the sake of my dear wife and children', Solomon sailed to join them. For want of a warrant, it was a year before Tasmanian officials could arrest him and send him back to England.

Solomon's trial at the Old Bailey was one of the sensations of the day. But unlike Fagin, Solomon did not hang. Found guilty on two counts of theft, he was sentenced to 14 years' transportation and promptly sent back to Tasmania. Solomon lived out the rest of his days there. The man said at one point to be worth £30,000 died in his sixties, estranged from his family and leaving an estate of just £70.

Dickens was renowned for his wit and his marvellous talent for mimicry. He developed an extraordinarily successful second career giving public readings of his works. His mammoth tours across England and America sold out in every city. He turned his flock of offspring into an amateur theatrical troupe, performing plays in which he generally took the starring role. In the course of these ventures he met Ellen Ternan, the young actress who was the great love of his later life.

He had a reputation for oddity. He was obsessed with light, filling his brightly painted room with mirrors. When Dickens was a child, his father pointed out to him a house that, he said, would demonstrate a man's having made it in life. So in 1856 the adult Dickens bought it – Gad's Hill Place in Higham, Kent. He was a demanding father, while his total repudiation of his wife Catherine after over 20 years of marriage was undeniably cruel.

Dickens' masterpiece was *A Tale of Two Cities* (1859) set in the French Revolution, which ends with Sydney Carton, rogue-turned-saviour, giving his life for that of a better man, saying 'It is a far, far better thing that I do now, than I have ever done; it is a far, far better rest that I go to, than I have ever known.'

Sir Richard Burton
1821–1890

He was one of those men in whom nature runs riot; she endows him with not one or two but twenty different talents.

Alan Moorehead

Sir Richard Burton was a Victorian explorer, scholar, eccentric and gifted maverick. He travelled into the undiscovered heart of Africa and was the first European known to have successfully made the pilgrimage to Mecca. He was the scholar who translated the *Arabian Nights* and the *Kama Sutra* in all their unexpurgated glory. Scandalous and courageous, Burton spent his life breaking down the barriers erected by geography and society.

Burton was a master of disguise. A brilliant linguist who spoke over 40 languages and dialects, he had an anthropologist's fascination with other cultures, particularly those of the East. Combined with his swarthy appearance, these talents allowed him on many occasions to pass for a native. His time as an undercover agent for the East India Company, which involved masquerading as a trader, prepared him for his most dramatic and dangerous escapade: making the pilgrimage to Mecca (*haj*) disguised as a Muslim. Burton underwent circumcision in order to perfect his subterfuge. Had his fellow pilgrims detected him, he would undoubtedly have been killed. He successfully reached Mecca in 1853, and his account of his astonishingly audacious achievement remains legendary.

As an explorer, Burton sought out the most dangerous places on earth. On an expedition to Somalia, an ambush by tribesmen left him with a javelin skewering his face. The resulting scar only added to his reputation as a devil-may-care adventurer. On his three-year journey into the heart of East Africa to discover the source of the Nile (1856–60), Burton nearly died from a variety of diseases and was often too ill to walk. This expedition, in which he discovered Lake Tanganyika, is as famous for his subsequent betrayal by his second in command, John Hanning Speke. Returning to England before Burton, Speke presented their findings to the Royal Geographical Society as exclusively his own. Disregarding his own frequent incapacitations (for part of the journey he was temporarily blind), Speke dismissed Burton's role as that of a sickly appendage. Burton stoically endured Speke's vicious campaign to smear his name, displaying a nobility of spirit that his fellow explorer so conspicuously lacked.

Speke's ability to mobilize opinion against Burton had much to do with society's perception of the latter as an immoral outsider. The son of an army officer who had been retired from active service after offending his superiors, Burton spent most of his peripatetic childhood on the continent. Educated by private tutors, Burton's university career was short-lived. Clashing with the dons after attending a forbidden steeplechase, he was sent down from Oxford in 1842. He abandoned England once more to join the army of the East India Company. The result was that Burton remained forever outside the 'old-boy network' that dominated Victorian England. He spent most of his life abroad: as an officer, as an African explorer, and as a consul to Fernando Po, Damascus and Trieste, where he eventually retired. England was 'the only country where I never feel at home' – merely a place to recover between adventures and to drum up much-needed cash.

Burton both outraged and fascinated the British establishment with his refusal to conform to petty social conventions. His contempt for small-mindedness and refusal to kowtow to authority were construed as arrogance. Fellow officers in India suspiciously regarded his empathy with other cultures as 'going native'. Burton's open-mindedness towards other cultures – in particular sexual practices, which he recorded in detail in his travel journals – outraged Victorian morality. Rumours abounded about the diabolical 'Ruffian Dick' – about his sexual experimentations, his hard-living habits and his apparently murderous

The adventures of Jane Digby – Dorset to Damascus

In 1869 Richard Burton took up the position of consul in Damascus. Here, he and his wife Isabel became close friends with one of the most extraordinary and adventurous women of the 19th century: Jane Digby (1807–81). The daughter of an admiral, Lord Digby, and grand-daughter of the Earl of Leicester, Jane Digby was blessed with blue eyes, alabaster skin and golden hair and grew up to be one of the reigning beauties of Regency society. But she was also a true original: highly intelligent, curious, witty, daring and lasciviously uninhibited (she possessed a modern enthusiasm for what she called 'the rapture'). She was also a gifted painter.

While still a young girl, Jane was almost destroyed by the grossly unjust marriage laws of her day. At the age of 17 she was disastrously married to Edward, Lord Ellenborough, a man twice her age who was a successful if dull politician and later governor-general of India. She soon embarked on a series of adulterous affairs, first with a cousin, Colonel George Anson, and then with the great romance of her early years, Prince Felix Schwarzenberg – an Austrian magnate, young diplomat and (later) the chief minister of the Habsburg Empire, who rescued the empire during the great crises after the 1848 revolutions. When this affair was revealed in her subsequent divorce from Ellenborough, the case became the sensational media scandal of the age.

instincts. He did little to dispel such gossip. Challenged once by a doctor who asked disapprovingly, 'How do you feel when you have killed a man?', Burton replied: 'Quite jolly, what about you?' Many saw him as a hero; others would leave a room if he entered it.

Burton's literary legacy illustrates his extraordinary unconventionality. Having collaborated on the translation of the *Kama Sutra* (1883), he turned his attention to the Eastern masterpiece *Arabian Nights*. His translation (1885) retained the full sexual content of the Arabic original, while his extensive footnotes displayed a lifetime's wealth of knowledge of Eastern culture and practices. It is a work of genius, to this day the pre-eminent translation in English. Unable to find a publisher, Burton printed it himself and was quick to notice the irony in its scandalous success: 'I have struggled for forty-seven years, distinguishing

Jane's destiny as an outcast was now ensured, as the relationship with Schwarzenberg collapsed and she was forced to live abroad, but it was her gift to turn such early misfortune into a fascinating cosmopolitan adventure. She settled in Munich, where she became the friend and mistress of King Ludwig I of Bavaria, a romantic aesthete who had a weakness for such adventuresses (he later lost his throne because of his love for the ruthless courtesan Lola Montez). Jane then married a German nobleman, Baron Carl Venningen, and bore him two children, one of them almost certainly the natural daughter of King Ludwig. But she soon fell in love again and eloped with a young Greek cad, the 'dangerous' Count Spiros Theotoky, with whom she travelled to Athens. She bore him a beloved son, Leonidas, but the boy died tragically in an accident and the relationship with Theotoky foundered.

Jane's next love was an Albanian warlord Xristodolous Hadji-Petros, the king of Greece's governor of Albania and northern Greece. After this she embarked on a series of daring excursions, often mounted on horse or camel, in the Middle East, where she fell in love with the Arabic and Bedouin way of life. Middle-aged but still beautiful, she visited Jerusalem, Baghdad and the ruins of Palmyra. She enjoyed affairs with various Arab chieftains until she settled in Damascus as the wife of the true love of her life, Sheikh Medjuel el Mazrab, who was 20 years her junior. She adopted an existence unique for a woman both then and now, assuming the Bedouin nomadic life in the desert for half the year and living in her palace for the other six months. She died in Damascus, where she lies buried.

myself honourably in every way that I possibly could. I never had a compliment, nor a "thank you", nor a single farthing. I translate a doubtful book in my old age, and I immediately make sixteen thousand guineas. Now that I know the tastes of England, we need never be without money.'

After Burton's death in 1890, his wife Isabel tragically burnt all his papers. A devout Roman Catholic who fell in love with Burton at first sight and waited ten years to marry him, Isabel was his greatest champion. Her campaigns for consulates and a knighthood for her husband have been criticized as pushiness. But it is fairer to say that Isabel, who built for her husband a marble tomb shaped like a Bedouin tent, rightly sought recognition for a man who was as talented and unconventional as he was heroic.

Florence Nightingale 1820–1910

What a comfort it was to see her pass. She would speak to one, and nod and smile to as many more ... we lay there by the hundreds, but we could kiss her shadow as it fell and lay our heads on the pillow again content.

An anonymous soldier in the Crimean War

With unsurpassable dedication and courage, Florence Nightingale devoted her life to a mission that has had an incomparable effect on the lives of millions. Tenaciously single-minded, the Lady of the Lamp overcame obstacles and obduracy to transform the state of medical care in the British Army and to establish nursing as a trained and respectable profession for women.

Named after her Italian birthplace, Florence Nightingale was raised in England and educated at home by her father to a standard well above that considered advisable for women of her era. By the time the bright and bookish Nightingale reached her teens, she was well aware that marriage and a life in society – the usual prospects for a girl of her class – held little appeal for her.

When, at 16, she heard God's voice informing her that she had a mission, Nightingale set about escaping from the family fold into a life of her own. But it was several years before her parents allowed her to enter the socially disreputable profession of nursing. She became an expert on public health and hospitals until finally, at almost 30, she persuaded her parents to let her go to Germany to one of the few institutions that provided training for nurses.

When the Crimean War broke out and newspapers began graphically reporting the terrible condition of the wounded British soldiers, Nightingale, by now the superintendent of the Institution for the Care of Sick Gentlewomen in London, was one of the first to respond. Sidney Herbert, an old friend and secretary of state for war, asked her to lead a party of nurses and to direct nursing in the British military hospitals in Turkey. In November 1854 Nightingale and her party arrived at the Barrack Hospital in Scutari, near Istanbul.

When she sailed back to England two years later, the 'Lady of the Lamp' was a national hero. Battling against filthy conditions and a chronic shortage of supplies, faced with insubordinate nurses who were frequently drunk and intransigent doctors reluctant to acknowledge the authority of a woman, Nightingale transformed the military hospitals. She personally attended almost every patient, administering comfort and advice as she made her nightly rounds. The mortality rate of wounded soldiers when she arrived was 50 per cent; by the time she left, it was just 2 per cent.

Nightingale constantly set herself new and ever more ambitious goals. Within a year of taking up her first London post she was longing to escape 'this little molehill'. After nursing the sick in Turkey for a while, she set her sights on the greater goal of transforming the welfare of the British Army as a whole. It was a task to which she dedicated the rest of her life. She pushed for the establishment of royal commissions on the matter and produced reports that were instrumental in the foundation of the Army Medical School. When she turned her attention to army health in India, she became so supreme an authority on the subject that successive viceroys sought her advice before taking up their posts.

'The very essence of Truth seemed to emanate from her,' wrote one contemporary, awed by 'her perfect fearlessness in telling it'. Undaunted by resistance, Nightingale triumphed over the Scutari doctor who initially refused to allow nurses into the wards; the inspector-general of hospitals who tried to argue that her authority did not extend to the Crimea; the government officials who were tepid about her mission to improve the health and well-being of the British soldier.

The woman appointed general superintendent of female nursing in the military hospitals abroad transformed nursing into a respected profession. On her return to England she promoted training for midwives and for nurses in workhouses, and in 1860 she established the world's first school for nurses, at St Thomas's Hospital in London.

Austere to the point of asceticism, Nightingale rejected her status as heroine, refusing official transport home from the Crimea and

The charge of the Light Brigade

On 25 October 1854, in the heat of the Battle of Balaclava during the Crimean War, the gorgeously attired Light Brigade obeyed the order of their commander, James Thomas Brudenell, Lord Cardigan, to charge along the valley in front of them. With Russian artillery holding the heights on either side and another battery lying at its end, it was, as Tennyson described it, a mile-long 'valley of Death' into which the 673 cavalrymen rode: 'Into the jaws of Death / Into the mouth of Hell'.

The order was a tragic mistake, the result of miscommunication and personal rivalries. From his hilly vantage point, the army's commander-in-chief, Lord Raglan, had ordered the Light Brigade to disrupt Russian troops attempting to remove some captured guns. But six hundred feet below on the plain, the cavalry's commander, Lord Lucan, could only see the Russians in their impregnable position at the far end of the valley. When the mystified and notoriously slow Lucan queried the order, Captain Nolan, the messenger, lost patience: 'There, my Lord, there is your enemy! There are your guns!' he cried. Gesturing angrily in the general direction of the Russians, he rode off.

Lucan delivered the order to the irascible Cardigan, who was also his despised brother-in-law. When the Light Brigade's commander protested, personal enmity stiffened Lucan's resolve. He declared that the order must be obeyed. Muttering loudly 'Well, here goes the last of the Brudenells!', Cardigan rode off to set in motion the suicidal mission.

rebuffing all suggestions of public receptions. Back in England, she sequestered herself, rarely leaving her house. The invalidism of the world's most famous nurse is considered to have been largely psychosomatic. Nevertheless, attended by a constant stream of important visitors, Nightingale was able to devote herself tirelessly to an extensive network of causes.

Her single-mindedness bred a certain ruthlessness. Driven by a sense of divine mission, Nightingale was impatient with those whom she considered to lack the necessary zeal. When the dying Herbert had to curtail his involvement in some or other charitable cause, she cut him off. But it was this tenacity that enabled her to bring about such extraordinary changes in the nursing profession.

The enemy guns were silent as the Light Brigade began its advance. But as Nolan, realizing the mistake, galloped in front of Cardigan shouting unintelligibly, the Russians opened fire. He was the first to be killed by the batteries that let fly a ceaseless barrage of shells and shot as the cavalry rode on steadily and unflinchingly 'while horse and hero fell'.

Frozen in horror, war correspondents and soldiers watched from the hills above. 'I am old, I have seen battles, but this is too much,' said one French officer. A compatriot nearby, General Pierre Bosquet, murmured one of history's most famous asides: 'It is magnificent, but it is not war.'

Seeing the Light Brigade's destruction, Lucan refused to sacrifice the Heavy Brigade too. Cardigan abandoned his men halfway through, refusing as a general to fight among 'the private soldiers'. Only a charge by the French cavalry saved the Light Brigade from total destruction. The bedraggled survivors stumbled back through the cannon smoke, their brightly coloured, fur-trimmed uniforms unrecognizable through the blood and dust. Almost half their number had been killed or wounded. When the horrified Raglan berated Cardigan for leading such an insane attack, the latter replied that he was simply following orders.

It was, announced *The Times*, 'an atrocity without parallel'. Even the enemy could not at first believe what they had seen, supposing that the British must be drunk. 'You are noble fellows,' the Russian commander Pavel Liprandi told a band of prisoners, 'and I am sincerely sorry for you.' 'When can their glory fade?' said Tennyson of the 'Noble six hundred'.

In 1910 the 90-year-old Nightingale, blind for a decade, died in London. At her express wish, the offer of a national funeral and burial in Westminster Abbey was declined. With extraordinary compassion and strength of will, Nightingale had effectively created her profession. A woman who was, for a nation, the exemplar of heroism, she brought comfort to millions.

Louis Pasteur 1822–1895

There are not two sciences: there is science and the application of science; these two are linked as the fruit is to the tree.

Louis Pasteur

The French microbiologist Louis Pasteur was a scientist whose varied and innovative studies made a massive contribution to the battle against disease in humans and animals. He did much pioneering work in the field of immunology, most importantly producing the first vaccine against rabies. His investigations into the micro-organisms that cause food to go bad were of vital importance to French and British industry, while the process of pasteurization he developed is still extremely important in preserving food and preventing illness.

Pasteur came from a family of tanners. As a child he was a keen artist, but it was clear to his teachers that he was academically very able. In 1843 he was admitted to the fine Parisian training college the École Normale Supérieure. He became a master of science in 1845, and in 1847 he presented a thesis on crystallography which earned him a doctorate.

With such a prestigious academic background and some ground-breaking research into physical chemistry behind him, Pasteur gained a professorship in the science faculty at the University of Strasbourg. Here he met Marie Laurent, the daughter of the university rector; they were married in 1849 and had five children together, two of whom survived childhood.

After six years in Strasbourg, Pasteur moved on to Lille. He held the firm view that the theoretical and practical aspects of science should work hand in hand, so he began teaching evening classes to young working men in Lille and taking his regular students around nearby factories. He also began to study the process of fermentation; one of his early achievements, in 1857, was to show that yeast could reproduce in the absence of oxygen. This became known as the Pasteur effect.

By 1857 Pasteur was back at the École Normale Supérieure. Here he continued his research into fermentation and demonstrated with unusual experimental rigour that the process was driven by the activity of minute organisms. In 1867 the French emperor Napoleon III relieved Pasteur of his teaching duties and granted him a research laboratory. With a new freedom of study, Pasteur set about resolving, once and for all, the great scientific debate over spontaneous generation – the question of whether germs and micro-organisms could simply 'appear' from nowhere. He found that germs were in fact transported in air and that food decomposed because it was exposed to them.

In 1862 Pasteur first tested the process, now known as pasteurization, by which milk and other liquids are heated to remove bacteria. In time this process would revolutionize the way food was prepared, stored and sold, and so save many people from infection. Pasteur also applied his theoretical work to the French vinegar and wine industries and the British beer industry, allowing the businesses concerned to produce goods that did not perish so quickly. It was as a result of a suggestion from Pasteur that the British surgeon Joseph Lister began in the 1860s to adopt antiseptic methods during operations.

In 1865 Pasteur saved the French silk industry by helping to identify and eradicate a parasite that was killing silkworms. By 1881 he had developed techniques to protect sheep from anthrax and chickens from cholera. He observed that creating a weakened form of a germ and vaccinating animals with it gave them effective immunity. It was an important development of Jenner's earlier use of cowpox germs to vaccinate against smallpox.

The most important vaccination Pasteur produced was against rabies. By manipulating the dried nervous systems of rabid rabbits, he created a weakened form of the terrible disease and managed to inoculate dogs against it. He had treated only 11 dogs in 1885 when he took dramatic action to save the life of a nine-year-old boy who had been bitten by a rabid dog. It was extremely risky but totally successful. Pasteur remained a hero of the medical establishment until his death, after a series of strokes, in 1895. He was buried in Notre Dame Cathedral in Paris, then reinterred in a crypt at the Pasteur Institute.

Jenner and smallpox

Smallpox was a contagious and deadly disease that had killed thousands of people a year throughout history. It caused plagues that swept through the Roman Empire in the 2nd and 3rd centuries AD, was a constant blight on the people of Europe, and wiped out millions of Native Americans in the New World. The turning point in the fight against the disease came in 1796, when the Gloucestershire physician Edward Jenner discovered how to give people immunity by inoculating them with cowpox.

Born in 1749 and raised in the countryside, Jenner was 20 when he went to London to be the house pupil of John Hunter, who was soon to become one of the country's most prominent surgeons. From Hunter, Jenner gained an enthusiasm for practical experiment, learning to collect specimens and to rely on observation rather than theory. When he returned to a country practice in 1773, he took these principles with him. During his career Jenner wrote medical papers on angina, ophthalmia and valve disease of the heart. In 1788 he was admitted to the Royal Society for a paper on the nesting habits of the cuckoo.

In the 18th century, smallpox was a common and grievous disease; causing large pustules and blisters all over the body, it was disfiguring and often fatal. The only known way to prevent infection was a method that had originated in Asia known as variolation, in which a healthy person was infected with matter from someone who had only suffered a mild bout of

Pasteur was one of many scientists who have performed medical miracles that have done so much to alleviate human suffering. Edward Jenner was one of the first, immunizing a child against smallpox in 1796. From the 1860s Joseph Lister (1827–1912) began his pioneering work on asepsis in surgery, using carbolic acid as an antiseptic to reduce the risk of infection. Operations had already been rendered far safer in the preceding decades by the physician John Snow (1813–58), who had introduced the use of anaesthesia to enable pain-free operations. Snow was also responsible for reducing the incidence of cholera by tracing its cause to contaminated water supplies.

In 1895 the German physicist Wilhelm Röntgen (1845–1923) discovered X-rays, thereby paving the way for vast improvements

the disease. This was risky and sometimes fatal: the 'mild' strain did not always stay mild and the infected person could pass on the disease to others.

Jenner noted the country wisdom that a man in search of a pretty wife should marry a milkmaid. He observed that dairy workers who had contracted cowpox – a trivial condition with slight similarities to smallpox – were generally free from the severe scarring that marked out smallpox survivors. Deducing that cowpox infection gave immunity to smallpox, in 1796 Jenner undertook a momentous experiment that would nevertheless be quite unthinkable today. A milkmaid named Sarah Nelmes had caught cowpox from a cow called Blossom. Jenner took pus from one of Sarah's blisters and inoculated it into eight-year-old James Phipps. Six weeks later Jenner inoculated the boy with smallpox; he remained healthy.

Jenner now devoted his life to promoting his vaccine. Despite medical scepticism, mistakes by other practitioners, and a lack of willing subjects for experiment, the project was soon a huge success. Parliament granted Jenner funds in 1802 and 1806. In 1805 he joined what would become the Royal Society of Medicine. Now a hero of the medical profession, he was appointed physician general to George IV in 1821. He died of a stroke two years later. In 1979/80 the World Health Organization formally declared that smallpox had been eradicated worldwide. The only threat from the disease is now thought to come from biological terrorism.

in the treatment of internal injuries. In 1928 Alexander Fleming (1881–1955) discovered penicillin, the first antibiotic, when he noticed that the mould in a dirty lab dish prevented bacteria from growing. In the 1950s the work of the French immunologist Jean Dausset (b.1916) led to great advances in our understanding of how the body fights disease. In 1953, Francis Crick (1916–2004) and James Watson (b.1928) discovered the double-helix shape of DNA. All those who worked on these projects deserve to be remembered as heroes of medicine.

Leo Tolstoy 1828–1910

When literature possesses a Tolstoy, it is easy and pleasant to be a writer; even when you know you have achieved nothing yourself ... this is not as terrible as it might otherwise be, because Tolstoy achieves for everyone. What he does serves to justify all the hopes and aspirations invested in literature.

Anton Chekhov

Leo Tolstoy is, in the opinion of many, the greatest novelist of all time. His two masterpieces, *War and Peace* and *Anna Karenina*, certainly rank among the finest novels ever written. He was also a skilful writer of short stories and essays, a powerful historian and a mystical philosopher who developed unusual yet influential Christian ideas about the human condition and moral improvement.

The essence of Tolstoy's greatness is his masterful grasp of human behaviour and motivation, which he combined with a natural gift for storytelling and an astonishing breadth and universality of vision. Though he was a deeply complex man, tormented by his failure to live up to his own standards, he had one of the sharpest and most original minds in the history of literature.

Count Leo Tolstoy was born into a prominent aristocratic family on his ancestral estate, Yasnaya Polyana, some 100 miles south of Moscow. His childhood was upset by the early deaths of both his parents, yet he still remembered it in idyllic terms. He was educated at home by tutors, but when he enrolled at the University of Kazan in 1844, it became apparent that he was neither a willing nor a diligent student, preferring to drink, gamble, womanize and socialize, and he left in 1847 without taking a degree.

He returned to Yasnaya Polyana with the intention of educating himself and improving the lot of his serfs, but his resolve soon weakened. In 1851 he went to the Caucasus, joined the army and used his experiences to write stories such as 'Hadji Murat', his best shorter work. It is a story of nobility, courage and betrayal in the life of a daring Chechen fighter during the thirty-year Russian war to defeat the legendary Chechen/Dagestani commander

Imam Shamyl and conquer the northern Caucasus. Tolstoy also served during the combined Anglo-French-Italian siege of the chief Russian naval base in the Crimea, Sebastopol. An 11-month campaign of appalling slaughter and incompetence ended in 1856 with the Russians sinking their ships, blowing up the garrison and evacuating. The experience was the basis for three literary sketches in which Tolstoy refined his technique of minutely analysing thoughts and feelings. 'The hero of my tale,' the author wrote, 'whom I love with all the power of my soul … is Truth.' In 1862 he married Sofia Andreyevna Behrs and again returned to his estate, this time with a plan to teach and learn from the simple peasant children.

Tolstoy's most productive period came between 1863 and 1877. From 1865 he was working on *War and Peace*, which he finished in 1869. This vast work is both domestic and political. It consists of three main strands: the monumental struggle of Russia and France, Alexander I versus Napoleon, between 1805 and 1812, particularly the French invasion and retreat from Moscow; the interlinked tales of two aristocratic Russian families, the Rostovs and the Bolkonskys; and lengthy essays on history. It is clear that Tolstoy identified himself with the curious, diffident and doubting, but kind, direct and moral character of Pierre Bezukhov.

Tolstoy has an original view of the wars he describes. He portrays Napoleon as a bungling egomaniac, the Russian tsar Alexander I as a man of fine words, obsessed with his own legacy, and the maligned Russian commander Mikhail Kutuzov as a wily old man of war. Combat itself is seen as chaos, without any overall connection or intrinsic structure. The fictional characters all to some extent see life in the same way and find solace only through what would become Tolstoy's main philosophy: salvation through devotion to family and the tasks of everyday life.

War and Peace, with its acute understanding of individual motivation and action, may have redefined the novel, but Tolstoy's next major project, *Anna Karenina*, was no less influential. Written between 1875 and 1877, it applied the principles of *War and Peace* to family life. 'All happy families resemble each other,' he wrote; 'each unhappy family is unhappy in its own way'. At the centre of the story lies the tragic affair of Anna with Count Alexei Vronsky, an army officer.

Russian heroes: Suvorov and Kutuzov

On 7 September 1812, about 70 miles west of Moscow, Russian troops under Field Marshal Prince Mikhail Kutuzov attempted to halt the invasion of Russia by Napoleon's *Grande Armée* in one of the bloodiest battles in history. The indecisive carnage involved a quarter of a million soldiers and more than 1000 guns. There were some 75,000 casualties, as thousands of men were cut to pieces by deadly cannon bombardments.

At Borodino Napoleon gave one of his poorest battlefield displays. Though he encouraged his men to match the spirit of his magnificent victory over the Russians at Austerlitz in 1805, he was himself dogged by ill health and failed to exploit Kutuzov's stretched resources and tactical weaknesses. Fighting began in the early morning and see-sawed back and forth over a series of earthworks, until by evening both sides were exhausted. The Russians withdrew at nightfall and soon afterwards the French occupied Moscow unopposed.

Many historians have seen Borodino as a missed opportunity for the French, who were hobbled by Napoleon's illness and indecisiveness. But in *War and Peace* Tolstoy, adopting his unique perspective on war, gives a radically different account of the battle:

At the battle of Borodino Napoleon shot at no one and killed no one. That was all done by the soldiers. Therefore it was not he who killed people.

In vivid detail Tolstoy paints Anna's mental contortions under the pressure of society's hypocrisies and her inner struggles (ultimately in vain) to rationalize her own behaviour.

Like *War and Peace*, *Anna Karenina* was a vehicle for Tolstoy's moral convictions. From 1877 he became more and more obsessed with the spiritual side of his life and suffered various crises of faith. He was excommunicated from the Orthodox Church in 1901 for his distinctive reinterpretation of Christianity, in which he emphasized pacifist resistance to evil, love for one's enemies, extreme asceticism and avoidance of anger and lust. He soon had a growing band of disciples across the world.

Tolstoy continued to write, using the profits from his third major

> *The French soldiers went to kill and be killed at the battle of Borodino not because of Napoleon's orders but by their own volition ... Had Napoleon then forbidden them to fight the Russians, they would have killed him and have proceeded to fight the Russians because it was inevitable.*
>
> *And it was not Napoleon who directed the course of the battle, for none of his orders were executed and during the battle he did not know what was going on before him.*

The cunning old one-eyed Kutuzov was always reluctant to fight, preferring to preserve his forces. After the slaughter at Borodino, Napoleon failed because Kutuzov's army was still intact: Kutuzov fell back cautiously, letting winter and delay force Napoleon's disastrous retreat from Moscow.

Having driven the French from Russia, Kutuzov died in 1813 very much a military hero in a distinctly Russian mould. He joined a pantheon of others, including Alexander Nevsky, the young Prince of Novgorod (1220–63), who defeated invading Swedes and Livonian knights; and the eccentric scarecrow-like Field Marshal Prince Alexander Suvorov (1729–1800), probably the greatest ever Russian commander, who never lost a battle. Suvorov defeated the Turks and the French, created aphorisms on tactics in his book *The Art of Victory* for his troops to learn, and in 1799 led his army over the Alps, matching Hannibal's feat of centuries earlier. (By way of exercise he also liked to do his gymnastics naked every morning in front of his army.) In 1942 Stalin created Orders of Nevsky, Kutuzov and Suvorov for military courage.

novel, *Resurrection* (1899), to help the persecuted Doukhobor Christian sect to emigrate to Canada.

Deeply unhappy in his marriage and his divided court of disciples, the ailing Tolstoy escaped from home with one of his daughters and a doctor but collapsed and died in the winter of 1910 in a railway station, refusing to see his wife. He had a simple burial on his family estate. Though frequently eccentric, his moral, ethical and spiritual ideas became highly influential; Gandhi, for one, was impressed by his doctrine of non-violent resistance. But it is his contribution to literature that towers above all else.

Pyotr Ilyich Tchaikovsky 1840–1893

Truly there would be reason to go mad were it not for music.

Tchaikovsky, on the fundamental importance of music to his existence

Pyotr Ilyich Tchaikovsky is one of the most enduringly popular composers in the Western tradition, whose symphonies and concertos have been recorded more often than those of any other composer, and whose ballet scores are among the most famous in the world.

While weathering the strains of an intensely difficult personal life, Tchaikovsky rejected the folk-based styles of other Russian composers of his age to create soaring, sweeping and heartbreakingly poignant Romantic works that contrast vividly with the brilliant but bleak operas of Wagner or the impassioned restraint of Brahms. From the 'Romeo and Juliet' Overture and *Swan Lake* to the '1812' Overture and his great opera *Eugene Onegin*, Tchaikovsky's music is as widely loved today as when it was written.

Like Beethoven and Mozart, Tchaikovsky showed early musical talent. He played the piano from the age of five and composed songs for his siblings, as well as reading and writing in French and German. His father was a mining engineer – comfortable but not wealthy – and the young Tchaikovsky was marked down for a career in law, attending the St Petersburg Imperial School of Jurisprudence from the ages of 12 to 19, then going straight into a civil service job at the ministry of justice. As he grew older, his talent for music grew ever more evident. He enrolled at the new St Petersburg Conservatory of Music in 1862 (resigning his job the next year) and, after maturing astonishingly quickly, left in 1865, already a fully developed musical personality. The following year he moved to Moscow, where he taught musical theory at the Russian Musical Society.

By 1870 Tchaikovsky had produced his first great work, the concert overture 'Romeo and Juliet'. It passed almost unnoticed when it premiered in Moscow but had more success in an 1872 revised version in St Petersburg. It was an abstract orchestral work that nevertheless told a story – one perfectly suited to Tchaikovsky's tragic and passionate temperament. His life had been affected by tragedy since 1854, when his beloved mother had died of cholera. He later wrote, 'I have attempted with love to express both the agony and also the bliss.'

In love lay Tchaikovsky's personal agony. From the late 1860s he was passionately involved with several young male students, and one of his favourites, Edouard Zak, killed himself in 1873. This had a profound effect on Tchaikovsky. A few years later, perhaps in an attempt to purge himself of homosexual tendencies but more likely to avoid gossip and scandal, he married an obsessive ex-student, Antonina Miliukova. She had plagued him with letters and threatened to kill herself if he did not return her affection. Despite clear warning signs that it was a completely inappropriate match, Tchaikovsky proposed to her in May 1877 and wed her in July that year. By September the marriage was over in all but name.

Despite this tumultuous period in his romantic life, Tchaikovsky was in fluent composing vein. He produced the ballet score *Swan Lake* in 1875–6. In 1877–8 he composed his outstanding Fourth Symphony and his greatest opera, *Eugene Onegin*, a musical interpretation of Pushkin's famous verse story. At first *Onegin* was not well received, but as time passed it came to be recognized as an operatic masterpiece – and when the piano score was published it sold in hatfuls. A lifelong Francophile, Tchaikovsky's music shows the clarity and lightness of French models rather than the more sombre and introverted tones of his German contemporaries.

With his marriage over, Tchaikovsky entered another important phase of his life: his relationship with the wealthy philanthropist Nadezhda von Meck. Though the pair never properly met, she bankrolled his career with an annual salary of 6000 roubles. This allowed him to quit his job and devote his life to composing. Meck supported him from 1876 until her abrupt severance of links in 1890, the period when Tchaikovsky composed some of his most famous works. In 1880 he wrote his overture '1812', with its bombastic finale that includes 16 cannon and the ringing of church bells. It premiered in Moscow two years later. By this time Tchaikovsky's fame was beginning to peak. He was commissioned

The Russian dancer

Tchaikovsky was the first symphonic composer to turn his hand to ballet, and *Swan Lake*, which premiered in Moscow in 1877, was an important stage in this art form's advance. Ballet developed from the Renaissance court spectacle, which had been reinvigorated by France's Louis XIV in the 1660s. Pointe work, or the art of dancing on the very tips of the toes, led to the emergence of the ballerina in the early 19th century. From the 1830s to the 1850s, a rise in the popularity of ballet coincided with a decline in its standards everywhere except for Denmark and Russia. Moscow's Bolshoi Ballet was founded in 1776 by the city prosecutor Prince Peter Urusov and an English entrepreneur Michael Maddox, but the Imperial Ballet in St Petersburg was backed by the imperial family and invigorated by the brilliant choreographer Marius Petipa (1818–1910), whose revolutionary, sometimes orientalistic, ballets included *The Pharaoh's Daughter* (1862), *The Talisman* (1889), *The Sleeping Beauty* (1890, music by Tchaikovsky) and *The Nutcracker* (choreographed by Lev Ivanov, under Petipa's supervision, music again by Tchaikovsky) (1892). The ballerinas became artistic and social stars in St Petersburg: one prima ballerina, Mathilde Kschessinska, became the mistress of the future Emperor Nicholas II, and was then shared between the grand dukes Sergei and Andrei, becoming so rich that she built her own palace.

Outside Russia, the most popular company was Serge Diaghilev's Ballets Russes, which took Russian ballet across Europe and the Americas.

to write the Coronation March for Tsar Alexander III in 1883, and his presence as a conductor was sought across Europe.

He wrote his Fifth Symphony in 1888 and followed this with two ballets – *The Sleeping Beauty*, completed in 1889, and *The Nutcracker*, completed in 1892. He also composed an opera, *The Queen of Spades*, unveiled in Moscow in 1890. All these works benefited from a more stable emotional environment, the lack of financial worries, and a strict work regime. By this time his fame had spread to America, where he was asked to conduct his *Coronation March* at the opening concert in New York's Carnegie Hall.

Like his mother, Tchaikovsky died most probably from cholera, contracted from drinking contaminated water in a St Petersburg

Diaghilev, who worked closely with the young composer Igor Stravinsky on *The Firebird* (1910), *Petrushka* (1911) and *The Rite of Spring* (1913), caused uproar with his challenging productions, which melded together the ideals of art, music, dance and drama. It was Diaghilev who made famous Vaslav Nijinsky (1890–1950), renowned as much for his athletic leaps as for his scandalously daring performances in the Paris premieres of *The Afternoon of a Faun* (1912) and *The Rite of Spring* (1913), both choreographed by the dancer himself.

The Russian ballerina Anna Pavlova (1881–1931) toured the world for 20 years, first with the Imperial Ballet, and from 1913 with independent productions. Her 'Dying Swan' was one of the finest individual performances known, devised by the respected choreographer Michel Fokine, who took ballet's pretty athleticism and added historical authenticity, drama and expression.

After 1917, the new Soviet government appreciated the prestige of ballet, renaming the Imperial as the Mariinsky until 1934 when the Soviet dictator Stalin named it after his assassinated henchman, Kirov. Stalin patronized ballerinas such as Maya Plisetskaya and Galina Ulanova. But after Nijinsky, the most famous male dancer of the century was Rudolf Nureyev (1939–93) admired for his animalistic grace and athletic beauty, who defected in 1961, becoming a huge star in the West. His partnership with Margot Fonteyn for many represented the height of ballet performance in the 20th century.

restaurant in October 1893. It was just days after the premiere of perhaps his most outstanding and tragic work, the Sixth Symphony, the 'Pathétique'. Requiem services and tributes were held throughout Russia in his memory. He created a passionate, highly charged, intensely emotional musical world, which still has an immediate appeal to listeners everywhere.

Sarah Bernhardt

1844–1923

There are five kinds of actresses: bad actresses, fair actresses, good actresses, great actresses — and then there is Sarah Bernhardt.

Mark Twain

Born in Paris, the actress famed across the world as 'the Divine Sarah' was as tempestuous in life as she was on stage. With boundless resilience – possibly a result of her insecure childhood as the illegitimate child of a Dutch courtesan – she was first a successful actress in France, before storming the London stage in 1876. Even the loss of her leg in later life posed no major obstacle to her flamboyant acting. And as soon as she had recovered from the amputation, she made a morale-boosting tour of the First World War front, conveyed about in a litter chair. She entertained no thoughts of retirement but just made sure that henceforth her parts could be played sitting down.

Convent-educated but in fact Jewish, as a young girl Bernhardt toyed with the idea of becoming a nun. But her mother's influential lover, Charles, Duc de Morny (1811–65), apparently decided otherwise. A brilliant French statesman, now undeservedly forgotten, he was the son of Queen Hortense of Holland and Emperor Napoleon III's half-brother, as well as a natural grandson of Prince Talleyrand. A financier, racehorse-owner and aesthete, not to mention an enthusiastic lover, he married a Russian princess. He was the mastermind of Napoleon III's coup and regime, and president of the Corps Legislatif, but his early death helped doom the Second Empire. It was entirely appropriate that this personification of French power, worldliness and style should have launched (and possibly fathered) the most famous French actress before the era of film.

Morny secured Bernhardt a place at the Paris Conservatoire and a job at the Comédie Française, where she made her debut in 1862, having already won student prizes. Gripped by stage fright, Bernhardt might have seemed better qualified as courtesan than actress. After six years of hard slog, she made her breakthrough and was acclaimed for her roles as Cordelia in a French translation of *King Lear* and the minstrel Zanetto in *Le Passant*, a verse play by François Coppée. Her success in the latter was such that she was commanded to reprise her performance in the presence of Napoleon III.

Audiences clamoured to experience her inimitable stage style, suffused with stormy outbursts of wild emotion, tears and grief. For many it became unimaginable that her most famous roles, Marguerite in Dumas's *La Dame aux camélias* and the title roles in Racine's *Phèdre* and Scribe's *Adrienne Lecouvreur*, could be played by anyone else.

Victor Hugo, in whose tragedies she starred, was entranced by her 'golden voice', while Sigmund Freud marvelled that 'every inch of that little figure lives and bewitches'. Yet Bernhardt was denounced by priests, not only for the risqué content of the plays she herself produced but also for her many lovers and unabashed sexuality. She lived life on her own terms, claiming to be 'one of the great lovers of my time'. Her promiscuity was notorious: 'My dear, when one has sat on a rose bush and pricked oneself, one cannot say which thorn was responsible,' was the response of her lover the Prince de Ligne (descendant of the 18th-century grandee and courtier) when Bernhardt revealed that she was pregnant with his child. Other lovers included Hugo and Gustave Doré. Her middle-aged marriage to the young actor Jacques Damala ended when he ran up extensive debts and deserted her to join the French Foreign Legion. Perhaps her beloved son Maurice was the only man who never let her down.

In the early 1880s she left Paris to begin long international tours through Europe and America, where she not only took the leading female roles in productions of both the classics and modern French plays, but also acted male parts, her slight build making her convincing as Hamlet, for example. A brilliant self-promoter, she conquered Paris, then the world, and was 'too American not to succeed in America', as the writer Henry James wryly commented. Bernhardt was the first international star of the pre-cinematic age – and did star in several early silent movies, among them *Queen Elizabeth* and *La Dame aux camélias*, from 1912.

The actor-managers

When Bernhardt formed her own company to put on plays in her later years, she was following in the tradition of great actor-managers, instigated by the likes of David Garrick (1717–79) and Colley Cibber (1671–1757) and reaching its heyday in the Victorian and Edwardian eras. A celebrated actor would lease a theatre and create a company specifically as a vehicle for his or her own leading performances in the plays produced.

The actor-manager was the undisputed star of the show. One of the first female actor-managers, Madame Vestris (1797–1856), drew the crowds with her famously good legs, shown to best advantage in 'breeches' roles in burlesques. Marie Bancroft (*née* Wilton, 1839–1921) and her devoted husband wooed the late Victorians at the Haymarket Theatre with their 'drawing-room' dramas. And when the national idol Sir Henry Irving (1838–1905) was taken ill at the end of his career, his company was forced to tour without him and profits plummeted.

These actor-managers knew how to create a box-office hit. Audiences flocked to see the unforgettable partnership of Irving and the enchanting Ellen Terry (1847–1928), just as they did to marvel at the great character actor Sir Herbert Beerbohm Tree (1853–1917). Tree, transforming George Bernard Shaw's *Pygmalion* out of all recognition, declared to his disgruntled playwright, 'My ending makes money, you ought to be grateful.' Actors, rather than authors, ruled the theatre. Shakespeare was a favourite choice simply because of the number of virtuoso parts his work offered.

The exuberant productions and painstaking sets were also pure

---

The multi-talented Bernhardt was also a gifted writer and sculptor, a skilful editor and translator of many plays. She herself became an actor-manager, organizing her own profitable tours. When her histrionic style went out of fashion, she simply directed her own theatre company, renting the Théâtre des Nations in 1898 (later renamed the Théâtre Sarah Bernhardt).

Bernhardt mythologized everything, constantly changing the story of her paternity, and she was probably the healthiest 'consumptive' ever to have lived (on at least one occasion, coughing 'blood' that was actually red liquid from a concealed bladder). But she was

theatre. At Irving's Lyceum each fabulous production outdid the last, with the new stage designs for his *Faust* proving particularly popular. At Her Majesty's Theatre, Tree put real rabbits, real grass and an entire farmyard of animals on stage for *A Midsummer Night's Dream*, and his shipwreck in *The Tempest* was so realistic that audience members felt seasick.

But the actor-managers also wrought monumental changes in the world of theatre. William Charles Macready (1793–1873), the volatile tragedian who managed Covent Garden and Drury Lane, rejected bowdlerized versions of Shakespeare and introduced proper company rehearsals. Previously the leads had unleashed their performances on audiences and cast members alike for the first time on opening night – 'Stand upstage of me and do your worst,' declared the great actor Edmund Kean (1787–1833) to his supporting cast. And Irving, who in 1895 became the first theatrical knight, entertained the great and good at after-show supper parties as lavish as his performances, and immeasurably raised the social status of actors. When he died, ten years later, he was internationally mourned by presidents and public alike.

By the early 1920s the era of the actor-manager was largely over, although a few successors – such as Gerald du Maurier (1873–1934) and matinée idol Sir Laurence Olivier (1907–89) – continued the tradition. Sir Donald Wolfit (1902–68) was about the last of the breed, his declamatory style regarded as risible by some. From thenceforth stage-managers, then directors, took over the production of a play, and the movies appropriated the glamour of the star players.

unremittingly loyal. Hearing that her runaway husband was now living in drug-addicted squalor, she personally rescued him, paying for private nursing. She was a fervent French patriot and mesmerized audiences to the very end.

Guy de Maupassant
1850–1893

Monsieur de Maupassant ... possesses the three essential qualities of the French writer: clarity, clarity and clarity. He exhibits the spirit of balance and order that is the mark of our race.

Anatole France, in *La vie littéraire* (1888)

Maupassant was the French writer who almost single-handedly made the short story an art form. A famous hedonist and sportsman, he shocked many with his 'immoral' literature. His work recognized the appeal of sensuality and human nature's ambivalence towards it. It is this sensitivity, combined with prose of exquisite clarity, that makes him a writer of greatness.

In 1880 Émile Zola decided to publish a collection of stories inspired by the recent Franco-Prussian War. Maupassant's contribution, 'Boule de Suif', was a masterpiece in miniature that ensured its author overnight success. It was typical of his style and originality, a tale of how a prostitute is exploited and betrayed by the hypocritical middle class in wartime. Many regarded such writing as little more than padding for newspaper columns, but Maupassant went on to develop the short story as a distinctive genre that was taken up by a series of later writers from James Joyce to Ernest Hemingway, and from Anton Chekhov to Somerset Maugham.

Born of impoverished Norman nobility, Maupassant gave up his unrewarding post in the civil service to embrace life as a writer. His genius was to reveal, in simple narrative, fundamental human truths with a skill that rivalled – and sometimes even surpassed – that of the finest novelists. The concision, elegance and humanity of the 300-plus short stories he produced over the ensuing decade demonstrate his mastery of the form.

Maupassant sought to present not 'a banal, photographic view of life ... but a vision more complete, more gripping, more searching than reality itself'. In this, he owed much to the tutelage of the great novelist Gustave Flaubert (1821–80). Flaubert, a friend of Maupassant's mother, took the young man under his wing when he returned to Paris after serving in the Franco-Prussian War of 1870–1.

Flaubert introduced him to the leading writers of the day, saying, 'He's my disciple and I love him like a son.' In turn Flaubert was a surrogate father (some murmured a real one) to Maupassant, whose own parents had separated when he was 11 and whose father was always a remote figure. Maupassant's style was honed under Flaubert to such an extent that the Russian master Tolstoy was moved to praise his searing insight and his disciplined, beautiful prose as the marks of genius.

At the same time Tolstoy deplored Maupassant's immorality. He was perverse and witty: one story told of a hungry gentleman in a stranded train on a very hot day who finally availed himself of the milk of a breast-feeding peasant. Another tells of a respectable upper-class lady who, looking out of her window, is mistaken for a call-girl by a good-looking young blade and afterwards seeks forgiveness by buying her husband a present with the proceeds. His work was often set in brothels or boudoirs; yet he was equally fascinated by war, by the shrewd peasants of his native Normandy, by finance and journalism, and by the strange twists of fate. The writer's fascination with sex (one critic described him as a 'complete erotomaniac') reflected a phenomenal promiscuity in life. Indeed, his boating trips with hedonistic Parisian girls inspired his short story 'Mouche', and his literary success financed the maintenance of several mistresses. Maupassant's best-selling novel Bel-Ami (1885) is a masterpiece, probably the best account ever written of that very modern world where journalism and politics meet, and the author went on to name his yacht after it.

Maupassant believed that the artist's duty was not to be a moral arbiter but to present society with its own reflection and leave people to draw their own conclusions. He declared, 'for a writer there can be no halfway house: he must either tell what he believes to be the truth, or tell lies'. The resulting incisiveness of his writing highlights the contrast between appearance and reality, illustrating how vanity and pride lead to self-deception and falsehood. Maupassant wrote of betrayal and seduction; of fortune favouring

Isaac Babel

One of Maupassant's greatest admirers was the Soviet author Isaac Babel (1894–1940). He ranks alongside the Frenchman (indeed he wrote a story called *Guy de Maupassant*) as one of the most gifted short-story writers of all – and his fate was even more tragic. Babel's passionate, tender, original, sensual, violent and witty stories exemplify the beauty and power of the genre. His gift as a writer is encapsulated in the comment of his friend the poet Osip Mandelstam: 'It is not often that one sees such undisguised curiosity in the eyes of a grown-up.'

Babel was born in the Jewish streets of the cosmopolitan port of Odessa in the Ukraine. The Jewish underworld of gangsters, whores and rabbis he observed there is vividly depicted in his *Tales of Odessa*. Babel's life was spent defying persecution. As a child, he had seen Odessa's Jews murdered in a pogrom. When he moved to St Petersburg to study literature – a city where Jews were banned along with 'traitors, malcontents and whiners' – he had to assume a false name.

Babel fought briefly on the Romanian front during the First World War, but he was injured and discharged. It was his experiences as a correspondent for the Red Army's savage and primitive Red Cossacks, during Lenin's 1920 war to spread revolution into Poland, that inspired his greatest collection of short stories, *Red Cavalry*. These tales of the brutality of war made Babel, in the words of his daughter, 'famous almost overnight'. However, various Soviet commanders close to Stalin were

the ruthless and the selfish; of societies based on collective hypocrisy; and of madness. He did not shy away from the deep ambiguities hidden within ourselves, while his writing has the power to dispel society's myths.

Maupassant himself was living proof of such ambiguities. On the one hand, he was a man of action, a passionate oarsman who could comfortably row 50 miles in a day, who once saved the English poet Swinburne from drowning. His military service and his love of the sea influenced many of the narratives and settings of his work. On the other hand, he was prone to anxiety and morbid thoughts and was increasingly gripped by the depression from which his mother had also suffered.

In his early twenties Maupassant discovered he had syphilis but

disgusted by the frank and rambunctious portrayal of the Red Cossacks and became dangerous enemies.

Babel flourished in the relative liberality of the 1920s, but as Stalin's Terror intensified, he ceased to write as a sort of protest: 'I have invented a new genre,' Babel told the Union of Soviet Writers in 1934, 'the genre of silence.' In the 1920s his wife and daughter had moved to France, his mother and sister to Brussels; but despite increasing repression and censorship Babel kept faith with Russia's revolution and chose to remain. He was a raconteur and bon viveur. He was also fatally fascinated by the Terror and rashly but characteristically set about writing a novel about the secret police. Babel had had a long affair with the flirtatious wife of Nikolai Yezhov, Stalin's poison dwarf and secret-police boss at the height of the Terror. When Yezhov fell from power, his wife was driven to suicide and all her lovers, including Babel, were dragged into the case and destroyed.

In 1939 the Soviet secret service arrested Babel at his cottage in the writers' colony of Peredelkino, leaving behind his new wife and baby. Interrogated and tortured, he confessed to a long-held association with Trotskyites and to anti-Soviet activity. Tried in prison, he was shot on Stalin's orders for espionage in January 1940. His family was told that he had died in a Siberian prison camp. In 1954 Babel was posthumously cleared of all charges. His reputation as a great writer has risen steadily ever since.

refused to have it treated. Mentally he became increasingly unstable, as his frantic existence accelerated his physical deterioration. In 1892, a year after his brother (also suffering from syphilis) died insane, Maupassant attempted suicide. He was committed to a nursing home, where he died less than a year later – aged just 43.

In just over a decade as a writer, Maupassant produced some 300 short stories, six novels, three travel books and a volume of verse. His frenetic life and work matched each other. Ultimately, it is the way that Maupassant cast light – often lurid, always truthful – on our own lives that marks him out as a great writer.

Oscar Wilde 1854–1900

*From the beginning Wilde performed his life and continued
to do so even after fate had taken the plot out of his hands.*

W.H. Auden, in the New Yorker (9 March 1963)

Oscar Wilde – poet, playwright, aphorist, novelist and writer of
childrens' stories, aesthete, victim of prejudice and hypocrisy, and
insouciant, irrepressible wit – treated his own life as a work of art; he
was its hero – and should remain ours. A lover of paradox and a
connoisseur of life's absurdities, he effortlessly skewered the pretensions,
prejudices and hypocrisies of his age. His destruction by the society that
had lionized him was a tragic echo of the themes he explored with such
charm and forensic skill in his own work.

Wilde's plays, such as *A Woman of No Importance* and *The Importance of Being
Earnest*, are rarely off the stage. His dazzling wit is enduringly quotable:
'I take my diary everywhere I go. One must always have something
sensational to read on the train,' declares Gwendolyn to Cicely in *The
Importance of Being Earnest*, a play that is said to be the most perfect comedy
ever written. More than any other writer of the time, his satire
deconstructs the pompous edifice of late Victorian society and does so
with considerable *élan*. But under the glittering surface lies the potential
for tragedy, and much of his work shimmers on the edge of darkness.
The Picture of Dorian Gray, the novel Wilde published in 1889, pushed the
limits of respectability with its themes of decay, cruelty and illicit love,
causing Wilde's wife, Constance, to remark that 'since Oscar wrote that
book no one invites us anywhere any more'. Yet it is a timelessly sensitive
and affecting evocation of our fears of death and ageing. Even his fairy
tales, *The Happy Prince* and *The Selfish Giant*, do not shy away from the
unpalatable reality of cruelty going unpunished and heroism
unrewarded; each is heartbreaking in its tragic beauty.

Wilde was born in Dublin of Anglo-Irish parents, but his desire to
be centre stage prompted him to pursue an education and a life in
England. The archetype of a *fin de siècle* aesthete, Wilde cultivated a
flamboyant appearance and a quick and cutting way with words,
turning himself into a celebrity long before his writing confirmed
that he was worth all the attention. 'The only thing worse than being

The Ballad of Reading Gaol

In May 1895 Wilde was sentenced to two years' hard labour for immoral acts. While he was serving out his time in Reading Gaol, a fellow inmate, Trooper Charles Thomas Wooldridge, convicted of murdering his wife by cutting her throat with a razor, was hanged. It was to 'C.T.W.' that Wilde dedicated his last great work, the elegiac *Ballad of Reading Gaol*, written in exile in France after his release in 1897. The poem had to be published under a pseudonym, 'C.3.3' (his prison number), due to the notoriety of his own name.

The Ballad of Reading Gaol has none of the anger or recrimination of *De Profundis*, the work that he wrote in prison raging against his lover's betrayal. Intermingling light and shade, the poem expresses a longing for innocence, beauty and redemption even in the mire of despair, and at the same time calls for forgiveness and understanding.

> *I never saw a man who looked*
> *With such a wistful eye*
> *Upon that little tent of blue*
> *Which prisoners call the sky,*
> *And at every drifting cloud that went*
> *With sails of silver by.*

The poem concludes:

> *And all men kill the thing they love,*
> *By all let this be heard,*
> *Some do it with a bitter look,*
> *Some with a flattering word,*
> *The coward does it with a kiss,*
> *The brave man with a sword!*

The Ballad of Reading Gaol is a far cry from the apparent frivolity that made Wilde infamous, a fitting epitaph for one who knew all too well that 'each man kills the thing he loves'.

talked about is not being talked about,' he said. By his early twenties the tall, drawling Oxford graduate, got up in a velvet suit with Regency-style knee-breeches, was notorious. Even the Prince of Wales demanded an introduction, declaring: 'Not to know Mr Wilde is to be not known in society.' From celebrity came a career: caricatures of the dandy who declared art to be the highest form of action began to appear on the London stage. When an enterprising producer took one of these plays on an American tour, he decided to take Wilde on a parallel lecture tour on the subject of aestheticism. Wilde – who reportedly arrived at US Customs with the comment 'I have nothing to declare except my genius' – became as famous across the Atlantic as he was in England. It was only in the half decade before his fall that Wilde fully became the writer he had always planned to be.

Wilde's homosexuality has become as famous as his work. He was a butterfly broken on a wheel. His provocative effeteness had prompted rumours about his sexuality for years, but Wilde was a married father who only became actively homosexual in his thirties after his marriage hit a bad patch. 'The only way to get rid of temptation is to yield to it,' said Wilde famously. Caught up in a vendetta between his preposterously vain and destructive lover Lord Alfred (Bosie) Douglas and Douglas' father, the lunatic martinet the Marquess of Queensberry, Wilde found himself the subject of a sustained campaign of childish abuse. Queensberry sent him phallic bouquets of vegetables, and the note he left at Wilde's club in February 1895 accusing him of being a 'posing somdomite' [sic] was the final straw. Urged on by Bosie, Wilde sued for libel.

It was a terrible mistake. Under cross-examination Wilde was as flippantly witty as ever, playing to his new audience, the occupants of the court's public gallery. But even his eloquent defence of immorality in his work could not cancel out details of his dalliances that he called 'supping with panthers'. The establishment could not tolerate such revelations. Wilde lost the case and was immediately tried and sentenced to two years' hard labour for gross indecency. Cries of 'shame' filled the galleries. Queensberry called the bailiffs in to repossess Wilde's house in lieu of costs. His son, who had fled to the Continent to escape indictment, publicly bemoaned his suffering, at a safe distance.

In prison Wilde wrote De Profundis, a bitterly brilliant 50,000-word letter to Bosie, a testament to his destruction by his great love. He never recovered, physically or psychologically, from his imprisonment. Ostracized by society, unable to see his beloved sons, he spent his final years wandering the Continent. His wit was undiminished to the last: 'I am dying,' he declared, 'beyond my means.' Shortly before his death, as he lay in a dreary room in Paris, he is said to have murmured, 'Either that wallpaper goes, or I do.'

Society's conflicted fascination with Oscar Wilde endures to this day. Finally, in 1995, a memorial window to Wilde was unveiled in Westminster Abbey's Poets' Corner.

David Lloyd George 1863–1945

How can I convey to the reader any just impression of this extraordinary figure of our time, this siren, this goat-footed bard, this half-human visitor to our age from the hag-ridden magic and enchanted woods of Celtic antiquity.

John Maynard Keynes, quoted in R.F. Harrod, *The Life of John Maynard Keynes* (1951)

Much of the fabric of modern British society rests on the achievements of David Lloyd George. Known as the 'Welsh Wizard' for his oratory, and as 'the Goat' for his womanizing, he was a passionate Welshman of radical politics and modest beginnings. As chancellor of the exchequer, he established the foundations of the welfare state, and as prime minister during the First World War he led the country to victory.

Lloyd George often found – and cast – himself an outsider in Westminster politics. One of his first causes, during the 1890s, was that of Welsh freedom. Yet with his great powers of oratory he rose fast through the Liberal Party. From 1899 he fiercely opposed the Second Anglo-Boer War.

In 1905 Lloyd George was appointed to the Cabinet as president of the board of trade, and in 1908 he was promoted to chancellor under the new prime minister, H.H. Asquith. As chancellor, he proved to be a bold reformer with a strong social conscience, pushing through legislation introducing old-age pensions.

In 1909 he went even further and announced the 'People's Budget', which he intended to 'wage implacable warfare against poverty'. The aim was to introduce a tax on land and higher-rate taxes on higher incomes to fund pensions, public works such as road-building, and new battleships to face the perceived threat from Germany. The House of Lords hated Lloyd George's proposals, and their rejection of the budget led to a constitutional crisis and ultimately the 1911 Parliament Act, which abolished the Lords' right of veto. Lloyd George extended the welfare state with the National Insurance Act of 1911, which introduced a way for working people to insure against future unem-

'Tiger' Clemenceau

Lloyd George's great contemporary in France was the charismatic and fiery Georges Clemenceau. They worked closely together during the First World War and when drawing up the Treaty of Versailles. Clemenceau's bullishness, his lifelong tenacity and his insistence on this punitive settlement with Germany earned him the nickname 'The Tiger'.

Clemenceau was born in a village in the Vendée, in western France, in 1841. He grew up among peasants and received his political education from his father, who shaped his republican views. In 1861 he went to Paris to study medicine, where he became involved in radical republican politics and journalism, critical of the regime of Emperor Napoleon III, and thus attracted the attention of the police.

In 1870–1 France lost the Franco-Prussian War. Clemenceau was involved in the overthrow of Napoleon III and elected to the provisional government. He vehemently but unsuccessfully opposed the imposition on France of a harsh treaty, by which France lost the provinces of Alsace and Lorraine to the new German Empire. In May 1871 Clemenceau tried, but failed, to mediate between the government and the rebels of the Paris Commune.

Throughout the 1880s and 1890s Clemenceau continued to serve in both politics and journalism. One of his triumphs was his support between 1894 and 1906 of the young Jewish army officer Alfred Dreyfus, a victim of anti-Semitism in the government, army and press, who was wrongly accused of being a German spy. Clemenceau's newspapers exposed the corruption and

ployment and to provide for their health care. Though unpopular with some at first, it made Lloyd George a hero to many.

During the First World War, Asquith's sleepy, passive conduct of the conflict contrasted with the tireless dynamism and the driving charisma of 'LG'. As minister of munitions and then as secretary for war, Lloyd George mobilized almost the entire population in the war effort, drafting women to take over factory work traditionally reserved for men, who were now away fighting. As a result of this and other measures, there was a great leap in productivity. But Lloyd George became increasingly critical of Asquith's handling of the war, and in December 1916 he allied himself with the Conservatives and some members of his own party to replace Asquith as prime minister, thereby splitting the Liberal Party.

injustice in that notorious case. In 1902 he was elected as a senator.

Clemenceau served as prime minister in 1906–9. In the lead-up to the First World War he argued for rearmament against Germany, and after war broke out he became a vociferous critic of successive governments and of the military high command, hurling accusations of ineptitude, defeatism and closet pacifism.

In November 1917, at the age of 76, Clemenceau accepted the invitation to become prime minister. Ruthless and belligerent, he forced through his belief in 'war until the end' and dealt severely with those he regarded as traitors and defeatists. He insisted on a unified Allied command under General Foch as the only way to win the war. By November 1918 his views had been proven right.

At the Paris Peace Conference of 1919, Clemenceau remembered the events of 1870–1, and in negotiations with Lloyd George and President Woodrow Wilson he insisted on Germany being disarmed, accepting 'war guilt' and agreeing to pay massive reparations. He made sure that the treaty was signed in the Hall of Mirrors at Versailles, the very place where Wilhelm I, having humiliated France, had declared himself German emperor in 1871. Clemenceau's force of character and decency made him a fighter for justice and a superb war leader, but his vindictive demands at Versailles were a mistake.

Clemenceau lost the presidential election of 1920 and retired. Before he died, nine years later, he published his memoirs, in which he predicted another war with Germany, some time around 1940.

Lloyd George led the war effort by sheer force of personality, but he was unable to overcome the rigidity and stupidity of the generals or prevent the colossal human losses of trench warfare. He agreed with his French counterpart, Clemenceau, that the Allies desperately needed a unified command, which came about in April 1918. By November 1918, Germany having exhausted itself in its final offensives in the spring and summer of that year, the war was won. In the subsequent peace negotiations, Lloyd George attempted to find a compromise between the idealistic, conciliatory Americans and the vengeful French.

Following the war, Lloyd George – long a believer in female emancipation – extended voting rights to women. He went on to help bring an end to the war of independence in Ireland, which had broken out in January 1919. In 1921 he negotiated a treaty allowing 26 southern counties to form the Irish Free State. But six northern counties remained part of the United Kingdom as Northern Ireland, with violent consequences for another 80 years.

Despite these achievements, Lloyd George found himself in political difficulties. His reputation was marred by scandals surrounding the sale of peerages, and the Conservatives in his coalition government opposed his plans to increase public expenditure on housing and social services, forcing him to resign in October 1922. Although he became reconciled with the main bulk of the Liberal Party and returned as their leader in 1926, the Liberals were now a spent force, eclipsed by the rise of the Labour Party.

After 1922 Lloyd George's vanity and folly undermined him. His visit to Hitler handed the Nazis a propaganda coup, though he later came to oppose appeasement and called for rearmament. He had resigned as leader of the Liberals in 1931 because of ill health, but continued to sit as an MP, declining Churchill's offer of a cabinet position during the Second World War on the grounds of his age. Long married to Margaret Owen, he had many mistresses, above all his secretary Frances Stevenson, whom he married in 1943. In that year he also voted for the last time in Parliament, in support of the Beveridge Report, which outlined the 'cradle-to-grave' extension of the welfare state that Lloyd George had done so much to create. It was a fitting farewell to politics. Early in 1945 he was raised to the peerage, but he died before he could take his seat in the House of Lords.

Henri de Toulouse-Lautrec 1864–1901

He did not overturn reality to discover truth, where there was nothing. He contented himself with looking. He did not see, as many do, what we seem to be, but what we are. Then, with a sureness of hand and a boldness at once sensitive and firm, he revealed us to ourselves.

From Toulouse-Lautrec's obituary in the *Journal de Paris*

Vicomte Henri de Toulouse-Lautrec, the iconic chronicler of Parisian nightlife, confronted society with a vibrant celebration of humanity in all its distortions. He is world-famous today principally for his posters, but while these are undeniably superb, they have obscured his brilliance as a painter and portraitist who brought poignant sensitivity to his studies of the women of the *demi-monde*. In truth he was the Rembrandt of the night.

Toulouse-Lautrec's art illuminates Paris's artistic quarter in all its glory, immortalizing the chorus girls and entertainers who crowded its streets, cabarets and cafés. It was a ground-breaking departure in art. His work caused outrage, but he did not do it to shock. Rather, he wanted to 'depict the true and not the ideal'. In so doing, he humanized his subjects because they were people he knew so well, giving them a nobility that society had always denied them.

Toulouse-Lautrec's style – clear, economical lines, bright colours and vigorous, often ironic representations – was as revelatory as his subjects. After he decided to become an artist, his wealthy aristocratic family arranged for him to be tutored by a family friend and society painter. Toulouse-Lautrec developed his distinctive style almost in spite of his training. Notwithstanding his eagerness to please, he found himself unable to copy a model exactly. 'In spite of himself,' a friend recalled, 'he exaggerated certain details, sometimes the general character, so that he distorted without trying or even wanting to.' A subsequent tutor found this freedom of expression 'atrocious'. Aged 19, he was given an allowance to set up his own studio, whereupon he moved to Montmartre and began to paint his friends.

Toulouse-Lautrec soon became famous for his lithographs. Bold and clear, their elegant style anticipates Art Nouveau. They showed that art did not have to consist solely of oil on canvas, and as posters they turned advertising into an art form. The vast audience this gave him

The *grandes horizontales*

Toulouse-Lautrec was not alone in being fascinated by the *grandes horizontales* and *demi-mondaines* – the decadent and scandalous courtesans who ruled the *demi-monde* of late 19th-century Paris. These charismatic and exuberant women made conquests of the royal, the aristocratic and the rich of Europe; but they also inspired and often patronized the great artists of the period, from Manet and Lautrec to Offenbach the composer, Zola and Proust the novelists, to other painters such as Renoir, Degas and Cézanne. They knew the heights of incredible wealth and the depths of loneliness and tragedy. They served as artists' models and poets' muses, famed not only for their sexual allure but also for their sparkling wit, outrageous ostentation and high living. Not exactly heroines – they were, at root, too greedy and debased for that description – they were nevertheless an important charismatic presence at the heart of France's political and artistic culture.

Apollonie Sabatier, known as La Présidente, held a salon for artists and writers and was the lover of the poet Baudelaire (inspiring some of *Les Fleurs du mal*) and a model for the sculptor Clésinger. The ethereal Marie Duplessis, who died at just 23, was immortalized by one of her lovers, Alexandre Dumas *fils*, in *La Dame aux camélias*. She spent 500 francs a day in an age when a schoolteacher earned 300 a year.

'She has slept with everyone,' commented one contemporary of the captivating Blanche de Païva, a Russian Jewess who kept the name of the Portuguese marquis she married and built herself the most extravagant palace in Paris. Well into middle age, La Païva was said to be a witch for her irresistible hold over men. She eventually settled down with the Prussian industrialist Count Guido Henckel von Donnersmarck. She died rich and a countess.

The most famous of all was Emma Crouch, from Plymouth, the 'English

transformed his career. 'My poster is pasted today on the walls of Paris,' he declared proudly of his first lithograph in 1891. His lithographs showed the great singing, dancing and circus stars of the Parisian night, especially the Moulin Rouge: *Aristide Bruant dans son cabaret* or *Moulin Rouge – La Goulue* and *Jane Avril sortant du Moulin Rouge* are now pasted on walls across the world. His paintings are remarkable for their humanity: his debonair boulevardier Louis Pascal shows that he could render men

beauty of the French Empire' who took the name Cora Pearl. Her admirers ranged from the Prince of Wales (the future Edward VII) to Plon-Plon, Prince Napoleon. But her favourite lovers were the most talented: Napoleon III's half-brother, the Duc de Morny, and the artist Gustave Doré. 'She had the head of a city worker,' wrote 'Zed', 'fiery blond, almost red hair, a vulgar and unbearable accent, a raucous voice, exceedingly common manners and the tone of a stableboy,' but she had the gift of making 'bored men laugh' and adored practical jokes. She once dyed her dog blue to match her outfit and used make-up to render her nipples a perfect rose-pink when she served herself up naked on a silver platter at the Café Anglais. A consummate horsewoman, she spent so much on her stable of 60 horses and carriages that one admirer described it as 'a form of rational insanity'. But when the Second Empire came crashing down in 1870, Cora stayed on in Paris and spent her money turning her mansion into a hospital for soldiers. She died in 1886, penniless, and typically with a joke: 'I am still Cora but minus the Pearls.'

The 'last courtesan', La Belle Otero, held sway until 1914. So many lovers killed themselves on account of this Spanish dancer, who had been kidnapped by admirers on a regular basis since the age of 14, that on a trip to New York she was billed as the 'Suicide Siren'. Carolina Otero was 'the most scandalous person since Helen of Troy', yet 'had the most regal and wonderful dignity'. Her lovers included the French politician Aristide Briand, Alfonso XIII of Spain, Wilhelm II of Germany, supposedly the young Tsar Nicholas II (before his marriage) and three Russian grand dukes, the Duke of Westminster ('Bendor'), the Italian poet-politician D'Annunzio, and the Prince of Wales – as well as several Balkan kings. She announced her wish 'to retire in full beauty' and ended her days in a tiny Nice apartment, her fortune and vast collection of jewels long since gambled away on the gaming tables. Astonishingly, she lived until 1965.

masterfully too, while his study for *The Medical Inspection* catches the pathos of whores queuing up in the surgery. Some of his most beautiful paintings show these women relaxing together or alone, such as *Abandon*, the *Two Friends* or the touching *Red Haired Woman Washing*. Both the stars and the ordinary girls were his friends and lovers.

Like the rest of his family, Toulouse-Lautrec was enthusiastically sporty, but at the age of 13 he broke his left thigh bone and a year later his right. Despite a long convalescence and numerous painful treatments, his legs never grew again. With a man's torso on dwarfish legs, he never exceeded 5ft (1.52m) in height. The cause was a bone disease, probably of genetic origin.

There is a clear irony in the contrast between the energy and physicality of Lautrec's paintings and his own atrophied state. He was never reconciled to his condition. His compositions often hide the legs of his figures. Surrounded by unusually tall friends, 'he often refers to short men,' commented one acquaintance, 'as if to say "I'm not as short as all that!"'. But the 'tiny blacksmith with a pince-nez' was under no illusions about himself: 'I will always be a thoroughbred hitched to a rubbish cart' was just one of a litany of self-deprecating remarks.

Even in the raffish, boozy world of Montmartre, Lautrec's alcohol consumption was legendary. He helped to popularize the cocktail. The 'earthquake' – four parts absinthe, two parts red wine and a splash of cognac – was a particular favourite. Syphilis accelerated his physical and mental decline, and when his beloved mother left Paris suddenly in 1899, it precipitated a total mental collapse. He was sent to a sanatorium, where he produced one of his greatest series of drawings, *At the Circus*. But after a brief spell he returned to Paris.

Toulouse-Lautrec degenerated into a haze of alcohol, the 'earthquake' giving way to an esoteric diet of 'eggs, which Monsieur eats raw mixed with rum'. Removed to one of his family's chateaux, he was reduced to dragging himself along by his arms as his useless legs failed to work. Almost paralysed and nearly totally deaf, Toulouse-Lautrec was just 36 when he died.

'He would have liked the elegant, active life of all healthy sports-loving persons,' wrote his father after his death. His son achieved in art all the vitality missing from his life. The man who did more than any other to create the image of *fin de siècle* Paris imbued his works with an astounding energy.

Gandhi 1869–1948

I know of no other man in our time, or indeed in recent history, who so convincingly demonstrated the power of the spirit over things material.

Sir Stafford Cripps, British Labour politician, speech at the Commonwealth Prime Ministers' Conference, London (1 October 1948)

Mohandas Karamchand Gandhi was 'the father of the Indian Nation', whose use of peaceful protest to achieve political independence has served as an inspiration for generations of political leaders seeking an end to oppression. The embodiment of man's capacity for true humanity, Gandhi came to be known by the name of Mahatma, meaning 'Great Soul'.

Gandhi never had a clearly defined role in Indian politics. But Indian independence was as much his achievement as it was of the politicians in the Indian National Congress. Gandhi's leadership forged a national identity among the Indian people. The tools of his protests – boycotts and non-cooperation – could be taken up by all. From spinning and weaving one's own cloth in preference to buying British textiles, to 250-mile (400-km) mass marches protesting against monopolies, Gandhi's methods of political involvement transcended the boundaries of age, gender, caste and religion.

No longer was political activism confined to the literate elite. Inspired by this small, frail figure dressed in homespun cloth, millions participated in the peaceful protests which reached their zenith in the 'Quit India' campaign of 1942. As the British authorities arrested hundreds of thousands of protesters, it became apparent that their rule was increasingly untenable. Some contemporaries criticized Gandhi's methods of protest as 'passive' – incapable of achieving anything of real import. The achievement of Indian independence in 1947, and the triumph of countless civil rights movements since, proved them wrong.

Gandhi's fragile appearance belied his iron will. Although he came from a distinguished family – his father served as prime minister in several princely states – as a youth Gandhi displayed little promise in any sphere. His politicization began in earnest when he was a young lawyer working in South Africa. Here Gandhi experienced

Midnight's children and Nehru's democracy

'At the stroke of the midnight hour, when the world sleeps, India will awaken to life and freedom.' On 15 August 1947 Jawaharlal Nehru declared the fulfilment of the goal for which, as president of the Indian National Congress, he had fought for so long. India had thrown off the rule of the British Raj to become an independent nation.

But some hours before that stroke of midnight, Mohammed Ali Jinnah, the leader of the Muslim League, had declared the independence of another state: Pakistan. It was a development that the British government and Congress and Gandhi himself had done everything to stop: the partition of India along religious lines.

During the 1930s friction had grown between the predominately Hindu Indian National Congress and the Muslim League. Fearing that they would become an impotent minority in a unified independent India, by the 1940s the Muslim League was adamant that the end of colonial rule must usher in an independent Islamic state. As tensions turned to violence, the British viceroy, Lord Mountbatten, brought forward independence to avoid an outright civil war.

As it turned out, partition increased the violence. When the mixed states of Bengal and the Punjab were divided along sectarian lines, it led to

discrimination at first hand when he was thrown off a train after a white traveller complained about the presence of an Indian in her carriage. Gandhi set about campaigning for Indian rights and in so doing developed the philosophy of protest that came to define him. *Satyagraha*, the 'truth force', was an all-consuming discipline that involved non-violent resistance to an oppressive authority. It required vast inner strength that could only be achieved by extreme self-control. Gandhi pursued it in every aspect of his life. Despite being happily married he adopted celibacy – and then tested his control by sleeping naked with attractive disciples. As a law student in London he had become an ardent practitioner of vegetarianism, and fasting became a frequent practice of his, which he used for both spiritual advancement and to attain political goals. Setting up ashrams, where he lived with his wife and followers, he abandoned

bloodshed on an unprecedented scale. An estimated two million men, women and children were massacred, and over ten million Hindus, Sikhs and Muslims fled for their lives. Washing their hands of the messy demarcation, the British walked away. At the same time, India and Pakistan fought the first of several wars, over the disputed territory of Kashmir.

Yet out of this disaster Nehru, as India's first prime minister, managed to achieve the seemingly impossible – he skilfully turned the world's second most populous country into its largest parliamentary democracy. Gandhi's heir and the idol of his people, Nehru was an extraordinary mixture: an Old Harrovian lawyer trained at Cambridge who had a love affair with Edwina Mountbatten, the last viceroy's intelligent and fascinating wife; like Gandhi, a champion of the poor; a believer in equality for women and reform of the caste system; one of the creators of the Non-Aligned Movement; and a champion of a new national identity to supersede racial and religious differences. Prime minister until his death in 1964, he founded a democratic political dynasty: his formidable daughter Indira Gandhi served as prime minister 1966–77 and was elected again in 1980, dominating Indian politics until her assassination in 1984. Her son Rajiv Gandhi was in turn prime minister from 1984 until 1989. He was assassinated in 1991. His Italian widow became the arbiter of the family's political party, the Congress Party, and their son Rahul is already a member of the Indian parliament.

his worldly goods and reduced his dress to the homespun dhoti – a type of loincloth. One of the few possessions that Gandhi left at his death was a spinning wheel.

Gandhi's campaigns against discrimination and injustice were many and varied. He fearlessly challenged social, religious and political practices in the pursuit of justice for the oppressed, be they women, peasants or nations. Visiting London in 1931 for a conference on constitutional reform, Gandhi chose to stay with the poor of the East End. A devout Hindu, he was nonetheless steadfast in his calls for a reform of the caste system and an end to the practice by which certain groups of people, by virtue of their birth, were stigmatized as 'untouchable'. For Gandhi there was 'no such thing as religion overriding morality', and his deep religious belief never closed his mind to the merits of the beliefs of others: he considered himself not just a Hindu but 'also a Christian, a Muslim, a Buddhist and a Jew'. The bungled partition of the subcontinent into India and Pakistan on religious lines and the descent into sectarian massacres deeply distressed him, and one of his last actions was a personal fast during the Indo-Pakistan war of 1947.

Gandhi always displayed remarkable personal courage. He endured imprisonment by the British government several times, and he demonstrated more than once his willingness to risk death to secure the future of the Indian nation. As Hindu–Muslim violence threatened to consume India, Gandhi made an unarmed and unprotected pilgrimage through the heart of the unrest in Bengal in an effort to quell it. His assassination in 1948 by a Hindu extremist who resented his conciliatory stance towards Pakistan so shocked his people that it helped stop the slide into mayhem and restore order: he therefore died both a martyr and a peacemaker. 'My service to my people,' he once said, 'is part of the discipline to which I subject myself in order to free my soul from the bonds of the flesh ... For me the path of salvation leads through the unceasing tribulation in the service of my fellow countrymen and humanity.' Gandhi was open-minded, tolerant and unfailingly amiable and even-tempered in his dealings with his opponents, and his profound respect for all men – and women – was a mark of his unparalleled nobility of spirit.

Marcel Proust
1871–1922

And suddenly the memory revealed itself. The taste was of the little piece of madeleine ...

Marcel Proust, Du côté de chez Swann (Swann's Way, vol. 1, 1913), translated by C.K. Scott-Moncrieff and S. Hudson, revised by T. Kilmartin

It is said that Marcel Proust spent the first half of his life living it, and the second half writing about it. The result was À la recherche du temps perdu, a semi-autobiographical novel sequence that is perhaps the most complete evocation of a living world ever written, and also a meditation on the nature of time, the self, memory, love, sexuality, society and experience. Proust's work was originally translated under the title *Remembrance of Things Past* (a quotation from Shakespeare), but a more recent translation, published in 1992, is more accurately entitled *In Search of Lost Time*.

In 1909 Marcel Proust, the dilettante son of a wealthy Jewish bourgeois family, ate a madeleine (a type of small sponge cake) dipped in tea and was instantly transported back to his grandfather's house in the country, where he had spent much of his childhood. Overwhelmed by the completeness of the memory, by its sights and smells, Proust found a purpose to the writing that he had dabbled in since he was a youth. At the age of 38, Proust began the work that was to become *À la recherche du temps perdu*.

As Proust embarked upon his re-creation of a world long gone, he withdrew completely from the world of the present. In his youth he had used his childhood asthma as an excuse to avoid any kind of career other than that of avid socialite. But when he began *À la recherche*, he shut himself off from society, sealing himself up in a cork-lined room. He became an obsessive invalid, his deteriorating health exacerbated by hypochondria. He insisted that his morning post be steamed in disinfectant, and he ingested nothing but handfuls of opiates and barbiturates.

Proust's approach baffled some: one publisher rejected his first volume, believing that an author did not need thirty pages to describe turning over in bed before going to sleep again. Discarding the notion of a plot-driven work, Proust takes his reader on an almost stream-of-consciousness journey back through his life. He digresses, for pages at a time, on some aspect of philosophy, or history, or art, in a manner that is yet incandescently beautiful, poetical and tragic but also hilarious, outrageous and frivolous. The mundane – drinking a cup of tea, lying awake at night – is just as important as the dramatic. Proust hypnotizes his readers, immersing them in a world as real as their own.

As his writing gathered pace, the neurasthenic, eccentric Proust adopted an exclusively night-time existence. His staff had to maintain complete silence as he slept during daylight hours. He would pay calls on friends well after midnight or expect them to accompany him on early-morning visits to the cathedral of Notre-Dame, dressed in a fur coat over his nightshirt.

Proust had an almost hysterical need to be the focus of attention. His invalidism was just one way of securing the attention of his mother; later on his self-enforced seclusion ensured the same concern from his friends. The desperation of the child when his mother goes out for the night in *À la recherche* vividly evokes Proust's almost Oedipal love for his mother. He tried to buy affection, employing his male lovers as staff, but he drove them away with his obsessive attentions.

A brilliant conversationalist and mimic, Proust was completely without malice. His extravagance was legendary: he financed a male brothel and once hired out the entire floor of a hotel in his compulsive search for silence. His long-suffering staff were extremely well paid, and handsome waiters handsomely tipped. Even after he had sequestered himself away, he still sent food parcels to the soldiers at the front in the First World War.

Proust was, in his youth, a terrible snob. But the desperate need of this Jewish homosexual to be accepted in Parisian high society did not prevent him from demonstrating real courage in the face of that society's virulent anti-Semitism. At the time of the Dreyfus Affair, Proust stood up as a prominent supporter of the Jewish army officer wrongfully convicted of treason – a move that risked social ostracism. And while he was always afraid in life of being rejected for his sexuality, he was not afraid to approach it in his writing, asserting that he needed to be as precise about Baron Charlus' sexual forays as the Duchesse de Guermantes' red shoes.

He achieved his goal. Proust's delicate, life-like descriptions are astoundingly complete. His fascination with the shifting nature of perception produced some of the most exquisite characterizations ever committed to the page. Over two thousand characters, in all their life-like ambiguity, people *À la recherche*. And they are described in some of the most beautiful prose ever written: every one of the novel sequence's eight million words seems to have been precisely chosen.

Proust was still correcting manuscripts a few hours before his death. Otherworldly in life, in death 'he was totally absent', commented one friend. But the notebooks into which Proust had poured his memory, his health and his soul seemed, to the writer Jean Cocteau, 'alive, like a wristwatch still ticking on a dead soldier'.

The great Modernist dinner party

On the night of 18 May 1922, Violet and Sydney Schiff held a dinner party at the Hotel Majestic in Paris to celebrate the world premiere of Igor Stravinsky's twenty-minute ballet-opera *Renard*, performed by Serge Diaghilev's Ballet Russes. But really it was a chance for Schiff, a wealthy American patron of the arts and celebrity groupie of the first order, to bring together over dinner his idols, the brightest lights of Modernism.

His guest list was stellar: the brilliant Russian ballet impresario Diaghilev, Igor Stravinsky, the composer of the *Rite of Spring*, the Cubist artist Pablo Picasso and the Irish writer James Joyce, author of the novel *Ulysses*. At the pinnacle of his wish list was Marcel Proust, the man to whom the heterosexual Schiff once wrote: 'A letter from you would be for me the answer to a prayer which my lips never stop sighing for.'

It was the great Modernist dinner party. But genius does not necessarily lend itself to sparkling conversation. Only Diaghilev, the master of ceremonies, wafting the aroma of almond blossom from his brilliantined hair, really rose to the occasion. Schiff, panicking that his A-listers would not turn up, drank too much champagne.

Joyce, embarrassed by his lack of evening clothes, didn't arrive until the diners were drinking coffee and was even more drunk and nervy than his host. Proust did not come until 2.30 am, missing by hours the menu of asparagus, *boeuf en gelée*, almond cake and pistachio ice cream, all selected in homage to his work.

Although exquisitely dapper in black evening dress and white kid gloves, Proust had retreated too far into his hermetic world to reassume the mantle of a socialite. On his arrival, one French princess stormed out, convinced that she was the model for an unattractively stingy character in his work. His conversational foray to Stravinsky, praising the greatness of Beethoven, did little to endear him to the composer edgily waiting for the first reviews of his latest work. 'I hate Beethoven,' snarled Stravinsky and turned away.

As for the conversation between the age's greatest men of letters, reports differ, but by all accounts it was not a success. 'Our talk,' Joyce later recalled, 'consisted solely of the word "no". Proust asked me if I knew the duc de so-and-so. I said "no". Our hostess asked Proust if he had read such-and-such a piece of *Ulysses*. Proust said "no".' After competing over their various maladies, the two giants of the literary avant-garde did eventually reach some kind of accommodation over their common liking for truffles, but Joyce ruined this new-found accord on their departure by jumping uninvited into Proust's taxi and lighting a cigarette. Proust did not ask him back to his apartment, and he never mentioned the encounter again.

Sir Ernest Shackleton 1874–1922

Difficulties are just things to overcome, after all.

Shackleton, in the journal of his South Polar journey (11 December 1908)

Sir Ernest Shackleton cut the most exciting and inspirational figure of all the extraordinary explorers of the early 20th century. He was a natural leader and an ambitious and dynamic adventurer, with great concern for the men who served him and an escapologist's streak of luck that usually pulled him and his colleagues out of danger. His exploits are legends of survival amid Nature's most extreme conditions.

Ernest Shackleton was born to Irish parents who settled in England, and at the age of 16 he joined the merchant navy. His voyages took him all around the world, until in 1901 he was appointed to serve on board the *Discovery*, a steam vessel specially built for work in the ice, which was carrying Commander Robert Falcon Scott to Antarctica. Scott chose Shackleton to accompany him and Edward Wilson on a dog- and man-hauled sled journey towards the South Pole.

On the journey – during which temperatures dipped below −80°C – all three men eventually became ill with scurvy, but Shackleton, coughing up blood, seemed worst affected. Although he was invalided home, where he briefly tinkered with politics, he never gave up the dream of a further attempt on the South Pole. In 1907 he returned to Antarctica, this time as leader. He had bought a ship, raised funds and engaged a crew of seamen and scientists. The expedition broke new ground. One party reached the South Magnetic Pole, another made the first ascent of Mount Erebus, an active volcano. In late 1908 Shackleton led another, heroic sled journey towards the geographic South Pole. Despite bitter conditions, in January 1909 the party came within 100 miles of their destination – further south than any man had ever been before, although his party did not quite make it to the Pole. On his return to Britain, Shackleton was lauded as a hero and knighted by the king.

In 1911–12 two expedition groups bettered Shackleton by reaching the South Pole. Robert Falcon Scott arrived second, beaten to the prize by the Norwegian explorer Roald Amundsen.

In 1914 Shackleton set out in charge of the British Imperial Trans-Antarctic expedition. His aim was to cross Antarctica from the Weddell Sea to McMurdo Sound, via the South Pole. However, the voyage of the *Endurance* was overtaken by misfortune. The enormous rafts of floating ice in the Weddell Sea closed in on the ship, and after 10 months of drifting with the pack ice the *Endurance* was crushed, without even having reached the expedition's jumping-off point on the coast. All of the men aboard were forced onto the surrounding ice floes, where they camped for another five months as they drifted north with the ice. In April 1916 they made their way to the northern edge of the ice floe and embarked in three small boats; after six days they reached Elephant Island in the South Shetlands.

From there, Shackleton and a handful of colleagues decided to head to the island of South Georgia, 800 miles away. They completed the hazardous journey across the stormy Southern Ocean in a tiny boat, reaching the island's south coast in 17 days. Even then, they had to climb an uncharted mountain range in the middle of the island to reach a Norwegian whaling station on its northern coast. In a single push over two days, Shackleton and two companions made it. From there, Shackleton organized the rescue of the rest of his men on Elephant Island, reaching them at the fourth attempt. Incredibly, not a single life had been lost.

When Shackleton returned to England, he was too old to be conscripted to fight in the First World War, but he volunteered anyway. A diplomatic mission to try to woo Chile and Argentina to the Allied war effort was a failure, as was a covert mission to establish a British presence in Norwegian territory. Shackleton returned to England in 1919 to lecture and write. In 1921 he set out on a voyage to circumnavigate Antarctica but died of a heart attack on board his ship, the *Quest*, in 1922, at South Georgia.

The polar historian Apsley Cherry-Garrard wrote, 'for a joint

Antarctic rivals – Scott versus Amundsen

Ernest Shackleton's gallant attempt on the South Pole in 1908–9 narrowly preceded the battle between his former comrade Robert Falcon Scott and the Norwegian Roald Amundsen, which would become one of the most famous races of discovery in history.

Scott joined the Royal Navy in 1880, when he was just 12 years old. By 1897 he had become a first lieutenant. He led the 1901–4 mission to Antarctica and was recognized as a dedicated scientific investigator and navigator. When he returned to England he was promoted to captain.

By 1910, having seen Shackleton overtake him in the bid to journey ever deeper south, Scott – still a national figure – raised the funds for a private expedition of scientific and geographical discovery, with the ultimate aim of reaching the South Pole.

At the same time, Amundsen had established his name as commander of the first vessel to sail through the sought-after Northwest Passage – a route joining the Atlantic and Pacific oceans across the top of North America – and was also intent on reaching the North Pole. When he heard in 1909 that others had claimed the North Pole, he decided to turn south.

During his time in the Arctic Amundsen had learned a lot from the indigenous people about survival in the harsh cold, and he had become expert in using dogs to pull sledges. This, combined with careful

scientific and geographical piece of organization, give me Scott … for a dash to the pole and nothing else, Amundsen; and if I am in the devil of a hole and want to get out of it, give me Shackleton every time'.

The Arctic explorers were the successors of the heroic 19th-century African explorers: David Livingstone (1813–73) was the Scottish Presbyterian missionary who, on an expedition through the interior of Africa in 1852–6, discovered the Victoria Falls, but in 1866 lost contact with the world. The remarkable adventurer Henry Morton Stanley (1841–1904), who found Livingstone in

planning, meant that when his party set out for the South Pole in October 1911, even severe conditions and the choice of a new, untrodden route could not prevent them reaching their destination on 14 December. Amundsen left behind a tent, with a note for Scott to confirm that he had been there. The Norwegian was a brilliant planner and student of Arctic life but also showed heroic endurance – and he should be celebrated just as much as Scott.

Scott's party was less skilled in polar travel, and they reached the Pole more than a month after the Norwegian. Despite physical fortitude, Scott's return journey was hampered by some of the severest Antarctic weather ever known, injuries to members of the party, and ill-placed food depots.

It became clear in mid-March 1912 that their party was doomed. One man had already died of an infection. Then, on 17 March, a second man, Captain Oates, left the tent, saying 'I am just going outside and may be some time,' a comment of classic English understatement, and crawled into a blizzard, hoping that his certain death would increase his companions' chances of survival.

But Oates's sacrifice was not enough. The group was pinned to their tent by blizzards and they froze to death just 11 miles from the next food depot. All the while, Scott kept recording his moving journal of events. 'Had I lived, I should have had a tale to tell of the hardihood, endurance and courage of my companions which would have stirred the heart of every Englishman,' he wrote in his final entry. 'These rough notes and our dead bodies must tell the tale.'

1871 on the shores of Lake Tanganyika, was born illegitimate as John Rowlands, raised in a workhouse, went to fight on both sides in the American Civil War, prospered as a journalist, traced the Congo to the sea and rescued the Sudanese official Emin Pasha in 1888. On finding Livingstone, Stanley supposedly said, 'Dr Livingstone, I presume.'

Winston Churchill

1874–1965

He mobilized the English language and sent it into battle.

President John F. Kennedy, conferring honorary US citizenship
on Winston Churchill (9 April 1963)

Churchill was one of the most remarkable men ever to lead the
British people. This extraordinary leader rallied Britain in her dark
hour, when Europe was dominated by Hitlerite Germany, and he
inspired and organized the British conduct of the war, against all
odds, until victory was achieved. After a meteoric career spanning
the first half of the 20th century as self-promoting adventurer,
bumptious young politician, mature minister and then lone prophet
of Nazi danger, serving in almost every major government position,
he emerged from isolation and proved as superb a warlord as he
was a writer, historian and orator. Perhaps even more so than Nelson,
he is regarded as Britain's national hero.

Churchill's father scolded him when he was a schoolboy for
idling away his time at Harrow and Sandhurst, and warned him
of an impending career as a 'mere social wastrel, one of the hundreds of public-school failures'. He need not have worried. As a
young soldier in the Sudan and as a war correspondent in southern
Africa during the Anglo-Boer War, Churchill devoted himself to
swashbuckling charges and escapes, journalism and self-promotion,
but he also devoured the great British historians of the past, such
as Macaulay and Gibbon, and adopted their elegant – sometimes
portentous – style as his own.

Churchill was elected a Conservative MP, but in 1904 he scandalized his party by crossing the floor to join the Liberals. He also married his wife Clementine that year, and for the rest of his long life
she was to provide him with unwavering support – and frank criticism when she felt it was necessary. Churchill became home secretary in 1910 and First Lord of the Admiralty the following year.
During the First World War, Churchill ensured the fleet was ready

but took the blame for the failure of the Gallipoli campaign, which cost the lives of 46,000 Allied troops. He resigned to serve at the Western Front, returning to become Lloyd George's minister of munitions in 1917.

In 1919–21 Churchill was secretary of state for war and air, then, switching allegiance to re-join the Conservatives, chancellor of the exchequer in 1924–9. In the 1930s he was out of office again, almost in political exile, but from the backbenches he foresaw the dangers of Hitler and German rearmament. His warnings were ignored by the appeasing government of Neville Chamberlain and much of the press. It was not until the Second World War broke out that he returned to favour and was brought into the War Cabinet, returning to his old position as First Lord of the Admiralty in 1939: 'Winston's back!', the Admiralty signalled to the fleet.

When, in May 1940, Chamberlain resigned in the face of the Nazi onslaught on Western Europe, there was a political feeling that Britain should make peace with Hitler. In one of the clearest cases of how one man can change history and save not just a nation but a way of life, Churchill insisted on defiance, and he became prime minister. He rose to the occasion. Just after becoming prime minister he addressed Parliament: 'I say to the House as I said to ministers who have joined this government, I have nothing to offer but blood, toil, tears, and sweat ... What is our policy? ... to wage war against a monstrous tyranny, never surpassed in the dark, lamentable catalogue of human crime. ... What is our aim? ... Victory, victory at all costs, victory in spite of all terror; victory, however long and hard the road may be; for without victory, there is no survival.'

With British troops evacuated from Dunkirk and a German invasion of the homeland apparently inevitable, Churchill told the House of Commons: 'We shall fight on the landing grounds, we shall fight in the fields and in the streets, we shall fight in the hills; we shall never surrender.' Two weeks later, as he announced the fall of France, he again addressed the House: 'Let us therefore brace ourselves to our duties, and so bear ourselves that, if the British Empire and its Commonwealth last for a thousand years, men will still say, "This was their finest hour."'

He kept his nerve as the RAF defeated the Luftwaffe in the Battle

The last charge at Omdurman – Gordon and Kitchener

As a young man, Churchill rode in the cavalry charge – the last of its kind by the British military – at the Battle of Omdurman in 1898, a heroic action by the 21st Lancers that earned three men the Victoria Cross and the regiment a royal cipher.

The Battle of Omdurman ended a long conflict in Sudan. In 1881 Muhammad Ahmed, who styled himself al-Mahdi, the prophesied saviour of Islam, led a rebellion against British rule. The Mahdi and his successor, the Khalifa, and their army of fanatical dervishes repeatedly defeated the British forces. London sent out the ultimate Victorian Christian-military ascetic, General Charles Gordon, who became an imperial hero-martyr, killed when the Mahdi took Khartoum in 1885. This almost brought down Gladstone's government. In 1898 Lord Salisbury dispatched an army led by the gifted but strange General Herbert Kitchener to avenge Gordon, who was Kitchener's own hero. Kitchener, who spoke Arabic and had made his name on espionage missions into the desert dressed as a Bedouin, was an inscrutably severe soldier and a superb planner, nicknamed the 'Sudan Machine'; he was also a connoisseur of interior decoration and an avid porcelain collector.

Churchill wrote a vivid account of the resulting battle, and the famous cavalry charge:

The trumpet jerked out a shrill note, heard faintly above the tram-

of Britain, making a Nazi invasion impossible. In the Cabinet war rooms, Churchill directed the war with energy and imagination, whether travelling abroad to visit troops and foreign leaders or holding meetings from his bed in the morning and pushing his exhausted officials until 3am or 4am, drinking large volumes of champagne and brandy as he worked. He worked hard to develop a good relationship with President Roosevelt, and he engaged positively with Stalin, despite his innate dislike of communism. At a

pling of the horses and the noise of the rides. On the instant all the sixteen troops swung round and locked up into a long galloping line, and the 21st Lancers were committed to their first charge in war.

The pace was fast and the distance short. Yet, before it was half covered, the whole aspect of the affair changed. A deep crease in the ground – a dry watercourse, a khor *– appeared where all had seemed smooth, level plain; and from it there sprang, with the suddenness of a pantomime effect and a high-pitched yell, a dense white mass of men nearly as long as our front and about twelve deep ...*

The Dervishes fought manfully. They tried to hamstring the horses. They fired their rifles, pressing the muzzles into the very bodies of their opponents. They cut reins and stirrup-leathers. They flung their throwing-spears with great dexterity. They tried every device of cool, determined men practised in war and familiar with cavalry; and, besides, they swung sharp, heavy swords which bit deep ... Then the horses got into their stride again, the pace increased, and the Lancers drew out from among their antagonists. Within two minutes of the collision every living man was clear of the Dervish mass.

Gordon was avenged. The Mahdi's tomb was destroyed, the Khalifa killed. Earl Kitchener of Khartoum went on to oversee the defeat of the Afrikaaners in the Boer War of 1899–1902, but his creation of concentration camps, where many died of disease, demonstrated his ruthlessness. In the First World War he became war secretary. He was one of the few to understand that this would be a long conflict and a new type of war: his famous face on posters that read 'Your Country Needs You' was used to raise a million-strong army. He died in 1916, when his ship, en route to Russia, hit a German mine.

series of summit conferences, he agreed with both leaders not only the strategy against Hitler but also the shape of the postwar world.

In the election held in July 1945 after the defeat of Germany, Churchill and the Conservatives lost power. The following year he described, presciently, the 'Iron Curtain' now descending across a Cold War Europe. He returned as prime minister from 1951 to 1955. The 'greatest living Englishman' remained an Edwardian romantic imperialist with an Augustan style and vision, but he never

lost his impish wit. When his grandson once asked him if he was
the greatest man in the world, he replied, 'Yes! Now bugger off!'
When accused of drinking too much, he responded, 'I've taken
more out of alcohol than alcohol has taken out of me.' His writing
was as fine as his leadership; he was the only political leader in
history to have won the Nobel Prize for Literature. On his death
in January 1965, Churchill received a state funeral, an honour rarely
accorded those outside the royal family.

Albert Einstein

1879–1955

*To raise new questions, new possibilities, to regard old
problems from a new angle requires creative imagination
and marks real advances in science.*

Einstein on the essence of scientific creativity

It is no coincidence that Einstein's name has become all but synonymous with genius. He was the most important physicist of the
20th century – some would say of any century. His discoveries,
both building on and supplanting the classical mechanics of Newton,
marked a paradigm shift that radically transformed our understanding of the universe.

Einstein's theory of relativity may be one of the most famous
and fruitful scientific insights of all time, but the man behind it
was far more than just a scientist. Throughout his life Einstein was
committed to social issues and pacifism, speaking out against tyranny
and persecution and despairing at the creation of the atomic bomb.
Fifty years after his death, he remains an instantly recognizable
figure, his face famously etched with wit and good humour.

Born into a family of secular middle-class Jews, Albert Einstein
was brought up in Germany. As a child he was slow to develop (he
was nicknamed *der Depperte* – 'the dopey one'), but a magnetic com-
pass given to him when he was five and a book on geometry he

The theory of relativity

Einstein's theory of relativity has been described as the towering intellectual achievement of the 20th century.

The special theory of relativity of 1905 changed the way people understood the laws that govern the universe. According to this theory, nothing can move faster than light, the speed of which is constant throughout the universe. It also showed, via the famous equation $E = mc^2$, that energy (E) and mass (m) are equivalent and bound together in their relationship by the speed of light (c). Special relativity does away with the idea of absolute time; it proposes instead that time is relative, its measurement dependent on the motion of the observer. Space and time are all part of the same thing, a single continuum known as space–time.

What special relativity did not account for was the effect of gravity upon space–time. Einstein spent the years between 1905 and 1915 struggling to find a theory that resolved this problem. The result was the general theory of relativity.

According to this theory, the presence of objects of mass curves or warps space–time. Like a bowling ball placed in the middle of a trampoline, a large object such as a planet or star causes other objects to move through space–time towards it. So the earth, for instance, is not 'pulled' towards the sun; rather, it follows the curve in space–time caused by the sun and is prevented from falling into it only by its own speed.

Einstein's prediction that light from a star passing close to the sun's gravitational field would be deflected, causing the star's apparent position in the sky to change, was confirmed by observations during a solar eclipse in 1919. Another peculiar effect predicted by Einstein and later confirmed by observation is time dilation: the idea that time is not absolute but slows down at speeds approaching the speed of light. One upshot of time dilation is the bizarre 'twins paradox'. If one of a pair of twins stays on earth while the other travels at close to the speed of light on a round trip to a distant star, the latter will have aged less than the stay-at-home sibling.

In this and numerous other ways, the theory of relativity continues to confound our common-sense ways of looking at and understanding the world around us. Nevertheless, it is today firmly established as the fundamental conceptual platform on which the physical sciences are built.

received when he was 12 pricked his intellectual curiosity in a way that the rigid German school system could not. Sent to boarding school in Munich, at the age of 15 the boy ran away from both school and impending military service and joined his parents, who had moved to Italy in search of work.

Unimpressed by the arrival of their dissolute, draft-dodging son, the Einsteins welcomed Albert's enrolment at university in Zurich, where he spent some of his happiest years. Here he met his first wife, Mileva Maric, a Serbian and fellow physicist whom he married in 1903. The same year he ended a long search for employment with an appointment to the patent office in Berne.

Analysing patents was undemanding work that left Einstein time to apply his mind to mathematical and scientific problems. He was struck in particular by the apparent incompatibility of Newton's laws of motion and James Clerk Maxwell's equations describing the behaviour of light. In 1905 he published a momentous series of scientific papers dealing with the movement and behaviour of light, water and molecules. The most important proposal was the special theory of relativity. The central insight of this was that the speed of light is constant and independent of the motion of the light source and the observer. One conclusion of the theory is that a body's mass is a measure of its energy content, the equivalence of energy (E) and mass (m) being expressed by the famous formula $E = mc^2$, where c is the speed of light.

Few people noticed Einstein's revolutionary theories until Max Planck, the German scientist and father of quantum theory, helped to publicize them. By 1913 Einstein had risen in the academic world to become director of the Institute of Physics at the University of Berlin. During all this time he wrestled with the one major deficiency in the special theory – its failure to account for the effect of gravitation. In 1915, in a series of lectures at the University of Göttingen, he finally resolved this problem by outlining his general theory of relativity, in which gravity is interpreted as an effect of the curvature of space–time. Early confirmation of this monumental discovery was given in 1919, when deflection of starlight passing the sun – predicted by the theory – was observed during a solar eclipse.

While Einstein's fame rocketed during this period, his personal life was in turmoil. After a lengthy separation he finally divorced Mileva in 1919 and promptly married his cousin Elsa Löwenthal.

Einstein was now the most famous scientist in the world. He met and corresponded with many of the world's leading scientists and artists, including Sigmund Freud, the Indian mystic Rabindranath Tagore and Charlie Chaplin. 'The people applaud me,' Chaplin once told Einstein, 'because everybody understands me; they applaud you because no one understands you.'

Though he was far from religiously orthodox and his theories seemed to cast doubt on religions, Einstein always believed in some form of higher principle or spirit. 'The scientist is possessed by the sense of universal causation,' he wrote. 'His religious feeling takes the form of a rapturous amazement at the harmony of natural law, which reveals an intelligence of such superiority that, compared with it, all the systematic thinking and acting of human beings is an utterly insignificant reflection.' He maintained a belief in what he called *der Alte* – 'the Old Man'.

In 1931 the rising Nazi Party attacked Einstein and his 'Jewish physics'. He left Germany for ever the following year, realizing his life was in danger. He settled in the USA at the University of Princeton. His pacifism – which had led to his open opposition to the First World War – weakened in the face of Nazi tyranny. He supported rearmament against Hitler, and in 1939 he co-wrote a letter to President Franklin D. Roosevelt in which the dangers of the development of nuclear weapons by the Nazis were pointed out. This prompted the Allied powers to collaborate in the Manhattan Project in order to produce the first atomic bomb themselves.

When the Second World War ended in 1945 with the destruction of Hiroshima and Nagasaki, Einstein turned sharply and publicly against further nuclear development and favoured international restrictions. He was even monitored by the FBI for his pacifist views. In 1952 he was offered the presidency of Israel; though he was a lifelong Zionist, he respectfully declined. When he died in 1955, Einstein had not achieved his long-term goal of finding a unified theory that would provide a comprehensive explanation of the fundamental forces governing the universe and so offer (as he figuratively put it) an insight into the mind of God. Such a goal has continued to elude succeeding gener-ations of scientists, whose work has nevertheless been revolutionized by Einstein – a colossus of science and the most humane of men.

Atatürk 1881–1938

We shall attempt to raise our national culture above the
level of contemporary civilization. Therefore, we think and
shall continue to think not according to the lethargic
mentality of past centuries, but according to the concepts
of speed and action of our century.

Atatürk, speaking at the 10th Anniversary of the Turkish Republic (29 October 1933)

Atatürk – the name adopted in 1934 by Mustafa Kemal – means 'Father of the Turks'. He was a leader of immense vision, who created a new Islamic secularism, led Turkey out of the ruins of the moribund Ottoman Empire and transformed it into a modern, Westernized republic. He became a military hero in the First World War and subsequently led the Turks to victory over an invading Greek army, sometimes with ruthlessness. He went on to become Turkey's first president, leading the country until his death in 1938. He was by far the greatest of the strongmen of the inter-war period. In our own time of challenge from Islamist fanaticism, Atatürk's vision has never been more important or relevant.

Atatürk was born in what is now the Greek city of Thessaloniki. He was an academically gifted child and attended military schools from the age of 12. Once he had been commissioned as an army officer, he joined the group known as the Young Turks, who were critical of the Ottoman regime and eager for reform and progress. Atatürk was one of those leaders who was as gifted a politician as he was a military commander. During the First World War, he was the victor of Gallipoli, defeating the Allied attack there. He also served in the Caucasus, Sinai and Palestine. He demonstrated a talent for winning the ultimate loyalty of his troops. 'I don't order you to attack,' he told them, 'I order you to die.'

At the end of the war Atatürk found himself on the losing side. As many of the Arab lands once ruled by the Ottomans were dis-tributed among the victorious Allies, he became involved with a national movement to create a modern nation out of the Turkish heartland of the defunct empire. British prime minister David

Lloyd George and the Allies believed in a Classically-inspired Greek empire, assigned much of Anatolia (the Asian part of Modern Turkey) to the Greeks, and encouraged its premier, Eleftherios Venizelos, to invade, thus launching a recklessly unnecessary war. Atatürk resisted ruthlessly and brilliantly, culminating in victory at the Battle of Dumlupinar in 1922 – and atrocity at the Great Fire of Smyrna, in which Turkish troops were responsible for conflagration, rapine and murder, destroying one of Europe's most cosmopolitan cities and killing 100,000 people. Commander-in-Chief Atatürk must bear some responsibility. Turkish independence was assured, however – confirmed in 1923 by the Treaty of Lausanne.

With the military struggle over, another challenge arose: to secure the modernization of a new secular Turkish state. In October 1923 the Republic of Turkey was declared, and Atatürk became president. As a nationalist, one of his first aims was to purge the country of foreign influence. As a progressive, his next priority was to separate the Islamic religion from the state.

The last Ottoman sultan had been deposed in 1922, and in 1924 Atatürk abolished the caliphate – the institution by which successive sultans had claimed rule over all Muslims. In place of an autocratic theocracy, Atatürk embraced, at least in theory, the principles of democracy and a legal code based on European models. Although Turkey remained a single-party state virtually without respite throughout the 1920s and 1930s, Atatürk tried to operate as an 'enlightened authoritarian' – ruling without opposition but with a progressive and reforming agenda.

Economically, Turkey lagged behind much of the Western world in the 1920s. Atatürk set up state-owned factories and industries, built an extensive and efficient rail service, and established national banks to fund development. Despite the ravages of the Great Depression after 1929, Turkey resisted the moves towards fascist or communist totalitarianism that took hold elsewhere.

Atatürk declared that Turkey 'deserves to become and will become civilized and progressive'. A major part of that drive was in the cultural and social field. The restrictions of Islamic custom and law were lifted. Women were emancipated – Mustafa Kemal's adopted daughter became the world's first female combat pilot – and Western dress was strongly encouraged, at times by official rules. Panamas and European hats replaced the traditional fez, which was banned by law. Education

Powerful corpses, embalmed leaders

Some political leaders are as powerful in death as in life, or even more so; and some achieve, in their corporeal mummification, a bizarre if creepy immortality. Atatürk's mausoleum at Anitkabir, in Ankara, remains the national shrine of Turkey. It takes its inspiration from one of the seven wonders of the ancient world, the original Mausoleum near modern-day Bodrum, the tomb of Mausolus, a satrap of the Persian Empire.

Although Atatürk's mausoleum is a place where his memory is revered, his actual body is not displayed. This is not the case with many other dead leaders, especially in totalitarian communist states, where people are encouraged to pay homage to the embalmed corpse as part of the cult of hero worship.

The body of Lenin, the founder of the Soviet Union, is on display in Red Square, Moscow, where it has lain since his death in 1924. The original wooden mausoleum erected days after his death was replaced in 1930 with a permanent display, which has been visited by tens of millions of people. Stalin lay next to Lenin from his death in 1953 until 1961, when he was buried in the necropolis outside the Kremlin, near other Soviet heroes.

In 1949 the Bulgarian communist leader Georgi Dimitrov, who had survived Nazi persecution in the 1930s and brought Bulgaria into close alliance with the Soviet Union, died – perhaps of poisoning – near Moscow. His body was embalmed and displayed in a mausoleum in Sofia until the fall of communism in 1990, when it was buried in the city's Central Cemetery. The mausoleum was torn down in 1999.

The Mongolian communist revolutionary Khorloogiin Choibalsan, a ruthless follower of Stalin who purged his enemies and executed thousands of

was transformed in towns and rural areas alike, and a new Turkish alphabet (a variant on the Roman alphabet) was introduced. Literacy levels rose from 20 per cent to 90 per cent.

Atatürk encouraged the study of earlier civilizations connected with the heritage of the Turkish nation. Art, sculpture, music, modern architecture, opera and ballet all flourished. In every area of Turkish life, Atatürk pressed forward his modernizing, nationalistic mission, and a new culture began to emerge. In the process he rode roughshod over non-Turkish minority groups, suppressing the Kurds, among others.

Buddhist monks, died in Moscow in 1952 and was embalmed in the massive mausoleum in Ulaanbaatar, styled on Lenin's mausoleum. It also housed the body of Damdin Sukhbaatar, a fellow revolutionary who died in 1923. Both corpses were removed and burned in 2004, and the mausoleum replaced with a monument to Genghis Khan, a national hero in Mongolia.

Several Czech communist leaders were interred in the Žižkov Mausoleum, in Prague. They included Klement Gottwald, who led the country from 1948 to 1953. His preserved remains were put on public display, but his body putrified and, despite being re-embalmed every 18 months, finally went yellow-green and was cremated in 1962.

Neither China's communist leader Mao Zedong nor Vietnam's Ho Chi Minh wished to be embalmed. Ho said it was unhygienic and a waste of farmland. Nevertheless, both remain on show. Mao, who died in 1976, rests in Tiananmen Square, Beijing, and Ho, who died in 1969, is in a Hanoi mausoleum. Mao's enormous crystal coffin was a massive feat of engineering, and 700,000 Chinese worked voluntarily on the construction of his tomb.

Two less well-known embalmed communist leaders are the Angolan ruler Agostinho Neto, who died in Moscow in 1979 and remains in a bizarre, spaceship-like mausoleum in Luanda, and Forbes Burnham, the Guyanan president who died in 1985. Burnham's body is in the Guyana Botanical Gardens in Georgetown.

Finally, North Korea's tyrant Kim Il-Sung died in 1994, and his body lies in state in a public mausoleum at the Kumsusan Memorial Palace in Pyongyang. After Kim's death, there was a three-year mourning period in North Korea, in which failure to grieve sufficiently was a punishable offence.

Their innards removed, their bodies stuffed, their skins constantly treated with preservatives, Mao, Ho and Kim, and to a certain extent Lenin, remain as sinister symbols of the power of their state systems long after their deaths.

Dramatically good-looking, Atatürk was an extraordinary and eccentric leader, a vigorous womanizer and a heavy drinker. His Herculean workload combined with these prodigious appetites to bring about a collapse in his health, and in 1938 he died of cirrhosis of the liver. He was only 57. He was loved by his people for his charisma, his energy and his personable style, and his funeral brought forth a massive wave of grief across the country. His memory is still revered; today in Turkey there are portraits and sculptures of him everywhere, and it remains a crime to insult the visionary father of the nation.

Pablo Picasso

1881–1973

Painting is not made to decorate apartments.
It's an offensive and defensive weapon

Pablo Picasso, in a letter (1945)

Art today would not be the same without the genius of the Spanish painter Pablo Picasso. In a career spanning nearly 80 years, Picasso – ever vigorous, ever full of *joie de vivre* – showed himself to be the most versatile and inventive artist not just of the 20th century but perhaps of all time, a master of painting and drawing as well as other media, such as collage, set design, pottery and sculpture. But his talent was not simply aesthetic. His most famous painting, *Guernica*, captured the total horror of war, while in his simple etching of the dove of peace he pointed the way for a happier future.

Picasso was born in Malaga to an artistic but conventional family. Inspired by his father, he showed exceptional talent for painting from a very young age. By the age of 14 he had his own studio and was already exhibiting in public and receiving praise from the critics. Before he was out of his teens, he was in Paris, mixing with the European avant-garde.

In 1901 Picasso embarked on a phase known as his 'Blue Period', in which his paintings – still relatively naturalistic – were dominated by shades of blue. The paintings from this time are mainly melancholy, lonely portraits, often depicting extreme poverty. Much of Picasso's dark mood was influenced by the suicide of a close friend, Casagemas. In a brilliant but gloomy self-portrait from this period, Picasso looks haggard and intense, far older than his 20 years. Soon, though, the mood lifted and Picasso moved into his 'Rose Period', in which his subjects – often circus people or acrobats – were depicted mainly in shades of pink.

In 1907 Picasso struck out in a bold new direction, influenced by Cézanne and African masks, and produced one of the first masterpieces of modernism, *Les Demoiselles d'Avignon*. It is a striking and wildly angular and distorted depiction of five aggressively sexual women in a brothel. Thus Picasso gave birth to Cubism, a completely new mode of capturing the essence of the subject on the canvas. Traditional perspective is abandoned in favour of multiple perspectives, as if the subject is seen from a number of different angles simultaneously. It was a revolutionary way of seeing. 'I paint objects as I think them,' Picasso said, 'not as I see them.'

After his Cubist phase, Picasso moved on to a neo-classical period, in which he painted monumental human figures in Mediterranean settings, influenced in part by Ingres and Renoir, and then, in the 1920s and 1930s, he became loosely associated with the Surrealist movement, experimenting further with distortions of the human face and figure, exploring the depiction of sexuality, and letting his imagination conjure up strange monsters.

Picasso supported the Republicans during the Spanish Civil War, his painting *Guernica* expressing his outrage at the violence of fascism, and in 1944 he joined the French Communist Party. Around this time he wrote: 'What do you think an artist is? An imbecile that only has eyes, if he is a painter; ears, if he is a musician; or a lyre in the deepest strata of his heart, if he is a poet? Quite the opposite, he is at the same time a political being.' In 1949 he absurdly contributed his famous design of the dove of peace to the communist-sponsored World Peace Congress held in Stalinist Poland. Picasso always had sympathy with the sufferings of the oppressed, even if his flirtations with Stalinist tyranny were misguided. He was not at heart a political animal.

In the decades that followed, Picasso continued to produce large quantities of work in a great variety of media, often exploring and reinventing great works of art from the past, such as Velasquez's *Las Meninas* or Delacroix's *Women of Algiers*. By now he was the most famous living artist in the world, his pictures purchased for large sums by galleries and rich private collectors. Sometimes Picasso would pay for an expensive meal in a restaurant by drawing a few lines on a napkin – and it is astonishing what he could convey with just a few lines.

Throughout his long career Picasso had a ravenous appetite for life and all its pleasures. Over the years he had a succession of wives and mistresses, sometimes overlapping each other, and in his later

Guernica

Guernica is Picasso's best-known work, created in the aftermath of the horrific bombing of the Spanish town of the same name in 1937. The vast canvas presents a twisted mass of dark colours, contorted bodies, screaming heads and terrified animals – a vision of wartime apocalypse. The masterpiece is both a memorial to the helpless people killed in this action during the brutal Spanish Civil War (1936–9) and a warning of the wider horrors that war brings, then and now.

In 1931 a leftist republic replaced Spain's overthrown monarchy, and in 1936 it faced an army coup. The ultimately victorious Nationalists, led by General Francisco Franco, were backed by Hitler's Nazis and Mussolini's Fascists. The Republic, increasingly dominated by communists and anarchists, was backed by Stalin's Soviet Union and thousands of young anti-fascist idealists. Both sides committed appalling atrocities, and thousands died. Franco subsequently ruled Spain as dictator until his death in 1975.

Guernica, the ancient capital of the fiercely independent Basque country, is a small town near Bilbao in northwest Spain. A Republican stronghold, it was a key target for the Nationalists. There were around 7000 people in Guernica on 26 April 1937, a number swelled by the fact that Monday was market day. At around 4.40 pm, bombs began falling. The planes came in low through the skies, exploiting the fact that Guernica had no air defences and the Republicans had no planes.

Several hours of bombing resulted in a firestorm in which many people were burned alive. Planes strafed the roads out of town, mowing down fleeing peasants. More than 1000 people died and only 1 per cent of the town's buildings survived.

The English journalist George Steer observed the aftermath of the

works he often depicts himself as some kind of satyr, or Olympian god, enjoying wine, women and *la vie en rose* beside his beloved Mediterranean. It seemed he would live for ever. When he did eventually die, at the age of 91, he was hailed around the world as the grand old man of modern art.

bombing, bringing it to international attention through an article published in both the London *Times* and *New York Times*. Steer wrote: 'Guernica was not a military objective – the object of the bombardment was seemingly the demoralization of the civil population and the destruction of the cradle of the Basque race.'

What Steer also revealed was that German and Italian planes were responsible for the bombing of Guernica. The Condor Legion of the German Luftwaffe, led by Generalfeldmarschall Wolfram Freiherr von Richthofen, had dropped the bombs, calling the mission Operation Rügen. Steer was able to demonstrate that Germany, Italy and Franco's Nationalists had banded together in gross defiance of an international non-intervention pact intended to prevent the Spanish Civil War from becoming a theatre for the brewing European struggle between fascism and democracy.

Steer was soon scared into silence, and Nationalist propaganda claimed that the Republicans had burned Guernica as part of a scorched-earth policy. But international outrage was stirred. Picasso, working on his great anti-war mural painting in Paris, decided to change its name to commemorate the town's awful fate.

Picasso remained so enraged with Franco's regime that he refused to allow the painting to be taken to Spain while the dictator was still alive. It finally reached Madrid in 1981, where it remains, too fragile to be removed to the Guggenheim Museum in Bilbao, despite Basque requests.

The bombing of Guernica was the first internationally recognized example of total war, openly targeting civilians in an attempt to terrorize a population into submission. It would become all too common in the world war that followed.

Franklin D. Roosevelt 1882–1945

His life must ... be regarded as one of the commanding events in human destiny.

Winston Churchill, following the death of Roosevelt

Franklin Delano Roosevelt, in his unparalleled four terms as US president, pulled the country out of the depths of the Depression, commanded the American military effort in the Second World War and helped create the 'American century', with his colossal, rich nation as the arsenal of freedom. A genial, decent man of tolerant liberal convictions, immense personal courage and ruthless political cunning, Roosevelt's determination to secure democracy at home and abroad makes him one of the greatest leaders in the history not only of America but also of the world.

Roosevelt was first elected president in 1932 by a country in the grip of a terrible economic slump, with 30 million out of work. As soon as he took office, he set about implementing the 'New Deal' he had promised the American people, setting them back on the path to economic prosperity. Unprecedented levels of government intervention in agriculture, trade and industry allowed capitalism to recover from the blows dealt it by the Wall Street Crash.

Roosevelt's administrations took on unheard of levels of responsibility for the people's welfare. In the face of bitter opposition from free-marketeers, he introduced social security, protected workers' rights to organize trade unions, and regulated working hours and wages. At the same time, through the 1930s, he oversaw the restoration of America's economic strength, so re-establishing the faith of Americans in their political system and their way of life – and giving the country the muscle to face the trials of global war that were to come.

Roosevelt wanted his country to be 'the good neighbour' to the world and sought for the United States a new role as a guarantor of freedom around the world. He recognized early the barbaric evil of Nazi Germany and knew that neutrality in the Second World War would, in the long term, damage US interests, but such was the strength of isolationist feeling that he was obliged to fight the 1940 presidential election on the promise of keeping America out of the war.

At the same time, Roosevelt did everything he could to support the Allies, instituting a 'Lend-Lease' programme of economic and military support that helped Britain to fight on alone against the Nazis after the fall of France. In January 1941 he enunciated the 'Four Freedoms' for which he stated America would be willing to fight: freedom of expression, freedom of worship, freedom from want and freedom from fear. In August 1941 he met Churchill and the two issued the Atlantic Charter, which asserted the universal right to national self-determination and security and laid down the principles of what was to become the United Nations.

The Japanese attack on Pearl Harbor in December 1941 ended US isolation. For Roosevelt, it was not enough to defeat Germany and Japan: 'It is useless to win battles if the cause for which we fight the battles is lost,' he declared. 'It is useless to win a war unless it stays won.' During the conflict, Roosevelt not only laid the foundations of the United Nations, but also, with Churchill and Soviet dictator Stalin, became an architect of the postwar world. He has been criticized for yielding too much of Eastern Europe to Stalin during these discussions, but since Soviet forces were in occupation there already, it is probable that only another war would have liberated them.

Roosevelt's belief that the weak should be defended against the predations of the rich and powerful had been drummed into him since childhood. Although he had had a privileged upbringing in the patrician society of the East Coast, an inspirational headmaster had instilled in him a deep sense of social responsibility. This was later enhanced by his marriage to his distant cousin Eleanor. A bluestocking of progressive social ideals, she was an indefatigable campaigner on behalf of the disadvantaged right up until her death in 1962.

Roosevelt's genius lay in his handling of people. To the millions of Americans who listened as he outlined his policies on the radio in his avuncular 'fireside chats', it seemed as though he was personally guaranteeing their well-being. 'We have nothing to fear but

American heroes – GIs and Medals of Honor

Franklin D. Roosevelt WAS A skilful commander-in-chief, and part of his genius was in spotting and promoting two of America's most unflashy but brilliant military organizers, George Marshall (1880–1959), who became his chief of staff (and later secretary of state), and Dwight D. Eisenhower ('Ike'; 1890–1969), who would be the supreme commander for the Allied invasion of occupied France that began on D-Day (6 June 1944) and later US president. Less senior, but heroic none the less, 464 ordinary American servicemen won the Medal of Honor during the Second World War, many of the awards going to General Infantry – or GIs.

The United States instituted the Medal of Honor in 1862, to recognize 'conspicuous gallantry and intrepidity at the risk of life, above and beyond the call of duty, in action involving actual conflict with an opposing armed force'. (Its civilian equivalent is the Presidential Medal of Freedom.) The criteria for its awarding were tightened in 1916, and again after the Second World War. The medal is given in the name of the US Congress, even though presented by the president, so it is popularly known as the Congressional Medal of Honor. Winners, no matter what their rank, must be saluted by all other ranks, even by five-star generals and the commander-in-chief himself.

Around 3459 medals have been issued to date. Nearly half of these – 1522 – were awarded during the Civil War that wracked the nation in 1861–5. A further 124 were awarded during the First World War, 131 during the Korean War and 245 during the Vietnam War. Two medals were awarded posthumously for the ill-fated peacekeeping operation in Mogadishu, Somalia, in 1993: to Master Sergeant Gary I. Gordon and Sergeant First Class Randall D. Shugart of Task Ranger Force. More recently, the Medal was awarded posthumously on 4 April 2005 to Sergeant First Class Paul R. Smith of the US Army's Third Infantry Division ('Rock of the Marne') for 'extraordinary heroism and uncommon valor' during the battle for Baghdad International Airport.

The United States also awards a medal for servicemen 'wounded in action as a direct result of enemy actions'. Instituted by George Washington on 7 August 1782, and re-established in 1932, the Badge of Merit is popularly known as the 'Purple Heart'.

fear itself,' he reassured them. Roosevelt's relationship with Churchill, his ally in the darkest war years, was one of genuine affinity; he once ended a long and serious cable by telling the British prime minister: 'It is fun being in the same decade as you.'

After the 'Big Three' Allied leaders met at Yalta in February 1945, Roosevelt appeared to the press in a wheelchair, apologizing for his 'unusual posture' but saying it was 'a lot easier' than carrying 'ten pounds of steel around the bottom of my legs'. It was his first public acknowledgement of the paralytic effects of the polio that he had contracted at the age of 39, and which he had battled and concealed by wearing leg braces and by other means. This was both a defence against public perceptions of weakness and a truly heroic personal refusal to let a debilitating ailment wreck his determination to carry out his presidential tasks.

Roosevelt's sudden death from a massive cerebral haemorrhage in April 1945, just before the first meeting of the UN, stunned the world. In his 12 years as president he had transformed the United States from an isolationist country in economic paralysis into a thriving superpower, the international champion of the values of freedom and social justice that Roosevelt, a man of immense humanity, optimism and courage, had done so much to secure.

David Ben-Gurion
1886–1973

In Israel, to be a realist you must believe in miracles.

David Ben-Gurion, in an interview (1956)

David Ben-Gurion was the architect and defender of the fledgling state of Israel, and its first prime minister. A fiery but highly pragmatic visionary, Ben-Gurion transformed the political map of the Middle East, creating the first land for the Jewish people for two thousand years. Not only did he manage to build up and defend this precarious homeland against attacks of overwhelmingly superior

Middle Eastern peacemakers

The Arab-Israeli conflict is the most intractable in the world: even though the means of resolving the conflict – Israeli and Palestinian states living side by side – is clear. So vicious is the bitterness, so complex the actual map, and so ruthless the interference of outside powers, that only statesmen with the vision and courage to risk their lives can ever make peace in the region.

On 16 May 1948, on the basis of a 1947 UN decision, Israel declared independence. The United States and the Soviet Union immediately recognized it, but five Arab nations – Jordan, Syria, Iraq, Lebanon and Egypt – declared war on the infant state. In the ensuing war of 1948–9, Israel managed to establish more practically defensible borders, but the country remained technically at war with its neighbours and under constant attack by terrorists. In 1956 Israel invaded Sinai to stop these attacks, but was forced to withdraw.

In 1967, when Israel's existence was openly threatened by Egypt and Syria, it decided to launch a pre-emptive air strike against them. The country's forces were led by two of the heroic generation of Israel's founders: Defence Minister Moshe Dayan, whose eye-patch and glamour seemed to symbolize his dynamic young country, and the blond, blue-eyed chief of staff Yitzhak Rabin. Both were Labour moderates who believed in Jewish coexistence with the Palestinians.

Israel wiped out both the Egyptian and the Syrian air forces on the ground. Jordan, gulled by mistaken reports of Arab victory, declared war. In six days, Israel defeated Egypt in the Sinai, which she occupied, and took the Golan Heights from Syria and the West Bank from Jordan. In Jerusalem, Israeli paratroopers took the Old City: the Western (Wailing)

force from every side, but he also created the only liberal democracy in the entire Middle East, an achievement that still stands today. The sheer force of Ben-Gurion's vitality was evident in every aspect of his life. As well as devoting himself to the building of a nation, he had a voracious desire for knowledge, teaching himself Ancient Greek to read Plato, and Spanish to read Cervantes.

Already a committed Zionist and socialist when he arrived in

Wall was in Jewish hands for the first time in 2000 years.

Golan and the hills around Jerusalem remain vital to Israeli security, but the mistaken decision to occupy, and build Israeli settlements in, the West Bank has created insecurity for Israel and suffering for the Palestinians.

In October 1973 Syria and Egypt attacked Israel on Yom Kippur, the holiest day in the Jewish calendar. The Israelis were caught off guard. Reinforced by US supplies, in a brilliant strategic move, Israeli forces crossed the Suez Canal and encircled an Egyptian army. On the Golan, the Israelis broke through and headed for Damascus.

In 1979, after a session mediated by US President Carter at Camp David, President Anwar Sadat of Egypt and Prime Minister Menachem Begin of Israel signed a peace agreement that earned them the Nobel Peace Prize. Sadat, Egyptian dictator and architect of the Yom Kippur War, opened negotiations with a dramatically courageous trip to Jerusalem. King Hussein of Jordan followed Sadat's example and made peace. Sadat paid for his courage when he was assassinated by Islamist extremists in 1981.

In the Oslo Accords of 1992, watched over by US President Bill Clinton and King Hussein, the Palestinian leader Yasser Arafat, Israel's prime minister Rabin and his foreign minister, Shimon Peres, showed courage in agreeing a land-for-peace solution: Rabin accepted Palestinian self-rule, and Arafat recognized Israel. But Rabin's heroic gamble provoked his assassination in 1995 by a Jewish extremist. A later Israeli premier, Ehud Barak, offered the Palestinians a practical deal, but Arafat's courage failed; his corruption and indecision opened the door to the Islamic radicals of Hamas, who have consistently refused to recognize Israel's right to exist. The peace treaties with Egypt and Jordan endure to this day. Hussein died in 1999, Arafat in 2004 and Peres was elected Israeli president in 2007.

Ottoman-controlled Palestine from Poland in 1906 as an impoverished youth of twenty, David Gruen soon adopted the Hebrew version of his name: Ben-Gurion. Under this name, the ascetic, ambitious, secular idealist rose from a position as a promising political activist challenging Turkish rule to head of the Zionist Executive in British Palestine. Ultimately, with his declaration of Israel's independence on 15 May 1948, Ben-Gurion became prime minister of the new Jewish state – a position he was to hold, save for a two-year interlude in the 1950s, for the next 15 years. His drive undiminished by age, he remained in parliament until three years before his death in 1973.

Ben-Gurion united a historically disparate and divided people in a state of their own. As the Second World War broke out in Europe, he masterminded the smuggling of thousands of Jewish refugees into Palestine, while the nations of the world closed their doors to them. His directive to Palestinian Jews to join the British Army to help fight the Nazis, at the same time as the British tried to bar Jewish immigration into Palestine, inspired international sympathy for the Zionist cause.

During the period of British rule, Ben-Gurion helped to create institutions – trade unions, agricultural associations, military forces – that would provide the skeleton of an independent Israel. He effectively created a shadow Jewish state within British Palestine, ready to assume power at a moment's notice. Without this structure in place, it is hard to imagine that Israel would have been able to combat the simultaneous attacks of five Arab nations that took place within hours of the new state's declaration of independence.

Ben-Gurion's leadership during the post-independence years shows his great skill as a statesman. Even in the most heightened of crises Ben-Gurion – who was by nature something of an autocrat – refused to implement emergency measures that might undermine Israel's commitment to democracy. The settlement of the Negev, once a desert but now one of Israel's most prosperous regions, was instigated on his initiative. Having begun his life in Palestine as a farm-hand, Ben-Gurion always believed that Zionism involved the conquest of land by Jewish labour, and when he retired he went to live on the kibbutz that he had helped to pioneer as a younger man.

Bold, mercurial, but unswerving in the courage of his Zionist and democratic convictions, Ben-Gurion's decisions – not least his declaration of Israel's independence – often seemed impossible or were in defiance of international pressure. He was a political moderate willing to be ruthless to secure the survival of the state. His secret agreement in 1956, by which Israel would invade Sinai to give Britain and France a pretext for seizing the Suez Canal, met with international condemnation. But Ben-Gurion defended the validity of his actions, and, in the event, it secured for Israel another eleven years of peace.

Ben-Gurion's vision did not blind him to political reality, nor did his single-mindedness preclude empathy with Israel's enemies. He was one of the first to recognize the validity of Arab objections to Zionism, and he consistently tried to accommodate the Arabs, despite accusations of treachery and opportunism from both sides of the Israeli political spectrum. After the Six Days' War, he was a lone voice, wisely arguing that Israel should renounce its vast territorial gains, apart from a united Jerusalem and the Golan Heights.

Ben-Gurion sought to create a state that would be 'A Light unto the Nations', and, despite the difficulties presented by the demands of politics and security, he never abandoned a desire to abide by the highest moral standards. The role that this stubborn, fervently optimistic, resolute Zionist played in securing and defending a homeland for the Jewish people cannot be underestimated. Israel's existence and democracy are a tribute to the tenacity of David Ben-Gurion.

Mikhail Bulgakov
1891–1940

There is no such thing as a writer who falls silent.
If he falls silent it means he was never a true writer.

Mikhail Bulgakov

Mikhail Bulgakov, the Soviet writer who was sometimes favoured but often banned during his lifetime, left as his legacy one of the greatest novels of the 20th century. *The Master and Margarita* is a madcap, searing satire of Soviet Russia, defying tyranny and despotism, and a celebration of the ability of the human spirit to triumph over dictatorship.

The plot of *The Master and Margarita*, which took Bulgakov over a decade to write, is complex and fantastical. In one strand Bulgakov tells how the Devil (Voland, based on Stalin) and his henchmen, including a giant gun-toting cat, wreak havoc in 1930s Moscow, while in another, set in Jerusalem in AD 33, Bulgakov explores Pontius Pilate's role in the crucifixion of Christ. Meanwhile the Master, a writer persecuted by the Soviet authorities for his novel about this very subject, has retreated to a lunatic asylum, which seemingly offers a saner refuge than the outside world. His mistress, Margarita, refuses to despair, but dances with the Devil to save the Master.

Bulgakov was well aware that his masterpiece could never be published in his lifetime. As well as exploring the complex interplay between good and evil, courage and cowardice, innocence and guilt, the novel champions the freedom of the spirit in an unfree world. Demonstrating the inability of those in power to legislate for the souls of the people they control, Bulgakov's work fundamentally challenged Stalinist Russia.

Doctor-writers — from Chekhov to Conan Doyle

Mikhail Bulgakov's early experiences as a doctor inspired an early collection of short stories, *Notes of a Country Doctor*. When in 1919 he decided to abandon medicine for a life of literature, the doctor-writer joined a long and eminent list. This is no coincidence: the training of a doctor, with its emphasis on observation, imagination, analysis and diagnosis, is in many ways similar to that of a writer.

The German poet and dramatist Friedrich Schiller (1759–1805) was an army surgeon, the Scottish novelist Tobias Smollett (1721–71) a naval one. The exuberant French Renaissance writer François Rabelais (1494–1553) broke his vows as a monk to become an eminent physician, and the poet John Keats (1795–1821) abandoned his position as a junior house surgeon to become a leading light of Romanticism. The bestselling Michael Crichton's (1942–2008) early thrillers paid his way through Harvard Medical School, while its 19th-century dean, Oliver Wendell Holmes (1809–94), was widely celebrated as a poet and humorist. The American Modernist poet William Carlos Williams (1883–1963) worked as a general practitioner in New Jersey all his life. 'I was determined to be a poet,' he said. 'Only medicine, a job I enjoyed, would make it possible for me to live and write as I wanted to.'

The Master and Margarita was first published after Stalin's death, in magazine instalments in 1967. Despite being heavily censored, it was an instant success. Its continued success is living evidence of its own premise that art will triumph over tyranny. In the 1960s Mick Jagger based the Rolling Stones song 'Sympathy for the Devil' on the book.

Born in Kiev, the son of a professor, Bulgakov qualified as a physician in 1916 and served as a field doctor with the White Army during the Russian Civil War. His refusal to flee his homeland, or to become a mouthpiece for communist propaganda, rendered him, in his own words, 'the one and only literary wolf' in the Soviet Union. In his first ten years as a writer, hostile notices outweighed the good by 298 to 3. His plays – even the less controversial adaptations and the historical works that he thought might be allowed to pass unnoticed – were stifled. He himself burned an early draft

---

W. Somerset Maugham (1874–1965) was the most successful writer in the world during his lifetime, but he too was a doctor. The success of his first novel enabled him to abandon medicine for a full-time career as a writer. Maugham wrote *Liza of Lambeth* (1897) while he was at St Thomas's medical school – the same hospital in which Keats had once practised – and the novel draws on Maugham's experiences treating the inhabitants of London's slums.

Sherlock Holmes's creator, Arthur Conan Doyle (1859–1930), the son of an indigent alcoholic, became a doctor to help his struggling family. Conan Doyle found his training at Edinburgh University 'one long weary grind'. But while he was a student he met Dr Joseph Bell, whose extraordinary ability to deduce a patient's history from their behaviour and appearance inspired literature's most famous detective.

It was the bankruptcy of his father that drove Anton Chekhov (1860–1904), then a medical student at Moscow University, to write. He published his early work under a pseudonym, intending to reserve his real name for the medical career that he considered his true vocation. 'Medicine is my lawful wife, and literature is my mistress,' wrote Chekhov. 'When I get fed up with one, I spend the night with the other.' Even after the success of such plays as *The Seagull* (1896) and *The Three Sisters* (1901) and his brilliant short stories, Chekhov never abandoned his love for the profession, giving free medical treatment to the peasants on his rural estate – a mark of the humanity of the man.

of *The Master and Margarita*, temporarily overwhelmed by the futility of writing the unpublishable. In a letter to the Soviet government in 1930, requesting permission to emigrate, Bulgakov outlined the fate he was facing as a banned writer: 'persecution, desperation and death'. His contemporaries believed that his death in 1940, from inherited kidney disease, was as much attributable to his treatment by Stalin, who had personally suppressed Bulgakov's final work, *Batum*, a play about the dictator's early life.

Bulgakov's work, when the authorities allowed it to be aired, was unremittingly popular. He had risen to prominence in post-Revolutionary Russia as a journalist and a playwright for the Moscow Arts Theatre. His smash hit *Days of the Turbins*, an adaptation of his superb Civil War novel *The White Guard*, was premiered in 1926. Based on Bulgakov's own happy upbringing in a large and loving upper-middle-class family, *Days of the Turbins* was the first play since the Revolution to give a sympathetic portrayal of the counter-revolutionary Whites. Under duress, Bulgakov had changed the play's title and provided an ending loosely sympathetic to the communist cause. It was enough to convince Stalin, who, enjoying its portrayal of family life in the Civil War, interpreted the play as a demonstration of the overwhelming strength of Bolshevism. It became Stalin's favourite play; he saw it 15 times.

In the last decade of his life Bulgakov, increasingly ill and disillusioned, had two lifelines. The first was Stalin, who saved Bulgakov from total destitution while at the same time stifling his career. Stalin recognized Bulgakov's brilliance as much as his political unreliability; if he had known that Bulgakov was writing *The Master and Margarita* in secrecy, he would have had him liquidated. Stalin's demand that his favourite play become part of the Moscow Arts Theatre's repertoire provided Bulgakov with almost his only income. And in response to Bulgakov's open letter of 1930, Stalin secured him a position as assistant director at the Moscow Arts Theatre. Bulgakov's second lifeline was his third wife, Yelena Sergeyevna, the model for Margarita, whose unconditional love sustains and saves the persecuted Master. Yelena ensured the survival of Bulgakov's masterpiece, safeguarding the manuscript until its publication just before her death in 1970.

Bulgakov was not a dissident as such: he survived in Stalinist Russia in order to write. He was in this sense an ordinary writer, not a political campaigner. Like the other creative geniuses of Stalinist Russia – the poets Anna Akhmatova and Osip Mandelstam, the poet-novelist Boris Pasternak (author of *Dr Zhivago*), the composer Dmitri Shostakovich, and the novelist Vasily Grossman (author of *Life and Fate*, another work that survived to undermine tyranny) – he made his compromises with the system in order to survive (though Mandelstam was finally crushed after his scabrous poetic attack on Stalin himself). Many other writers were killed by Stalin, yet as Bulgakov famously wrote: 'Manuscripts don't burn!'

Marshal Zhukov
1896–1974

In the constellation of World War II generals,
Marshal Zhukov is undoubtedly the brightest star.

Pavel Grachev, Russian defence minister (1995)

The Soviet general Georgy Zhukov is much less famous in the West than generals such as Eisenhower and Montgomery, but he was undoubtedly the greatest commander of the Second World War, turning the tide against the Nazi invaders at Moscow, Leningrad and Stalingrad, and then leading the Red Army in its bloody counter-offensive all the way to Berlin. Without the heroic Soviet effort, with its sacrifice of 26 million lives, the war might have ended very differently. Zhukov was a communist and a ruthless Stalinist general, who placed results far above his concern for individuals and casualties. Yet he was also an honest, decent, uncompromising and gifted leader, who represents not the cruelty of his master, Soviet dictator Stalin, but the heroism of the Russian people.

Military service dominated Zhukov's life. Conscripted as a private in the First World War, this son of peasants was decorated and promoted. He then fought for the Bolsheviks in the Russian Civil War of 1918–21. Further promotions followed in the 1920s, and Zhukov became known both as a strict disciplinarian and as a diligent

The machine that won the Second World War

The Soviet T-34 tank was probably, in its simplicity and effectiveness, the decisive machine of the Second World War. This single tank played a crucial role in defeating the German invasion of the Soviet Union, and in the counteroffensive that ultimately led to the fall of Berlin.

In 1938 Mikhail Koshkin, the lead designer at the locomotive factory in Kharkov, Ukraine, convinced Stalin to let him design a heavily armoured tank, which he said would be the tank of the future. The result was a 30-tonne, four-man vehicle, over 22ft (6.75m) long. It had thicker armour than its predecessor and a compact diesel engine that could deliver speeds of up to 34mph (55kph). It was equipped with a 3-inch (76.2mm) main gun, plus two or three machine guns. In March 1940 Koshkin invited the military to turn their guns on one of his prototypes, but not a single shell penetrated the tank's 2.8-inch (70mm) armour. The T-34 went into production at the end of the month. In September Koshkin died of pneumonia, but development was continued by his deputies.

When the Germans invaded the Soviet Union in 1941, they were shocked and demoralized to find the Soviets equipped with tanks that could outmanoeuvre theirs and punch holes in their armour from up to

planner. When Stalin slaughtered the officers of the Red Army in the 1937 Terror, Zhukov survived and was promoted.

In 1939 Zhukov commanded the Soviet army against the Japanese on the Khalkin-Gol River. His daring use of tanks led to the defeat of the Japanese within three days. The invaders lost as many as 61,000 of their 80,000 men, and the shock put them off attacking Russia ever again. Zhukov earned the title of Hero of the Soviet Union and in 1940 was appointed chief of staff, but staff work did not suit him: he was a fighting general. When Hitler invaded the Soviet Union in June 1941, Zhukov formed a tempestuous, but ultimately successful, partnership with Stalin. The Soviet dictator recognized Zhukov's brilliance and professionalism, accepting him as his military mentor and making him deputy supreme commander-in-chief.

1.25 miles (2km) away – four times the German range. The Germans despairingly referred to their anti-tank guns as 'doorknockers' – unable to penetrate the T-34's armour and only serving to give away a unit's concealed position.

Desperate for parity, the Nazis developed the Panzer (Panther) and Tiger tanks, which had better firepower, stronger armour and an equivalent range of fire. By 1943 the playing field had been levelled. The inevitable collision came in July of that year, at the Battle of Kursk. It was the greatest tank battle ever seen, involving around 6000 tanks, 2 million troops and 4000 aircraft. Various technical improvements to the T-34 and its superior manoeuvrability led to a bloody victory for the Soviets. The T-34 was able to move directly alongside the Tigers and Panzers and blow holes in their sides from point-blank range. The battlefield turned black from explosions and burning tanks.

Kursk began a Soviet counteroffensive that demanded vast firepower. By the end of the war more than 60,000 T-34s had been produced, leading the Soviet advance west across eastern Europe and into the German Reich.

The T-34 remained in use long after the Second World War and saw action in the Korean War and the Arab–Israeli conflicts of 1956 and 1967. By 1995, when the 50th anniversary celebrations of the end of the Second World War were held, Eastern Europe and the former Soviet bloc contained more than four hundred monuments to the brutal, iconic T-34.

Stalin used Zhukov as a troubleshooter, as the Germans thrust deep into Russia, taking millions of prisoners. When Minsk fell and Stalin almost lost his nerve, Zhukov – the toughest general in Russia – burst into tears. In July, after a row with Stalin, Zhukov was sacked as chief of staff. But he went on to command and save Moscow and Leningrad. In the latter, he bolstered the besieged city's defences so that the city did not fall. In Moscow, he took over the defences as the Germans advanced. With the loss of one quarter of the 400,000 men at his disposal, Zhukov managed to halt the German blitzkrieg in the freezing winter of 1941, just saving the capital and driving the Germans back 200 miles (320km). It was a vital victory.

The next task was to organize the Soviet counterattack in the most dreadful battle of the war – Stalingrad. Zhukov, along with

Marshal Vasilevsky and Stalin himself, conceived of the plan to lure German forces into Stalingrad. With a million men, more than 13,000 guns, 1400 tanks and 1115 planes, Zhukov oversaw the encirclement of the German Sixth Army. The average life expectancy of a Soviet soldier brought into the long battle was little more than 24 hours, and around a million men from both sides were killed. But Stalingrad turned the tide of the war.

Promoted to marshal, Zhukov next led the Red Army to victory in the greatest tank battle ever fought, at Kursk in 1943. The Red Army pushed ever westward, into Poland and then into Germany itself, where the last great battle of the European war was fought through the streets of Berlin. Stalin typically took overall command of the Battle of Berlin himself, forcing the two commanders, Zhukov and Marshal Konev, to compete in the race to the Reichstag. In the early hours of 1 May 1945 Zhukov telephoned Stalin to inform him that Hitler was dead. The next day the city surrendered.

When the war was over, Zhukov was a national and international hero. The Soviet military rank-and-file idolized him, and Western generals thought extremely highly of him. Ironically, all this made him a political threat: Stalin had him accused of Bonapartist tendencies and demoted him, but he ensured Zhukov was not arrested.

After Stalin's death in 1953, Zhukov was brought back to the centre of Soviet politics as defence minister. He helped Nikita Khrushchev become Stalin's heir by arresting Lavrenti Beria, the head of Stalin's secret police, but he was independent and had a fractious relationship with the new leader. In 1957 he again supported Khrushchev, helping to defeat the old Stalinists, but afterwards he was sacked, once more accused of Bonapartism.

Zhukov, who died in 1974, was tough and brutal and sometimes made costly mistakes. He believed in Stalinist methods and was arrogant about his own ability. Yet Zhukov played a more pivotal role than any other Allied commander in the defeat of Nazism. Ultimately, he represents native Russian military genius. Now Zhukov's statue on horseback stands just outside the Kremlin near Red Square. He is not just a Soviet giant but a Russian hero, standing alongside the two field-marshal princes Suvorov and Kutuzov.

Ernest
Hemingway 1899–1961

Man is not made for defeat. A man can be destroyed but not defeated.

The essence of man's – and Hemingway's – indomitable spirit captured
in *The Old Man and the Sea* (1952)

Ernest Hemingway was arguably the most important American writer
of the 20th century. His novels and short stories, rejecting the stuffy
19th-century values he saw in his own family and in the world
around him, introduced a new and powerful style of writing:
sparse, economical, tough, masculine prose that captures the horrors of war and the trials of love, and advocates a strong moral
code for conducting life in a complex world of pain and betrayal.
Hemingway could be unpredictable, violent, bad-tempered, vainglorious, ridiculous and drunken, but these were all aspects of a
troubled yet brilliant mind. He was awarded the Nobel Prize in
recognition of his work and his distinctive and unique contribution to literature.

Hemingway grew up in a Chicago suburb. His father, the physician Dr Clarence Hemingway, urged him towards manly outdoor
activities like hunting, shooting and fishing. His mother, Grace,
instilled in him a familiarity with literature. He used to claim that
the first words he said as a baby were 'Afraid of nothing! Afraid of
nothing!', probably untrue but typical of his famed machismo. As
a young man Hemingway went to Italy to serve in the First World
War. He was blown up by a mortar in 1918, but, despite being
injured by shrapnel and coming under machine-gun fire, he managed to carry two comrades to safety.

Though he later embellished this experience, it was an outstanding act of bravery for which the Italian government awarded
him the Silver Medal of Honour. While recuperating, Hemingway
fell in love with a Red Cross nurse, Agnes von Kurowsky, who

declined to marry him. He never forgot the experience.

When he returned to America, his mother reprimanded him for his 'lazy loafing and pleasure seeking', accusing him of 'trading on his handsome face' and 'neglecting his duties to God'. Hemingway had always despised his mother's written style, her sermonizing and her religion, which he saw as running counter to human happiness. Now he began to despise her wholesale. The breach with his family was never reconciled, and when in 1921 Hemingway took a job as foreign correspondent on the *Toronto Star*, based in Paris, he cut himself free and became his own man.

In Paris Hemingway fell in with prominent literary figures such as Gertrude Stein, Ezra Pound, and his friend F. Scott Fitzgerald, author of *The Great Gatsby* and the other American literary genius of the time. In 1924–5 Hemingway published his short-story cycle

The Dance of Death

'Life, death, ambition, despair, success, failure, faith, desperation, valour, cowardliness, generosity, meanness – all condensed into the actions of a single afternoon.' Such is the mesmeric attraction of bullfighting, captured by a celebrated matador. To the initiated, the *corrida* (bullfight) is a metaphor for life, a microcosm of the human condition – a terminal struggle of man against nature and man against himself.

The *corrida* was a lifelong obsession for Ernest Hemingway, who understood its elemental fascination better than most non-Latins. Few human activities have stirred up such passion among supporters and opponents alike, and rarely can the opposing sides have so thoroughly misunderstood each other.

'Should an animal be tormented and killed for sport?' asks the opponent rhetorically, but for Hemingway and other devotees the *corrida* is not sport at all but an art form – 'the only art in which the artist is in danger of death', as Hemingway explains in his classic account *Death in the Afternoon*. The object of sport is winning, but in bullfighting style and method are all – the final kill is always secondary to the manner in which it is accomplished; victory in itself is never enough. Hemingway again makes the essential point: 'We [non-Latins], in games, are not fascinated by death, its nearness and its avoidance. We are fascinated by victory and we replace the avoidance of death by the avoidance of defeat.'

In Our Time, and in 1926 the successful novel *The Sun Also Rises*, which dealt with the lives of the aimless socialites of America's post-war 'Lost Generation', who decadently drifted around Europe without purpose.

Hemingway's first masterpiece was *A Farewell to Arms*, published in 1929. It was heavily autobiographical, telling a love story set in the First World War. A young ambulance man, Frederic Henry, falls in love with Catherine Barkley, an English nurse tending to his recuperation. After Henry deserts his post, the couple flee to Switzerland, but Catherine and her baby die in childbirth, leaving Henry desolate.

Spain played a dominant part in Hemingway's life and works. He wrote a sensitive study of bullfighting, *Death in the Afternoon*, in 1932, and when the Spanish Civil War broke out in 1936, he

---

The *corrida* has been described as a tragedy in three acts, floodlit by the sun and played out in an arena of sand and blood. In the first act, the *picadors*, the matador's mounted assistants, lance the bull with pikes. In the second act, the foot soldiers – the *banderilleros* – perform some initial capework and spear barbed darts into the bull's neck. And in the closing act, the maestro – the matador himself – works the bull in a series of graceful passes with the *muleta* (red cape), establishes his mastery over his adversary, and at last dispatches him with a clean thrust of the sword between the shoulder blades.

The matador is not only artist but also priest, dressed in ceremonial costume and assisted by his team as he presides over the proper observance of the rites. The skill and bravery of a top matador is beyond question. Although the bull is weakened before the final act, it is still enormously powerful and dangerous. No matador escapes many serious gorings in a career, and nearly a third of all matadors are killed in the arena. The leading matadors win enormous popularity and are fabulously celebrated and rewarded for their skills.

It has been said that bullfighting, the primordial dance with death, opens a window into the soul of Spain: brave yet brutal; heroic yet barbaric. In capturing the contradictory essence of Latin machismo, it is easy to see how the *corrida* bewitched Hemingway and continues to fascinate and appal in equal measure.

became deeply involved in the Republican cause, raising money to assist the struggle against General Franco's Nazi-backed Nationalists. His experience was the basis for his second masterpiece, *For Whom the Bell Tolls*, published in 1940. Set during the Civil War, this tells the story of an American volunteer guerrilla, Robert Jordan, who is sent to blow up a railway line in support of a Republican attack. Jordan's love for a Spanish girl, Maria, develops in a narrative that skilfully explores the Spanish character and the brutality of war.

Hemingway covered the Second World War as a journalist, flying several missions with the Royal Air Force, seeing action on D-Day and taking part in the liberation of Paris. After the war he spent most of his time working at Finca Vigía, his home in Cuba. The jewel of this final period was *The Old Man and the Sea* (1952), the tale of an elderly fisherman and his struggles to land an enormous marlin. This short book won Hemingway the Pulitzer Prize in 1953 and the Nobel Prize the following year.

Alcohol, age and various serious accidents, including two plane crashes, took their toll on Hemingway. During the 1950s he spiralled into depression, and the more unpleasant aspects of his nature – he could be sour, quarrelsome, prone to violence – all came to the fore. Forced from Cuba in 1960 by Fidel Castro's revolution, Hemingway settled in Ketchum, Idaho. Aware that his creative powers were in terminal decline, and realizing that the electric-shock therapy he was receiving for depression was useless, he killed himself with a shotgun in 1961. He was 62 years old.

Hemingway may have been a troubled and troublesome character, but he was also a figure of enormous energy and dynamism who left an indelible mark not just on modern literature but on language too. He was a master of the short story and an outstanding novelist, whose sparse and understated style became a model for later writers. Truly, he was the all-American action hero of 20th-century writing.

George Orwell

1903–1950

In Burma and Paris and London and on the road to Wigan pier, and in Spain, being shot at, and eventually wounded, by fascists — he had invested blood, pain and hard labour to earn his anger.

The novelist Thomas Pynchon

Of all the writers of the 20th century, none did more to shape the way ordinary people think and speak than George Orwell. His novels *Animal Farm* and *Nineteen Eighty-Four* not only offer stark warnings of the dangers of tyranny and state control; they shifted political perceptions and enriched the English language itself. He was also the greatest English-language essayist of his century, always original, penetrating and eloquent. Orwell's politics were consistently left-wing, but he scathingly cut through the rigid conventions of leftist sympathy for Stalinist mass-murder. His principled criticism of the horrors of totalitarianism marked him out as an intellectual icon for people of any political hue. Even the word 'Orwellian' has become part of the English language.

George Orwell was the pen name of Eric Arthur Blair. He was born in 1903 to an English family posted in Bengal, where his father was an officer working in the opium department of the British Civil Service. Although Orwell moved back to England while still an infant, the experience of imperialism left a deep impression that is visible in much of his work.

In 1922 Orwell joined the Indian Imperial Police and was posted to Burma. His time there was the basis for brilliantly observed essays such as 'A Hanging' and 'Shooting an Elephant', as well as the poignant and gripping novel *Burmese Days* (1934). His strong sense of conscience led him to resign in 1927, and he came back to England highly disillusioned with the realities of imperial power.

It was in such a state of mind that Orwell set about turning himself into a writer. In the late 1920s and early 1930s he took a number of grim menial jobs in Paris, often as a *plongeur* in hotel kitchens, then returned to London and 'went native', living as a tramp in hostels and boarding houses. The lice, dirt, greasy pan-scrubbing and toe-rags were all condensed into his first narrative, *Down and Out in Paris and London* (1932). It laid bare the misery of the very poor in Europe and started a lifelong obsession with the living conditions of the working classes.

The old school tie

George Orwell went to school at Eton, but he did not seem to enjoy it much and looked back on his young self as an 'odious little snob'. In the light of his later life he was a rather unusual Etonian. The world's most prestigious places of education are more used to turning out great political leaders.

Eton has, to date, produced 18 prime ministers of Britain and one of Northern Ireland. The first was Sir Robert Walpole (prime minister 1721–42); others have included William Pitt the Elder (1766–8), Arthur Wellesley, Duke of Wellington (1828–30, 1834), and William Gladstone (1868–74, 1880–5, 1886, 1892–4). The last was Alec Douglas-Home (1963–4). The current Conservative leader, David Cameron, hopes to be next on the list.

Eton's great rival, Harrow, has produced seven prime ministers, including Robert Peel (1834–5, 1841–6), Lord Palmerston (1855–8, 1859–65) and Winston Churchill (1940–5, 1951–5). Jawaharlal Nehru, the first prime minister of independent India (1947–64), was also a Harrovian.

If Eton and Harrow have dominated the early education of British prime ministers, then their higher education has been largely monopolized by England's two ancient universities, Oxford and Cambridge. Even since the start of the 20th century – an age of increasing diversity in higher education – ten of Britain's prime ministers went to Oxford and three to Cambridge.

Six others did not go to university at all, including the two greatest leaders of the period, Churchill (1940–5, 1951–5) and Lloyd George (1916–22). The only exceptions to the Oxbridge rule are Neville Chamberlain (1937–40), who studied at Mason College, later the

His next book, *The Road to Wigan Pier* (1937), gave a vivid and powerful account of the everyday living conditions of miners in the urban heartlands of northwest England, with telling insights into the hardships of unemployment and poor housing. It also includes a personal account of Orwell's own progress towards socialism. Even before the book was published, Orwell decided to put actions before words and set off for Spain in 1936 to join the Republicans in the struggle against Franco's right-wing Nationalists. The experience of fighting in the Spanish Civil War provided the

University of Birmingham, and Gordon Brown (from 2007), who went to Edinburgh University. The paradoxical inference is that it is easier to become prime minister with no higher education at all than with a degree from somewhere other than Oxbridge.

France's equivalent of Oxbridge in terms of political output is the specialized and elite École Nationale d'Administration (ENA), founded in 1945, which has educated no fewer than four presidents and seven prime ministers, including the presidential/prime ministerial double-act of Jacques Chirac and Dominique de Villepin (2005–7). The dominant position of these *énarques* (as alumni are known) in French government has itself become a political issue, and the election of Nicolas Sarkozy as president in May 2007 may have something to do with the fact that he is a lawyer rather than an *énarque*.

Harvard and Yale, the two most prestigious universities in the United States, have between them educated 11 US presidents. Harvard was the Alma Mater of John Adams (president 1797–1801), John Quincy Adams (1825–9), Rutherford B. Hayes (1877–81), Theodore Roosevelt (1901–9) – who kept in his college room a small zoo including lobsters, snakes and a giant tortoise – Franklin D. Roosevelt (1933–45) and John F. Kennedy (1961–3).

Alumni of Yale include William Taft (1909–13), Gerald Ford (1974–7), George H.W. Bush (1989–93) and Bill Clinton (1993–2001). Only George W. Bush (2001–08), who was an undergraduate at Yale and took an MBA at Harvard, managed to go to both. While America has its private high schools too, there is nothing comparable to the unique hold on British political power that Eton and Harrow have traditionally wielded.

raw material for an account of his involvement, written in the first person – *Homage to Catalonia* (1938).

During his time in Spain, Orwell was shot in the neck, after which he returned to England. During the Second World War he took a job making BBC propaganda for the Far East, but he soon quit and concentrated his energies on writing *Animal Farm* (1945), an allegorical, anti-Stalinist tale of a farmyard where the pigs take over from the humans, before gradually slipping into tyrannical and corrupt ways. The pigs' slogan – 'all animals are equal, but some animals are more equal than others' – is among the most famous lines of 20th-century literature.

Orwell's greatest contributions to the English language are found in his powerful political novel *Nineteen Eighty-Four* (1948). In this chilling warning against the perils of state control, which reveals an astonishingly truthful understanding of the cruelty and wicked-ness of how communism really worked, he introduced a plethora of suggestive concepts, including the Thought Police, Room 101, Big Brother, Doublespeak and Groupthink. The novel was completed shortly before Orwell died of tuberculosis at the age of 46, having suffered ill health for most of his adult life.

At the same time as writing his novels and other books, Orwell was producing an uninterrupted flow of columns, essays and book reviews. He dealt with all manner of topics. One of his finest essays, 'Politics and the English Language', was an extraordinary argument in which he linked lazy use of words with political oppression. But these complex ideas were always expressed in the most elegant, laconic phrases. Every essay he wrote, even when he was impassioned and angry, was delicately phrased and accessible to every reader.

Orwell left a huge body of work. His books have never been out of print since his death and collections of his essays continue to be published. Many of the ideas expressed in his novels are still as fresh today as ever. His bitter criticisms of the Soviet Union and the repres-sive nature of communism were fully vindicated by the collapse of the Soviet Union from the late 1980s. Orwell's astonishing clarity of vision, combined with an unerring ability to convey challenging ideas in ways that are accessible to all, has ensured that his standing as a great writer of and for the people is uncontested.

Oskar
Schindler 1908–1974

I hated the brutality, the sadism, and the insanity of
Nazism. I just couldn't stand by and see people destroyed.
I did what I could, what I had to do, what my conscience
told me to do. That's all there is to it. Really, nothing
more.

Oskar Schindler

A womanizing, heavy-drinking war profiteer, Oskar Schindler was responsible for one of history's greatest acts of selfless heroism. His decision to save over 1000 Jewish slave labourers from death at the hands of the Nazis has been immortalized in literature and film – an act of individual nobility that epitomizes the triumph of humanity over evil. Like Dickens's sinner-hero Sydney Carton in *A Tale of Two Cities*, Schindler demonstrates that real heroes are often not pious and conventional but worldly rogues, eccentrics and outsiders.

Oskar Schindler was an extravagant and genial businessman from Moravia, in what is now the Czech Republic. He was born into a wealthy family, but his various enterprises were destroyed by the Great Depression that spread through Europe in the 1930s. A wheeler-dealer who excelled at bribery and manipulation, Schindler became one of the first to profit from the Aryanization of German-occupied Poland. In 1939 he took over a Kraków factory from a Jewish industrialist and filled it with Jewish slave labour.

In the late 1930s, sensing which way the political wind was blowing, Schindler had worked for German intelligence – an action that had seen him briefly imprisoned in his native country. When the Germans invaded Czechoslovakia in 1938, Schindler, now set free, joined the Nazi Party. His boozy bonhomie earned him a swift rise. But after watching yet another Nazi raid on the Kraków Ghetto, which adjoined his factory, he decided to use his considerable influence to counteract his party's anti-Semitic policy and to save as many Jews as he could.

The very qualities that made Schindler a successful profiteer enabled him to save his workforce of over 1000 Jews. A consummate actor, Schindler used his charm to deflect his fellow Nazis from sending his Jews to the extermination camps. Gestapo officers arriving at his factory, demanding that he hand over workers with forged papers, would reel drunkenly out of his office three hours later without either workers or their papers. He was arrested twice for procuring black-market supplies for his Jews, but his bribes and his easy manner secured his release. 'Whatever it took

Righteous Gentiles and resistance fighters

The Nazi German project to eliminate the entire Jewish race, using industrial methods of gassing and burning, ranks as the most evil in history. Most people did nothing because either they believed this was right or they feared for their lives. Yet some astonishing and heroic individuals did act to save the Jews or destroy Hitler. Over 20,000 people are honoured by Yad Vashem, Israel's Holocaust memorial, as Righteous Gentiles: non-Jewish men and women who risked their lives to save Jews.

Stationed in German-occupied Denmark, in 1943 the Nazi attaché Georg Duckwitz warned King Christian X's government of the impending deportation of Danish Jews. The king wore the Yellow Star that marked Jews. An underground operation smuggled most of Denmark's 7500 Jews to safety in Sweden.

Frank Foley, the British vice-consul in Berlin, Dr Feng Shang Ho, the Chinese consul in Vienna, and Dr Aristides de Sousa Mendes, the Portuguese consul-general in Bordeaux defied their government's official instructions on the eve of war, issuing life-saving visas to tens of thousands of Jews.

Within months of Germany's invasion of Hungary in 1944, over 400,000 Jews had been deported to Auschwitz. But thanks to the Swiss consul Carl Lutz, the Italian businessman Giorgio Perlasca and the Swedish diplomat Raoul Wallenberg, over 100,000 of Budapest's Jews

to save a life, he did,' his lawyer later said. 'He worked the system extraordinarily well.'

When 300 of his female workers were sent by administrative error to Auschwitz, Schindler secured their release with a hefty bribe. He forbade anyone, including officials, to enter his factory without his express permission. He spent every night in his office, ready to intervene in case the Gestapo came. As the Nazis retreated and the 25,000-strong population of the nearby labour camp at Plaszów was sent to Auschwitz, Schindler pulled every string to have his factory and all his workers moved to Moravia. Even though he was now himself in danger, he stayed with his Jews until the

---

were saved. Wallenberg was kidnapped by Soviet agents in 1945, dying in a Soviet prison.

In German-occupied North Africa some Arabs helped protect the 1.5 million Jews resident there. Muhammed V, sultan of Morocco, declared to the Nazis, 'there are no Jews, only Moroccans'. When the cosmopolitan Tunisian nobleman Khaled Abdulwahab heard that German officers were planning to rape a local Jewish woman, he hid her and other local Jews on his farm.

The continuing examples of genocide have given rise to modern-day Schindlers. As the international community turned its back on the bloodshed in Rwanda in 1994, Paul Rusesabagina, a hotel manager, protected over 1000 terrified Tutsis and moderate Hutus like himself in the Hôtel des Mille Collines. When his Tutsi wife and children were offered safe passage abroad, he refused to abandon those he was protecting. Now living safely in Belgium with his family, Rusesabagina's actions have also been immortalized in film.

Resistance fighters heroically fought Nazi barbarism across Europe. The young Czechs Jan Kubiš and Jozef Gabčík assassinated Reinhard Heydrich, mastermind of the Holocaust, in Prague in 1942. Even in Germany, there was some resistance, though it only gained momentum when the war was already lost. The bravest of the German resisters was Dietrich Bonhoeffer, a Lutheran pastor, who both rescued Jews and conspired to assassinate Hitler, but he was arrested in 1943 and hanged in 1945. Count Colonel Claus von Stauffenberg heroically planted a bomb to kill Hitler at his Wolf's Lair HQ on 20 July 1944. The bomb exploded but Hitler survived. Stauffenberg and 200 other plotters were executed.

Russians arrived in May 1945 and he knew that they were safe.

Schindler rarely talked about his motivation. As a child, his best friends had been the sons of a rabbi who lived nearby. 'It didn't mean anything to me that they were Jewish,' he said later when asked why he acted against Nazi policy, 'to me they were just human beings.' When pressed to explain his apparent volte-face, his reasoning was astounding in its simplicity: 'I believed that the Germans were doing wrong ... when they started killing innocent people ... I decided I am going to work against them and I am going to save as many as I can.' 'I knew the people who worked for me,' he told another. 'When you know people, you have to behave towards them like human beings.'

Many are still confounded by why this unlikely hero would sacrifice everything to save these people. But for Schindler, who began saving Jews long before the tide of war had turned, it was simply a matter of conscience. In the words of another man he saved: 'I don't know what his motives were, even though I knew him very well. I asked him and I never got a clear answer ... but I don't give a damn. What's important is that he saved our lives.'

The opportunistic Schindler ended the war penniless. He spent his vast fortune to protect lives, even selling off his wife's jewels. His marriage to the long-suffering Emilie finally broke down in 1957. 'He gave his Jews everything,' she later said. 'And me nothing.' He was shunned in Germany after the war, his actions a constant challenge to the collective self-deception that nothing could have been done. His postwar business ventures flopped. The Jews whom Schindler had saved came to the support of their erstwhile benefactor. A Jewish organization funded his brief, unsuccessful stint as a farmer in Argentina and his short-lived German cement factory. From all over the world the Schindler Jews sent money. He died of liver failure in 1974. He is buried, according to his wishes, in Jerusalem, 'because my children are here'.

Odette Sansom

1912–1995

*I am a very ordinary woman to whom a chance was given
to see human beings at their best and at their worst*

Odette Sansom, reflecting on her experiences

Although she was awarded the George Cross and the Légion d'honneur for her work behind enemy lines during the Second World
War, Odette Sansom described her occupation in *Who's Who* as 'housewife'. Known simply as 'Odette', she never viewed her unflinching
bravery in Nazi-occupied France as anything out of the ordinary.

Born in France, in 1931 Odette Brailly, as she then was, married
an English hotelier, Roy Sansom, whom she had met when he stayed
at her Picardy home to improve his French. The couple subsequently
settled in England and had three children together. Almost a decade
later Odette, living a quiet life as a London housewife, responded to
a War Office request for all French-born residents to provide any
photographs they might have of their homeland. When Odette sent
in her holiday albums, the War Office called her in to see whether
she might be able to help them with more than snapshots. She was
asked to join the First Aid Nursing Yeomanry, where she received
her basic training, but this was a really a cover for her recruitment
into the Special Operations Executive (SOE), the covert British
organization that sent agents to occupied Europe to work as spies
and saboteurs.

Although her recruiters had been impressed by her vivacity, her
intelligence and her desire to redeem France from the disgrace of its
capitulation in 1940, her trainers at SOE were at first doubtful that
Odette had what it took to be a secret agent. But eventually, noting
her steely determination, they selected her for work in occupied France.

She was landed by boat in Antibes in October 1942, where she
met her group leader, Peter Churchill. Odette was meant to join a
new circuit in Burgundy, but Churchill, with whom she would fall
in love and eventually marry, instead secured permission for her to

stay with his circle. Using the code name Lise, Odette worked as Churchill's courier for over a year, helping him to transmit vital information to and from England.

In April 1943 Odette and Churchill were betrayed by a double agent. Odette had been suspicious of 'Colonel Henri' as soon as she met the German officer who claimed that he wanted to defect to the Allies. Churchill, when he returned by parachute from London where he had been receiving instructions, was equally suspicious. But by then it was too late. A more indiscreet member of their circle had already confided in Sergeant Bleicher of the Abwehr (German military intelligence), and Odette and Churchill were arrested.

In 14 separate interrogations in Fresnes Prison in Paris, as her toenails were torn out and her spine branded with a red-hot iron, Odette refused to alter her story, or to reveal the identities or where-

Violette and Hannah – female spies and the SOE

From 1940 to 1945 the Special Operations Executive (SOE) – founded, in the words of Winston Churchill, 'to set Europe ablaze' – poured hundreds of undercover agents into occupied Europe to work with resistance groups opposing the Nazis.

Following in the footsteps of Edith Cavell – the nurse who was shot by the Germans during the First World War for helping Allied soldiers to escape from occupied Belgium – the women of SOE were prepared to risk everything for a cause they believed in. Odette was just one of 39 women sent into France, the most important area of operations for SOE. Among this number were a dancer, a fashion designer, an Indian princess and another French-born housewife, Violette Szabo (1921–45).

Violette, whose actions were immortalized in the 1958 film *Carve Her Name with Pride*, volunteered for service after the death of her husband, a French Foreign Legion officer, at the Battle of El Alamein. Recruited by SOE, Violette left behind her infant daughter and was parachuted into France in April 1944. In Cherbourg she reorganized a network the Germans had smashed, and then sabotaged enemy communication lines in Limoges. She escaped twice after being arrested, and when she was finally cornered, she refused to surrender quietly, firing her Sten gun until

abouts of two other SOE officers whom the Gestapo were determined to find. Sticking obdurately to the quickly fabricated story that she was married to Peter Churchill, she insisted that she, not Churchill, was the leader of the group. She managed to convince her interrogators of the truth of this by agreeing that she, rather than Churchill, should be shot. As a result, Churchill was only interrogated twice. Odette was sentenced to death.

In 1944 she was transferred to Ravensbrück concentration camp, where she was to be executed. That she survived was partly down to the fact that she and Churchill had convinced the Gestapo that his uncle was the British prime minister, Winston Churchill. Nevertheless, Odette was held in solitary confinement and treated brutally. When the Allies landed in France, she was kept in complete darkness for three months as a punishment. But believing her to be well-connected, the camp commandant used Odette as a

---

eventually she dropped with exhaustion. Violette maintained her silence during months of torture. With her fellow agents Denise Bloch, Cecily Lefort and Lilian Rolfe, the 23-year-old Violette was executed at Ravensbrück in February 1945.

The women of SOE came from all over the world. Many were British with a French father or mother, or themselves French-born, while others were Greek, Dutch, Norwegian, Italian, Polish – even American.

The Hungarian-born Jewish poet Hannah Senesh (1921–44) joined the SOE from Palestine, where she had emigrated as a teenager. Aged only 22, she was parachuted into Yugoslavia in 1944 to engineer the rescue of the Jews of Hungary. Her two male colleagues, when they heard of the German invasion of Hungary, decided the mission was too dangerous, but Hannah, determined to 'bring my mother out', pressed on alone and crossed the border. She was arrested, and her radio transmitter discovered.

Despite months of torture in a Budapest prison, Hannah refused to tell her captors what they wanted to know. She transmitted signals to the other Jewish prisoners with mirrors and signs drawn in the dust, trying to keep their spirits up. Even when her captors brought her mother into her cell and threatened to torture her, Hannah refused to reveal any information. She was tried for treason and executed by firing squad – just one of many women agents who paid the ultimate price.

hostage when he fled before the advancing Red Army. As soon as they reached Allied lines, Odette denounced him.

Odette emerged from prison gaunt, ill and, in the words of a doctor's report, 'in a state of high nervous tension due to maltreatment'. Yet in the years after her release she refused ever to indulge in bitterness or recrimination and instead devoted herself to working with charities dedicated to healing the physical and mental wounds of war. She made an emotional return to Ravensbrück in 1994 to unveil a plaque to her SOE comrades who had died there.

Odette was awarded the George Cross, England's highest non-military honour, and appointed to France's Légion d'honneur. She was idolized in the press, and her actions were immortalized in the 1950 film *Odette*. But she remained a self-effacing heroine, stating that she accepted the George Cross only on behalf of all those who had fought in the war, adamant that it was the luck of her survival, and not any particular bravery, that had secured it.

Odette married Churchill in 1947, but the marriage was not a success. She was, however, blissfully happy with her third husband, Geoffrey Hallowes, another ex-SOE man, until her death in 1995.

John F. Kennedy
1917–1963

Democracy is a difficult kind of government. It requires the highest qualities of self-discipline, restraint, a willingness to make commitments and sacrifices for the general interest ...

John F. Kennedy, speech in Dublin (28 June 1963)

The 35th president of the United States was a gifted and charismatic man, the youngest – after Teddy Roosevelt – to reach the White House, and the only Roman Catholic to do so. In the three short years of his presidency he gave America and the world a vision of a peaceful and prosperous future. His assassination in 1963 was met with grief across the globe.

John F. Kennedy was the son of Joe Kennedy, a ruthless self-made business tycoon who had made fortunes in whiskey during the Prohibition era and in movies and real estate afterwards. As President Roosevelt's ambassador to London, he was discredited by becoming a shameless appeaser of Nazi Germany. But his children overcame this stain on the family's reputation to become almost American royalty. His son John ('Jack') Kennedy joined the US Navy in September 1941, shortly before the USA joined the war, and went on to serve in the Pacific theatre. He was decorated with the Navy and Marine Corps Medal for saving the crew of his PT (patrol torpedo) boat after it was rammed by a Japanese destroyer off the Solomon Islands.

Not long after leaving the navy, Kennedy entered politics, serving as a Democratic Party congressman between 1946 and 1952, when he was elected to the Senate. In 1960 he defeated Senator Lyndon B. Johnson of Texas to become the Democratic candidate for the presidency. Running with Johnson as his vice-presidential candidate, Kennedy beat the Republican Richard Nixon, partly as a result of his superior gift for public speaking and his ability to look good on TV. When he was inaugurated as president in 1961, he gave an inspirational speech: 'Ask not what your country can do for you,' he told his fellow Americans. 'Ask what you can do for your country.'

Kennedy's presidency was a glamorous one, full of youthful idealism, in which the White House played host to many artists and cultural figures. Even though Kennedy himself was an obsessional lothario, having affairs with the film star Marilyn Monroe, society women and Mafia molls, none of this was known or revealed at the time; he and his elegant first lady Jackie created an American 'court' such that it came to be known as Camelot. Politically Kennedy's presidency was dominated by the Cold War, the global struggle for supremacy between the democratic free world, led by America, and the communist dictatorships of the Soviet Union and its allies. In 1961 Kennedy authorized the CIA-led invasion of Cuba at the Bay of Pigs, a fiasco in which Cuban exiles unsuccessfully tried to overthrow Fidel Castro.

The Cuban Missile Crisis

Since the 1959 revolution Cuba had been ruled by Fidel Castro, a Soviet ally. Nikita Khrushchev, the Soviet leader, felt Russia was losing the arms race, so he recklessly bet his foreign policy on changing the balance of power. He had decided to place nuclear warheads in Cuba, which America traditionally considered part of its 'back yard'.

On 14 October 1962 an American U-2 spy plane overflew Cuba, taking aerial photographs. The courage of a CIA spy in the Russian military, Colonel Oleg Penkovsky, who was later exposed and shot in 1963, enabled American analysts to identify medium-range ballistic missiles near San Cristóbal, only 90 miles (145km) from the coast of Florida.

President Kennedy was briefed on 16 October. The next day American military units began to move southeast. Meanwhile, a second U-2 mission identified further construction sites and between 16 and 32 missiles already on Cuba. On 18 October, without revealing that he knew about the missiles, Kennedy warned the Soviet foreign minister, Andrei Gromyko, of the 'gravest consequences', should the Soviet Union introduce significant offensive weapons to the island.

Four days later, having ruled out an air strike against the missile sites, Kennedy went on national television to reveal the discovery of the Soviet missiles and announce a naval 'quarantine' (blockade) of Cuba, which was only to be lifted when the weapons were removed. On 24 October American ships moved into position. Though Khrushchev had declared the blockade illegal, Soviet freighters heading for Cuba stopped dead in the water.

In an exchange of telegrams between Kennedy and Khrushchev that

Matters escalated in 1962 with the Cuban Missile Crisis, in which Kennedy became involved in a nuclear stand-off with the Soviet leader, Nikita Khrushchev, spelling acute danger not only for America but also for the world. As the superpowers teetered on the brink of mutual destruction, Kennedy stood firm, steering the world through the worst international crisis since the Second World War.

Khrushchev backed down over Cuba, but in 1963 there were still great tensions in Germany, where Western and Soviet forces

evening, neither side gave ground. But American military defences were moved, for the only time in history, to DEFCON 2, a heightened state of readiness for imminent attack.

On 25 October the United Nations called for a 'cooling-off' period between America and the Soviet Union. Kennedy firmly refused. The next day Khrushchev offered to remove the missiles in exchange for American assurances not to invade Cuba.

On 27 October Khrushchev made another offer: removal of Soviet missiles from Cuba in exchange for the removal of American missiles from Turkey, which bordered the Soviet Union. Then, around noon, a U-2 spy plane was shot down over Cuba by a Soviet missile, and the pilot killed. At a meeting with his military advisers, Kennedy agreed to hold back from an immediate military response and to offer terms in accordance with Khrushchev's initial suggestion. But there was no expectation that Khrushchev would now accept. Kennedy warned America's NATO allies to expect war the next day.

However, when the next day dawned, Khrushchev announced that the Soviet Union would remove its weapons from Cuba. Kennedy had negotiated a deal whereby the US missiles in Turkey would be removed in secret. Though few in Moscow, Washington, Cuba or Turkey were entirely satisfied with the outcome, the crisis was over.

Kennedy emerged from the crisis with immense credit. He had been tough but not rash and had called Khrushchev's bluff. The Soviet leader, by contrast, was criticized for his recklessness and lost face: in 1964 he was overthrown in a Kremlin coup by Leonid Brezhnev. The rest of the world was simply relieved that the greatest nuclear crisis in history had somehow been averted.

faced each other on either side of the divided country. Kennedy gave one of the great speeches of modern times in Berlin, where the Soviets had recently built the infamous wall to prevent East Germans escaping to the West. 'Freedom has many difficulties and democracy is not perfect, but we have never had to put up a wall to keep our people in,' he said. In the same speech, he used the famous phrase 'Ich bin ein Berliner', calling for solidarity across the Western world.

As well as being involved in a military stand-off, the USA and the Soviet Union were in competition in the space race. In 1961 Kennedy persuaded Congress to vote $22 billion to put an American on the moon before the end of the 1960s. When Neil Armstrong and Buzz Aldrin landed on the moon in 1969, it was testament to Kennedy's far-sighted commitment to space exploration. Less far-sighted was his commitment to increasing amounts of military support for South Vietnam in its battle with the communist North, a policy that was to mire America in a decade-long conflict that in the end it had to abandon. However, there is some evidence that Kennedy, had he lived, planned to withdraw from Vietnam after the 1964 election.

On the home front, Kennedy was initially slow to give his complete backing to the civil rights movement. But in 1962 he sent 3000 troops to the University of Mississippi to allow a black student, James Meredith, to enrol for classes. By 1963 he had thrown his whole weight behind civil rights and gave a stirring speech on national television. After his death, the Civil Rights Act of 1964, which he had proposed, became law.

Kennedy's assassination in Dallas, Texas, in 1963 was a moment that stopped the world in its tracks. He was gunned down while being driven through the city in an open-topped car, probably by Lee Harvey Oswald, who was himself murdered days later by Jack Ruby, a dubious nightclub-operator. The wealth of conspiracy theories provoked by Kennedy's death is testament to the glamorous and optimistic effect that this young and charismatic president had on the world he helped save from annihilation.

Nelson Mandela

b.1918

*I have fought against white domination, and I have
fought against black domination. I have cherished
the idea of a democratic and free society in which
all persons live together in harmony and with equal
opportunities. It is an ideal which I hope to live for
and to achieve. But if needs be it is an ideal for
which I am prepared to die.*

Nelson Mandela, defending himself at the Rivonia Trial (1964)

In his fight for freedom against South Africa's apartheid system
Nelson Mandela has inspired millions across the world with his
courage, endurance and nobility of spirit. The transfer of South Africa
from apartheid to black rule could have led to vindictive massacres,
similar to the slaughter when India became independent, but, thanks
to one politician, this revolution was essentially tolerant, peaceful,
orderly and bloodless. This is the towering achievement of a man who
embodies South Africa's journey towards democracy and racial equality.

On 11 February 1990 Nelson Mandela walked out of the gates
of the Victor Verster Prison in the Dwars Valley near Cape Town. It
was the first time that he had been free for 27 years, a triumph of
hope that signified the beginning of a new era for a country riven
by apartheid since 1948. It was Mandela who in 1994 became
South Africa's first democratically elected president.

The privileged son of a Tembu chieftain of royal descent, Mandela
grew up in rural Transkei and had a boarding-school education that
exposed him to little of the discrimination that most of South Africa's
black population faced. Before Mandela fled his home to avoid an
arranged marriage, his most significant experience of oppression
had been his designation as 'Nelson' by a primary-school teacher
who found his African name too difficult to pronounce.

n Johannesburg the young lawyer began to live
 me: Rolihlahla, or 'troublemaker'. Mandela became
freedom fighters for the African National Congress
as repeatedly arrested and imprisoned for his non-
ests throughout the 1950s. When the ANC was out-
dela – the 'Black Pimpernel' – went on the run, drumming
as support and military training for the organization. In
196. e became the leader of the ANC terrorist wing, Umkhonto
we Sizwe (Spear of the Nation), planning violence against

Sotho, Xhoso and Zulu

When Nelson Mandela was inaugurated as South Africa's president in 1994, he was accompanied by an *imbongi*, a 'praise-singer' who lauds, and sometimes rebukes, the clan chiefs of the Xhosa tribe. As the Xhosa prince Mandela was made president of South Africa's multiracial democracy, the *imbongi* by his side was a sign that the nation's diverse black peoples could openly renew their pride in their heritage and history.

During the near half-century of racist apartheid, the black African inhabitants of South Africa were treated as a single inferior racial group. In fact, there are three main black African peoples in South Africa, each with its own language, culture and origin. Sothos are descended from those who migrated from the north in the 15th century. They lived peacefully as highly skilled craftsmen in a farming society based around villages ruled by chiefs, but this way of life was destroyed by British and Boer annexation in the 19th century. Nevertheless, many of their traditional practices remain, particularly in the rural areas of Lesotho, an independent kingdom completely surrounded by South Africa. Modimo, the Sotho supreme being, is still honoured, as is Moshoeshoe, the powerful 19th-century chief who, until his death, protected the Southern Sotho peoples from colonization. Songs and folktales of magic and monsters abound; elaborate rites of initiation into adulthood, involving seclusion and intricate decoration of the body, are still practised; and rural Sothos still wear traditional brightly coloured blankets instead of coats.

In the Xhosas' move south they adopted from the indigenous Khoisan people (or 'Bushmen' as Europeans called them) their distinctive lin-

military/government targets. He regarded terror as a last resort to be used only when peaceful methods seemed hopeless, but he later confessed that the increasingly violent ANC terror and guerrilla campaigns also abused human rights. After being arrested and jailed in 1962 for leaving the country, in the Rivonia Trial of 1964 Mandela was sentenced to life imprisonment.

Mandela's speech from the dock echoed through the townships from the Cape to the Paarl. It helped to politicize a people who had had every opportunity for education, advancement and

---

guistic click. But by the late 18th century their willingness to trade and interact with other societies had led to *mfecane* – 'scattering'. They were pushed west by the Zulus and east by the British and the Boers. It has been argued that the territorial displacement of this cattle-breeding people fostered a degree of political engagement that is reflected in the predominance of Xhosas in politics.

Under the gifted but destructive king and commander Shaka (c.1787–1828), a small people named the Zulus overwhelmed their neighbours, conquering most of the Natal region and creating an empire guarded by their fearless warriors. Equipped with a short-handled, long-bladed dagger rather than the traditional spear, the *Impi* – regiments formed of every Zulu man between 19 and 40 – wrought havoc on their enemies. Unencumbered by heavy weapons or baggage, the 'running army' could cover up to 50 miles (80km) a day. Their remarkable military prowess increasingly brought them into conflict with the martial technology of the British Empire. Under Shaka's successors, the Zulu warriors used their 'beast's horns' formation to outflank and surround their British enemy at Isandhlwana (1879), but with their large cowhide shields they were powerless if they failed to breach the British defences, as at Rorke's Drift.

By the end of the 19th century the Boers and the British had annexed the Zulu empire, crushing their rebellions. In the second half of the 20th century, forced to live in the special Zulu 'statelet' of Kwazulu under apartheid, the Zulus still gloried in their identity, expressed politically through the Inkatha Party. After years of apartheid-encouraged conflict with the ANC, the Zulu Chief Buthelezi joined Mandela's first government until his falling out with the ANC in 1999. But pride in Zulu culture and history, and their revered ancestors, remains strong.

independence taken away from them by the apartheid policies of the Afrikaaner Nationalist government, which had crushed their rights and dignity. His words gave them hope.

Mandela is a man of awesome obduracy. Sentenced to hard labour in a stone quarry on Robben Island, Mandela transformed his prison camp into the 'Island University', assigning instructors to educate the teams of inmates as they toiled at their back-breaking work. He put on plays and distributed books to fill the hours. After 27 years' waiting, Mandela delayed his final departure from prison by one more day: 'They are going to release me the way I want to be released,' he explained, 'not the way they want me to be released.'

As Mandela's stature grew across the world, the apartheid government, under hardliners like P.W. Botha, tried to do deals with this prisoner who had become their Achilles' heel. They offered to release him if he would denounce the ANC; Mandela refused: 'Until my people are free, I can never be free.' Peace takes men of vision and courage on both sides, and in 1989 the new South African president, F.W. de Klerk, was courageous enough to take the necessary risks. In 1990 he lifted the ban on the ANC just days before he released Mandela. And once free, Mandela almost immediately renounced violent action, thus making the vow he had refused to undertake while imprisoned.

Mandela has never indulged in racism. At his trial he called for freedom regardless of colour, and on his release he refused to stir up racial tensions. As president (1994–9) he included representatives of all ethnic groups in his multi-party government. He established the Truth and Reconciliation Commission to investigate human rights abuses. The Madiba – the honorific tribal name by which South Africans know him – shared the 1993 Nobel Peace Prize with de Klerk. His one embarrassment was the violent gangsterism of his wife Winnie, whom he divorced. He later married the widow of President Machel of Mozambique. Mandela has recognized that during his presidency he did not do enough to combat the AIDS epidemic. In retirement he has taken every step to redress his mistake. With characteristic honesty, Mandela has since admitted that his own 1960s militancy, no less than apartheid, violated human rights and he has refused to let his followers suppress this fact.

'My life is the struggle,' said Mandela.

John Paul II 1920–2005

His name became part of our history, his thoughts will be an always present inspiration to build ... a more peaceful world for all of us.

Chilean president Ricardo Lagos, on the death of John Paul II

In 1978 the Polish cardinal Karol Wojtyla became Pope John Paul II. He was the first non-Italian pontiff for 455 years. During his long tenure, he became a hero of the struggle for freedom over tyranny. He was a champion of liberty in Eastern Europe, particularly in his native Poland, and a supporter of oppressed people all over the world.

A tireless traveller and a master of modern media, John Paul II was a relentless critic of totalitarian tyranny and of the inequalities created by materialism. He strove to build bridges between the Catholic Church and the Jewish and Islamic peoples. And in old age he battled bravely against illness and frailty, dying a truly iconic spiritual leader for people throughout the world.

As a young man in Poland, Wojtyla knew the harsh reality of totalitarian rule. After the Nazis invaded his country in 1939, he was forced to take on menial work, such as labouring in a limestone quarry. It was a time when the Vatican under Pope Pius XII failed to show moral leadership and equivocated over Nazi oppression in Poland and elsewhere in occupied Europe. Wojtyla put his life at risk to smuggle Jews out of Poland and was placed on a Nazi death list. Fortunately he escaped detection during a Gestapo raid on the Archbishop of Kraków's house in 1944 and survived the Second World War.

In 1946 Wojtyla was ordained as a priest. He rose rapidly through the Church ranks to become Archbishop of Kraków in 1963 and a cardinal in 1967. By this time he was established as one of the most important religious figures in Poland, where he was frequently at odds with the communist authorities. He was no unthinking firebrand, but he was more than willing to stand up to the authorities, as when he supported industrial workers in Nowa Huta in their efforts to build a new church.

Wojtyla's profile increased rapidly at the Vatican, where he was a trusted adviser to Paul VI. So when Paul and his successor, John Paul I, both died in 1978, it was he who won a tight ballot of the cardinals. At the age of just 58 he became pope.

International attention was lavished upon the first non-Italian pope for nearly half a millennium. This suited John Paul II, who set about spreading a global message of freedom for those in need. On his first foreign trip, to Mexico, he spoke up for the unemployed and oppressed, though he held back from advocating political regime change.

After bringing great pressure to bear on the authorities, in 1979

Polish heroes – Sobieski to the Warsaw Uprising

Surrounded by powerful empires, Poland has often been the target of their carnivorous appetites: partitioned thrice in the 18th century, finally consumed by Russia, Prussia and Austria in 1795, re-created in 1918, at war with Soviet Russia in 1920, invaded by Nazi Germany and partitioned with Soviet Russia, then brutalized by the Nazis, who committed their wickedest deeds there, until 'liberated' by Stalin, swallowed by the Soviet Empire for over forty years, now free again. No wonder this perpetual struggle has thrown up such heroes.

Jan Sobieski (1629–96), the last great king of Poland, was a superb military commander, nicknamed the Lion of Lehistan by his Turkish enemies, whom he defeated at the Battle of Chocim. Elected king as John III in 1674, he commanded 80,000 Poles and Austrians in the total defeat in 1683 of Kara Mustafa's 130,000 Turks, winning the title of 'Saviour of Vienna and Western Civilization'.

Prince Józef Poniatowski (1767–1813) was the king Poland never had. Son of an Austrian-Czech princess and nephew of the last Polish king, Stanislas-Augustus, he fought the Russians, with Tadeusz Kosciusko, during the Polish revolution of 3 May 1791. He rejoined the remarkable Kosciusko in the 1794–5 rebellion, but the Poles were defeated and the country partitioned. He re-emerged in 1807 as war minister in Napoleon's Grand Duchy of Warsaw, defeating the Austrians repeatedly in the 1809

John Paul was permitted to return to Poland, becoming the first reigning pope to visit a communist country. Announcing his arrival as a 'pilgrim', he was given a rapturous welcome that was broadcast around the communist world. The sight of crowds chanting 'We want God' caused an international sensation. Having shaken up the communist authorities, John Paul then visited a number of countries on the other side of the Iron Curtain. In Ireland he denounced sectarian violence and terrorism, and in America he spoke passionately against the selfishness of consumerism and capitalism.

In 1981 John Paul was shot at close range in Rome by a Turkish gunman, Mehmet Ali Ağca. The pope had fiercely criticized communism, and it later emerged that the gunman had connections to

war, joining Napoleon's invasion of Russia, and fighting at Borodino. Napoleon promoted him to marshal, but he was drowned after the Battle of Leipzig in 1813.

Adam Mickiewicz (1798–1855), handsome, Romantic, mystical icon of Polish patriotism and the greatest Slav poet along with Pushkin, is the Polish national bard. A defiant patriot, he was exiled by the Russians. Polish chivalry and martyrdom (and Russian villainy) fill his works. During the Crimean War he travelled to Istanbul, where he died while raising a Polish Jewish legion to fight Russia.

Jozef Pilsudski (1867–1935) was the swashbuckling anti-communist and opponent of Russian rule who, in 1918, became the first leader of an independent Poland for 123 years. During the Russo-Polish War of 1919–20, when Lenin's Russia hoped to invade Europe, Marshal Pilsudski defeated the Russians at the Battle of Warsaw, thereby saving the West from Bolshevism. As head of state until 1922, and then dictator from 1926, he worked for an inclusive Poland, protecting Jews and other minorities.

The greatest of all Polish heroes, though, must be the fighters of the Warsaw Ghetto in January–April 1943 and the Warsaw Uprising of August–October 1944. The Nazis enclosed Polish Jews in the ghetto to await liquidation. After 254,000 of them had been murdered at the Treblinka death camp, Jewish secret armies in Warsaw fought back but were brutally destroyed, with 56,000 killed. As the Soviet Red Army approached Warsaw, the Polish Home Army rose to defeat the Nazis and assert Polish sovereignty. Unaided by the Soviet forces, 200,000 Poles were slaughtered by the Nazi SS and their Ukrainian henchmen, and the city of Warsaw was gutted.

the Bulgarian secret police, and therefore to the Soviet KGB. The bullets missed his vital organs by millimetres, which he took as a sign from God to continue his work. He publicly forgave his attacker.

Throughout the 1980s John Paul continued his spiritual opposition to communism. After the peaceful revolution of 1989 and the fall of the Berlin Wall, the Soviet leader Mikhail Gorbachev – who admitted that without John Paul II there would have been no such speedy end to communism – paid a humble visit to the pontiff in Rome, opening diplomatic relations between most of the former Soviet capitals and the Vatican.

During the next decade John Paul took on the task of extending the branch of peace to the Jewish and Islamic peoples. He allowed the first mosque to be built in the Vatican, and in 1993 he signed an agreement to open relations with Israel. In 2000 he made a high-profile trip to the Holy Land and visited a Holocaust memorial. He also promoted many cardinals from the developing world.

Throughout his long pontificate John Paul stood up for freedom with unwavering resolve. His inspiring voice carried huge authority. His condemnation of Paraguay's dictator Alfredo Stroessner helped to bring down the latter's regime, while a speech opposing the death penalty led to its abolition in Guatemala. An appearance on Italian television led to a Mafia don surrendering himself.

Pope John Paul II was generally inflexible over doctrine, remaining doggedly conservative in matters such as the ordination of women and the use of contraception, even in the face of Africa's AIDS epidemic. Nevertheless, he will be remembered as one of the most outstanding popes in history. To the end he was an inveterate opponent of oppression and inequality. This man of peace used his position nobly and made the papacy relevant again – even for non-Christians.

Andrei Sakharov

1921–1989

The party apparatus of government … cling tenaciously to their open and secret privileges and are profoundly indifferent to the infringement of human rights, the interests of progress, security, and the future of mankind.

Andrei Sakharov, memorandum to Leonid Brezhnev (5 March 1971)

Andrei Sakharov, the physicist who was once called the 'Father of the Soviet H-bomb', became the most prominent political dissident in the world, protesting against the evils and contradictions of Soviet totalitarianism. He represents both the peaks of Russian science and intellectual achievement and the courage of an individual to stand up to rampant tyranny. That stand led to rejection, maltreatment, exile and hardship. Yet, unlike most dissidents, Sakharov survived to see his efforts bear fruit.

Andrei Sakharov was an intelligent child, who was able to read by the age of four. His father encouraged his interest in physics experiments, which he later called 'miracles I could understand'. At Moscow University in the 1940s he was recognized as one of the brightest young minds of his generation. In 1948 he was recruited to join a nuclear research team under the personal control of Stalin's ruthless henchman Lavrenti Beria, and he spent much of the next decade involved in top-secret projects in Turkmenistan.

The project in which Sakharov played the pivotal role was the creation of a hydrogen bomb – a weapon much more powerful than the atom bombs dropped on Hiroshima and Nagasaki in 1945. The Americans tested their first H-bomb in 1952; the Soviets followed in 1953. As the Cold War arms race between America and the Soviet Union accelerated, Sakharov believed that his work was contributing to world peace by helping to maintain a balance of power.

But as the years passed, he began to have doubts about 'the huge material, intellectual and nervous resources of thousands of people' which were being 'poured into the creation of a means of total destruction, capable of annihilating all human civilization'.

In 1961 Sakharov, now in a very prominent position as his country's pre-eminent nuclear scientist, urged the Soviet leader Nikita Khrushchev to stop atmospheric nuclear tests, believing that the radioactive fallout could ultimately lead to the deaths of hun-

Courageous Soviet bloc dissidents

Among the many brave dissidents and campaigning writers in the Soviet bloc and the Russian Federation, those detailed below are particularly worthy of mention. As Sakharov once asked, 'What kind of country is this, cruel and without a soul, that destroys its best citizens ...?'

Aleksandr Solzhenitsyn (1918–2008) fought in the Red Army with distinction during the Second World War, but after criticizing Stalin he was sent to a labour camp, recalling his experiences there in the novel *One Day in the Life of Ivan Denisovich* (1962). This, together with later novels such as *The First Circle* (1968), with its brilliant portrait of the postwar terror and Stalin himself, earned him the 1970 Nobel Prize for Literature. His subsequent non-fiction work *The Gulag Archipelago* (1974–8) was an exhaustive account of the Soviet Union's system of penal camps. This exposé guaranteed reprisals from the authorities, and in 1974 he was exiled from his own country. He did not return until 1994, after the collapse of the Soviet Union, when despite the apparent liberalism of his work, he seemed to emerge as an ultra-conservative nationalist.

Václav Havel (b.1936) has led an extraordinary life, swapping the theatre, the pen and the prison to become his country's head of state and a shining international symbol of the peaceful transition from communist repression to vibrant democracy. A dramatist at Prague's famous Theatre on the Balustrade in the 1960s, he evolved, after the suppression of the liberal thaw of the Prague Spring, into Czechoslovakia's leading dissident. He was imprisoned several times and his works banned, but he was never forgotten either at home or abroad, where other writers such as Tom Stoppard championed his cause. After another brief incarceration in 1989 and the dissolution of the communist government, his people elected him president of

dreds of thousands of people. After agreeing to look into the matter, Khrushchev simply ignored him. From this point onwards, Sakharov grew more critical of the Soviet regime. Despite a US–Soviet agreement in 1963 to refrain from detonating nuclear devices in space, underwater or in the atmosphere, there was little political commitment to non-proliferation, let alone disarmament.

The arguments about nuclear weapons led Sakharov on to broader

Czechoslovakia (and later of the Czech Republic when the country split), his humility and informality giving him a unique style.

Lech Walesa (b.1943) was the brave electrician in Gdańsk, Poland, who in 1980 founded the anti-communist Solidarity, the first independent trade union to be created within the Soviet empire. Solidarity attracted 80 per cent of the Polish workforce within a year, and the communist leader General Jaruzelski instituted martial law, imprisoning Walesa for a year. Walesa won the Nobel Peace Prize in 1983, and after four years of house arrest he re-emerged as Solidarity leader as the Soviet empire crumbled. In 1989 he was triumphantly elected as the Polish president, serving in 1990–5. Unpopular as president, he nonetheless helped to free Poland.

Anatoly (Natan) Sharansky (b.1948) is now a major political figure in Israel, where he moved following his release from nearly a decade of imprisonment and forced labour in Russia between 1978 and 1986. He had been a prominent dissident, and worked as a translator for Sakharov. His case became an international cause célèbre, resulting in great embarrassment for the Soviet Union.

Anna Politkovskaya (1958–2006) was a fierce critic, and ultimately victim, of authoritarianism and gangsterism in post-Soviet Russia. She devoted her life to exposing despotism, corruption and cruelty, particularly in the war in Chechnya. Her harangues against creeping state power and the diminishing of democracy, her high-profile role as a negotiator in the Dubrovka theatre siege of 2002 – when brutal Chechen terrorists held over a thousand hostages and many were killed as the theatre was stormed – and her respected position in the West, all earned her powerful enemies. She was mysteriously poisoned on her way to negotiate with Chechen terrorists holding hundreds of schoolchildren at Beslan (where again the bungled storming cost the lives of many). She was shot dead outside her Moscow apartment in 2006.

political questions. In 1966 he urged the new Soviet leadership, under Leonid Brezhnev, to turn away from rehabilitating the reputation of Stalin. He was rebuffed – though Stalin was not in fact fully rehabilitated.

The Soviet leadership could not ignore Sakharov's next move. In 1968 he wrote a book entitled *Progress, Coexistence and Intellectual Freedom*, which denounced the oppressive Soviet regime and argued for closer links with the West. It caused a storm in Moscow's dissident circles, and an even greater reaction when it was read abroad. Sakharov was a marked man. But he was not cowed and continued to protest – against the persecution of the dissident writer Aleksandr Solzhenitsyn, in favour of the rights of national minorities, and against the mistreatment of political prisoners. In 1975 he won the Nobel Peace Prize, but he was forbidden to leave the country to collect it. His second wife, Yelena Bonner, herself a courageous dissident, collected it on his behalf.

In response to the Soviet invasion of Afghanistan in late 1979, Sakharov called for an international boycott of the 1980 Moscow Olympics. In January 1980 he was arrested by the KGB and transported to internal exile – and grim living conditions – in the city of Gorky. Only Bonner's trips between Moscow and Gorky from 1980 to 1984 – during which time she was harassed and publicly denounced – gave him a lifeline to the outside world. In 1984 she too was arrested, for slandering the regime, and was sentenced to five years' exile in Gorky. Bonner joined her husband on long and painful hunger strikes in order to secure medical attention for their family.

In 1985 a new and reforming Soviet leader, Mikhail Gorbachev, came to power, determined to end the stagnation and oppression that Sakharov had so long criticized. The following year Sakharov was released and invited back to Moscow. He returned as a hero and was elected to the Congress of People's Deputies, the Soviet Union's first democratically chosen body. He went on to play a prominent part in the democratic revolution that was sweeping the Soviet Union and remained in Russia until his death from a heart attack in 1989.

Yelena Bonner is still alive, a vocal critic of Russian atrocities in Chechnya and of the return of Russia to KGB-style authoritarianism. She and her husband remain beacons of the struggle against tyranny.

Margaret Thatcher

b.1925

I am extraordinarily patient, provided
I get my own way in the end.

Margaret Thatcher

Margaret Thatcher first entered Parliament in 1959, making her maiden speech a year later. Interviewed in 1970, by that time education secretary, she said 'it will be years before a woman either leads the Conservative Party or becomes Prime Minister. I don't see it happening in my time.' Nine years later she succeeded Labour's James Callaghan as prime minister and went on to spend 11 years and 209 days at 10 Downing Street, during which time she transformed the British political, economic and social landscape. She was the longest-serving prime minister for more than 150 years and the first woman to hold the post in Britain.

Born Margaret Roberts in 1925, daughter of a Grantham shopkeeper who was also a Methodist lay preacher and a town alderman, she was grammar-school educated and middle class. After a scholarship to Oxford and a brief career as a research chemist (during which she helped to develop the first soft ice cream), she trained as a barrister. She took the Conservative seat of Finchley in the 1959 election, encouraged by Denis, her shrewd, wealthy businessman husband, who steadfastly supported her career. The very qualities for which the company ICI had criticized her in a post-university interview, reporting that 'this woman is headstrong, obstinate and dangerously self-opinionated', surely aided her swift ascent at Westminster.

Emerging to lead the party in 1975, as the dark horse challenger to the then leader Edward Heath, she was at first conciliatory but gradually moved towards radical free-market policies in Opposition, as the country under the Labour government succumbed to waves of industrial strikes, culminating in the so-called 'Winter of Discontent'. This was enough to win the Conservatives the general election of 1979, and Margaret Thatcher became prime minister. Britain then was rotten and enfeebled, the sick man of Europe, but she rejuvenated the country.

With the Labour Party beset by extremism and in disarray, Thatcher's brand of non-paternalistic Conservatism appealed to aspirational working-class voters, and she would win two more elections.

Great women leaders

Boudicca was queen of an early celtic people of eastern England, the Iceni, the widow of a king who had seized power, but was humiliated and whipped by the Roman governors under Emperor Nero. In AD 60 she led her people in a bloody uprising against the Romans, who had usurped her rightful kingdom. She defeated a legion, commanding from her chariot, and burned Colchester, St Albans and London before being defeated at the Battle of Watling Street, after which she probably took poison.

Much later, but with similar force of character, Maria Theresa (1717–80), archduchess of Austria, Holy Roman empress, and queen of Hungary and Bohemia, disproved all those who argued a woman could not, and should not, rule. On the death of her father, Charles VI, in 1740, the Prussian King Frederick the Great invaded her province of Silesia, almost leading to the break-up of the Habsburg Empire in the War of the Austrian Succession. But the young empress held her empire together and proved herself an inspiring, shrewd, competent and tough leader in her 40-year reign. With her husband, Francis I, Holy Roman emperor, she had 16 children; later, she ruled jointly with her son Joseph II.

Elizaveta (1709–61), empress of Russia, daughter of Peter the Great and Catherine I, seized power by *coup d'état* in 1741. Renowned for her amorous enthusiasms, her blonde Slavic beauty and her unparalleled dress collection, she appeared frivolous but was actually an astute auto-crat, laying the foundations for the achievements of Catherine the Great, whom she chose as the wife for her heir and brought to Russia. Elizaveta founded Russia's first university in Moscow, outlawed the death penalty, and was the backbone of the anti-Prussian alliance in the Seven Years' War. Only her death in 1761 saved Frederick the Great from apparently inevitable destruction.

Modern times have seen more female leaders, some brought to power by the assassination of their husbands. Sirimavo R.D.

'The lady's not for turning,' she declared famously at her party conference in October 1980, when all around her were encouraging compromise. She unhesitatingly broke with what she saw as political defeatism in the years since 1945, and successfully injected a new Churchillian pride and vigour into national life. She privatized badly run state industries, trying to roll back state involvement

Bandaranaike (1916–2000), a socialist, served three terms as prime minister of Sri Lanka over two decades, the world's first democratically elected female leader, after her husband prime minister, Solomon Bandaranaike, was assassinated. Similarly, Cory Aquino (b.1933) took over from her assassinated husband Benigno, and was elected president of the Phillipines in 1986 after 'people power' overthrew dictator Ferdinand Marcos. She set her nation on the path of democracy. Benazir Bhutto (1953–2007) succeeded her father, Zulfikar Ali Bhutto, as leader of the Pakistan's People's Party after he was hanged by the country's military dictator, President Zia. She was elected Pakistani prime minister twice (1988–90 and 1993–6) and was twice removed from power. Two years after the death of the Indian prime minister Jawaharlal Nehru in 1964, his daughter Indira Gandhi herself became premier. She served three consecutive terms (1966–77) and a fourth term from 1980 to 1984.

Golda Meir (1898–1978), one of the greatest modern female leaders, owed her position to no one. Born in Kiev, she served as Israel's foreign minister very successfully in 1956–66, becoming its first female prime minister in 1969. She was austere, loyal and lion-like in her defence of her people. In 1972 Meir (who during her ministry kept secret her 12-year struggle against leukaemia) authorized the Mossad intelligence agency to take vengeance for the terrorist massacre of Israeli athletes at the 1972 Munich Olympics. But Meir herself was devastated by the outbreak of the Yom Kippur War in 1973. Israeli leader David Ben-Gurion used to say she was 'the only man in my cabinet'.

Some countries almost have a tradition of women succeeding their men: the charismatic but ruthless Eva Duarte Perón, wife of Argentine dictator Juan Perón (president 1946–55), wanted to be her husband's vice-president but died of cancer. On his death, his second wife, Isabel, ruled disastrously in 1974–6 and was removed by the military. In 2007 the democratically elected Argentine president Néstor Kirchner (2003–7) announced that, on his retirement, his wife Cristina would run for president.

in the economy and people's lives. Her declaration that 'there is no such thing as society' is frequently taken out of context. But, nonetheless, she staunchly believed that the individual should bear the burden of responsibility for his or her welfare.

When the Argentine military junta invaded the Falkland Islands in 1982, it seemed impossible that Britain could launch a war across 8000 miles of ocean; but Thatcher ordered the creation of a Task Force, inspired the nation to defeat tyrannical aggression, and reconquered the Falklands.

Her political partner abroad was Ronald Reagan, US president 1981–9, a genial unintellectual ex-actor, much mocked in Europe, though he was a superb orator. Ironically, with his clear, big ideals and gentle charm, and despite the folly of the Iran-Contra scandal, he turned out to be one of the greatest modern presidents, his hatred of Soviet totalitarianism – the 'Evil Empire' – leading to the arms race that won the Cold War and in turn to the dissolution of the Soviet Empire. Reagan died in 2004, but his diaries attest to his close partnership with Thatcher. She shared Reagan's anti-Sovietism, earning the nickname 'the Iron Lady' from the Soviet press, which she relished. (French President François Mitterrand once described her as having the 'eyes of Caligula and the mouth of Marilyn Monroe', a unique mixture of aggression and femininity that was frequently caricatured by satirists.) Reagan and Thatcher engaged with the new Soviet leader, Mikhail Gorbachev, whom she called 'someone we can do business with', encouraging his reforms and retreat from oppression and empire.

In 1984–5 she was faced with the miners' strike, launched in response to plans to close many pits. This strike, which she regarded as an attempt to topple her government, was quelled by wearing the miners down, breaking the grip of trade unionism, and mobilizing police and army to control rioting strikers. It was a test of her leadership but also the final attempt by undemocratic trade unions to dominate British government using strikes as blackmail.

But later her new 'community charge' (dubbed the Poll Tax) caused riots. Her opposition to closer cooperation within the European Community undermined her credibility. Her chancellor had already resigned. When her deputy, Geoffrey Howe, resigned, his speech triggered a 1990 Conservative leadership election. She was overthrown by a palace coup, abandoned by almost all of her Cabinet, and left Downing Street in tears. Baroness Thatcher now sits in the House of Lords, her late husband receiving a baronetcy.

With President Reagan, Thatcher was instrumental in engineering the triumph of capitalist democracies over communism in the Cold War; she helped to draw back the Iron Curtain and gave freedom to millions. She won a seemingly impossible war, transformed sclerotic Britain into a healthy and reinvigorated country, made London Europe's financial centre, broke the power of the unions, and became a global political star. There was no one else like her. Labour Prime Minister Tony Blair admitted he was, in many ways, her heir. And if you live in Britain today, the society around you is in no small part a creation of Margaret Thatcher, the greatest British leader since Churchill.

Anne Frank
1929–1945

I hear the ever approaching thunder, which will destroy us too, I can feel the suffering of millions and yet, if I look up into the heavens, I think that it will all come right, that this cruelty too will end, and that peace and tranquillity will return again.

Anne Frank (15 July 1944)

The diary of a Jewish girl in hiding during the Second World War has become a totemic symbol of the Holocaust, a monument to the 6 million Jews killed and a talisman for victims of persecution across the world. But Anne Frank was far more than a symbol. She was a teenager whose refusal to be broken by fear or despair in the face of the blackest persecution is a triumph of humanity, the mark of a truly heroic soul. She also became, in spite of her youth, a great writer, an observer and recorder of the terrible events of her dark time and her family's struggle to survive. Hers was not the only such diary to emerge, but it was the finest – an immortal classic.

On 6 July 1942 Anne Frank, her parents Otto and Edith, and her elder sister Margot left their house on the Merwedplein in Amsterdam. Wearing layers of clothes and carrying no suitcases to avoid arousing suspicion, they made their way to Otto Frank's office building on the Prinsengracht. At the top of the stairs there was a door, later concealed behind a false bookcase. It led to what Anne named the 'Secret Annexe' – four rooms where the Franks, with another family, the van Pels, and a dentist called Fritz Pfeffer, would hide for the next two years.

The Franks were German Jews who had emigrated to the Netherlands a decade earlier, following Hitler's rise to power. A lively and

A lost and refound masterpiece

In 2004 a newly published work was hailed as the 20th century's *War and Peace*. Written, like Anne Frank's diary, amid the chaos of war, *Suite française* – the posthumous masterpiece of the Jewish novelist Irène Némirovsky – is a jewel that lay undisturbed for over 50 years.

Irène Némirovsky was born in Kiev in 1903 to wealth and privilege. Her adored father, one of St Petersburg's richest bankers, neglected her in favour of work and the casino, while her mother hated her, blaming Irène for the loss of her own youth. When the revolution broke out in 1917, the teenage Irène and her family fled to France, where they quickly re-established their fortunes. Irène herself – a sparkling socialite of just 26 – became a literary sensation on the publication of her first book, *Daniel Golder*. Wealthy, successful, happily married to a successful banker and the mother of two adored young daughters, Irène's life appeared to be idyllic in every way.

But when the Germans invaded France in 1940, Irène and her daughters' pre-war conversion to Catholicism counted for nothing. The Nazis classified them as Jewish and foreign; her husband, Michel Epstein, was forbidden to work, while her income dwindled to nothing. When the Germans entered Paris, Irène and Michel abandoned the city to join their daughters in the isolated village of Issy-l'Évêque.

Far away from her glittering Parisian life, Irène walked for hours every

vivacious girl, Anne was given a red-checked cloth-bound book on her 13th birthday. Addressing her first entry 'to Kitty', she hoped that 'I shall be able to confide in you completely, as I have never been able to do in anyone before, and I hope that you will be a great comfort and support to me'.

The German occupation of the Netherlands was two years old when Anne began her diary. By 1942 Jews were subject to a curfew and made to wear yellow stars on their clothing. They were forbidden to take the tram, to ride bicycles or to take pictures. On 5 July 1942 16-year-old Margot received papers ordering her to report for transportation to a work camp. At 7.30 the following morning the Franks left their house.

The Annexe's occupants had prepared themselves for a long stay.

---

day to find a patch of wood or a field where she could work. 'I have done a lot of writing', Irène wrote sardonically to her publisher on 11 July 1942. 'I suppose they will be posthumous works, but it helps pass the time.' Two days later she was arrested and a month later she died in Auschwitz. 'Could you please find out if it would be possible for me to be exchanged for my wife?' wrote Michel in desperation in September; within weeks he too had been arrested, soon to die in Auschwitz's gas chambers. The police searched for their daughters, but their governess hid them for the duration of the war.

Fifty years were to pass before Irène's daughter, Denise Epstein, could bear to read her mother's notebook, which she had carried with her since fleeing Issy-l'Évêque. When she did, she realized that it was not the diary she had thought it to be but the first two volumes of an extraordinary novel. Trapped in wartime France, Irène had begun a literary symphony charting the nightmare engulfing her adopted country – a nightmare she knew she would not survive.

Irène Némirovsky held up a mirror to France at its darkest hour. Writing against the ticking clock presaging her own death, she described the panic of an invaded Paris; valour, spinelessness, betrayal and humble nobility; the muddled ambiguity of human nature. Her uncompleted masterpiece is the legacy of an extraordinary heroine, a woman who, in the midst of persecution, understood the atrocities that humans, driven by fear, apathy or weakness, can be moved to commit against their fellows.

Anne's parents had been making secret trips to the hiding place for months. But nothing could have prepared them for the oppressive reality of hiding away from the world. Their survival was dependent on their 'helpers', four loyal employees of Otto Frank's who risked their lives to bring them food, clothes, books and news. Absolute silence had to be maintained during the day to avoid rousing the suspicions of the workers in the store downstairs. 'We are as quiet as baby mice,' wrote Anne in October 1942. 'Who, three months ago, would have guessed that quicksilver Anne would have to sit still for hours – and what's more, could?'

Anne was a talented writer, funny, quick and possessed of a somewhat caustic eye. But her diary is also the work of a normal teenager – bright, impetuous, moody and impatient. She struggled between the 'good Anne' she would like to be and the 'bad Anne' she felt she more often was. She was insightful, unstintingly honest and, increasingly, wise.

'There is no way of killing time,' she wrote in 1943. But she refused to give up hope. 'It's really a wonder that I haven't dropped all my ideals, because they seem so absurd and impossible to carry out,' she wrote on 15 July 1944. 'Yet I keep them, because in spite of everything I still believe that people are really good at heart.'

Three weeks later the German police stormed the Secret Annexe. It is still unknown who betrayed them. The Annexe's inhabitants were sent to Westerbork, then to Auschwitz. In October Anne and Margot were transferred to Bergen-Belsen. They died of typhus within days of each other in March 1945, just a few weeks before the British liberated the camp.

Otto Frank was the only one of the Annexe's inhabitants to survive. When he returned to Amsterdam after the war, Miep Gies, one of their loyal helpers, gave him the diary that she had found scattered on the Annexe's floor. Asked later for his response on first reading his daughter's diary, Otto replied: 'I never knew my little Anne was so deep.'

While she was in hiding, Anne became convinced that she wanted to be a writer. Anne was not the only Jewish child diarist of the Holocaust. Probably there were many. A gifted Czech boy, Peter Ginz, kept a witty diary in Prague during 1941–2: 'When I go to school,' he wrote, 'I counted 9 "sheriffs"' – referring to Jews made to wear the yellow star. He was gassed in Auschwitz in 1944. These gifted diarists were not the only ones to turn hell into literature: *Night* by Elie Wiesel (b.1928) and *If This is a Man* by Primo Levi (1919–87) are the two masterpieces of this European Dark Age.

A year before she died, Anne Frank wrote of her desire 'to be useful or give pleasure to people around me who yet don't really know me. I want to go on living even after my death!'

Elvis Presley
1935–1977

The colored folks been singing it and playing it just like I'm doin' now, man, for more years than I know ... They played it like that in their shanties and in their juke joints and nobody paid it no mind 'til I goosed it up.

Elvis Presley, in an early interview

Elvis, the King. Thus the United States, that most republican of nations, dubbed its favourite musical son, ensuring that his pre-eminence would remain inviolate. He didn't invent rock 'n' roll, he didn't write many songs, he never toured abroad, and he has since been eclipsed in almost every bald statistic of popular-music success. But all that is irrelevant. His sublimity of voice – startling in its reach from raunch and rebellion to the angelically tender – his devastating good looks, and the pulsating charisma of the performer entranced millions. He was a global star, and, by carrying the black music of blues and gospel to a white audience in a way that was unthinkable before, he enabled the musical synthesis that remains the bedrock of popular music today.

Elvis Aaron Presley had a poor Southern upbringing and was much closer to his lively and impressive mother than his shirking, petty-criminal father. He was a shy teenager, often bullied for being a mother's boy. When he left school, he started driving lorries, just as his father did. But it was not long before his remarkable voice came to the attention of the record producer Sam Philips. Philips was looking for a white man to sing 'Negro' songs, and when he heard Presley's self-funded singles, recorded in 1953 as a birthday present for his mother, Philips felt he had found his man.

In 1954 Presley recorded 'That's All Right', a blues song. Radio stations in Tennessee immediately began playing it, and Presley went on a tour of the Southern states. He came up against the ingrained prejudice of many white Americans opposed to seeing blacks and whites mixing together or sharing culture. But even this generations-old legacy of separateness could not compete with the adoration from the young and more colour-blind fans that Presley began to attract. By 1956 pressure from white teenagers had forced

Immortal heroism: Elvis to Anastasia

To describe an iconic figure as a 'living legend' is a cliché. It has an oddly literal resonance, though, in the case of Elvis, where the murky circumstances of his early death combine with the power of belief to ensure a lively rumour mill that the King still lives.

The theories vary. 'Evidence' includes the fact that his middle name is spelled incorrectly on his grave and that 'Elvis' is an anagram of 'lives'. And Elvis has been 'spotted' working as a gas-station attendant or a hamburger waiter the length and breadth of the United States. Some believe he was abducted by aliens, while one man claims to be Elvis reincarnated, helped along by a beam from a UFO. The so-called 'Elvis Presley Jr' has performed in Las Vegas and released his second album, 'Elvis Presley Armageddon Angel', in 2003.

In the longer view, the tradition of immortal heroism begins with the semi-divine kings of ancient civilizations, who were believed to join the ranks of the gods on their deaths. It is at the core of Christianity, and the medieval church was rich with the cults of saints whose corpses or body parts never decayed – a sure sign of their incorruptibility.

Subsequent ages saw political pretenders claim to be supposedly dead rulers. An imposter in Scotland claimed to be the murdered Richard II. The Tudor king Henry VII had to contend with two such impostors – Lambert Simnel and Perkin Warbeck. In Russia's 'Time of Troubles', three different impostors, the so-called False Dmitrys, pretended to be the youngest son of Tsar Ivan the Terrible, murdered in 1591. One False Dmitry actually ruled

radio stations nationwide to play Elvis' singles – hits such as 'Heartbreak Hotel' (1956), 'Love Me Tender' (1956) and the title song to the film *Jailhouse Rock* (1957) – and he remained completely frank about his musical influences. In some quarters black critics accused him of 'stealing' their music; in contrast, Little Richard called Elvis 'a blessing', who 'opened the door' for black music. What was undeniable was that his momentum was unstoppable.

Elvis signed a management deal with 'Colonel' Tom Parker, to whom he turned over all of his business affairs. Parker was a shadowy character, but he was a master merchandiser and turned Elvis into the greatest musical brand the world had ever seen. Under his

---

as tsar, 1605–6. In the 18th century, at least two men claimed to be Catherine the Great's murdered husband, Peter III: one of them, an Illyrian quack, Stephen the Small, ended up ruling Montenegro for six years, while the Cossack rebel Emilian Pugachev led a rebellion that engulfed much of southern Russia. In 1825 the unexpected death of the mystic Tsar Alexander I led to an abundance of sightings of wandering peasants said to be the tsar. The murder by the Bolsheviks in 1918 of Tsar Nicholas II and his family, including his daughter Grand Duchess Anastasia (1901–18), led to the most famous 20th-century impostor claiming to be Anastasia. Anna Anderson (c.1896–1984) convinced even some remaining Romanovs, but she was exposed after DNA tests as a Polish charlatan.

It is not just heroes whose deaths have been disputed; for quite different reasons, the notorious cast a long shadow. The outlaw Jesse James, shot dead by his accomplices in 1882 in Missouri, was 'seen alive' in Alabama as late as 1948, when he would have been 101. Two years later J. Frank Dalton, who claimed to be James, was buried in Guthrie, Texas, his body later being DNA tested (he was almost certainly a fraud). Dystopian fantasies that Hitler outlived his Berlin bunker in 1945 have prompted books and films aplenty.

Returning to the world Elvis knew, musicians continue to be a ripe source of death-defying feats. The Doors' eccentric singer Jim Morrison is still sometimes 'sighted'. In the 1990s the murders of American rappers Tupac Shakur and Notorious B.I.G. were shrouded in mystery, exacerbated by the fact that Shakur released a posthumous album espousing a theory developed by the Renaissance political philosopher Niccolò Machiavelli: that the best way to flush out an enemy is to fake one's own death.

guidance, Elvis found that he could draw crowds and audiences on a phenomenal scale. He broke records for sales of singles and albums, and he could attract 80 per cent of the American television audience for his TV appearances. Young men wanted to be him, young women wanted him, and older generations were scared and shocked. In the city of Liverpool, John Lennon recruited Paul McCartney to the band that had Elvis as its lodestar and that wanted to be 'bigger than Elvis'.

Back home, as Elvis' music and high-energy stage act grew ever more popular, conservative America became more disgusted and worried that its offspring were being irrevocably corrupted. His habits of shaking his legs, rolling his tightly leather-clad hips, thrusting and throwing himself about in front of the microphone were considered the height of obscenity. As a result, there were many who saw Elvis' draft into the US Army, and subsequent posting to Germany in 1958, as something of a relief. When he returned to America in 1960, he was a more subdued character, and during the 1960s, as the era of the pop groups burgeoned, he chose to concentrate on a lacklustre film career rather than return to music. But he reinvented himself for a musical comeback in 1968, adopting some of the influences of the Beatles and the Rolling Stones, the very stars who had re-interpreted his kind of music and sold it back to America.

Elvis's popularity remained huge throughout the 1970s, and he sold out enormous venues across the United States, particularly in Las Vegas, albeit in a new persona where the performer was now encased in the outré outfits of the cabaret scene. He still made it into the charts, for example with 'Always on My Mind' (1973). But his health and state of mind declined alarmingly. He grew fat, gorging himself on fast food. He also became addicted to prescription drugs. He slept for most of the day and cut a bloated figure on stage – although that voice remained mesmerising.

Elvis died on 16 August 1977. He suffered heart failure at Graceland, his mansion in Memphis, Tennessee. His funeral was a massive event, watched by millions. He ranks with the American singer Frank Sinatra, those English bands the Beatles and the Rolling Stones, and the French singer Edith Piaf as musical giants who have moved beyond the realm of music into the conscious identity of nations.

Muhammad Ali

b.1942

I'm the greatest thing that ever lived. I'm so great I don't have a mark on my face. I shook up the world.

Cassius Clay, soon to become Muhammad Ali, after defeating Sonny Liston in 1964

Muhammad Ali was not just the greatest boxer of his generation, he is one of the greatest sportsmen of all time. As a fighter, he displayed a prodigious, sublime talent, but he also transcended the world of sport. Deep-felt conviction, outspoken politics, courage, wit, style, sheer chutzpah, all have combined to create a living legend. Since retiring, Ali has triumphed as an iconic figure who lit the torch at the 1996 Atlanta Olympics and has spoken poignantly about non-violent Islam in the post-9/11 world.

Cassius Clay, as Ali was named at birth, took up boxing as a 12-year-old. He had an exceptional amateur career, winning 134 bouts and losing only seven. He went to the Rome Olympics in 1960 and won a gold medal at light heavyweight, impressing with his speed and lightning reflexes. The Miami boxing trainer Angelo Dundee took Clay on as a young professional and had little to do to improve his brazen style. He kept a low guard, relying on his speed to dance around opponents. Early in life he would proclaim himself 'the greatest'. When he destroyed the great heavyweight Sonny Liston in two fights – the second a severe pounding in May 1965 – it seemed that he was set to fulfil his own prophecy.

Outside the ring, Clay was undergoing a transformation that would shape the rest of his life. He became involved with Malcolm X and the Nation of Islam – a radical black Islamic movement. It appealed to Clay because of the racism he had experienced growing up in the Southern states of the USA. Soon the outspoken young man had changed his name to Muhammad Ali. By the time of the rematch against Liston and a subsequent savaging of another big-name heavyweight, Floyd Patterson, Ali was as divisive outside the ring as he was brilliant in it.

The combination of Ali's extravagant fighting style, his forthright talk and his refusal to join the US Army in 1966 ('Man, I ain't got no quarrel with them Vietcong,' he explained at the time) rapidly made him a hate figure for white America. He declared himself a conscientious objector, and in 1967 he was stripped of his world title and banned from fighting in America for three years. Undeterred, Ali delivered more than 200 anti-war speeches condemning the actions of the USA in East Asia.

When Ali returned to the ring, he took part in three of the most famous fights of all time: the Fight of the Century (1971), which he lost to Joe Frazier; the Rumble in the Jungle (1974), in which he reclaimed the heavyweight crown then held by George Foreman; and the Thriller in Manila (1975), which represented redemption

---

'I have a dream'

Muhammad Ali was a potent symbol for the black civil rights movement of the 1960s, but its greatest figure was the Baptist minister Martin Luther King Jr (1929–68). In 1963, having led a march to Washington, D.C., he stood on the steps of the Lincoln Memorial and gave one of the most famous speeches ever delivered, 'I have a dream':

I am happy to join with you today in what will go down in history as the greatest demonstration for freedom in the history of our nation ...

Now is the time to make justice a reality for all of God's children ... This sweltering summer of the Negro's legitimate discontent will not pass until there is an invigorating autumn of freedom and equality ...

We must conduct our struggle on the high plane of dignity and discipline. We must not allow our creative protest to degenerate into physical violence. Again and again we must rise to the majestic heights of meeting physical force with soul force ...

We can never be satisfied as long as the Negro is the victim of the unspeakable horrors of police brutality. We can never be satisfied, as long as our bodies, heavy with the fatigue of travel, cannot gain lodging in the motels of the highways and the hotels of the cities ... No, no, we are not satisfied, and we will not be satisfied until justice rolls down like waters and righteousness like a mighty stream ...

against Frazier. In the Foreman fight, held in Zaire (now the Democratic Republic of the Congo), Ali used his 'rope-a-dope' tactics, hanging back for seven rounds and allowing Foreman to punch himself out, then countering in the eighth to knock out his younger opponent.

The Thriller in Manila is probably the most celebrated of all Ali's fights. In the build-up to the contest he taunted Frazier with various slurs and poems. The two men battered one another for 14 rounds, until finally Frazier's corner threw in the towel. Afterwards Ali said of his own heroic efforts: 'That must be what death feels like.' He had thrown everything into an incredible victory, and – history having vindicated his stance on Vietnam – he had earned redemption in the eyes of the world.

Ali fought on until the early 1980s, by which time his powers

---

I say to you today, my friends, so even though we face the difficulties of today and tomorrow, I still have a dream. It is a dream deeply rooted in the American dream.

I have a dream that one day this nation will rise up and live out the true meaning of its creed: 'We hold these truths to be self-evident: that all men are created equal.'

I have a dream that one day on the red hills of Georgia the sons of former slaves and the sons of former slave owners will be able to sit down together at the table of brotherhood.

I have a dream that one day even the state of Mississippi, a state sweltering with the heat of injustice, sweltering with the heat of oppression, will be transformed into an oasis of freedom and justice.

I have a dream that my four little children will one day live in a nation where they will not be judged by the colour of their skin but by the content of their character ...

When we allow freedom to ring ... we will be able to speed up that day when all of God's children, black men and white men, Jews and Gentiles, Protestants and Catholics, will be able to join hands and sing in the words of the old Negro spiritual, 'Free at last! Free at last! Thank God Almighty, we are free at last!'

Within five years Martin Luther King had given his life to the struggle, a victim of the assassin's bullet.

---

had visibly declined. However, in spite of the sad end to his career, he is rightly remembered as one of history's greatest ever sportsmen. Only the footballer Pelé and a very few others can be said to have dominated their sports in the same manner. World champion three times, he was the quintessence of glamour and glory in his sport, thanks to his skill and guile in the ring and his psychological mastery of his opponents.

But Ali was more than just a superb sportsman. He was a principled man who stuck by his beliefs even when threatened. Though his pronouncements on race were not always well judged and he could be cruel to his opponents, Ali transcended such indiscretions and won over almost all his critics with his bravery and charisma.

Since the 1980s Ali has been progressively affected by the symptoms of Parkinson's disease. The sight of his quavering hand lighting the Olympic torch in Atlanta in 1996 touched the world; the transition from angry young man to symbol of world unity was complete. In 1999 he was voted Sports Personality of the Century. Despite his frailty, he still travels the world supporting a range of humanitarian causes.

Aung San Suu Kyi
b.1945

The quest for democracy in Burma is the struggle of a people to live whole, meaningful lives ... It is part of the unceasing human endeavour to prove that the spirit of man can transcend the flaws of his nature.

Aung San Suu Kyi's words, spoken by her son, at the Nobel Peace Prize ceremony in 1991

Since she returned to Burma in 1988, Aung San Suu Kyi has been consistently repressed by the Burmese military dictatorship. Under almost permanent house arrest, she has been denied access to her family and her supporters, she has been threatened, and the government has tried to bribe her. All without success: they cannot stifle her – a prisoner of conscience whose determination to fight for her country's freedom has prompted her to sacrifice her own.

Aung San Suu Kyi is the daughter of one of Burma's most inspirational politicians, Aung San, who was assassinated in 1947 as he led the country to independence from Britain. Suu Kyi, who was just two when her father was killed, left the country as a teenager when her diplomat mother, Khin Kyi, was posted to India. After taking a degree at Oxford University, Suu Kyi settled in the city, marrying an academic, Michael Aris, and raising two children.

Suu Kyi's political career began in 1988, when a telephone call summoned her back to Burma to care for her mother, who had just suffered a stroke. 'I had a premonition that our lives would change for ever,' her husband later recalled. As she nursed her mother in Rangoon (Yangon), Suu Kyi was surrounded by the upheaval at the end of General Ne Win's 26-year-long dictatorship. When, instead of the referendum he had promised, Ne Win implemented another military coup, in which human rights were further eroded and thousands of unarmed pro-democracy demonstrators were massacred on the streets, Suu Kyi began to speak out. So began her road to becoming heir to her father as politician, a path also trod in the region by Pakistan's Benazir Bhutto (1953–2007) and India's Indira Gandhi (1917–84).

Within months of her return to Burma, Suu Kyi had helped to found the National League for Democracy (NLD). In the much-vaunted elections of May 1990, the NLD won by a landslide, gaining 82 per cent of the available seats. Suu Kyi, as the NLD's general secretary, was Burma's democratically elected leader. But it was a result that Burma's military government chose to overrule.

Just over a year after her return to Burma, Suu Kyi was, with her NLD colleagues, arrested without charge and placed under house arrest – a situation that has persisted, with breaks, ever since. She was released for five years in 1995 and for another year in 2002. On each occasion, however, the popularity of the nation's chosen leader, her command over its oppressed people and her inspirational addresses prompted the military junta to re-imprison the woman whose presence and personal sacrifice represent the greatest threat to their dictatorial rule.

In 1989 Suu Kyi stood alone in front of an army unit with its

People power

In recent years peaceful popular revolutions have overturned oppressive rule in countries across the world.

'This could be as close as the 20th century has come to the storming of the Bastille,' remarked a US reporter in 1986, as millions of people filled Manila's main street in the bloodless revolution that overturned two decades of autocratic rule in the Philippines. Spurred on by the imprecations of Manila's archbishop over the airwaves, the populace massed in support of the rebel politicians outraged at President Ferdinand Marcos' rigging of the presidential elections. On 25 February the democratic opposition candidate, Corazon Aquino, was inaugurated as president. Marcos made one final address, his flamboyant wife Imelda sang the couple's theme song one last time, and they fled.

The Velvet Revolution of 1989 was the peaceful revolt which ousted Czechoslovakia's communist government. Flower-carrying student protesters refused to be incited to violence by police attacks. The mass demonstrations across the country that followed, supporting the calls of the dissident leaders for change, caught the communist government completely off guard. The dissident playwright Václav Havel was soon installed as president.

In Lithuania's Bloody Sunday of 1991, Russian security forces attacked the non-violent protesters who were linking arms and singing folk songs. It was the culmination of Lithuania's, Estonia's and Latvia's Singing Revolution: mass demonstrations in which the nationalist songs banned under communist rule became tools of peaceful protest. When

rifles trained on her. She had motioned her NLD colleagues to step aside, presenting herself as a lone and easy target. Under house arrest she endured a hunger strike, refusing to accept any help from the government that had imprisoned her. This rendered her so malnourished that her hair fell out, her heart began to fail, and she developed a condition in which her spinal column began to degenerate. Every time she has been released from house arrest the fearless Suu Kyi has immediately spoken out against the government, calling loudly and repeatedly for democracy and liberation in a tyrannous state that violates human rights more than almost any other in the world.

The presence of one of the world's most famous prisoners of

the states unilaterally declared their independence of the USSR in 1990, international powers had hesitated to acknowledge them. Bloody Sunday earned them that recognition as their peaceful protest demonstrated the bankruptcy of Soviet rule.

When Slobodan Milosevic of Serbia rigged the presidential elections of 2000, protesters stormed and set fire to their parliament building and the state television station, assisted by the policemen who were meant to be restraining them. 'The Butcher of the Balkans', who had precipitated Yugoslavia's implosion into bitter civil war, was swiftly swept from the stage.

Between November 2004 and January 2005, the Orange Revolution of Ukraine supported the pro-Western election winner against Russian-backed fraud and thuggery. Even after he was mysteriously poisoned by Russian security agents, Viktor Yushchenko was inaugurated as president in January 2005.

In the former Soviet republic of Georgia, the Rose Revolution of 2003 acquired its name from the flowers that the opposition crowds carried as they marched on parliament. The isolated president (and former Soviet foreign minister) Edvard Shevardnadze resigned and was succeeded by young lawyer Mikheil Saakashvili, soon elected president.

The supporters of the Cedar Revolution in Lebanon blamed Syria for the murder of former prime minister Rafik Hariri in 2005. The demonstrators' protest eventually pressured Syria into removing its troops from Lebanon and brought about the fall of the pro-Syrian Lebanese government.

conscience – and one who was awarded the Nobel Peace Prize in 1991 – has become an increasing embarrassment for Burma's military government. They have done everything to force her out: denied visas to her family, cut her phone lines, intercepted her letters. Suu Kyi has undergone some of the worst trials that a wife and mother could face. Her children have grown up without her, and in 1999 her husband died of prostate cancer, denied the chance to visit his wife one last time despite every diplomatic effort. At the cost of untold personal suffering, Suu Kyi has refused every government attempt to bribe her with liberty in return for her permanent departure from the country.

Suu Kyi has sacrificed her own freedom in her struggle to gain it for her people. Her suffering brings to the attention of the world the plight of her country. She does not herself believe that she is a martyr or a hero or exceptional in any way. This extraordinary woman, whose writings reveal an undiminished zest for life, whose compassion and optimism have not been crushed by ceaseless persecution, sees herself simply as an ordinary person fighting for the freedom of the ordinary people of her country. 'It's no use standing there wringing your hands saying "My goodness, my goodness, this is terrible,"' Suu Kyi once declared when asked how she responded to suffering. 'You must try to do what you can. I believe in action.'

The Unknown Rebel

On 5 June 1989, as the Chinese Communist Party brutally crushed the Tiananmen Square student uprising, a column of tanks was held up by a solitary young man as it attempted to drive out of the square. Again and again he prevented the tanks from moving on, until finally they turned off their engines. He then jumped up onto the leading tank to scold the commander for shedding so much innocent blood.

Dubbed 'Tank Man' or the 'Unknown Rebel', the young man's real name was never discovered, nor his fate. Some said he was executed, others that he is still alive in China. Captured on film and broadcast around the world, the image of the man's astonishing courage summed up the tragedy of Tiananmen Square – the brutal suppression of the democratic student protesters and the reckless killing of thousands of innocents.

Tank Man's protest and the uprising as a whole failed to change China's destiny. Nevertheless, *Time* magazine named him one of the 100 most influential people of the 20th century. This anonymous figure came to symbolize the heroism of the simple impulsive acts of ordinary people.

The Tiananmen Square protests were a popular uprising aimed at changing the course of communist China. Soon after the death of Chinese dictator Mao Zedong in 1976, the tough pragmatist Deng Xiaoping – himself a victim of the orchestrated upheaval of Mao's Cultural Revolution (1966–1975) – emerged as China's 'Paramount Leader'. Deng followed a policy of economic liberalization combined with absolute political control by the Communist Party. The party's general secretary, Hu Yaobang, pressed for greater reforms but was sacked by Deng after student protests in 1987.

On 15 April 1989 Hu's death sparked student protests, which were at first small-scale but soon became widespread. This was the era of Mikhail Gorbachev's glasnost and liberalization in Russia, so Deng and the Chinese leadership were already nervous. Students and teachers were soon joined by workers. The protests became focused on Tiananmen Square in Beijing, which before long was occupied by vast numbers of protesters.

On 19 May General Secretary Zhao Ziyang addressed the seething student crowds on the square in a conciliatory spirit (but with a tone of warning too), telling them: 'Students! You talk about us, criticize us, it is all necessary. You are still young … you must live healthily … We are already old, it doesn't matter to us anymore …' On 30 May a statue of the Goddess of Democracy was erected. By now the elders of the Communist Party, led by Deng, still chairman of the Central Military Commission, and President Marshal Yang Shangkun, were convinced that stability and party control were threatened. Hardline premier Li Peng declared martial law. The 27th and 28th Armies were ordered into the city, and the assault started at 10.30pm on 3 June.

There was indiscriminate fire; it is believed that about 2600 were killed and 30,000 injured. Journalist Jan Wong, watching from Beijing Hotel on 5 June as the Unknown Rebel stopped the tanks, recalled: 'So the tank is turning, then the young man jumps in front of the tank, and then the tank turns the other way and the young man jumps down that side. They did this a couple of times. Then the tank turned off its motor. The young man climbed up onto the tank and seemed to be talking to the person inside. After a while, the young man jumps down, the tank turns on its motor and the young man blocks it again …' He had reportedly told the tank commander: 'Why are you here? You have caused nothing but misery.' Just then, two people on the sidelines pulled him into the crowd – perhaps to a life in hiding, perhaps to face a firing squad.

The following year President Jiang Zemin claimed that 'the young man was never, never killed'. Tank Man remains an inspiration: the unknown hero who represents all the other unknown heroes.

This book is for him and for them.

Index